*From Wilderness Vision
to Farm Invasions*

From Wilderness Vision to Farm Invasions

Conservation & Development
in Zimbabwe's Southeast Lowveld

William Wolmer
Knowledge, Technology & Society Team
Institute of Development Studies
University of Sussex

JAMES CURREY
OXFORD

WEAVER PRESS
HARARE

AFRICAN ACADEMIC PRESS
a Tsehai Publishers imprint
HOLLYWOOD, CA

James Currey
73 Botley Road
Oxford OX2 0BS
www.jamescurrey.co.uk

Weaver Press
P.O. Box A1922
Avondale, Harare
Zimbabwe
www.weaverpresszimbabwe.com

African Academic Press
a Tsehai Publishers imprint
PO Box 1881
Hollywood, CA 90078
www.tsehaipublishers.com

All rights reserved. No part of this book may be reproduced in any form, or by electronic or mechanical means, including information storage and retrieval systems, wihtout permission in writing from the publishers, except by a reviewer who may quote brief passages in a review.

© William Wolmer 2007
First published 2007

1 2 3 4 5 11 10 09 08 07

ISBN 978-0-85255-436-4 (James Currey)
ISBN 978-1-77922-045-5 (Weaver Press)
ISBN 978-1-59907-017-9 (Tsehai Publishers)

British Library Cataloguing in Publication Data
Wolmer, William
From wilderness vision to farm invasions: conservation & development in Zimbabwe's south-east Lowveld
1. Land use, Rural - Zimbabwe 2. Rural development - Zimbabwe
I. Title
333.7'616'096891

Typeset in 10.5/11.5pt Monotype Bembo
by Frances Marks, Harare
Printed and bound in Great Britain at the University Press, Cambridge

Contents

List of Maps, Figures & Boxes   viii
List of Abbreviations   ix
Acknowledgements   x

Part One Lowveld Landscapes

1
Landscapes of the imagination   1
The lowveld and its people   3
Landscape   6
The physical construction of 'cultural landscapes'   7
Imagined landscapes   8
    Landscape as a 'way of seeing'   8
    Landscape as text   10
    Social constructionism and critical realism 11
    Landscape and identity   12
Wilderness – a binary vision   12
Overview   15

2
The wilderness vision   20
Colonial perceptions of the lowveld landscape and its inhabitants
The landscape aesthetic – picturesque scenery and wilderness   22
A land of mystery, danger and scoundrels   24
Narratives on the Lost City   27
A land of adventure   29
Unfit for white habitation – except for pioneers   32
A new landscape aesthetic   35
Power over people   35
Celebrating wilderness   38
Wilderness threatened   40
Conclusions   41

3
Socialised, sacred and contested spaces   42
African landscapes in the lowveld
'Lived in' landscapes   43
Symbolic landscapes   48
Landscape and identity   48
Politicised landscapes   52
Sacred landscapes   56
Christian landscapes   64
Conclusions   66

Part Two The Productive Landscape

4
Lowveld livelihoods   68
The 'suitability' of dryland cropping in the landscape

Pre-/early colonial dryland agriculture	69
Other livelihood strategies	73
The colonial period: land alienation and its impact on African agriculture in the lowveld	78
Agricultural extension in the lowveld during the colonial period	82
Narratives concerning the suitability of dryland agriculture in the lowveld	85
Dryland agriculture in practice today	88
Policies in practice	91
Conclusions	92

5
'Backwater to breadbasket'   93
Irrigated agriculture in the lowveld

The lowveld sugar story	94
Large-scale irrigation, Rhodesian identity and a new landscape aesthetic	97
Commercial irrigated agriculture post-Independence	103
Irrigation in the communal areas	105
The micro-politics of irrigated landscapes	112
Conclusions	114

6
Cattle country   116
Livestock management in the ranches and reserves

The ranches	117
Supporting narratives	120
The 'reserves'	121
Cattle country and cattle people	126
Pasture science: veld management and destocking	126
The ranching model	129
Livestock diseases and landscape management	131
Livestock management in practice	137
Conclusions	141

Part Three The Natural Landscape

7
Manufacturing wilderness 142
Wildlife conservation in the lowveld
Gonarezhou National Park 144
District Commissioner Allan Wright 149
African evictions 152
The tsetse challenge 153
Gonarezhou National park after Independence: Wars, drought
and political intrigue 157
Commercial wildlife management in the lowveld 162
The wildlife landscape 171
Community-Based Natural Resource Management 176
Conclusions 183

Part Four The Politics of Land(scape)

8
Reclaiming the wilderness? 186
Farm invasions in the lowveld
An overview of 'the land question' post-Independence 187
Competing discourses concerning land 190
The land question in the lowveld 191
Farm invasions in the lowveld 193
Who were the invaders? 194
The dynamics of the farm invasions 198
Dryland agriculture and land 201
Water and land 204
Cattle and land 208
Wildlife and land 209
Conclusions 215

Bibliography 219
Index 239

List of Maps, Figures & Boxes

Maps

1.1	Zimbabwe's highveld, middleveld and lowveld, indicating study area	3
1.2	The south-east lowveld	4
1.3	Land use in the south-east lowveld	5
4.1	Categorisation of 'Natural Regions' in Zimbabwe	86
6.1	Foot and mouth disease zones in the lowveld	135
7.1	The Save Valley Conservancy and surrounding districts	164

Figures

2.1	A Caldwell illustration from *Jock of the Bushveld*	30
5.1	Lake Kyle, serving the lowveld sugar estates	100
5.2	Clearing bush in preparation for planting sugar cane	101
5.3	Land cleared for sugar cane and uncleared bush	102
6.1	Matibi II communal area livestock populations	122
6.2	Percentage of population near Chikombedzi owning livestock 1998	125
6.3	Changing composition of cattle holdings in Matibi II, 1993-1998	125
7.1	Lowveld Hall, Zimbabwe Natural History Museum	143

Boxes

3.1	Shangaan categorisations of landscape types	45

List of Abbreviations

Agritex	Agricultural extension service
ANC	Assistant Native Commissioner
ARDA	Agricultural Development Authority
BSAC	British South Africa Company
CAMPFIRE	Communal Areas Management Programme for Indigenous Resources
CBNRM	Community Based Natural Resource Management
CESVI	Cooperazionne e Svilupo
CFU	Commercial Farmers' Union of Zimbabwe
CNC	Chief Native Commissioner
CSC	Cold Storage Commission
DA	District Administrator
DC	District Commissioner
DFID	Department for International Development (UK)
DNPWLM	Department of National Parks and Wildlife Management
DNR	Department of Natural Resources
DVS	Department of Veterinary Services
ESAP	Economic Structural Adjustment
FMD	Foot and Mouth Disease
GEF	Global Environmental Facility
GKG	Gaza-Kruger-Gonarezhou
GTI	Gazaland Tourist Initiative
GTZ	Deutsche Gesellschaft für Technische Zusammenarbeit
IFC	International Finance Corporation
ISC	Imperial Cold Storage and Supply Company
IUCN	International Union for the Conservation of Nature
MDC	Movement for Democratic Change
MNR	Mozambique National Resistance
MRC	Masvingo Records Centre
MRLRP	Mwenezi Radical Land Reform Programme
NAZ	National Archives of Zimbabwe
NC	Native Commissioner
PRO	Public Records Office (UK)
RDC	Rural District Council
SADC	Southern African Development Community
SAFIRE	Southern Alliance for Indigenous Resources
SEDAP	South-Eastern Dry Areas Project
SELCC	South-East Lowveld Co-ordinating Committee
SDI	Spatial Development Initiative
SLA	Sabi-Limpopo Authority
SVC	Save Valley Conservancy
TTL	Tribal Trust Land
TFCA	Transfrontier Conservation Area
UDI	Unilateral Declaration of Independence
UNEP	United Nations Environment Programme
USAID	United States Agency for International Development
VIDCO	Village Development Committee
WADCO	Ward Development Committee
WNLA	Witwatersrand Native Labour Association
WWF	World Wide Fund for Nature
ZANLA	Zimbabwe African National Liberation Army
ZANU(PF)	Zimbabwe African National Union – Patriotic Front
ZAPU	Zimbabwe African People's Union
ZIPRA	Zimbabwe People's Revolutionary Army
ZNA	Zimbabwe National Army
ZWTAC	Zimbabwe Wildlife and Tourism Advisory Council

Acknowledgements

Special thanks are due to Jacob Mahenehene who has acted as my irreplaceable translator, guide, research assistant and host since my first visit to Chikombedzi in 1997, and without him none of this work would have been possible. I would also like to thank Ian Scoones and Melissa Leach who read numerous drafts of my chapters and provided many insightful comments. Ian deserves particular thanks, not least for introducing me to Zimbabwe. He was also a constant source of support and without him I would never have ended up in the fascinating nether reaches of the lowveld. I am very grateful for the patience and understanding of all those in Harare, Masvingo, Chikombedzi, Chiredzi, Mwenezi and elsewhere in the lowveld who gave up their time to be pestered by me.

This research was made possible by funding from the Economics and Social Research Council. I was hosted in Zimbabwe by the Institute of Environmental Studies at the University of Zimbabwe. I am extremely grateful for their assistance.

Many friends and colleagues have provided sounding boards for ideas, helpful comments and encouragement. These include Enrique Aldaz, Saul Dubow, Rosaleen Duffy, Buzz Harrison, Mike Holdgate, David McDermott Hughes, Patrick Moriarty, James Keeley, Gilles Kleitz, Gus Le Breton, Frank Matose, JoAnn McGregor, Billy Mukamuri, Jay Singh, Bev Sithole, Lucas Sorbara and the IDS Environment Group. Sara Rich Dorman kept me plentifully supplied with dispatches from the Zimbabwean press. Sue Ong guided me through the bureaucratic labyrinth surrounding a doctorate (on which this book is based) and Hazel Lintott of the University of Sussex Cartographic Unit drew the beautiful maps. My parents were loyally interested and supportive throughout and my mother's experience of doggedly completing a PhD and book in much more difficult circumstances was a source of inspiration. Finally I would like to thank Vicky Baum, not just for her valuable comments and editorial suggestions, but also for her unceasing support and understanding during the writing of this book.

Versions of sections of this book have appeared separately in journals. Thanks are due to the publishers of the *Journal of Southern African Studies* for the use of material from my article 'Transboundary conservation: the politics of ecological integrity in the Great Limpopo Transfrontier Park', 2003, Vol. 29 (1): 261-78. Parts of Chapters 7 and 8 appear in 'Wilderness gained, wilderness lost: wildlife management and land occupations in Zimbabwe's lowveld', in the *Journal of Historical Geography*, 2005, Vol. 31: 260-80.

PART ONE
Lowveld Landscapes

1

Landscapes of the imagination

In the first few years of the twenty-first century Zimbabwe has occupied an unusually prominent position in the international arena as race, politics and land have come together in a powerful headline-grabbing cocktail bringing the ever volatile 'land question' to the world's attention. Much media coverage has been devoted to the radical changes that have taken place in parts of the landscape. Alongside condemnation of Zimbabwe's degenerating human rights record and imploding economy particular outrage has been reserved for the seizure of largely white-owned commercial farmland, especially where this involved the despoliation of pristine wilderness areas by machete-wielding 'invaders' who chopped down trees, cleared fields and slaughtered wildlife. Typically apocalyptic headlines exclaimed: 'Wildlife die in African Crossfire', 'Zimbabwe's Killing Fields', 'Zimbabwe's Shame', and 'A Holocaust Against Our Wildlife'.[1] Yet neither the motives for the violent occupation of land in this manner, nor the shrill emotive response to it, can be properly understood without an understanding of the competing ways in which this landscape is and has been physically managed and invested with symbolic meaning.

This book explores the physical and imaginative construction of a particular Zimbabwean landscape. It asks how this landscape has been shaped, reshaped, imagined, reimagined, represented, and defined by different actors. It shows how one representation of this landscape has had dramatic consequences for the ways in which this landscape and its inhabitants have been acted upon, eliciting conflicts and struggles over meaning and cumulating in an equally dramatic rejection of this way of seeing and acting upon landscape. This is an inherently political debate, and as with many political debates in Zimbabwe it winds up being about land – power over land and the power to define what constitutes an appropriate land use.

---

[1] *The Observer*, 12 November 2000, *Environment and Wildlife*, February 2001, *Greenline*, No. 19, *Zimbabwe Standard*, 1 October 2000.

The landscape in question is in south-eastern Zimbabwe and is known as the 'lowveld'. Over the last hundred years differing notions of what the lowveld is and what it stands for, and the assumptions they entail, have played out in conflicts over what is the appropriate land use and management strategy. It has been variously seen as: cattle country suitable for ranching; wild bush for game ranching or national park; potentially productive land for irrigated sugar estates or smallholder farming; and the ethnic homeland of the Shangaan people and abode of their ancestral spirits.

Conservation and development programmes in Zimbabwe's south-east lowveld have been rooted in a particular 'way of seeing' this landscape – as wilderness. This wilderness vision derives from the colonial period and earlier and it has two facets which respectively encourage conflicting ways of acting on the landscape. On the one hand it came to be constituted in the imagination of colonial explorers and adventurers as a landscape of adventure, mystique and danger, which was simultaneously, to different actors, a disease-ridden, drought-ravaged, barren and fearful landscape to be battled and tamed. This is a potentially productive landscape. On the other hand the wilderness vision celebrates a pristine and glorious piece of national heritage that must be preserved or rehabilitated. This is essentially a 'natural' landscape. In both manifestations of this wilderness vision African people have been written out of the landscape.

The wilderness vision continues to be extremely influential in informing projects and plans for the lowveld. However, there has been one important change. The binary wilderness vision of separate productive and natural spaces has to some extent been conflated by the emergence of a game ranching industry and a discourse on sustainable utilisation of wildlife that holds that the lowveld landscape can be simultaneously natural and productive. The lowveld landscape has come to be represented as a wilderness asset to be exploited productively and sustainably by both the commercial and communal farming sectors in Zimbabwe. But, in the context of current economic imperatives, global environmental agendas and donor priorities, it is the way of seeing the lowveld as a pristine or natural landscape that has become the increasingly hegemonic facet of the wilderness vision, and has encouraged and underpinned particular conservation and development initiatives in south-eastern Zimbabwe including private wildlife conservancies and a transboundary protected area. The danger is that, rather than providing a means to stimulate an economically depressed and physically marginalised area, these initiatives rooted in the pristine wilderness vision have deepened antagonism over land and led to further coercive regulations on resource use at odds with people's livelihood strategies. Yet the farm and national park invasions in the lowveld in 2000 revealed starkly contrasting ways of seeing the landscape that often conflict with the wilderness vision. The turbulent dynamics around these land invasions and the associated fast-track land reform process may actually open space for these previously silenced notions of landscape to influence policy.

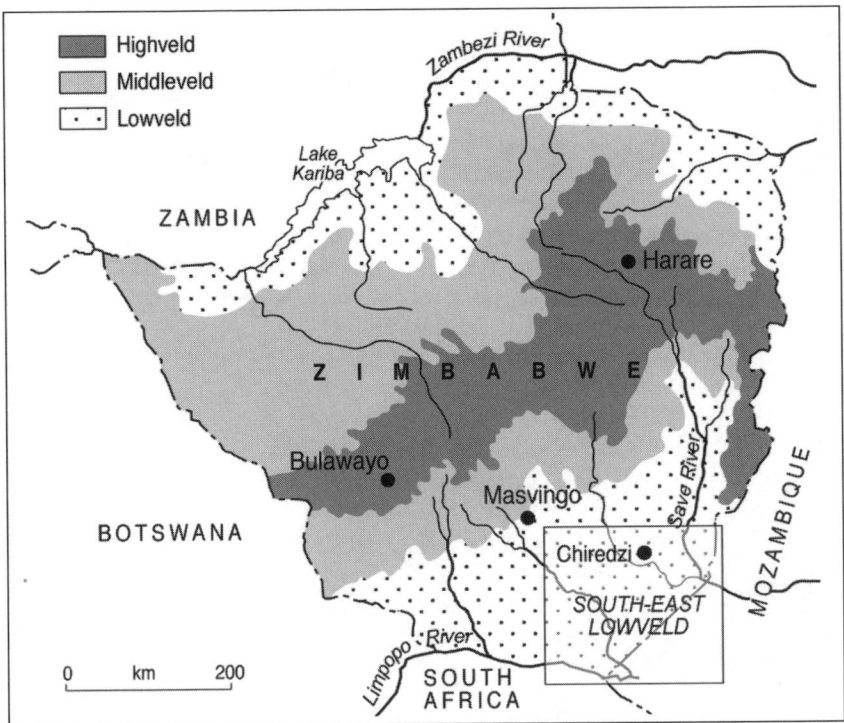

Map 1.1 Zimbabwe's highveld, middleveld and lowveld, indicating the study area

The lowveld and its people

Strictly speaking the lowveld is a botanical and geographical descriptor. Veld literally means 'pasture' and low means below 600 metres. Although this altitudinal band also encompasses much of the Zambezi valley in Zimbabwe (see Map 1.1), the term lowveld is generally only applied to the south-east of the country. The lowveld stretches across a swathe of country from Beitbridge, on the South African border, following the Limpopo to the border with Mozambique, and encompassing the Save valley to the north. There are three main categories of land represented in the south-east lowveld. In the argot of Zimbabwean land designations these are: state land (Gonarezhou National Park and Malipati Safari Area under the management of the Department of National Parks and Wildlife Management),[2] communal areas and large-scale commercial farms. The communal areas form a broad arc separating the national park from the commercial farms and extend west along the Limpopo river (Ndowoyo, Sangwe, Matibi II and Sengwe; and Chipise, Diti and Mtengwe respectively). Until the recent

---

[2] In 2003 this became the Zimbabwe Parks and Wildlife Management Authority. I shall refer to it as DNPWLM in this book.

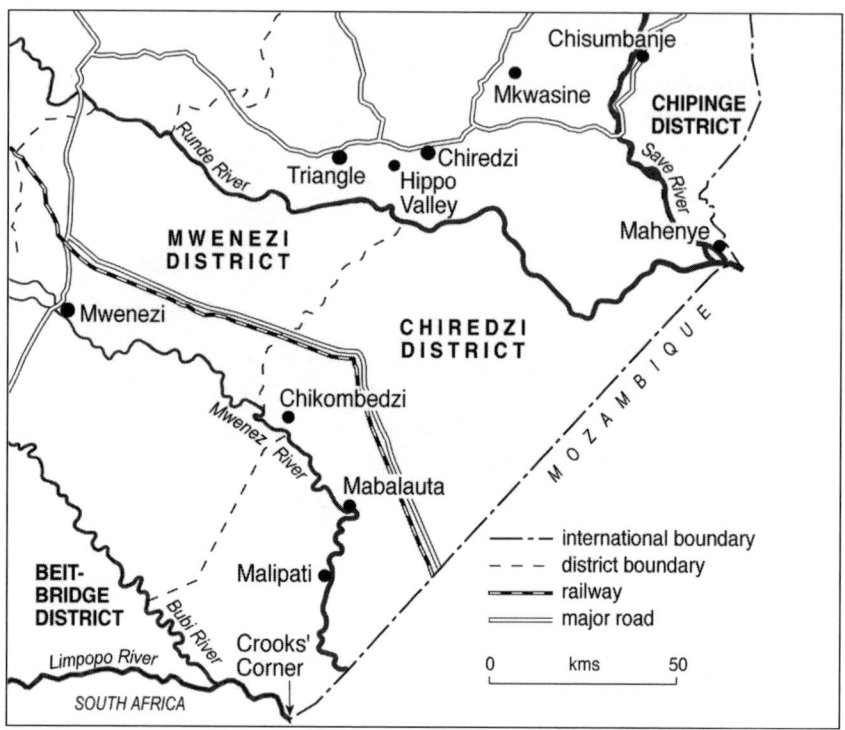

Map 1.2 The south-east lowveld

large-scale land reform programme commercial farms, in the main white-owned, covered the remainder of the lowveld. There are also smaller areas of small-scale black-owned commercial farms (Gonakudzingwa) and older resettlement areas (Chizirizvi and Nuangambe) (Cunliffe 1993) (see Maps 1.2 and 1.3). The terrain is relatively flat and typically characterised by large expanses of mopane woodland (*colophospermum mopane*). It is one of the driest parts of Zimbabwe with an average rainfall of below 450 mm. Major droughts have struck the lowveld on a number of occasions in recent decades, most notably in 1982-84 and 1991-92. Much of the lowveld, and in particular its communal areas, is very remote and only accessible via 'dust' roads through massive, until recently, unpopulated ranches. In January 2000 Cyclone Eline brought severe flooding and washed away many bridges making much of the region even more inaccessible.

The Zimbabwean (and formerly Rhodesian) lowveld differs in one important respect from the contiguous South African lowveld. Although vegetationally and topographically very similar, its political economy was not shaped by the discovery of gold. As a result there is much less infrastructure and it has always been a more physically and conceptually peripheral space.

The largest ethnic group in Zimbabwe's south-east lowveld have been variously described as Tsonga, Hlengwe or Shangaan/Changana/Shangani.

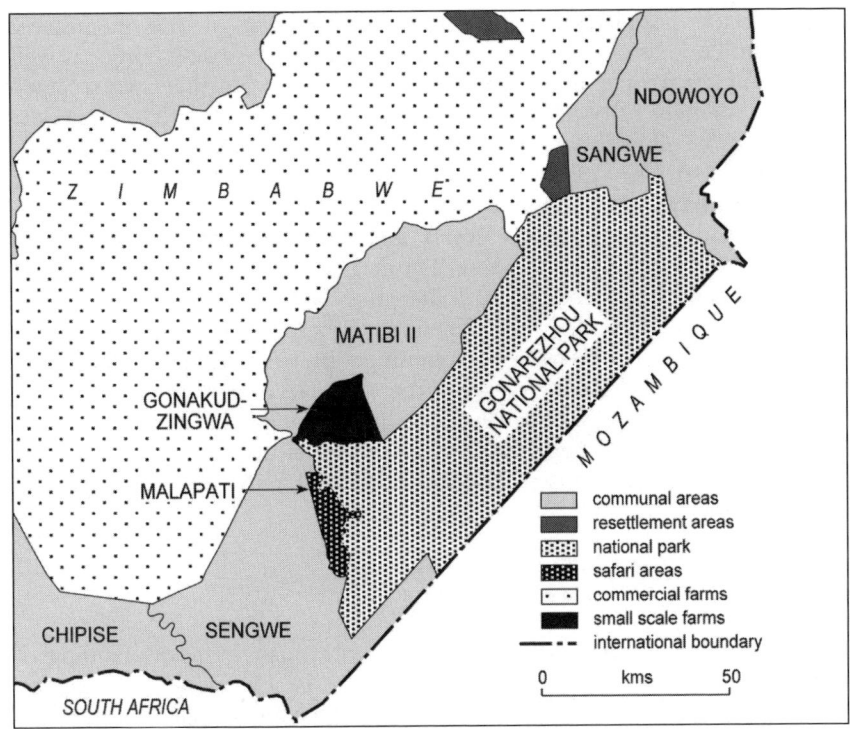

Map 1.3 Land use in the south-east lowveld

As elsewhere in colonial Africa these appellations owe much to the way in which officials and missionaries responded to cultural confusion by 'inventing' 'tribes' – employing the preconceptions and prejudices of their age to order the African world in their own image (see Ranger 1985; Harries 1989; Vail 1989; Worby 1994).[3] Nowadays in Zimbabwe the term Shangaan is commonly used to refer to any of the Ndau or Hlengwe inhabitants of the south-east lowveld to the east of the Bubi River (Cunliffe 1993). Although it is valid to argue that this appellation is not technically correct (Mtetwa 1976; Bannerman 1978; 1980) and, as a generic and popular way to embrace diverse peoples and chiefdoms with no common name, it is of little ethnographic value (Harries 1989), the fact remains that 'Shangaan' identity has been actively taken on by many of the inhabitants of the lowveld and strategically used to gain employment and mobilise politically. For these reasons I have used the label Shangaan in this book.

[3] As Said puts it: 'All cultures tend to make representations of foreign cultures the better to master or in some way control them' (1993: 120). In southern Africa enormous effort was invested in delineation reports, investigating lineages and establishing 'legitimate' chieftaincies in order to pigeonhole peoples' ethnicity and codify (or simply invent) traditions. Dividing Africans into tribes made them visible to Europeans and more easily administered. See, for example, National Archives of Zimbabwe (NAZ) S 2929/8/4 Delineation Reports Nuanetsi District.

The black population of the lowveld, however, is not exclusively Shangaan. There is a significant population of Ndebele and Karanga, as well as some Venda people along the Limpopo. In the 1950s there was a large-scale resettlement of Ndebele evictees from Gohlawayo Purchase Area near Filabusi to the alluvial pan west of the Mwenezi River in the Malipati area of Sengwe. Between 1952 and 1956 four other groups of 'outsiders' were settled in Matibi II communal area. These comprised a small group of Ndebele and Karanga from Victoria Reserve, Karanga from Gutu, and VaDuma from Chikwanda Reserve (Bannerman 1978). Other Ndebele and Karanga people displaced by land alienation for white farms made their own way to the lowveld. Post-Independence there was a continued flow of people into the region from surrounding districts such as Chivi, Zaka, Mwenezi, Gutu and Bikita, escaping the crowded communal lands of the plateau in search of more extensive grazing and arable lands. White immigration to the lowveld began in the early twentieth century and peaked in the 1960s as large amounts of land were alienated for 'commercial farming' and irrigated estates.

Landscape

The conceptual core of this book rests on a nuanced understanding of what it is we mean by 'landscape'. Landscape is a term with a complex etymology. Although seemingly more self-explanatory than 'culture' and 'nature',[4] it has been used in a variety of overlapping and competing ways in various disciplines. I do not wish to conflate the different strands of meaning of landscape, but (to use but one landscape metaphor) I have found it a useful viewpoint from which to survey the vast and rapidly proliferating theoretical literature on human constructions of nature and a helpful way into understanding the multiple layers of meaning of the Zimbabwean lowveld.

Two main types of question can be asked of landscapes, each reflecting quite different usages of the term. Ontological questions can be posed about the human creation of 'cultural landscapes': How have humans physically transformed the environment? Landscape, in this sense, is a portion of a natural and cultural environment – it is material, surrounding us, 'out there ... rather than in one's head' (Duncan 1995: 414). Secondly epistemological questions can be asked about landscape's attendant cultural, symbolic and political meanings: How is landscape mediated through artistic and cultural representations? How is landscape discursively constituted? How is it bound up with regimes of power and knowledge? In this usage landscape is as much imagined as 'real' – it is a 'way of seeing', or a text to be read. Taken together, but not conflated, these two usages of landscape

---

[4] Raymond Williams terms culture 'one of the two or three most complicated words in the English language' (1988: 87) and yet 'the idea of nature makes [it] seem relatively simple' (1980: 69).

constitute a useful analytical tool. As David Matless has argued:

> ... it is the 'duplicity' of landscape, as a cultural term carrying meanings of depth and surface, solid earth and superficial scenery, the ontological and the ideological, that gives it its analytical potential: 'not despite its difficulty as a comprehensive or reliable concept, but because of it'. (Matless 1998: 12; citing Daniels 1989: 197)

The notion of landscape enables one to move beyond sterile debates on nature-culture dualisms because it is both natural and cultural – a hybrid, reflecting the intertwined nature of social and ecological processes (see, for example, Descola and Palsson 1996; Braun and Castree 1998; Soper 1996; Lovell 1996). Landscape is the environment that people see, use, perceive, experience, interpret or understand, and because of this inherently phenomenological nature it encompasses the realm of human actions and imagination in a way that 'environment' does not. Landscape is a cultural process not an entity (Mitchell 1994; Hirsch and Michael 1995; Matless 1998; Layton and Ucko 1999).

The physical construction of 'cultural landscapes'

Landscape has been a central organising concept in geography for much of the twentieth century. The term 'cultural landscape' was coined by Carl Sauer in the 1920s to refer to the tangible record of human modification of the environment. Sauer and the Berkeley School of 'cultural geographers' sought to understand how rural peasants encoded their cultural values on the 'folk' landscape (Duncan 1995). They saw landscapes as the material outcomes of historical interactions between society and the environment. To Sauer 'the cultural landscape is fashioned from a natural landscape by a culture group. Culture is agent, the natural area the medium, the cultural landscape the result' (Sauer 1969: 343).[5] The focus of attention was on the material artefacts and visible forms in the landscape such as vernacular architecture, roads and crop patterns – landscape was conceived of as a palimpsest embodying the traces of people's past activities (e.g. Hoskins 1955).

The work of Sauer and other cultural geographers and environmental historians is particularly valuable in that it has contributed to a new understanding of the role of human agency in fashioning 'natural' landscapes. Any landscape presents a 'physiognomy shaped by man' (Warnke 1994: 10). This is most apparent when viewing agricultural landscapes where:

> Even the simplest topographical features are the results of political decisions. The size and disposition of the fields, the crops that are grown in them and the locations of the farms are determined by re-allocations, 'green plans', agricultural subsidies and control of the market. Fields, patches of woodland, dykes, pastures and meadows are all outcomes of agrarian policies. (Warnke 1994: 10)

---

[5] First published in Sauer (1925).

Even American wilderness areas, and Amazonian rainforests, those icons of unspoilt, pristine nature, uncontaminated by humanity, turn out on closer inspection to be – in a very material sense – profoundly human creations (Cronon 1996). Indigenous people have had a major impact on the structure and species composition of the 'pristine' forests of the Amazon region, for example, through a process of succession management over many centuries (Posey 1985). From the Sussex South Downs (Brandon 1998), to the American Great Plains (Cronon 1991), to the forests of West Africa (Fairhead and Leach 1996a), all landscapes are fashioned by human agency. In some cases 'natural' landscapes are deliberate artifice. Capability Brown's English landscape gardens and Frederick Law Olmstead's American parks and gardens, for example, sought consciously to improve on nature and shape it into more appropriately 'natural' configurations (Williams 1973; Whiston Spirn 1996).

Imagined landscapes

The second usage of the term 'landscape' lies in the realm of epistemology. Landscape, in this sense, has been defined as 'the symbolic environment created by human acts of conferring meaning to nature and the environment' (Greider and Garkovich 1994: 1). This implies a breaking down of the distinction between the physical dimension of landscape and its imaginary, representational sense (Demeritt 1994a). The axiomatic point of departure is that landscapes are more a social or cultural 'construction' than a reality 'out there' (Proctor 1998). They are as much imagined as 'real'. They are spaces with cultural, symbolic and political meaning that are socially constructed and perceived and interpreted from many different and contested viewpoints which reflect different actors' particular experience, culture and values (Blaikie 1995). This ties in with much work in the social sciences on the social construction of nature showing how the concept 'contains, though often unnoticed, an extraordinary amount of human history' (Williams 1980: 67), 'which has led different human beings to conceive of the natural world in very different ways' (Cronon 1996: 20).[6]

Landscape as a 'way of seeing'

An influential strand of research on imagined landscapes has grown out of British cultural geography and art history. This work stimulated a renewal of interest in 'landscape' as a category – although it is in a very different mould from the cultural geography of Sauer and the Berkeley School in

---

[6] Glacken's magisterial *Traces on the Rhodian Shore* identifies three key themes in Western attitudes to nature: the idea of a designed earth, the idea of environmental influence, and the idea of human beings as modifiers of nature (Glacken 1967; Ravi Rajan 1997; see also Collingwood 1945; Olwig 1984).

that it seeks to uncover landscapes' deeper meanings and symbolic qualities. Drawing on John Berger (1982) and Raymond Williams (1973), Dennis Cosgrove describes landscape as a 'way of seeing' – of representing, structuring or symbolising surroundings – that, with its basis in the mathematical technique of linear perspective, has affinities with the 'basic techniques of capitalist life' developed in the Renaissance (such as mapping and the surveying of land) (Cosgrove 1984: 70, 86; Daniels 1989: 205-206). The technique of perspective allowed artists to render depth realistically and establish a viewpoint for the spectator of the landscape (Rose 1992). This 'painterly' way of seeing is elitist, in part because it was the wealthy classes of Europe who commissioned paintings but also because the rural landscape itself was bound up with its representation. Estate owners paid landscape architects to design their properties to look like landscape paintings and then had them painted (Duncan 1995).

This way of seeing was closely associated with capitalist relations of production, as 'nature' was processed into an aesthetic commodity (Coetzee 1988: 41; Neumann 1998: 17; Andrews 1999). Daniels (1989: 206; following Cosgrove 1984) argues that 'the power of landscape was to give the impression that, far from being implicated in the commodification of land and any attendant class tensions, it represented [an illusory] world of nature'. Landscape, in this analysis, is a 'visual ideology which obscures not only the forces and relations of production' but also the less aesthetically pleasing or picturesque experiences of nature (Daniels 1989: 206). The English landscape garden, for example, was 'a rural landscape emptied of rural labour and of labourers ... from which the facts of production had been banished' (Williams 1973: 120).[7]

This way of seeing cast landscape as an object to be viewed by an externally located gaze – to be gazed upon from a single, perspectival and ego-centred viewpoint rather than 'experienced'. Specifically landscape was understood from the elite social position of the landowner whose property is spread before them (Rose 1992).[8] Furthermore, as Williams points out, 'the very idea of landscape implies separation and observation' (Williams 1973: 120). This notion of landscape equates with Foucault's panopticism – a visual regime that allowed surveillance and monitoring on a large scale (Foucault 1977). Nature took on a passive role, deprived of agency under a totalising gaze that created the impression of unity and control and accorded power to the viewer of the landscape to survey, discipline and control nature (Escobar 1999).[9] Feminist geographers have made the

---

[7] In the British context there is a considerable literature on 'natural' or nostalgic landscapes (such as enclosed fields, country estates, grouse moors and heritage museums) which mask exploitative social relations of production (e.g. Hewison 1987; Soper 1996).

[8] Anthropologists Hirsch and O'Hanlon (1995) similarly describe landscape as a restrictive way of seeing which privileges the point of view of 'outsiders' and sustains a radical split between insiders and outsiders on the land.

[9] As the object of expert scientific knowledge nature could be regularised, simplified, disciplined, and managed.

further point that this way of seeing (or gaze) is masculine, and the passivity of being looked at is the feminine position (Rose 1992).

Landscape as text

Reflecting the shifting intellectual currents in geography and the social sciences there was, in the 1980s and 1990s, a broadening of the scope of inquiry into landscapes and their meaning. With the poststructural turn in social theory, there has been a shift away from Marxist concerns with the emergence of a capitalist way of seeing, towards treating landscape metaphorically as 'text', 'icon', 'spectacle' or 'theatre' and examining how its reading or viewing is embedded within discursive formations.[10] Landscapes' multi-layered texts offer simultaneous readings and are culturally constructed through 'contested processes of signification' (Demeritt 1994a: 164).[11]

There has been a growing recognition that knowledge is multiple and positional and that landscapes are 'read' differently by different actors and are thus not simply an elite way of seeing. They are locales of meaning which are perceived and interpreted from many different and contested viewpoints which reflect different actors' particular experiences, culture and values at particular moments in time (Blaikie 1995), and the institutional context and power relations within which they are embedded (see Duncan 1990; Barnes and Duncan 1992; Duncan and Ley 1993). As Sullivan (2001b: 1) notes 'this polysemy confers tension to landscapes. As such, landscapes become the location and currency of claims and counterclaims, some of which relate deeply to the legitimacy and survival of identity among particular and variously defined groups' (see Peluso 1992; Berry 1993; Moore 1998).

Paraphrasing Mosse (1997: 255), historically contingent interactions between knowledge and power accord validity to particular readings of landscape to the exclusion of others (see Ferguson 1990). This relates to an eclectic body of research that is sometimes glossed as 'political ecology' which broadly focuses on the power relations implicated in the formation and function of ecologies and landscapes (Rocheleau 1999). Some of the themes in this work include: bringing local and global politics into the frame (Bryant 1992; 1997); querying and reframing accepted environmental

---

[10] A discourse is a way of thinking, writing or talking about a subject. All statements operate within a particular discourse which defines or limits how we think about things. In Foucault's (1972) terminology when sets of statements are linked together they become discursive formations, and when successfully established they are 'regimes of truth' (McDowell 1994). This is not to imply that discourses are all-encompassing and unchallengeable. As Grillo (1997) citing Seidal (1985: 44) points out, 'discourse is a site of struggle ... in which social meanings are produced or challenged'.

[11] Moore (1986) provides an early example from anthropology of a treatment of space as a cultural text which can be read and 'worked at' by members of the society who move through and act on it.

narratives (Thompson, Warburton and Hatley 1986; Anderson and Grove 1987; Behnke, Scoones and Kerven 1993; Tiffen, Mortimore and Gichuki 1994; Leach and Mearns 1996; Stott and Sullivan 2000); listening to differentiated local narratives[12] (Fairhead and Leach 1996a; Moore 1998); and drawing attention to the socially-constructed, historically-located and politically-partial nature of environmental science (Beinart 1984; Escobar 1996; Peet and Watts 1996; Roberson et al. 1996).

Social constructionism and critical realism

It is worth issuing a note of caution at this stage. The idea that landscape lies purely in the realm of the imagination has come under criticism from those who think the emphasis has moved too far away from material reality. As Demeritt puts it:

> ... metaphors of icon, spectacle and text tend to eclipse discussions of landscape changes *per se*. Landscape becomes interesting only in so far as it frames the social and provides a passive stage for an exclusively cultural drama. (1994b: 134)

The danger is also that landscapes can endlessly be matched to actors 'deriving as many meaningful landscapes as actors can be found to imagine and inhabit them' (Abramson 2000: 2). This reflects a broader philosophical debate on the merits and dangers of extreme 'social constructivist' approaches to nature (see Harvey 1993; Escobar 1996; Braun and Castree 1998; Proctor 1998; Escobar 1999). To counter this dilemma various writers have argued for a 'critical realist' approach that recognises the social construction of knowledge without disregarding the possibility of the independent agency of nature. As Gandy says: 'If we disentangle ontological and epistemological questions we can show that the world exists separately from us but our knowledge of it can only ever be partial and is mediated through social practice' (1996: 35).

Thus landscape is not simply *tabula rasa* where only human actions matter – and upon which we merely impose our gaze and interpretations – but is also an historical actor, existing independently of human perceptions of it. And, as Fairhead and Leach (1996a) show, considering landscape interpretations as in part socially constructed does not negate the fact that historical evidence might support some interpretations more than others (see also the criticisms of 'environmental orthodoxies' in Anderson and Grove (1987) and Leach and Mearns (1996)). Critical realism holds that some explanations are more adequate explanations of reality than others, though it concedes that all are always 'partial truths' (Proctor 1998).

---

[12] Narratives, in this context, are 'stories' or arguments 'of apparently incontrovertible logic which provides scripts and justifications for ... action' (Fairhead and Leach 1995: 1023). Their chief virtue is that they help to stabilise and underwrite the assumptions necessary for decision-making (Roe 1991).

Landscape and identity

Another strand of research in 'new' cultural geography and anthropology has been the investigation of multiple discourses about place and identity. Landscape has been a powerful idiom for representing national identity. Daniels, for example, examines the role of landscape art in envisioning changing notions of nationality in Britain and the United States, and Matless explores 'landscape and Englishness' (Daniels 1993; Matless 1998).

The imagined landscape of Africa was in large part a by-product of the making of modern European self-consciousness (Said 1978; Comaroff and Comaroff 1991; Harries 1997). As Luig and von Oppen point out, 'like other non-European parts of the world, [Africa] served as an important screen for European identities in formation, in a context of imperial quest for domination and control' (1997: 29-30).

> Imperial nationalists, almost by definition, have been intent to annex the home-lands of others in their identity myths. They have projected on these lands and their inhabitants pictorial codes expressing both an affinity with the colonizing country and an estrangement from it. It is often the very 'otherness' of these lands which has made them appear so compelling, especially as a testing ground for imperial energy and imagination. (Daniels 1993: 5)

African national parks were particularly symbolically important for the construction of racial and national identity for European settlers and legitimating conquest (Carruthers 1989; Neumann 1998; Ranger 1999). In southern Africa views of landscape were partially vernacularised and a significant element in whites' assertion of colonial identities distinct from those of Europe (Beinart 2000; see Haarhoff 1991; Carruthers 1995; Foster 1998; Bunn 1999; Noyes 2000).

Some writers have argued that a European visual aesthetic was brought to bear on African space in order to physically and symbolically appropriate it – to exert cognitive as well as physical mastery over the natural environment (Okoye 1997; see Comaroff and Comaroff 1991; Noyes 1991; Bunn 1994; Mitchell 1994; Harries 1997). However this Western gaze was never all-encompassing and was often resisted. Attempts have increasingly been made to uncover the previously ignored, often subversive, senses of place and notions of landscape that are constructed by the powerless rather than the powerful, in particular the post-colonial 'other', and enable the previously silenced to enter discourses about landscape (McDowell 1994; see, for example, Guha and Spivak 1988).

Wilderness – a binary vision

> Wilderness hides its unnaturalness behind a mask that is all the more beguiling because it seems so natural. As we gaze into the mirror [wilderness] holds up for us, we too easily imagine what we behold is Nature when in fact we see the reflection of our own unexamined longings and desires. (Cronon 1996: 71-71)

I have already outlined how wilderness areas have been physically modified by human action. Yet moving from the ontological to the epistemological realm, wilderness is also very much – and controversially – a cultural construction. A central argument of this book is that a particular imagined landscape or way of seeing, deriving from the European understanding of wilderness, has been applied to the lowveld. The history and associations of this conceptualisation merit a brief explanation.

Broadly speaking there are two senses of wilderness in Judaeo-Christian philosophy (Curtin 1964; Nash 1982; Coetzee 1988). These two senses are 'not discrete entities but combined in the tension of shifting ambiguity' (Short 1991: 10). They are sometimes convergent, but often in conflict (Broch-Due 2000). The first sense in which wilderness has been understood is as forbidden wasteland located in a realm over which God's sway did not extend (Coetzee 1988) and beyond human control. Descriptions of wilderness in this vein abound with negative connotations. It has been variously: alien, uncontrolled, chaotic, confused, lonely, fearful, forlorn, barren, dreary, degenerate, desolate, hostile, dangerous, evil, empty, uncivilised, cruel, savage, suffering, unimproved and untamed. This threatening space needed ordering using 'the cosmetics of European aesthetic formula and social systems' (Lammas 1996: 45). It was a terrain of struggle which humanity has long attempted to tame, subdue, domesticate, civilise and bring into the productive sphere. The conquest of this malign wilderness was a sign of human achievement, a measure of social progress (Short 1991). This is most clearly demonstrated in the New World notion of the extension of the frontier, where pioneers progressively established order in the midst of chaos and danger.

The second strand of thought about wilderness has also been influential. In their search for the roots of modern environmentalism historians have regularly landed on early nineteenth-century romanticism and primitivism, initially associated with the writing of Wordsworth and Rousseau and the painting of Claude Lorrain, that reacted pejoratively to the idea of progress and the worship of economic growth and connected creativity, happiness and fulfilment with proximity to unmodified nature (Beinart and Coates 1995). In unadorned nature was the *sublime* – in the spiritual sense that it inspired awe in the supernatural or God. The mountain and the forest, in particular, became symbols of the sublime (Schama 1995).

This wilderness is a place to be revered rather than feared. It is space of deep spiritual significance and a symbol of an earthly Edenic paradise (Short 1991); and a place of safe retreat into contemplation and purification (Coetzee 1988; cf. Mukonyora 2000). Wilderness has increasingly been positioned as the symbolic alternative to the human enterprise embodied by 'the decadent metropole' (Anderson and Grove 1987). It is a refuge or sanctuary in which those in need of consolation can find respite from the pressures of civilisation and modernity (Nash 1982); and a source of nostalgia that is somehow sullied or degraded by human contact (Van der Post 1984).

The nostalgic striving for contact with pure, unspoiled, authentic, original nature and yearning for sources of transcendence in the natural world is nowhere better illustrated than in the history of the idea of wilderness in the United States (Haila 1997).[13] Wilderness, in various guises, has always been a hugely powerful and emotive concept of nature in American culture.[14] Wilderness gained currency as a North American nationalist concept in reference to the mythic 'frontier' and started to be represented as a valuable feature of national heritage and as something distinct from European cultural monuments – a symbol of national identity with quasi-religious overtones (Short 1991; Haila 1997). This romantic image of wilderness was depicted in the epic paintings of Bierstadt and Moran, the writings of Emerson and Thoreau and made physically manifest in the American landscape with the establishment of the world's first national park at Yellowstone in 1872 (Nash 1982). This model in which wilderness was 'preserved' from the effects of human agency by gazetting a bounded space for nature was subsequently disseminated worldwide (Neumann 1998).

As Broch-Due (2000: 18) points out, the legacy of this ancient European obsession with wilderness is 'an ingrained ambiguity that continues to project two distinct sets of values'.

> On the one hand, to subdue wilderness is to establish order and perhaps re-create Eden by cultivating nature, human and nonhuman, in the mould of Christianity and/or capitalism. On the other hand, to feel awed is to celebrate wilderness in its originary form, a nostalgic mode that still travels with a wish to preserve nature as a way to preserve our common past (or *Our Common Future*) but is no less open to commodification and exploitation.

She makes the further important point that this past and present Western imagery does not just represent 'points of view' that are abstract figments of the imagination. Rather they become powerful and sometimes coercive realities on the ground, 'transforming the peoples and places they were originally intended to describe' (Broch-Due 2000: 18). In essence ways of seeing define ways of acting (Ranger 1999: 69).

Yet, whether envisaged as barren and unimproved, as immoral and savage, or as a spiritual refuge from the city, wilderness has always been fashioned as counterposed to civilisation. The wilderness premise is that nature, if it is to be truly 'natural', must also be pristine and by definition entirely outside the realm of the human – 'the place where we are is the place where nature is

---

[13] This has been the subject of numerous works by historians of environmental ideas. Key texts include Nash (1982) and Oeschlaeger (1991). The writings of Henry David Thoreau, John Muir and Aldo Leopold are judged to have been particularly influential. Ideas of wilderness continue to be particularly significant to the American, and global, environmental movement.

[14] The vitriol with which 'wilderness deconstruction' – and in particular the environmental historian William Cronon's writing – has been rebutted by defenders of a 'pure', unproblematic American wilderness is testament to the emotive power of the concept (see for example the essays in Soule and Lease (1995) and Proctor (1998)).

not' (Cronon 1996: 81). However the wilderness vision – binary or otherwise – is but one peculiarly Western way of seeing which requires the suppression of histories of inhabitation and a denial of other imagined landscapes. As touched on above, the Western gaze is not all-encompassing and there are dissenting visions. Some notions of landscape are fundamentally at odds with the Western perspectival construction of landscapes with its visual bias. These landscapes, instead, are dynamic, experienced and dwelled in. They are multi-layered constructions of social experience that can be thought of as sedimented history or socialised spaces (Fairhead and Leach 1996b; Sullivan 2001b). They are not simply a way of seeing, but a way of being in the world (Bender 1998). In this respect the concept of landscape is a useful entry point into understanding social processes.

Overview

In applying these ideas to the analysis of the lowveld landscape of southeastern Zimbabwe I will examine how the lowveld has been physically and imaginatively constructed by a range of actors and how the multi-layered ways of seeing, reading or experiencing the lowveld have influenced the ways in which it has been defined, represented and acted upon.

Moving beyond crude colonial/indigenous, white/black, rural landusers/government officials and local/global dichotomies a variety of actors come into focus. These include: Shangaan smallholder farmers (who themselves are socially and economically differentiated and rely on farming and migration remittances to varying extents); Shona and Ndebele in-migrants; white commercial farmers (cattle ranchers, game ranchers, and irrigators); black 'small-scale' commercial farmers; war veterans; Agritex (the government agricultural extension service);[15] the Veterinary Department; the Department of National Parks and Wildlife Management (DNPWLM); local and international NGOs; and the World Bank Global Environment Facility (GEF). There is no shared or uncontested 'local' or 'external' perspective on landscape.

I will attempt to uncover the range of different perceptions of the lowveld landscape that are and have been held by these and other actors. How do these perceptions reflect their needs, interests and values? How have they changed over time? How are they contested and maintained? To what extent are they bound up with social identities? What power relations are they embedded within? To what extent do they impinge on and influence policy discourses (and *vice versa*)? Who gains and who loses? Whose perspectives and knowledge count in defining policy agendas, and whose perspectives and claims are marginalised and at what costs to their livelihoods? And what policy spaces and alternative ways of framing debates on environment and development in the lowveld are opened up by allowing

[15] In 2003 Agritex was renamed Agricultural Research and Extension Services (AREX).

silenced perceptions and experiences to be heard?

Chapter 2 explores colonial perceptions of the lowveld landscape and its inhabitants. In part because of the difficulties inherent in applying a European picturesque and pastoral landscape aesthetic to the lowveld it came to be celebrated for its very divergence from this aesthetic – this was a wilderness vision that was expressed in two very different ways. Either it was a land of mystery, danger, lost cities, and adventure to be tamed and controlled by pioneers; or it was a pristine wilderness celebrated, threatened and protected.

Chapter 3 investigates African perceptions of the landscape that has come to be termed the lowveld. Shangaan, Shona and Ndebele-speakers' interpretations and representations of this place reveal more than a dualistic vision of wilderness that must be saved or pushed back. These are often rooted in a different paradigm that is not founded on the conceptual separation of nature and civilisation and does not approach landscape in purely visual terms. A variety of ecological and spiritual understandings, political struggles and livelihood strategies are brought to bear on and in the landscape – it is full of meanings and memories. This leads to a multi-layered constellation of porously bounded jurisdictions, each of which is very far from 'fixed' but continually made and remade. This chapter examines these multiple, overlapping, dynamic and contested African ideas and images of the landscape that have arisen out of daily interactions with this 'lived in' and symbolic space, and are bound up with identity, politics and religion.

Chapters 4, 5 and 6 explore different facets of the 'productive', or potentially productive, agricultural or pastoral lowveld landscape. Chapter 4 describes the history of dryland agriculture and other livelihood strategies in the lowveld and examines how land-use practices have changed with population movements, colonial land alienation, agricultural extension and legislation. It traces the way in which the landscape has been represented as unsuited to dryland agriculture and its inhabitants portrayed as non-farmers. In particular the lowveld has been rigidly defined as belonging to an agro-ecological category – or 'natural region' – in which rainfed cropping is economically and environmentally unsustainable. The chapter reveals the consistent mismatch between static, inflexible official recommendations for agricultural development and the dynamic realities of actual farming practice. Dryland farming has always been, and continues to be, a key livelihood strategy – alongside others – and recent environmental, economic and political dynamics have conspired to increase its importance.

In Chapter 5 I examine the actual and planned attempts to bring irrigation to the commercial and communal sectors in the lowveld. The physical transformation of the landscape is underpinned by a way of seeing that holds that the wild landscape could and should be battled, tamed and economically and aesthetically transformed from a backwater to a productive, lush breadbasket by heroic pioneers. In both sectors there has been a penchant for massive, engineering-driven, technocratic irrigation schemes but few of these have ever materialised (none in the communal areas). Small-scale irrigation schemes that have been developed in the communal areas of the lowveld have tended to have overly rigid prescriptions and to ignore the priorities of those who do not want to be full-time farmers but pursue irrigated agriculture as only one among many diverse livelihood strategies. The physical and imaginative transformation of the landscape has been bound up with issues of identity and with struggles for power at many levels as different landscape representations have been appropriated and used by different actors to gain control of water or exert influence.

Chapter 6 discusses the portrayal of the lowveld as cattle country – ideal ranching land. This way of seeing has underpinned attempts to transform the lowveld into a patchwork of hard-edged, fenced zones; to establish demarcated grazing lands and individual owner-managers of stock within communal areas; to encourage high 'off-take rates'; and to constrain livestock movement. The history of livestock husbandry in these communal areas runs counter to this way of seeing and acting. Smallholders' livestock management strategies have not been supported and have often been actively discouraged by policy. Opportunistic strategies such as livestock loaning arrangements subvert the ranching vision which portrays livestock management as a purely technical (rather than a social or political) issue.

Chapter 7 investigates an alternative wilderness vision – one that celebrates a 'natural' or pristine wilderness and has led to attempts to preserve or rehabilitate the wild landscape rather than tame it. It traces the conceptual battles around the establishment of Gonarezhou National Park, the wildlife conservancies, and a transfrontier national park. It shows how a strange alliance of ecocentric and neoliberal priorities has conspired to encourage a shift in the conservationist agenda from viewing protected areas as inviolate sanctuaries to looking to them increasingly as potential sources of revenue which should be extended across the landscape. In this respect any division between 'natural' and 'productive' spaces is an increasingly artificial one as the boundaries have blurred. Finally it asks whose interests are served by CAMPFIRE and other community wildlife utilisation schemes which to date have delivered minimal returns to communities and imposed further coercive restrictions on other livelihood activities.

Finally in Chapter 8 I explore these ways of seeing the lowveld landscape in relation to the highly charged politics of land in the lowveld and Zimbabwe more generally of recent years. I briefly trace the history of land reform in Zimbabwe before analysing in detail the dynamics of the farm invasions in the lowveld in 2000-2001. In relation to the themes of dryland agriculture, irrigation, livestock and wildlife management, I ask whether the land reform programme will improve the livelihoods of people in lowveld communal areas and incorporate their alternative perceptions of landscape. Does it have the potential to replace the wilderness vision with a new way of seeing and, consequently, acting? I conclude by arguing for the need for land reform to support flexible and mobile livelihood strategies that cut across single land-use zones and hard boundaries; and for opening a debate on the restitution of ancestral land in Zimbabwe's lowveld.

My introduction to the south-east lowveld of Zimbabwe came in 1997 when I worked on a collaborative research project on crop-livestock integration with the Institute of Environmental Studies at the University of Zimbabwe.[16] In the search for a 'low resource endowment' study site to contrast with the relatively well-researched plateau communal areas and Zambezi Valley we landed on the southernmost portion of Matibi II communal area near Chikombedzi township in Chiredzi District. My first impression was of a dusty and incredibly remote outpost where the beer-hall proudly advertised itself as 'The back of beyond – where they all come to drink'. I spent six months in the area in 1997 and 1998 where I became interested in the physical and symbolic lowveld landscape more broadly and decided to return for my doctoral research.

The fieldwork for this book took place in 1999 and 2001. In 1999 I spent six months in Zimbabwe conducting what might be termed a multi-sited ethnography (cf. Marcus 1995). My in-depth case study work was again carried out mainly in the vicinity of Chikombedzi township where I had already established local connections. This broadly 'village-based' research was interwoven with spells in Chiredzi, Masvingo and Harare (the district, provincial and national capitals). After a year back in the UK observing dramatic changes in Zimbabwe from afar I returned to the lowveld for a further three months. Together both spells of fieldwork involved approximately 200 interviews as well as on-site observation in Matibi II and Sengwe communal areas, Gonarezhou National Park, Gonakudzingwa small-scale farms and various commercial ranches. I also undertook a smaller amount of research in Sangwe communal area and on commercial ranches in Mwenezi District (see Maps 1.1 and 1.2). An effort was made to talk to a spectrum of people representative of the diversity of rural Zimbabwe: young and old; women and men; Shangaan, Shona, Ndebele, English and Afrikaans speakers; richer and poorer. I also interviewed informants from government, civil society and the private sector in Chiredzi, Masvingo and Harare – all these interviews were conducted in English. The majority of the 'village-based' interviews were, however, conducted in Shangaan or Shona. Despite my best anthropological intentions my language skills never reached the proficiency necessary to conduct an interview. I was immensely fortunate in this regard in my working relationship with Jacob Mahenehene who acted as my interpreter. We had already worked together since my first visit in 1997 and established a close rapport which I believe helped surmount some of the pitfalls inherent in the translation process. Given Zimbabwe's anguished racial politics there are many subjects that it is hard,

---

[16] Crop-Livestock Integration: The Dynamics of Change in Contrasting Agroecological zones – funded by the Renewable Natural Resources Research Strategy, Livestock Production Programme of the Department for International Development (see Wolmer, Sithole and Mukamuri 2003).

or even impossible, for a white, British researcher to broach — particularly in the febrile atmosphere surrounding the 2000 parliamentary election and farm invasions. Where it was inappropriate for me to conduct an interview Jacob did so instead (as the footnotes acknowledge). Where information might be judged potentially sensitive the names of interviewees have been omitted or disguised. Written material consulted included travellers' accounts, biographies, literature set in the lowveld, policy documents, scientific studies and archival records from the National Archives of Zimbabwe, the Masvingo Records Centre, and at the Royal Geographical Society and the Public Records Office in the UK. A methodological dilemma that must not be ignored is the tension inherent in using such sources both as 'representations' and as reflections of 'reality'. As Moore and Vaughan (1994) and Fairhead and Leach (1996: 17) note, the unease that this dualism provokes is inescapable — for sometimes they, and I, are reading 'colonial written accounts, for example, ... for what they say about representations of landscape and people at the time — for their place in discourse — and sometimes seeking in them the data about past landscape [and people] which they provide.'

2

The wilderness vision
Colonial perceptions of the lowveld landscape and its inhabitants

The lowveld has long been an extremely evocative concept in southern African white settler culture and the lowveld landscape continues to have a resonance for many who do not live within it or anywhere near it. In the last quarter of the nineteenth century the European visitors to the portion of the southern African lowveld that was to fall inside Rhodesia were few and far between. Those to record their journeys to the region included ivory hunters, political emissaries from Rhodes to the Gaza Nguni kings, agents for the British South Africa Company assessing the agricultural potential of the area for white settlers, and labour recruiters investigating the availability of labour for the Witwatersrand mines.[1]

The 'Pioneer Column' of white settlers arrived in what was soon to become Southern Rhodesia from South Africa in 1890. Initially Rhodes' British South Africa Company was intending to exploit the mining potential of the region and replicate the success of the Transvaal. However, mining proved to be less viable than hoped and the colonialists decided to focus on the agricultural possibilities of the country and land alienation began. White farming practices were forcibly mapped onto the country's highveld, the agro-ecological zone with the highest rains, most fertile soils and the largest agricultural potential (Moore 1999; see Palmer 1977; Moyana 1984; Moyo 1995).

Initially the dry and relatively inhospitable Rhodesian lowveld was not favoured for white settlement. Early 'pioneers' such as Dunbar and Moodie rapidly traversed a 'barren, deserted' and sparsely populated lowveld to reach the 'healthier' Eastern Highlands where agricultural labour was readily available (Oliver 1957; Hughes 2001). Early in the twentieth century the few Europeans frequenting the lowveld were perceived as adventurers or outlaws operating physically and legally on the margins, making a living by

---

[1] See, for example, Doyle (1891); Gillmore (1890); Longden (1950); and Oliver (1957).

poaching elephants and illegally recruiting labour for the gold mines of the Witwatersrand and other nefarious activities.[2] More substantial white settlement only came to the lowveld later in the twentieth century as a further, this time internal, migration took place when a second wave of 'pioneer' settlers left the highveld in search of extensive ranching land (see Chapter 6). In the resulting second phase of land alienation much of the lowveld was appropriated for ranching – the massive Nuanetsi Ranch occupying a large portion of it (over 2 million acres) – denying the resident, mainly Shangaan-speaking, population access to this land. Some of these ranches later established irrigation systems to grow sugar and citrus (see Chapter 5). More recently others have shifted their focus from cattle to game (see Chapter 7), but cattle production has historically been the main form of land use in the commercial (white) farming sector in the lowveld.

The Rhodesian lowveld was invested with conflicting and competing meanings by these European travellers, entrepreneurs and settlers. Often deeply ambiguous and contradictory notions coexisted in their imaginations. The landscape has variously been represented as a disease-ridden wilderness, a backward and primitive zone, a degraded wasteland, a rugged frontier, a lost kingdom, a politically unstable lair for insurgents, an ideal ranching territory, a potential agricultural breadbasket, a romantic Eden, and a hunting arena. These perceptions reveal much about the role of the lowveld in the shaping of the white Rhodesian psyche. But beyond this they have all had implications for the way in which the lowveld was framed as a target for particular interventions ranging from tsetse fly eradication programmes, to elephant translocations, to counter-insurgency bombing raids.

These diverse colonial perceptions of the lowveld landscape stem from one particular way of seeing the landscape – as wilderness. As described in Chapter 1 this wilderness vision has two facets – one pejorative, the other romantic. Embedded in and closely bound up with these views of the lowveld landscape are colonial representations of its African inhabitants. Notwithstanding this broad generalisation about how the lowveld was understood it is important to stress at the outset that colonial perceptions of this landscape were not monolithic.[3] Indeed:

... despite [European] culturally specific traditions about what [an African] landscape

---

[2] These mines had, however, brought substantial white settlement to the South African lowveld which came to be criss-crossed by wagon trails supplying the townships.

[3] An idea of the multiplicity of discourses associated with African landscapes by Europeans is given by a reading of Jean and John Comaroff's detailed study of the encounter between non-Conformist Christian missionaries and the Tswana in South Africa (Comaroff and Comaroff 1991: 395; 1997: 561). In the first volume the index cites the following references for 'Africa – European images/representations of': as antithesis of Europe; as dark; as degenerate; as desert; as Eden; as emasculated; as enchanted landscape; as female body; as garden; as mother; as slothful; as victim; as virgin landscape; as wasteland. And in the second volume: as camera obscura; as child-like; as degenerate; as dirty; as ethnicized stereotype; as fallen; as idle; as primitive forebears; as savage; as sick continent; as uncultivated.

had to consist of, their views were not uniform. The paintings, writings, photographs, monuments and place names produced [in colonial Africa] display utterly different, often contradictory views among Europeans themselves. Their endeavour of 'bringing culture' to Africa depended on their own social situations. (Luig and von Oppen 1997: 31)

The colonial encounter was therefore 'more a spiralling, many-layered conversation than a straightforward process of conversion or colonial domination' (Comaroff and Comaroff 1997: xvi). In this context the term colonial refers particularly to white southern African perceptions. I do not mean to suggest that colonial perceptions everywhere in the world fitted this mould. Also, as will become clear, 'colonial' perceptions are alive and well in the 'post-colonial' era. Indeed, in some respects, particularly given the current context of donor-driven development and conservation initiatives, these colonial perceptions could be said to be exerting an increasing influence over African environments today as parts II and III will illustrate (cf. Anderson and Grove 1987).

The landscape aesthetic – picturesque scenery and wilderness

As Chapter 1 described, the landscape 'way of seeing' was a specifically European visual convention where the land was ordered and arranged into scenery from the point of view of the beholder and terrain was viewed as the potential subject of a painting. Bringing this European visual aesthetic to bear on African space was a means by which it could be physically and symbolically appropriated (Okoye 1997).[4] In the case of the southern African lowveld this meant that early travellers frequently used painterly metaphors in their references to scenery, panoramas and landscapes; and these landscapes were aesthetically pleasing when their features were redolent of the stylistic conventions and pictorial principles of the European (and particularly English) visual landscape.[5] The 'park-like' nature of the landscape was frequently celebrated and explicit references to painting, colour and to English landscapes made:

> ... we descended into open rich grass land, covered with large trees, through which the river wound majestically in an uninterrupted course far into the distance – a splendid landscape, fresh, green and painted with the most vivid tints. (Elton 1873: 24)

---

[4] For more on this theme see Noyes (1991); Bunn (1994); Lammas (1996); Comaroff and Comaroff (1991); and Harries (1997).

[5] In particular the idioms of the 'picturesque' and the 'pastoral' were used as modes of organising the pictorial and literary representation of the English landscape. As Andrews (1999: 129) explains: 'The picturesque view of nature is one that appreciates landscape in so much as it resembles known works of art'. In this respect certain conventions of framing, perspective, and staging were invoked. Landscapes were composed in receding planes broken by objects such as ruins, rivers, trees and mountains, with some foreground interest such as a shepherd, and used a particular palette of colours.

> The beauty of the scene before us was almost a sufficient reward for our labour, for it was charming Devonshire hills repeated in altitude and incline, only occasional clumps of trees usurped the place of grass and gorse. (Gillmore 1890: 38)

> Eastwards, for as far as the eye can see, stretches a rolling expanse of tree-tops, in the foreground a medley of green, yellow, and russet-brown, but with increasing distance, merging into a carpet of blue-grey, which, as it recedes, assumes an even fainter hue, until at last it blends with the dim haze of the horizon. (Stevenson-Hamilton 1937: 23)

The counterpoint to this was that, as Harries (1997: 183) points out, when 'the landscape did not speak in a language understood by the viewers they described it in inverted and negative terms of what they knew. The land was empty, monotonous, colourless, treeless, silent, naked, devoid of perspective, unmarked by human enterprise and without God.' To Erskine (1890: 1st Journey, 10) and Hyatt (1917: 132) for example:

> The country is of the same unvarying flatness, covered with seedy looking 'Bush'.

> The low bush veld is simply deadly in its monotony. Practically the only tree you find in it is the mopani, and, though the soil is red sand and the leaves a rather bright green, the general impression you get is that everything is a horrible, dull grey.

A Chief Native Commissioner was later to comment on the site of the proposed Gonarezhou National Park: 'Away from the big rivers there is little scenery of interest. There are palm trees in some of the shallow valleys, and broken hilly country to the South East of Chipinda Pools. But the vast bulk of the area is very flat, dry and uninteresting country.'[6] Ranger (1999: 12-13) argues, in this vein, that the Matopos Hills of Zimbabwe 'struck the first [European] artist travellers as *almost* picturesque. But to be fully picturesque, and therefore paintable as landscape, they needed something which seemed lacking to European eyes. They needed a castle, or a hermitage, or some of the other signs of culture and history which marked the great nineteenth-century paintings of the picturesque. Without such human signs the Matopos were hard to see.' Similarly Coetzee (1988) describes how in the early nineteenth century the scientist and amateur painter William Burchell resorted to incorporating his caravan of wagons, oxen and sheep into the foreground of his sketches of the South African landscape in order to evoke the picturesque. Thomas Baines – who had had great difficulty 'articulating [South African] frontier space in picturesque terms' – made his way rapidly to the more sympathetic Victoria Falls which he repeatedly and famously painted in the picturesque idiom (Anderson 1993: 73; cited by Ranger 1999: 14).

---

[6] S 1542/G1/1 CNC to the Minister of Commerce and Transportation 13 November 1933. More recently, attempts have been made to re-evaluate the aesthetic qualities of Gonarezhou's plains which are: 'flat, endless and featureless at first sight, but in fact possessed of subtle changes in colour and texture, or browns, greys and ochres' (Pitman 1980: 2).

However, the endeavour to set African landscapes within European frames and stylistic conventions was often thwarted by their sheer otherness and exotic divergence from the northern European visual experience. African landscapes in general, and the flat, arid, southern African lowveld in particular, challenged the familiar tropes of nature and landscape of the arriving Europeans, as they could rarely be made to fit the picturesque landscape aesthetic (Coetzee 1988; Neumann 1998). These new arrivals 'lacked the visual conventions to "see", or make sense of, either the landscape or the indigenous population' (Harries 1997: 171). Instead, a way of seeing landscape that had more in common with emerging approaches to other New World landscapes in North America and Australia came to the fore – a schema of representation responsive to 'empty' country, liberated from the conventions of the picturesque. This is what I have termed the 'wilderness vision' (cf. Coetzee 1988).[7] Rather than attempting imaginatively to transform the landscape to fit European conventions, this vision emphasised the landscape's very difference from Europe – its exotic 'otherness' (cf. Lammas 1996).

As we have seen in Chapter 1, the wilderness vision is not a monolithic, unchallenged one. It has had many strands that have been woven together and unravelled at particular moments and in particular places. Colonial perceptions of the Rhodesian lowveld broadly fit a dualistic attitude to wilderness. The two basic manifestations of this visual code respectively encourage conflicting ways of acting on the landscape. Either the wilderness has been in some way malign, a 'Heart of Darkness' to be battled and tamed and converted to the conventions of the picturesque; or it has been a benign, even sublime, 'Eden' to be protected or returned to former glories.

A land of mystery, danger and scoundrels

Early in the twentieth century many colonial-era representations of the lowveld emphasised its darker side. The barbaric nature of the land and its inhabitants (both black and white) is dwelt on, portraying a savage land of mysticism, desperados and chancers. This is the lowveld described in T.V. Bulpin's *The Ivory Trail*, a heavily romanticised account celebrating the activities of an outlaw ivory poacher, gunrunner, smuggler and labour recruiter, Cecil Barnard (known as Bvekenya). Bvekenya operated from the point at which Southern Rhodesia, the northern Transvaal and Portuguese East Africa (Mozambique) intersected. This 'secluded and sinister wedge

---

[7] On the theme of wilderness in New World painting see, for example, Short (1991) and Tyler (1983). There were important differences between American and African ways of seeing landscape. One is that the notion of sublime landscape emerged to a far lesser extent in Africa. Coetzee (1988) and Harries (1997) argue that European settlers in southern Africa initially lacked the institutions and ideological apparatus that were necessary in America to harness the emancipatory potential of the sublime to an expansive colonial culture.

of land ... was a last home to many a curious and lawless character: a sanctuary from civilisation, whose solitary state was paradise to all those whose deeds or inclinations made imperative a retreat to some last stronghold of the lawless' and as such became known as 'Crooks' Corner' (Bulpin 1954: 20). This view is substantiated by administrative reports of the time including the Assistant Native Commissioner for Nuanetsi Sub-District who wrote in his Annual Report of 1927 that: 'It is no chimerical assertion that the country adjoining the Eastern and S.E. borders of the district is a veritable Tom Tiddler's ground and provides sanctuary for many doubtful characters both white and black.'[8]

Murray (1995) provides an account of the illicit labour recruiting or 'blackbirding' carried out by these 'doubtful characters'. The 'labour pirates' were attracted to this 'forsaken, isolated wasteland' by the steady stream of labour migrants from Southern Rhodesia, Portuguese East Africa and as far afield as Nyasaland en route to the Witwatersrand goldfields in search of work. Crooks' Corner was a point of entry for these clandestine migrants into the northern Transvaal and they converged on the area in large numbers. The isolation of this area and the expanding demand for low-cost labour enabled predatory labour recruiters to exploit the situation by using increasingly unscrupulous methods to 'recruit' large batches of migrants, smuggle them across the Limpopo and sell them on to licensed recruiting agents. They were also able to exploit the rugged landscape and proximity of three countries around a poorly defined border by slipping in and out of each country to evade arrest from the respective police forces. Bvekenya would even allegedly move the beacon marking the border from one side of his camp to another depending on the jurisdiction of the authorities looking for him. By the 1910s cut-throat (sometimes literally) competition had pushed the blackbirders northwards to encompass the whole Southern Rhodesian lowveld, penetrating inland as far as Ndanga, Chibi and Melsetter Districts (Murray 1995).

Crooks' Corner took on something of a Wild West image – a lawless frontier zone harbouring an assortment of white petty criminals, desperados, outcasts and fugitives who, as well as illicit labour recruiting, depended on gunrunning, extortion and poaching for their living (Bulpin 1954; Murray 1995). To official eyes these men had 'degenerated beyond the pale of civilisation' not only because of their nefarious activities but because they appeared to revel in their 'derelict lifestyle'; and from the blackbirders' point of view the 'harsh and disagreeable landscape offered convenient sanctuary from the probing glances of state authority ... and provided at least temporary respite from police detection and arrest' (Murray 1995: 376, 387-388).[9] In this way the characteristics of the landscape and the wayward

---

[8] NAZ S 235/505 ANC Nuanetsi Annual Report 1927.
[9] Alexander *et al.* (2000: 45) describe a similar colonial perception of Shangani Reserve in south-west Zimbabwe as a zone of violence and criminality: 'the site of battles; a refuge for bandits and murderers; a hide-out for those who wanted to avoid tax or missionary teaching.'

Europeans who inhabited it came to be bound up – both were marginal and dangerous.

This landscape was also perceived as a barren and inhospitable area. As one early traveller put it:

> I had heard of the 'Hlenga' [Shangaan] country as a term synonymous with thirst and hunger, and every privation pertaining to a desert; but until now I had not realised their proximity. (Erskine 1890: 2nd Journey, 12)

This was no place for the faint hearted for, as well as the physical dangers, this was a landscape invested with mystical threats:

> The wilderness in which Bvekenya hunted, between the Great Sabi and the Limpopo, from the Rhodesian border down to within fifty miles of the sea, was known to the Shanganes as the *Hlengwe* (The Place Where You Need Help) [sic]. It was a place where terror dwelt: a haunt of the wild animals, of sudden death, of ancient savagery, and the nameless ghosts of strange gods whose lore and rites were half-forgotten. ... The *Hlengwe*, in short was not an environment likely at any time to nurture a culture or mother some glorious civilisation. (Bulpin 1954: 110-111)

In part this representation of the lowveld as a land of 'ancient savagery' derived from the European accounts of the Gaza Nguni empire which encompassed the Zimbabwean lowveld in its hinterland and was raided extensively by the Nguni. The European term for this empire was 'Gazaland' and it was often translated as 'land of blood' and associated with intrigue, danger and savagery. The following account, written in the introduction to a children's book, is a typical representation of the Gazaland days:

> During the period of conquest [by the Nguni kings] blood flowed like water. For many years vultures, hyenas and other carnivora lived mainly on human flesh. It is impossible to fix even approximately the number of men, women and children who were exterminated by the Zulu hordes but they must number many tens of thousands. The Shangaans fled everywhere like antelopes. (Pirow n.d.: 7-8)

These representations draw on a long history of crude representations of Africa as the 'Dark Continent' rife with mystery and savages to which noble missionaries brought light and salvation.[10] Representations of the lowveld landscape as a place of mystery and danger were extended to colonial representations of its black inhabitants. Indeed, European perceptions of landscape have always been inextricably bound up with their representations of African society:

> The tribespeople who lived in this desert of bush and sand and swamp were a wild and unruly lot. They were sparsely scattered in the bush. The animals, fever, drought, hunger and their own passions kept their numbers down. Foul murders and dreadful barbarities marked the passing of their days, while the spectre of witchcraft haunted their thoughts like a continuous and horrible nightmare. (Bulpin 1954: 110)

---

[10] Famous examples include Stanley's *Through the Dark Continent* (1890) and Conrad's *Heart of Darkness* (1925) (see Curtin 1964; Comaroff and Comaroff 1991; Said 1993; Harries 1997).

Similarly Hyatt (1917: 132) associates what he perceives as the dullness of the landscape with the evolutionary level of its inhabitants: 'The kraals are in keeping with the scenery, and the natives, who are mainly the M'Hlengwi [Shangaan], a very low race, suit their surroundings admirably.' He asserts that 'the local heathen were a dangerous lot, always on the verge of revolt'.

However, alongside these derogatory descriptions of 'the Shangaan', were contrasting representations of them as noble warriors that were also bound up with the notion of the lowveld as a place of danger. These representations derive from the period of the Gaza Nguni occupation when the Hlengwe people became associated (in European eyes and often by themselves – see Chapter 3) with the Nguni conquerors. There is a long history of European celebration and romanticisation of the Nguni/Zulu as a noble, warlike and disciplined tribe. The writings of Rider Haggard are probably the most well known example of this – Europeans identified with the military discipline and control of the Zulu *impis* and Shaka was often described as a 'black Napoleon' (Hamilton 1998). The legacy of this perception is that, even today, it is not uncommon to hear both white and black Zimbabweans describing Shangaan and Ndebele as a 'manly' and 'loyal' people with a warrior heritage and by comparison denigrating 'Shona dogs' or the 'shifty Shona'.

Narratives on the Lost City

Alongside the notion that the lowveld was a primitive land of savagery that could never 'mother some glorious civilisation', lay contrasting colonial-era representations of this landscape depicting it as steeped in ancient history. This is the 'Land of King Solomon's Mines', or the location of an Arab citadel or 'White City of the Lundi'.[11]

A reclusive eccentric named 'Tommy' Blake-Thompson, a labour recruiter for the Shabani asbestos mine stationed at the isolated Marumbini (at the confluence of the Save and Runde Rivers) in the 1950s, is a key figure in the propagation of these stories (Saunders, *pers. comm.*). In correspondence with Roger Summers, the Curator of Archaeology of the National Museum, Bulawayo, Blake-Thompson passed on reams of notes concerning his theories on Arab careening docks in the Save River, a 'lost city' on Nyamatongwe Mountain (now inside Gonarezhou National Park) where Arab slave traders congregated, and the existence of Arab or Phoenician trading routes from Great Zimbabwe stretching across the lowveld as far as the coast.[12]

These stories were, and still are, common currency in some quarters and

---

[11] The whole of Rhodesia, and not only the lowveld, was depicted in this way to some extent. But the area of the lowveld running from Great Zimbabwe into the Save and Runde valleys was particularly associated with these narratives.

[12] NAZ TH 10/1/1 Blake-Thompson Papers.

various attempts were made to substantiate the rumours. In part these were attempts to bolster the racist Rhodesian argument that Great Zimbabwe was not of Shona origin. Ancient stone-walled cities were unknown in comparable European Iron Age sites, yet this could not be squared with the presumption that African cultures were inevitably less sophisticated than European ones. Hence the appeal of the theory that European races must have built these cities in a distant age (Steibel 2000).[13] Also, as Garlake points out, 'Cecil Rhodes recognised the considerable propaganda value that evidence of ancient foreign settlement, preferably white and successful and with Biblical origins, would have. It would give a precedent and respectability to the conquest and a promise of similar prosperity to the settlers and investors in the new colony' (1983: 1). Much later it was not surprising that the white minority Rhodesian Front regime of 1962-79 should seek to censor all material suggesting that Great Zimbabwe was of African origin as they were wary of promoting black cultural pride and political consciousness through any indication of the achievements of Zimbabwean history (Garlake 1983). Thus any supposed evidence of an exotic foreign civilisation's presence in the region was seized upon.

Notwithstanding the post-colonial debunking of the myths concerning the exotic origin of Great Zimbabwe, the stories concerning Arabic presence in the lowveld have proved remarkably persistent. This is revealed by the following quote from a senior member of the incipient lowveld tourism industry talking about the establishment of the Gazaland Tourist Initiative:

> One of the reasons [for the choice of the name Gazaland Tourist Initiative] is that Gazaland is a historical term and if you read the accounts of the hunters who traipsed over this part of the world hunting elephant and what have you, there's a great deal of romance and history attached to Gazaland and there are even stories about Arab traders coming up the Save – there's reputed to be mooring rings on the banks of the Save above Mahenye. This part of the country has old established trading links – ivory, slaves, with the coast going back hundreds of years. There is a bit of nostalgia and I think with some inventive marketing that could be a real bonus. We could really make something of it.[14]

Indeed, this has now happened; as these stories have been incorporated in tourist publicity literature to bolster the lowveld's 'mystique'. Each visitor to the Chilo Safari Lodge on the banks of the Save River has the following letter waiting for them in their rooms:

Dear Guest,

Cast your eyes up stream towards the sunset this evening and picture a scene from days gone by! An Arab dhow sails majestically up the Save River, laden with trinkets,

---

[13] However, it is important to note, as Garlake (1983) does, that some knowledgeable Rhodesian settlers and archaeologists were sceptical of these claims, seeing no reason to doubt that Great Zimbabwe was the comparatively recent work of local people (e.g. Selous, in McIver 1906: 341).

[14] Interview: Gazaland Tourist Initiative representative, Chiredzi 13 July 1999.

beads, cloth, muzzle loaders and knives for barter. The crew breathe a sigh of relief as they negotiate their way past the Deyseni Island where you now stand. As traffic controller you signal the Harbour Master with a Kudu Horn (which has been passed down in your family from generation to generation!) – "Dhow proceeding to Chilo Gorge – trade about to begin". The Harbour Master stationed on the cliff overlooking Chilo Gorge signals in return "message well received". The exhausted and weather-worn crew give you their usual friendly salute in passing. The sails are slackened and the dhow glides through Chilo Gorge and docks at Chivara Falls. What a spectacle!

This evocative description peoples the lowveld landscape with exotic actors who came from outside to bring scenery and civilisation to the wilderness. It is another powerful image that the European imagination has projected onto the lowveld. As District Commissioner Allan Wright writes of the 'lost city' in his memoirs, 'I had visions of great white walls lying in the red dust, conical towers and trinkets of silver and gold, rusted cannon and strange statuary' (1972: 44). This romantic imagery is now employed by the tourist industry as another means by which to market the lowveld. This, of course, is not a new phenomenon. Stanley Hyatt, writing early in the twentieth century, tells how:

> Rhodesia was conquered and exploited primarily as a mining country. It was, we were told, possibly with truth, certainly with a sufficient amount of truth for a company prospectus, the Ophir of the Old Testament. Some enthusiasts even went so far as to identify the Sabi [Save] River with Sheba... Ophir and Sheba were very useful. They brought millions of capital, if not into the country, at least into the promoters' pockets. (Hyatt n.d.: 110)

Again this exotic landscape was associated with representations of its contemporary inhabitants who were often described as having Arabic, 'Semitic' or 'Hamite' features. Carlaw (1962: 69), for example, describes 'the Shangaan people' thus: 'Their features are generally negroid but some have an Arab cast to them, which is not surprising since Arab dhows are said to have sailed right up the Sabi as far as the junction, and some years ago the remains of wharves were reported there'.[15]

A land of adventure

In the popular imagination of nineteenth- and early twentieth-century colonialists the lowveld was also a wild frontier for brave men seeking adventure. This is the 'bushveld' immortalised by Sir Percy Fitzpatrick in his famous book *Jock of the Bushveld*,[16] a romanticised account of the wagon

---

[15] Similar representations can be found in De Laessoe (1906), Junod (1927) and Wright (1972).
[16] *Jock of the Bushveld* was a school text for Rhodesian children – white and black – and has been physically inscribed in the South African landscape near Kruger National Park where a 'Jock' monument and museum now stand.

Figure 2.1 A Caldwell illustration from *Jock of the Bushveld*

transport riders who brought supplies across the Transvaal lowveld to the goldfields of the Witwatersrand. Their intrepid hunting exploits, illustrated by Edward Caldwell, went a long way toward defining the quintessential lowveld landscape for generations of white southern Africans (see Figure 2.1). The hero's first view of the lowveld landscape encapsulates this experience:

> Perched on the edge of the Berg, we overlooked the wonder-world of the Bushveld, where the big game roamed in thousands and the "wildest tales were true". (Fitzpatrick 1907: 15)

This was a 'hunter's paradise', where the landscape was most likely to be viewed down the barrel of a gun and where hunting was celebrated as a rite of passage. As early as the 1870s an English traveller was extolling the quality of the hunting in the lowveld and predicting its future:

> Nowhere in this part of Africa have I seen so much game. I shot a Sassabye, a Zebra and a Water Buck, and wounded several Gnus, sassabyes and zebra. Impala, rovi-bucks or Pullahs abound in troops but are exceedingly wild... Doubtless now that the Zulu country is shot out this will become the favourite resort of English sportsmen. (Erskine 1890: 2nd Journey, 17)[17]

Aspects of this reputation endured until quite recently. In the 1960s when the District Commissioner for Nuanetsi (now Mwenezi) was advertising

---

[17] Other hunters to sing the praises of the lowveld include Fernandes Das Neves (1879), Gillmore (1890), Chamberlain (1923), and Struthers (1991).

for a Field Assistant to be stationed in Matibi II communal area he received 120 replies and 'found that the reputation Nuanetsi had of being a big-game area where adventure was still to be found around every corner, acted as a magnet for many' (Wright 1972: 225).

Much has been written about the 'cult of the hunt' in Anglophone colonial Africa which transformed the hunting of wildlife from a means of survival to a socially exclusive pleasure pursuit. Hunting 'game' was a Victorian celebration of manliness in the face of Africa's 'savagery', and it was only properly done using certain methods and under particular rules (i.e. shooting, not trapping or spearing) and by Europeans. Conservation legislation was first employed in Africa to reserve areas of land, and certain quarry species, for European hunters and defend them from 'poachers' (MacKenzie 1988; Adams and McShane 1992; Beinart and Coates 1995; Adams and Hulme 1998). However, in contrast to the East African experience, white hunting in the southern African lowveld was never a particularly socially exclusive or elite pastime (cf. Neumann 1996; Carruthers 1989).[18] Hunting was considered by Rhodesian whites as a birthright and an important part of a boy's rite of passage to adulthood. As Chapter 7 describes, this notion of the lowveld as a hunting arena has been physically inscribed on the landscape through the creation of small designated hunting plots or 'shooting boxes' in the 1950s and with the current massive growth of the safari hunting industry on large- and small-scale commercial ranches.

Yet again, colonial representations of the lowveld as the land of the hunt also extended to perceptions of its African inhabitants. 'The Shangaan' were portrayed as quintessentially people 'of the lowveld' and, as such, they were a 'sturdy courageous race, bred in a land where wild animals abound' (Wright 1972: 22). At its most extreme this meant that they were dehumanised as simply another part of the fauna and metaphorically related to other animals, as Erskine (1875: 92) demonstrates:

> The [Shangaan] tribe are essentially people of the bush, more so than any others. In most parts of it they live entirely upon meat, and are like bloodhounds in the chase. Should an animal be hit so as to drop blood, they follow it, and sleep on the spore until they get it. They seem, like vultures to find meat apparently beyond human ken.

They came to be viewed as 'essentially a hunting tribe', who were 'skilled in bushcraft, highly observant naturalists, and fearless and effective hunters' (Wright 1972: 22). One writer argues that, because tsetse fly prevented widespread livestock ownership, 'all the close study the Africans usually reserve for their domestic beasts was lavished instead on the habits and intimate peculiarities of the wild animals they hunted' (Bulpin 1954: 77). The counterpoint to their perceived natural inclination to, and skill in, hunting was that they were held to have 'until quite lately not gone in for

---

[18] Although in Rhodesia a distinction was sometimes drawn between the mainly Afrikaner 'biltong hunters' and mainly English-speaking 'sportsmen' (e.g. Wright 1972).

agriculture' and 'even now it is only those who have Makaranga's [Shona-speakers] living with them who do so to any extent.' A typical description of Shangaans is as 'lackadaisical agriculturalists, untidy hut-builders and not even particularly good stockmen' (Wright 1972: 22, 201). Today these views are still held, as the following quotes from my interviews illustrate:

> A lot of the people in this part of the country are Shangaan and historically they were hunter-gatherers. They aren't pastoralists at all; cattle and cropping is a relatively recent phenomenon.[19]

> This part of world had tsetse fly and malaria – humans and cattle couldn't survive – only hardened people like Bushmen and Shangaans. They moved on a seasonal basis to hunt game and moved into safer regions higher up (around the Zimbabwe ruins) and came down for hunting sorties. There is no ancient evidence of farming here. People were basically nomadic.[20]

When someone is described as Shangaan in the lowveld tourist literature it is invariably as a 'Shangaan tracker'. Shangaan communities are still characterised as 'superstitious, traditional and resistant to change' with respect to the adoption of agricultural technologies, and 'less accommodative of change and new ideas' (Institute of Environmental Studies 1999; Sithole *et al.* 1999: 9). These perceptions, however, miss the deep importance of agriculture to livelihoods and ignore the fact that hunting was only one of many livelihood strategies (and was in part a strategic adaptation to Nguni raiding rather than a 'natural' predisposition). This will be explored in more detail in Chapter 4.

Unfit for white habitation – except for pioneers

One of the more pervasive early narratives attached to the lowveld was that it constituted an unhealthy, disease-ridden landscape that was 'unfit for white habitation'. Early in the twentieth century an emissary sent by Rhodes to negotiate with the Gaza king Gungunyana concluded that:

> … after a residence of nearly eight years in Southern Rhodesia, during which time I have been in all parts of the country and had a vast amount of malaria fever, and blackwater fever on two occasions, at present, owing to the unhealthiness of the country generally outside the towns, and [south-eastern] Mashonaland specially, it is hardly the place for the white man to choose to settle down in, and make a home like the other English colonies. One cannot make farming pay, as the expenses are great and the natives can raise all the grain required far cheaper than a white man, who can trade it from them and then sell it. This is generally done in preference to white men attempting to grow it. (Dickens 1907: 22-23)[21]

---

[19] Interview: Malilangwe, 13 July 1999.
[20] Interview: Rancher, Mwenezi, 12 August 1999.
[21] Dickens concedes that this is good ranching land – he continues: 'The country is very suitable

A little later, an English trader working in the Rhodesian lowveld during the dry season wrote:

> No white man could have lived through a wet season in the low veld. The damp heat would have been appalling; the rivers would all have been in flood, cutting him off from communication with his kind; the country would have been one vast swamp of black mud, alive with mosquitoes; whilst there would have been no trade of any sort doing, for all the natives would have been busy in their fields, sowing the new crops. … As practically every trader who tried to remain on his station throughout the summer died before he had a chance to tell any one about the horrors of his experience, not much is known of the subject of the weather and conditions generally; but we were quite ready to assume that these were disgusting. (Hyatt 1917: 165-66)

Yet this diseased and dangerous landscape, 'where whites lost sap and vigour' (Bunn 1999: 34), has had a perverse attraction for many Europeans. As a South African guidebook admits: 'it is the land of languor, malaria and heat, and … in an inverted sort of way, they are part of the lowveld's mystique' (Jenkins and Palmer 1978: 109-110). The challenge this very antithesis of a civilised landscape posed is part of the folklore of the 'pioneer' white ranchers of Zimbabwe's lowveld. Indeed, one early rancher's biography claims it was the very words 'unfit for white settlement' on a map that encouraged him to set out to prove the experts wrong and establish a ranch in the lowveld (Somerville 1976).[22] Another early white settler reminisces that 'to many the lowveld was uninhabitable, but to those who liked it, the question 'Why the lowveld?' could be answered in three words … its wealth, its fascination and its challenge' (quoted in Eastwood 1996: 31). The wildness and danger of the landscape was celebrated as proof of the pioneering spirit of those 'sturdy individualists' who had carved

---

[21 (ctnd)] for cattle and sheep farming, the grass being sweet and cattle thriving well on it. Many more farmers would settle and go in for it if the various cattle diseases the country has lately been visited with could be got rid of permanently' (Dickens 1907: 22-23) (and see Chapter 6).

[22] D.M. Somerville was the general manager of Devuli Ranch from 1935 to 1965 and one-time MP. He writes in his memoirs of Lucas Bridges' establishment of the million acre ranch: 'The First World War was over and Lucas Bridges – "rancher-explorer from the uttermost part of the earth" – was looking for a fresh challenge … While studying a map of Rhodesia in the offices of the British South Africa Company in London, Lucas Bridges noticed a large tract of land in the Sabi Valley, marked heavily in red "Unfit for white settlement". Officials explained that the dense bush country was unsuitable for farming. There were no roads, the heat was intense, and the area infested with lions, leopards, hyenas, jackals and snakes. Malaria, bilharzia and other tropical diseases were rife. A few hardy indigenous people lived in the Sabi Valley. But white men, accustomed to cold or temperate climates, could not hope to survive, let alone prosper. Lucas Bridges promptly set out to prove the experts wrong. Guided by the veteran hunter Ally Hamman, he walked down into the sweltering summer heat of the Sabi Valley to mark out the first rough boundaries of Devuli Ranch…' (Somerville 1976: 5). Bridges (1948: 513-514) himself says: 'On a large-scale map in Government House, I saw a district where the Devuli and Sabi Rivers joined. It was marked in red letters, 'Unsuitable For White Settlement.' When I had made sure that this condemnation was not due to the dreaded tsetse fly, of course I had to go there'.

farms from 'virgin bush'. This was a wilderness to be tamed and controlled rather than conserved.

Such pioneer discourses are typically characterised by an emphasis on the awful nature of the wilderness with its harsh and primitive conditions, the struggles and setbacks encountered by the pioneers, and 'pride in progress measured in terms of bringing order and productivity to the wilderness and of building a new community' (Moodie 1999: 1). As has been noted on the cattle stations of Australia, the spatial layout of rancher's homesteads 'reflects the adversarial nature of the relationship that the settlers created with the land and its inhabitants. ... [T]he main house is invariably cast as a sanctuary, placed at the heart of a series of barriers [such as fences, trees, gardens and other buildings] between it and "the bush"' (Strang 1999: 212), symbolically different from the disorder beyond.

Schmidt (1995) argues that evoking images of the frontier, of penetrating wilderness (a consciously sexualised metaphor) in order to gain open access to resources, was a means of legitimising European expansion in Zimbabwe. There are close parallels here with the North American experience of the frontier which both conferred legitimacy upon, and derived legitimacy from, the wilderness vision (Turner 1920; Nash 1982; Cronon 1996). The frontier myth has been integral to the identity of these settler societies (see Coetzee 1988; Haarhoff 1991; Anderson 1993). Crucially, it erased entirely the presence of indigenous people from the landscape prior to the arrival of European settlers and negated any claims indigenous people might have to the land (Robins 1994). Unknown and threatening 'empty' space was discovered and penetrated by pioneering explorers and this empty space became a 'place' as white setters filled it with their own names, knowledge, memory and identity (Luig and von Oppen 1997), and thus invested it with history.

The association between the Rhodesian lowveld landscape and the notion of the pioneer is particularly well illustrated by the heavily romanticised history that has grown up around the role of one individual, Thomas Murray MacDougall, in establishing the lowveld irrigated sugar estates (this is explored in more detail in Chapter 5). He is typically described as 'a legendary Scot, a man of vision and courage, who, at the beginning of this century, came from far off places to the wild lowveld, saw its great potential, and determined to tame it' (Saunders 1989: 1). MacDougall's story fits well into the Rhodesian pioneer discourse and the tendency from Rhodes to Smith to glorify 'hero leaders'.[23] Saunders (1989) subtitles his book *Murray MacDougall and the Story of Triangle* 'An epic of land, water and man'. On the inside of the cover is a print of a baobab tree (an iconic signifier of the lowveld) and the words:

Here was an idle corner of old Africa, devoured by anthills and long grass, tangled

---

[23] The story glosses over the less salubrious moments in MacDougall's lowveld career such as his time as a predatory labour recruiter.

with tall trees and chance-grown shrubs, inhospitable to man, parched and withered through long months, yet with wild waters wasting in their season. [It continues] And one man came with his wagons, accompanied by a Swazi youth, and he loved this land and made it his home.

These discourses were echoed in the 1960s when large-scale commercial irrigation schemes came to the lowveld and magazine articles deliberately invoked images of the earlier Rhodesian pioneers in describing the activities of the new settlers. Today in Zimbabwe these pioneer discourses have shaded into white nostalgia for a Golden Age (cf. Moodie 1999).

A new landscape aesthetic

A landscape that had seemed threatening and a site of disorder and danger came to be increasingly rendered in terms of scientific and technical mastery. This way of seeing the lowveld is encapsulated by the first President of the Lowveld Regional Development Association in South Africa's Eastern Transvaal, who wrote in 1954 of the South African lowveld: 'This book is the story of success, of the triumph of man over a wilderness; of the triumph of science over disease; of the conversion of a Valley of Death into a paradise. ... The stubborn thistle bursting into glossy purples, richer than the most voluptuous garden roses' (Webb 1954: v).

These pioneer settlers set out to transform the lowveld both physically and imaginatively until 'the savage landscape has been tamed into a gently-contoured panorama of green and brown that might be any countryside in Europe' (Lambert 1961: 13). In contrasting the 'old, unchanging greyness of the mopane woodland, and the thrusting new green of the sugar cane fields and citrus orchards fed by furrows or spinning jets of water' (Pollock 1968: 76) and celebrating the 'emerald green chequerboard of irrigated fields' that 'stretches away to the horizon',[24] writers were symbolically illustrating the transformation of barren wilderness to productive farmland through the emergence of a European pastoral landscape that fitted the conventions of the picturesque. The landscape which settlers initially lacked the visual conventions to see, had been physically and symbolically conquered as the wilderness vision gave way to this European visual aesthetic. A similar struggle over appropriate ways of seeing the lowveld landscape informed by, and influencing, different landscape aesthetics was played out between conservationists and the Veterinary Department, and will be explored in Chapter 7.

Power over people

As elsewhere in Rhodesia, and indeed in most colonial states, attempts to

[24] 'Fifty years of sugar production', *Sunday Mail*, 5 November 1989; cited by Mlambo and Pangeti (1996: 9).

tame and control the landscape were bound up with attempts to exert control over the people in the landscape. This was particularly apparent during the long process of land alienation, as land was classified along racialised lines. As we have seen, the British South Africa Company, on realising the country was not as rich as the Witwatersrand in minerals, had decided to focus on developing the agricultural possibilities of the country. Between 1908 and 1960 white settlers appropriated large tracts of the most productive agricultural land, denying Africans the right to occupy areas now designated as 'commercial land' or 'Crown Land' and confining them to 'Native Reserves'. These reserves were then subject to an array of interventions that were framed as attempts to modernise agriculture and prevent environmental degradation.

Within the 'Native Reserves' (later Tribal Trust Lands, then Communal Areas) the colonial authorities also set about reorganising space to impose control.[25] There has recently been much written on how missionaries and colonial administrations in Africa, in trying to implement their 'civilising mission' and development programmes, attempted to instill the 'appearance of order' on the landscape by superimposing the squares and straight lines of the 'rectangular grid of civilisation' on chaotic and sinuous space (Noyes 1991; Robins 1994; Comaroff and Comaroff 1997).[26] Villagisation programmes, land-use planning, national parks,[27] mission architecture and discourses on hygiene and domesticity, via physical reordering, enclosure, division and classification of space, have been mechanisms for surveillance and administrative and social control (Robins 1994; Munro 1995; Comaroff and Comaroff 1997; Scott 1998; cf. Foucault 1977). Missionaries in the lowveld, for example, tended to erect their houses on hills 'from where they cast an organising gaze on the land below' (Harries 1997: 187) and were able to subject the landscape to their cognitive control.[28]

In Zimbabwe one of the ways attempts at social control were played out was in the form of the centralisation programme of the 1930s and the Land Husbandry Act of 1951. This model for land reorganisation in the

---

[25] As the Native Commissioner for Ndanga put it: 'I am now in a position to state that the practice of living in isolated huts or groups of huts all over the reserve has ceased. In consequence the patrolling and administration of the District has been simplified and increased efficiency and control has been secured.' NAZ S 235/504 NC Ndanga Annual Report 1926.

[26] Geometry and reason were associated with the 'authority of man'; civilised space should be ordered: and have divisions and contrasts: with the separation of humans from animals, the private from the public, and high from low (Comaroff and Comaroff 1997).

[27] As with the restructuring of agricultural landscapes and domestic space, national parks offered, consciously or otherwise, very real opportunities for investigation, surveillance and control. Parks legitimated the resettlement of scattered populations into townships where they could be easily observed, the strict policing of areas to prevent 'poaching' and the collection of taxes and fees for grazing rights and other permits.

[28] The Swiss missionary Paul Rosset, for example, established a mission station on Dzombo mountain overlooking Grootvlei in what is now in Sengwe communal area in 1897 (Wright 1972).

communal areas involved the division of land into separate consolidated blocks for arable and grazing, with a line of resettled homesteads dividing the two. The reasons for and impacts of this have been well researched (see Drinkwater 1991; Scoones *et al.* 1996; Moore 1999; Wolmer and Scoones 2000). However, centralisation was not attempted in the lowveld, nor was the Land Husbandry Act implemented there, as these measures were not considered appropriate to the extensive nature of agriculture and livestock husbandry in the area (see Chapters 4 and 6).

But the communal areas of the lowveld were not to escape social control in the guise of spatial reorganisation. The notion that the lowveld was a lair of wild and unruly people who were beyond the sphere of governmental control and were perpetually on the verge of revolt, which was commonly applied in relation to both black and white inhabitants early in the twentieth century, was to resurface in the 1970s and 1980s. The liberation war was fought particularly bitterly in this corner of Zimbabwe, which came to be known as the 'Repulse operational area'. ZANLA guerrillas operated out of transit camps just inside Mozambique and Rhodesian security forces, including the notorious counter-insurgency Selous Scouts, patrolled the lowveld 'infiltration points', engaging in numerous bloody 'contacts' with each other on both sides of the border (Reid Daly 1982; Godwin and Hancock 1997). The landscape was scattered with the sites of violence – minefields, ambushes, bombing raids, train derailments, security force dirty-trick operations – and it was and remains scarred by memories of this violence (cf. Ranger 1999; Alexander *et al.* 2000).

In a mildly subversive aside, the British Director of Tsetse Operations, John Ford, writing in the 1970s, equated the lowveld with '*Grenzwildnis*' which he described as an area:

> ... avoided by the majority of people, especially the ruling class who tend to drive unwanted members of subject races into it, it serves as a wildlife reserve and reservoir of zoonotic infection, and also as a base of operations for dissident political groups. The Rhodesian political detainees as well as the freedom-fighter groups may be compared with the followers of the surviving brothers of interlake divine kings. (1971: 349)

The mention of political detainees was a reference to the construction of Gonakudzingwa Restriction Camp at which various ZIPRA freedom fighters, including Joshua Nkomo, were interned in 1964 in the – misplaced – hope that their spatial isolation would minimise their influence. The black civilian population of the area were also forced to move from their homesteads, which were burnt, into fenced 'Protected Villages' or 'keeps' – essentially concentration camps – to which they had to return at night in order to deny their support, in the form of shelter and food, to the 'comrades' in the bush. In this way, far more blatantly than by the centralisation programmes on the highveld of previous years, populations were relocated in the interests of surveillance and control. This strategy stemmed directly from the long-standing way of seeing the lowveld as a land of fear and insecurity over which dangerous elements moved freely.

These same narratives were to re-emerge not long after Independence when wild and unruly people again stalked the lowveld. This time it was MNR (Renamo) fighters from the civil war in Mozambique leading occasional bloody raids into the villages near the border, killing and abducting people, and destroying and plundering houses, shops and grinding mills, leading the MP for Chiredzi South to comment in 1989 that:

> In real terms the Game Park [Gonarezhou] has of late been turned into an 'MNR Barrack', from which MNR bandits launch their heinous attacks. They have a few kilometres and hours to attack and go back to their sanctuary without much interference, if any.[29]

This 'unfavourable security situation' was cited as a reason for an 'accelerated villagisation programme' in the district. Villagisation, with heavy echoes of colonial centralisation, was a top-down planning initiative to create 'more permanent and durable' planned villages.[30]

Celebrating wilderness

Popular media representations of the landscape of Zimbabwe's lowveld today are commonly characterised by symbols drawn from 'wild nature': the lone baobab tree or an endless expanse of mopane bush 'where the elephant roam and the roar of lions shatters the night'.[31] This is a rugged and 'pristine' wilderness from which all sign of humanity has been banished; it stands in sharp contrast to the 'thrusting green' cane culture celebrated by the eulogisers of the lowveld's irrigated agri-businesses (Pollock 1968) or the violent lair of dissidents which military intervention and spatial reorganisation sought to tame and make secure. This wilderness is not to be battled and tamed, but rather to be protected or rehabilitated. Its very difference from pastoral European landscapes is emphasised and glorified rather than feared and suspected.

This way of seeing African landscape is of course not confined to the southern African lowveld. Indeed one of the most powerful narratives colonialists brought to bear on African landscapes generally, with close parallels to the romantic visions of American wilderness outlined in Chapter 1, is that of Africa as Eden, idyllic and timeless, where Europeans could rediscover a harmony with nature perceived as 'no longer available in the despoiled and domesticated metropolitan landscapes of Europe' (Anderson and Grove 1987: 4; see Curtin 1964; Adams and McShane 1992). The lowveld came to be valued as a particularly authentic, unalienated wilder-

---

[29] Masvingo Records Centre (MRC) LAN/8: Letter from MP Chiredzi South (T.H. Mahileke) to Speaker of House of Assembly (D.N.E. Mutasa) 27 June 1989.
[30] MRC LAN/22/Chiredzi: Letter from Department of Physical Planning to DA Chiredzi 11/10/1989.
[31] URL: http:// www.peaceparks.org.

ness experience. General Smuts epitomised this romanticised, sublime, even sexualised, perception when he wrote:

> Wild Africa makes a very subtle appeal to our emotions, and fortunately for us much of Africa remains wild. Civilization has barely touched it at a few selected points, and in the course of the ages the contacts of Africa with civilization have never been permanent or long-lived. After a casual acquaintance with her sister continents she has always shaken herself free and returned to her wild ways. ... By turns gentle and soothing, hard and cruel, always baffling, mocking, and yet binding, the Spirit of the Wild is essentially feminine. Those who would successfully woo her must possess qualities of mind and body not given to all. Moral and physical weaknesses are sternly punished by her, and, like all else worthy of achievement, her conquest takes time and demands perseverance; but, once fairly won, she holds her successful suitor in thrall so fast that he remains her lover until he dies'. (Foreword in Stevenson-Hamilton 1929: 3)[32]

European ideas about African landscape are most strikingly revealed by the attempts made physically to recast the African landscape in the image of an imagined wild continent by the creation of protected areas from which 'unnatural' elements of the landscape, such as African people, were excluded (Neumann 1995). However, Neumann argues, using the case of Serengeti National Park, that initially the vision of African Nature 'could include the people who claimed customary rights of occupation and use. Those not evicted from game parks were dehumanised as primitive and part of fauna' (1995: 163). In this case the Maasai in Serengeti National Park had to remain 'traditional' (as defined by the park administration, and based on British interpretations or inventions of African culture) – therefore cultivation was not allowed, nor the use of weapons other than 'spears, swords, clubs, bows and arrows', nor fire-setting. 'Ultimately, however, the myth of the Maasai as 'natural' humans could not be sustained as the preservationists were increasingly confronted with the evidence of their labour and agency. Thus, nature, as represented in national parks, was produced by removing the people who, ironically enough, had influenced the ecology of the Serengeti through thousands of years of human agency' (1995: 163).[33]

The southern African precedent for the establishment of large-scale protected areas was Kruger National Park (formerly Sabi Reserve), in the Transvaal lowveld. The first head ranger of the park was James Stevenson-Hamilton. His influential views on (and of) the lowveld drew directly on the romanticised 'land of mystique' narratives and painterly metaphors outlined above.[34] Yet his was a more pantheistic spiritual view of a landscape which could not and should not be 'tamed'. He dedicated his book, *The Lowveld: Its Wildlife and its People*, to 'the Guardian Spirit of the Lowveld'

---

[32] See also Van der Post (1984).
[33] This discourse was applied to the Shangaan people living in Gonarezhou National Park in the Zimbabwean lowveld and is explored in Chapter 7.
[34] See Carruthers (1995) for a detailed account of the discourses surrounding the establishment of Kruger National Park.

and wrote with a metaphorical flourish:

> The Low-Veld resembles the vanished Bushmen, who once made it their hunting ground, in that it may be destroyed, but can never be truly tamed. It will never submit to be the docile adopted child of a utilitarian Western civilisation. There is no middle course, either it must remain Nature's enchanted garden, or, its finest fauna and flora all destroyed, its streams dried up, its Spirit fled, it will lie like a discarded shell, a repellent wilderness of rock and everspreading sand, scorched by the burning sun. Outraged Nature will quickly complete the destruction begun by man.
>
> Let us, then ... make it our duty to hand on this heritage of wild spaces and splendid animals intact to posterity. Thus alone may the South African of the future know his country as it was before civilisation seized it, and tore away its romance. (Stevenson-Hamilton 1929: 255).

North of the Limpopo the idea of an official game reserve in Zimbabwe's south-east lowveld dates from the 1920s. The story of the struggles for and against the eventual establishment of Gonarezhou National Park is told in Chapter 7. White Zimbabweans, conservationists, wildlife magazines and nature documentaries consistently echo Smuts and Stevenson-Hamilton's discourses on the 'call' or 'lure' of the lowveld. As with the East African savanna the southern African lowveld has come to stand for wild Africa in microcosm, as a particular European vision of Africa collapsed a diverse continent onto a particular space (cf. Adams and McShane 1992). This 'pristine wilderness vision' has become increasingly hegemonic in recent years and has encouraged and underpinned particular conservation and development initiatives in south-eastern Zimbabwe, which will be discussed in detail in Chapter 7.

Wilderness threatened

Another common theme in colonial, and post-colonial, representations of African landscape is the crisis scenario of unfolding environmental catastrophe (Anderson and Grove 1987; Leach and Mearns 1996). This spectre of eco-catastrophe has been used to legitimate highly interventionist prescriptions for the conservation of soil, water, forests, and wildlife.[35]

These environmental degradation narratives have been particularly prominent in Zimbabwe's lowveld because of the perceived uncertainty of its climate and general fragility of the environment. Drought has long been a concern of the colonial authorities. One District Commissioner, for example, deliberately echoed Grzimek's (1965) vision of 'Africa denuded and choked by sand' when he opined that 'semi-desert conditions ... seem to be creeping into the whole south-eastern corner of Rhodesia and neighbouring Transvaal' (Wright 1972: 69). In particular, African human nature has been frequently perceived as having a malignant effect on the nature of

---

[35] See, for example, Beinart (1984), Ranger (1985), McGregor (1995), and Scoones (1996).

wilderness (cf. Broch-Due 2000) and the communal areas of the lowveld are typically described as 'devastatingly degraded' (Kelly 1973). These narratives were bolstered by a particularly severe drought in 1992 which led to reports in the international media that Zimbabwe in general and southern Zimbabwe in particular was 'the next Ethiopia'.[36] Equally apocalyptic headlines accompanied coverage of the poaching associated with the farm invasions in 2000, as we shall see in Chapter 8.

Conclusions

An understanding of these 'colonial' ways of seeing the lowveld (as scenery, as wild, as mysterious, as exotic, as threatened, etc.) and its indigenous inhabitants (as unruly savages, as brave warriors, as skilled hunters, as good workers, etc.) is important not only because it gives a revealing insight into the role of this African environment in providing a screen onto which European identities and narratives were projected and adapted. These perceptions were to underlie longstanding attempts either to transform the wilderness landscape into a productive space or to preserve it and its wildlife in protected areas, as well as efforts to 'develop' its inhabitants. Moreover, 'colonial' perceptions exert an undiminished influence in donor-driven conservation and development initiatives today, as when the Chiredzi Rural District Council, for example, describes one of its key aims as to 'conserve the essential visual and social quality of the district that has evolved over many years'.[37]

The colonial wilderness vision that has been applied to the lowveld is inherently contested. There has been a long discursive struggle over the two opposing facets of this vision – wilderness as empty or degenerate to be tamed or developed versus wilderness as pristine nature to be conserved or rehabilitated. This struggle has been played out in the context of interventions in the lowveld landscape and the resulting discourses around the 'productive lowveld' and the 'natural lowveld' are discussed in Parts II and III respectively. However the wilderness vision is not just contested from within. It is also challenged by an entirely different paradigm – one that is not founded on the conceptual separation of nature and civilisation and does not approach landscape in purely visual terms. These alternative ways of relating to the lowveld landscape derive from African experiences of space and notions of located identity and are explored in the following chapter.

[36] Richard Boston, 'A country dying of thirst', *The Guardian*, 2 September 1992.
[37] Chiredzi Rural District Council, Master Plan, 1997.

3

Socialised, sacred and contested spaces
African landscapes in the lowveld

David Lan (1985: 112) writes of the Zambezi valley that the 'dim-sighted' visitor:

> ... is confronted by mile upon mile of apparently empty bush, a scattering of mud huts, a few gravel paths and precious little else; amongst many other absences the one that seems most striking is the absence of a record of the past. Mud huts decay, the sites of abandoned villages are soon lost in the dust, the traces of ancient civilisation are ploughed over time and time again.

In the lowveld, whether white settlers sought to tame or protect the landscape, they mistook the similar absence of an obvious record of the past for a lack of history. The landscape appeared homogenous, boundless, flat, and largely featureless – it was an empty canvas on which their fantasies (such as the notion of an ancient Arab 'lost city') were imposed. But this superficially empty bush conceals a lot of human history. For the lowveld's African inhabitants each hill, grove, pool, stream and fence is invested with meaning and memory. This landscape is a living cosmology in which the present and past, the living and dead, and the secular and religious are intertwined.

As Chapters 1 and 2 described, both the notion of a landscape aesthetic itself, and the wilderness vision, are explicitly European constructions. From tsetse control programmes to transboundary protected areas the wilderness vision has influenced ways of acting on the land, as Parts II and III will explore. There has been academic debate over whether landscape is simply a European construct that has been brought to bear on an empty Africa by missionaries, settlers, hunters and scientists, or whether Africans themselves possess a notion of landscape. Some have argued that the very notion of landscape necessarily focuses our attention on an externally imposed 'view'. It implies colonial involvement, as a European visual aesthetic was imposed on African space in an attempt to appropriate it physically and symbolically (Okoye 1997; see Noyes 1991; Pratt 1992; Bunn

1994). Others argue that Africans 'have not only developed an intimate knowledge of their environment in the course of day-to-day practice, but also visual perceptions and symbolic representations of nature which amount to an *aesthetic* of landscape' (Luig and von Oppen 1997: 23).

However, to focus on landscape solely as a visual aesthetic is, to my mind, overly reductive. As Chapter 1 explored, the strength of the concept of landscape is that it can be used more generally to characterise the outcomes of intertwined social and ecological processes, and the ways people experience and understand these. The lowveld landscape has been moulded and remoulded over many years by its African inhabitants. Shangaan, Shona and Ndebele people relate to this landscape in a range of ways. They are not simply living in and using the landscape's natural resources. It is a landscape inscribed with social memories and identities (cf. Cohen and Atieno Odhiambo 1989; Lovell 1996), with religious meaning (cf. Ranger 1999), and one in which the Cartesian separation of culture and nature is often replaced by holistic understandings of the human place in the landscape (cf. Croll and Parkin 1992; Descola 1996). This is a 'socialised landscape', not a wilderness emptied of all vestiges of humanity (Fairhead and Leach 1996b). African interpretations and representations of this place reveal more than a dualistic vision of wilderness that must be saved or pushed back, and they often stand in stark contrast to colonially-derived perceptions and policies. A variety of ecological and spiritual understandings, political struggles and livelihood strategies are brought to bear on and in the landscape. This leads to an overlapping constellation of porously bounded jurisdictions, each of which is very far from 'fixed', but rather continually contested and remade. This chapter will examine the multiple, overlapping, dynamic and contested African ideas and images of the space termed the lowveld that have arisen out of daily interactions with this 'lived in' and symbolic space, and are bound up with identity, politics and religion.

'Lived in' landscapes

An exploration of African uses, experiences and representations of the lowveld landscape points to a relationship to space quite at odds with the pristine or degenerate wilderness vision of space devoid of humanity. This dynamic landscape has acquired particular shapes and meanings (which are in turn continually contested) through everyday physical, social and political practice. As Luig and von Oppen (1997: 7) stress, such processes should be 'analysed not as a sedimentation of history, but as continuous reworking of past experience and future potentialities'. Landscape history, in this sense, can be understood as social history or lived history (Fairhead and Leach 1996b).

This is a landscape over which groups of people have moved – settling or raiding – and in the process have moulded and remoulded the physical appearance of space. Livelihood strategies have also been fluid in a risky environment subject to great alteration. Changing environmental and political dynamics over time have led to land-use transformations, as well as complex accommodations and adaptations such as changes in the social context and landscape location of agricultural practices. There has been both a social shift (towards smaller units of production) and a spatial shift (from riverbank cultivation to extensive cropping of outfields). As Chapter 4 describes, the erratic rainfall of the lowveld led to a sparse population settled along rivers, cultivating vegetables and small grains. Although agriculture has always been the livelihood staple, its relative riskiness meant that the population of the lowveld were forced to rely more heavily than their plateau neighbours on hunting (for subsistence and trade), fishing and gathering. Pre-colonial livelihoods were also much affected by Nguni raiding parties and it is possible that the fear and insecurity this engendered militated against more extensive, permanent cultivation and encouraged more flexible, mobile strategies focusing on shifting agriculture, hunting and gathering.

Far from being the landscape of 'the same unvarying flatness' and 'simply deadly in its monotony' encountered by some European observers this was, to its African inhabitants, a highly differentiated landscape of many vegetational, faunal and topographical niches. One early European traveller did acknowledge that:

> The different kinds of bush form to the Bush-man quite as distinctive landmarks of the country as to the dwellers therein as the mountains and rivers are to the inhabitants of the open country, and as the rocks do to the geologist in his maps of the surface. When you hear a native relate his hunting or tracking adventures he will tell you exactly each description of bush that he passed through on the way… The Hlenga [Hlengwe] in a pathless bush on these vast plains being entirely cut off from a view of the horizon will never lose his way even in strange parts. (Erskine 1890: 9)

An indication of the nuanced way in which different landscape types are characterised is given by the sample of land categories in Box 3.1.

These niches, spaces and micro-environments have specific uses, meanings and associations as elements in a vast lexicon of 'bushlore', and are exploited in different ways by different people in an opportunistic, dynamic manner for agriculture, livestock husbandry, hunting or other livelihood strategies (such as salt gathering) in this risk-prone environment. They are elements of a complex mosaic of key resources spread across the landscape (cf. Scoones 1997). This multi-faceted utilisation of landscape for agricultural production is explored in more detail in Chapter 4.

Implicit in the colonial perceptions of landscape outlined in Chapter 2 is the modernist or Cartesian separation of nature and culture. This conceptual division enables an ideology of mastery over nature, with the thinking subject having mastery over the unthinking and passive object. The landscape becomes a resource to be manipulated and controlled (or managed and planned). In this case the colonial gaze fixed the lowveld landscape as a wilderness that should either be preserved and rehabilitated

Box 3.1: Shangaan categorisations of landscape types[a]

Kutlhuma: thicket – favoured as hiding places by hyenas, leopards and lions.
Magamga: mountainous areas where rock rabbits hide themselves amongst the stones. Also favoured by snakes feeding on rock rabbits.
Mabhiripirini: riverbank gulleys – where pythons are found.
Mabvungurhi: canopied areas – where owls rest during the day.
Bhanyini: areas with tall grass and thorn trees where quelea birds nest.
Dhavhata: pan – where water collects, frogs and tadpoles are found.
Ndovolo: area of black fertile soil.
Mathlivi: stone depressions which collect water in the rainy season. Hunters, baboons, and birds drink from them.
Chihlahla: forested area – where animals graze during the day.
Patsa: open area where buffaloes graze.
Thlaveni: area of red, sandy soil – it is hard to bicycle because of the sand. Good for growing groundnuts and bambara nuts.
Kimgidzo: river bank where hippos graze.
Titshava: Mountain/hill that can be seen from a great distance.
Bhozeni: an area of the same type of trees that dominate other species.
Gutusimi: area where the trees are of the same size.
Magumbitsini: thicket that is hard to penetrate.
Thangava: portion of field in which women grown their own crops (such as groundnuts, beans, sweet reeds and water melons).
Madyelweni: grazing lands.
Handle: an uninhabited place.
Tidywaleni: stone floor – where flat stones extend over a large area.
Masimbiri: ironwood groves.
Tipala: Salt pans – where evaporation leaves salt crystals. The salt is often gathered and sold; also: plains – favoured by impala during moonlight as it is hard for predators to attack them.
Marhimakule: outfields – where people dig for tubers (*phombwe*) in drought years.
Chawunga/mananga: remote, quiet and fearful area where only birds and wild animals are found – popular with foreign visitors.
Chilweni: where baboons stay and sleep – usually along the riverbank where there are tall trees and grass.

[a] These are derived from numerous interviews during 1999.

or eradicated. A key theme of debate in recent anthropology has been the critique of this nature-culture 'false dichotomy' and dualistic thinking. Croll and Parkin (1992: 3) note the paradoxical nature of the relationship between humans and their natural surroundings in which 'humans create and exercise understanding and agency on the world around them, yet operate within a web of perceptions, beliefs and myths which may portray people and their environments as constituted in each other, with neither permanently privileged over the other.' Ethnographic studies show how, for example, people commonly attribute human dispositions and behaviour to plants and animals or expand the realm of non-human living organisms to include spirits and artefacts (Descola and Palsson 1996a). As we shall see below, the lowveld is no exception. Questioning conventional assumptions about human and non-human agency and the relations between humans and the landscape leads to the conclusion that humans and their changing environments are 'reciprocally inscribed in cosmological ideas and cultural understanding'; they are part of each other: 'the forest is the people, in the same way that ancestors can be, in a sense, extensions of the living' (Croll and Parkin 1992: 3; Vitebski 1993). These are what I have termed socialised landscapes (after Fairhead and Leach 1996a).

Going beyond the dualism of nature and culture opens up a new perspective in which states and substances are replaced by processes and relations (Descola and Palsson 1996a). This is encapsulated by the Shangaan concept of *tumbuluko*. Junod (1927) translates *tumbuluko* as 'Nature' and describes it as deriving from *ku tumbuluka* meaning 'to happen, to be formed.' Yet *tumbuluko* is also interpreted as being more akin to 'culture' or 'tradition'. Typical explanations of the concept I received include: 'our beginning – where we come from'; 'the beginning of our culture'; 'activities we have carried out since long back'; 'the way we were created by God'; 'something natural'. *Tumbuluko* can also be used as a badge of cultural identity which is deliberately contrasted with, and defended from, foreign influence: 'you Christians are following a European religion – it is not our *tumbuluko*'; 'educating our daughters is not our *tumbuluko*'; 'we have come a long way with our *tumbuluko*, we won't leave it for someone else's'.[1]

Another Shangaan concept which throws up a divergent way of understanding environmental resources in the landscape – and hence has implications for contemporary 'natural resource management' programmes – is *sviumbiwa*. This is akin to the Shona concept of *zvisikwa*, which Donald Moore dissects in his work in Zimbabwe's Eastern Highlands. He avoids the usual English translation of *zvisikwa* as 'natural resources' and describes instead how they are commonly understood as 'things created'. Unlike natural resources, *zvisikwa*:

> ... do not implicitly posit an ahistorical 'natural' essence eclipsing humans' symbolic and material interaction with a particular landscape. Rather, they arise through a range of cosmologies and religious idioms, fusing elements of Christianity, ancestral spirits of the lineage and family, and territorial guardian spirits. *Zvisikwa* are imbued with use-values and take on meanings through people's daily livelihood struggles: the collection of firewood, pasturing of cattle, drawing water from springs and streams, hunting and fishing. (Moore 1998: 387)

In this respect the European dualistic vision of the lowveld that has informed so many development and conservation schemes which will be described in Parts II and III is simplistic and problematic in that it obviates

---

[1] Interviews: Jane Ndlovu, Chikombedzi, 27 July 1999; Tsuvuka Dhumezulu, Chikombedzi, 28 July 1999; Mr. Gumbakumba, Masukwe, 19 September 1999.

these nuanced notions of landscape held by many of the lowveld's inhabitants. It would be incorrect, however, to portray caricatured 'imperialist' European and 'holistic' African notions of landscape as necessarily antagonistic and divergent. Indeed some African perceptions of the lowveld landscape have much in common with some of the European perceptions of the lowveld described in the previous chapter. Although Chapter 2 portrayed the 'wilderness vision' as a European way of seeing the lowveld, it would not be accurate to characterise the concept of wilderness as a peculiarly European convention with no parallels or overlaps with African concepts of nature. Notwithstanding ethnographic work that collapses the nature-culture dichotomy in a variety of contexts, many African societies have elaborated rich symbolic differentiations between wilderness and settlement, the wild and the tamed, forest and village (Gottlieb 1992; Luig and von Oppen 1997; Beinart 2000). The Shangaan term *mananga*, approximating in meaning to 'inhospitable wilderness', is applied to certain niches in the lowveld landscape. It is used to describe remote areas where there are no homes or fields, no water, no pathways, only wild animals – difficult and dangerous places to travel on foot, but highly valued as hunting grounds.[2] Some elderly Shangaan interviewees expressed nostalgia for 'lost' *mananga* – due to growing populations and encroaching homesteads – that was akin to contemporary environmentalist sentiments. In such narratives the blame for the erosion of these wilderness spaces tends to be directed at other ethnic groups who have migrated to the lowveld – 'in this place of ours there were plenty of *mananga* before the coming of outsiders'.[3] To Shona and Ndebele in-migrants, on the other hand, *mananga* were fearful spaces to be avoided, or tamed through intensive settlement.[4] This closely parallels the understandings of wilderness of migrants elsewhere in Zimbabwe. Alexander, McGregor and Ranger (2000), for example, write about how, in the eyes of 'modernised' Ndebele-speaking evictees from the Filabusi area (on the highveld plateau), the forests of Nkai and Lupane, where they were forcibly resettled, appeared 'dark', threatening, hostile, polluted and evil – a place of disease and suffering fit only for wild animals.[5] In the lowveld, the recent history of *mananga* is not simply one of the gradual erosion and disappear-

---

[2] Interviews: Hasani Mashavele, Phalela; Mr. Simango, Malipati, by Jacob Mahenehene 16 November 2000 and 23 November 2000. There are risks involved in hunting in the 'far bush' or *mananga*, however. One popular Shangaan folk story tells of how a hunter 'learnt his lesson' from straying into the *mananga* where he was attacked by spirits who looked like very old people with huge teeth, wearing clothes only on one side of their body (Stockil and Dalton n.d.).
[3] Interview: Mrs Manyise, Old Boli, by Jacob Mahenehene, 4 November 2000.
[4] Interview: Lawrence Moyo, Chishinya, by Jacob Mahenehene, 23 November 2000.
[5] A group of these evictees from Filabusi were resettled not in Nkai and Lupane but in Malipati in Sengwe Communal Area of the lowveld. According to the Provincial Agricultural Officer: 'When they came to see this country it was a good rainy season, the rivers and streams were running and they saw it was very good for cattle. They 'agreed' to move

ance of these 'wilderness' spaces. When, during the liberation war, large areas were temporarily depopulated as people were forcibly moved into 'protected villages' the newly empty areas came to be classified as *mananga*. The extensive sowing of minefields (particularly along the Mozambican border) meant that some of these places have remained as such.

Symbolic landscapes

Certain parts of the lowveld landscape also become explicitly socialised when they acquire temporary or permanent symbolic or ritual significance. Every few years, for example, particular out-of-the-way places, usually near rivers, acquire symbolic significance as the location of Shangaan circumcision ceremonies (*mula*). A circumcision lodge (*ngoma*) is built and men spend three or four months there going through initiation ceremonies. Women and uncircumcised men are strictly forbidden from approaching the place (Stevenson-Hamilton 1929: 236; Sparrow 1977). These days the doctor from Chikombedzi hospital camps with the initiates and performs the circumcisions. Men who have attended the *mula* take on a new name. The female equivalent is the girls' initiation ceremony (*tikomba*). As one woman explained: 'we were taken into the bush to be taught how to respect our elders, what to do when we were married and how to handle our husbands'.[6] These days *tikomba* are also attended by 'Shona' girls living in the lowveld.[7] The *mula* and *tikomba* are liminal spaces, both in the sense of representing a rite of passage to full adult status and as constituting an intermediary perception of space, set between the everyday and the sacred (Parkin 1991). These ceremonies point towards the ways in which the physical and imagined landscape, social identity and ritual authority are bound up. These connections are explored in more detail below.

Landscape and identity

In their ground-breaking work on the 'historical anthropology of the landscape' of the Luo in Siaya, western Kenya, Cohen and Atieno Odhiambo describe the mental mapping of landscape in various ways by different actors:

---

[5] (ctnd) there in preference to going to Chief Mabikwa in Lupane.' NAZ S 2929/8/4 Delineation Reports Nuanetsi District: T.W.F Jordon, Provincial Agricultural Officer to Provincial Commissioner, Victoria Province, 15 March 1973. The representation of a threatening wilderness landscape is found elsewhere in Africa too. Okoye (1997), for example, describes the tangled area of trees in Igbo villages where spent medical and ritual material is discarded. This is known as *ajo ofia* which translates as 'fearful wilderness' or 'bad bush' – the sites of 'things abnormal and pathological'.

[6] Interview: Mrs Makanami Muzimba, Chikombedzi, 3 August 1997.

[7] Interview: Mr Mahutse, Phahlela, by Jacob Mahenehene, 29 July 2000.

> For the person of Siaya, 'landscape' is not a reference to the physiognomy of the terrain. Rather, it evokes the possibilities and limitations of space: encompassing the physical land, the people on it, and the culture through which people work out the possibilities of the land. 'Landscape' means existence. Land is simultaneously and ambiguously *piny* (territory), *thur* (homeground), and *lowo* (reproductive soil). (1989: 9)

The Siaya landscape is not a bounded locality but constitutes the threads with which the diaspora of Luo-speakers weave 'useful and intimate identifications with social space' as they move around Siaya, Nairobi's urban region, and the Indian Ocean coast (Cohen and Atieno Odhiambo 1989: 44). In a similar fashion the landscape of Zimbabwe's south-east lowveld is riven with the memories and experiences of its Shangaan-speaking inhabitants. Mental maps of 'Shangaan space' do not consist of a bounded physical entity hemmed in by administrative and national boundaries, but define a range of overlapping or connected spaces spread out over what now constitutes commercial, communal and state land in Zimbabwe, Mozambique and South Africa. Writing early in the twentieth century of the 'Tsonga', Junod contended that:

> The geographical notions of the tribe are … very scanty. As a rule they do not think it possible to know a country, or place, where they have not travelled. Everyone must compile his own geography. (Junod 1927: 311)

However, then and now, the 'geographical notions' of Shangaan-speakers were very far from scanty. By the time Junod was writing, the long history of population movements, labour migration and kinship links across three nations meant that, even for those who had not travelled across national borders, their imaginative landscape also constituted threads woven from social interactions across space. One must be wary of depicting a universal, generalised 'Shangaan landscape' which is conceptualised in an identical fashion by all. Junod was right in that everyone compiles his or her own geography from everyday experience. Yet the lowveld landscape also invokes shared experiences or 'social memories' in its Shangaan inhabitants that implicate people *vis-à-vis* each other and the land (cf. Moore 1998; Bender 1999). Social memories revolve, in particular, around the experience of movement and migration over the landscape. The human history of the lowveld is one of ongoing large-scale movements of populations and micro-scale movement of individuals and families. Oral histories record how the ruins of families' former homesteads (*shubhi*) range broadly over the landscape, tracing a history of migration.[8] Mobility has always been integral to livelihoods – in the form of hunting and trading expeditions, opportunistic cropping and livestock management strategies, and long-standing labour migration. Movement has also been a forced response to Nguni raiding parties, colonial land alienation, and the disturbances of the liberation war.

---

[8] Interview: Kraalhead, Chikombedzi, 3 August 1997.

The moment of 'arrival' in what now constitutes the Zimbabwean lowveld is particularly integral to contemporary Shangaan identity. The Hlengwe peoples first advanced up the lowveld rivers[9] (Save, Runde, Chiredzi, Mkwasine, and Limpopo) from the coast of Mozambique into south-eastern Zimbabwe in the late eighteenth and early nineteenth century, 80-100 years before the turbulent *mfecane* and the rise of the Gaza kingdom.[10] They overcame or assimilated the Shona populations that were thinly scattered along rivers or permanent sources of water, or where higher relief meant there was slightly more rainfall (Beach 1994).[11] These Shona peoples either adopted the Hlengwe dialect and culture or withdrew into the highlands (Bannerman 1978; 1980; Cunliffe 1993). However many Shona river and place names were retained. This driving away of 'cowardly' Shona peoples to the refuge of the mountains (i.e. the highveld) by Hlengwe people arriving in the area that was to become the Zimbabwean lowveld figures prominently in oral histories, and these memories are embedded in landscape. The name of Gonakudzingwa, the ancestral shrine of the Mapokole lineage, for example, is derived from the phrase *ndago-nakudzingwa vangavarimo* meaning 'I chased them away'.[12]

The Hlengwe migration preceded that of Shoshangane Manukosi's Nguni. Shoshangane, and subsequently Mzila and Gungunyane, established the Gaza state from southern Mozambique which extracted tribute from a vast area, stretching from the Zambezi river in the north to south of the Limpopo, and inland as far as the south-eastern lowveld of Zimbabwe and the mountains west of the Limpopo. In the process it assimilated many of the Hlengwe and Ndau people of the region.[13] The term 'Shangana' came to be adopted by the Hlengwe as a praise name and persisted as they were proud to associate themselves with the heroic past of the Gaza empire and the Nguni warriors (Bannerman 1980); today oral histories commonly meld Hlengwe and Nguni identity.[14] A 'Shangaan' landscape has thus been constructed around the imagined heritage of a warriorly Nguni which can be counterposed with that of the conquered 'Shona'.

Layered over this imagined landscape are aspects of colonial mythology

---

[9] The Hlengwe expansion was probably caused by expanding dynasties and/or a movement of Sotho people into Mozambique causing land shortages (particularly of riverine land) (Bannerman 1978; 1980).

[10] One major drive followed the Sabi and Lundi rivers. The other ran parallel up the Limpopo into Pfumbi country dominated by Chief Matibi (Houser 1972).

[11] This 'Shona' population would have been Karanga-speaking to the west of the Chiredzi River and Ndau-, Romwe-, Duma- and Rembetu-speaking to the east of that river; they were collectively called *Nyai* (foreigner) by the Hlengwe invaders (Bannerman 1980).

[12] Interviews: Kraalheads, Chikombedzi, 11 September 1997 and 6 July 1999.

[13] These people, voluntarily or forcibly, adopted Nguni customs (such as ear-piercing and circumcision) and were recruited into the Gaza *mangas* (regiments) as scouts. NAZ HI S/3/CHIBI 'The Shangaans'.

[14] Interview: Chagwaliva, 1 October 1999.

which have been selectively appropriated in attempts to define Shangaan identity around a broader historical and geographical lineage; specifically, the mythology surrounding Solomon's Ophir and the diffusionist ideologies concerning the Middle Eastern origin of Great Zimbabwe described in Chapter 2. For example:

> King Solomon, from the bible, lived with Shangaan people long back. He stayed with them for 40 years in the Middle East. Shangaan people used to stay with Jewish people and their culture is more or less the same - they both practice circumcision.[15]

> Shangaan people originated from the Middle East near the Suez Canal. These Shangaan people were part and parcel of the Middle East and were forced to leave due to political problems. When they moved to this area they drove out the Hottentots who occupied this territory long back before the Rosvi people. The Shona were still in Tanzania.[16]

As Moore and Vaughan (1994: xviii) describe in relation to the Bemba people of Zambia, the Shangaan people 'were not simply represented by administrators, missionaries, and anthropologists, but they were actively engaged in representing themselves. They, or rather some of their representatives, had an interest in telling a particular story, constructing a view of their society, creating a set of customs, establishing a network of powerful symbols, and furnishing themselves with an ethnic identity and set of social institutions'.

The experience of labour migration was also integral to the formation of an ethnic identity for a mobile diaspora of 'Shangaan' people and hence the mapping of Shangaan space. After the late 1850s the anglicised version of Shangana – 'Shangane' or 'Shangaan' – had come to stand for Tsonga-speakers (mainly east coast Mozambican) who were recruited in batches to work in South Africa and had a stereotypical reputation as good mine-workers. Harries (1989: 102) suggests that, as well as being imposed on people, Shangaan identity was, in part, constructed by the miners themselves. Their work in ethnically defined teams at the rock-face, in highly dangerous conditions, and communal life in the compounds with its own rites and rituals, bred solidarity and co-operation and their newly shared identity took on some of the functions of an extended family:

> These 'sons abroad' ... developed an ethnic consciousness as a means of survival in an unfamiliar and competitive world and they spread their ideas and experiences into rural areas where people had little concept of the existence of a Tsonga or Shangaan 'people'. (Harries 1989: 103)

The mines also deliberately promoted divisions along ethnic lines by providing ethnically segregated barracks and fostering ethnic competition as a divide and rule strategy (Badenhorst and Mather 1997). Mtetwa (1976) goes

---

[15] Interview: Chikombedzi, 15 October 1999.
[16] Interview: Masukwe, 18 October 1999.

as far as suggesting that due to the good reputation of Shangaan labourers some people called themselves Shangaans simply in order to obtain employment in the Transvaal mines.[17] Today, labour migration is still considered a semi-obligatory rite of passage for young Shangaan men.

Thus Shangaan ethnic identity is a complex product of social memories of a romanticised Gaza empire, the shared experience of labour migration, and histories of mobility, which was subsequently codified and fixed by missionaries and colonial administrators.[18] In this respect the Shangaan landscape, as in Siaya, refers to far more than the 'physiognomy of the terrain' and is not a bounded locality. Rather it constitutes a web of people across space whose identity is inseparable from the ways in which this landscape is experienced, used and remembered (cf. Sullivan 2001a).

Politicised landscapes

In post-colonial Zimbabwe (as well as South Africa and Mozambique) Shangaan ethnic identity has been politicised. Some Shangaan politicians have increasingly sought to carve out an exclusively Shangaan space, deliberately differentiated from and contrasted with the space of the (latterly) plateau-dwelling Shona. As one councillor puts it: 'In Chiredzi Shangaan people should dominate Shona people because this is the place of Shangaan people'.[19] There is also a perception that a Shona-dominated central government is ignoring the Shangaan people – as one interviewee puts it:

---

[17] The NC Chipinga, for example, writes in 1943 that: 'As in the past most of the young men of this district have continued during the year to work in the Transvaal mines where their reputation as "Shangaan" mine boys is apparently as good as ever' (NAZ S 1563 NC Chipinga Annual Report 1943). In a similar vein Ranger (1989) describes how labour migrants would call themselves 'Manyika' in order to maximise their chances as domestic servants in the labour market.

[18] Henri-Alexandre Junod, a missionary from the Swiss Mission in Lourenço Marques (Maputo) and an entomologist turned early ethnographer, played a key role in fixing the ethnic identities of a diaspora of peoples living around the confluence of southern Mozambique, north-eastern South Africa and south-eastern Zimbabwe. Junod wrote a detailed ethnography of the 'Tsonga tribe' first published in 1898 (Junod 1927) which was lauded as a classic anthropological monograph by generations of anthropologists (Harries 1993). Junod and his colleagues' attempts to define and delineate the Tsonga stemmed in large part from a desire to establish for the Swiss Mission a separate and distinct constituency from that of the German missionaries who had already laid claim to, and excluded the Swiss from, the autochtonous chiefdoms in the northern and eastern Transvaal (and who had become conversant in their Pedi and Venda-based dialects) (Harries 1988; 1989). The Swiss now had *their* people too. The development and delineation of the Tsonga language was thus the product of the evangelising drive of these missionaries. There was a pragmatic need for a standardised proselytising language to avoid expensive duplication of their texts and in addition 'a linguistic monopoly gave the Swiss an important edge over other missions in their drive to save African souls' (Harries 1988: 41-42).

[19] Interview: Councillor, Chikombedzi, 21 December 2000.

'we are not considered as a people like the Shona and Ndebele, our place is really underdeveloped'.[20] Indeed Chikombedzi 'growth point' in Matibi II communal area remained unelectrified until 2001 and no roads are tarred. Some councillors in Matibi II and Sengwe communal areas – angered that their wards provide much of the district's revenue (via the CAMPFIRE scheme, see Chapter 7) yet receive very little development assistance, other than occasional drought relief – want to disassociate from the Shona-dominated Chiredzi Rural District Council (RDC) and (re)merge with Mwenezi RDC (re-establishing the boundaries of the former Nuanetsi District).[21] A further bone of contention is the lack of any provision for teaching in Shangaan. Until the late 1960s Shangaan textbooks from South Africa and Mozambique were used in the lowveld. The Rhodesian government banned the use of teaching materials from other countries in the liberation war and they have yet to be reintroduced.[22] In 2000-2001 lowveld politicians made much of the threat of Shona people taking 'Shangaan land' in the farm invasion process (see Chapter 8). However, notwithstanding these rumblings of discontent, the ZANU(PF) government has been very successful in co-opting Shangaan politicians to its broadly nationalist cause and, unlike in Matebeleland, the government's exclusive official version of heroic nationalism has gone largely unchallenged (cf. Alexander et al. 2000).

Ethnic affiliation is not the only aspect of social identity inscribed in the landscape of the lowveld. Another is the chiefdom. Particular areas and features in the landscape represent links with dead ancestral kin and reflect sets of rights to land and resources. Each lineage relates to a particular chief's area and, as Neumann puts it, their 'locally lived geography is as much an expression of identity as a declaration of rightful possession' (1998: 176). Shangaan society can be divided into three lineage groupings: Chauke (the ruling clan); Hlungwana/Sono; Nyai and Baloyi. The former two were Tsonga-speaking and the latter two were tribute-paying 'foreigners' including Shona and Pfumbi – some of whom were acculturated into Shangaan society (Bannerman 1980).[23]

As Patrick Harries points out, Tsonga social identity was rooted in the

---

[20] Interview: Chikombedzi, by Jacob Mahenehene, 12 March 2000. In the case of Shangaan-speakers in South Africa, Bunn (1999: 29) argues that their cross-border clan alliances have ironically meant they have not had the same base for political mobilisation against state control as other ethnic groups.

[21] Interview: Councillor, Chikombedzi, 20 August 1997.

[22] Interview: Shangaan Chief, 19 September 1999. This chief made representations to the Constitutional Commission of 1999 for Shangaan language provision in schools.

[23] According to Bannerman's investigations the Chauke lineage trace their common ancestry to Matsena (died c. 1751). Matsena's son Xigombe gave rise to the Sengwe, Chikwarakwara, Vurumela, Chitanga and Magudu dynasties south of the Runde river, whilst the eastern dynasties of Chisa, Tsovani, Chilonga, Magatsi and Mahenye descend from Zhari, son of Mangule and grandson of Matsena (1978; 1980).

institution of the chiefdom and not simply the clans or lineages (*lishaka*). The latter were, in a sense, social constructs that provided their members with a sense of temporal and spatial belonging. But a high degree of migration and social incorporation of captives and refugees meant that the following of one individual chief was never restricted to the 'pure' descent group of a single clan or extended family. Rather it was an open institution attracting and incorporating outsiders prepared to subjugate themselves to the chief. The absorption of *kukondza* (tribute) people into chiefdoms is still common. For example refugees from the Mozambican civil war in the 1980s became *kukondza* to chiefs in the Zimbabwean lowveld and were employed at minimal or no wages to herd cattle, plough, fetch firewood or do housework.[24] This institution thus provided a measure of security for uprooted groups and a means for big men to increase their power through increasing the size of their followings and hence military strength and food production capacity (Harries 1994). The chiefdom had a physical and intellectual spatial unity and a political unity represented and embodied by the chief himself.[25] Its members identified themselves as being 'from the land of' the lineage dominating a specific chiefdom. They shared an intimate knowledge of the landscape and its living and dead inhabitants, expressed in ritual, songs, proverbs and riddles (Harries 1994).[26] The physical landscape is in a sense a mnemonic device from which people are able to read a perceived shared past. Each hill, forest grove, river pool and valley is associated with a chiefdom, and these places are the idiom through which the chief's claims to authority and to ownership of land, as well as claims to control the character of agricultural production, were and are expressed (cf. Ranger 1987). Also, as we shall see, the chiefly ancestral spirits reside in these places, giving them religious, as well as political, significance.

In this respect the landscape is constitutive not only of ethnic identity but also of one's sense of belonging to a chiefdom.[27] However, during the colonial period there was a massive and long drawn-out process of alienation from these ancestral lands. Almost without exception oral histories gathered

---

[24] Interview: Mrs. Manyise, Old Boli, by Jacob Mahenehene, 4 November 2000.

[25] Junod refers to the chiefdom as 'the true national unit' (cited by Harries 1994: 6).

[26] As Beinart (2000) notes, local narratives in the form of folktales, songs, stories and proverbs are a rich source of insights into African understandings of nature and landscape in the lowveld. These moral tales and explanatory myths present local forms of knowledge and wisdom and explore encounters with the natural world. Metaphors and observations are drawn from nature that offer a mirror to human society, reflecting social and agrarian change. Common themes in Shangaan folk stories include moral tales about the hare as a trickster who gets his comeuppance, and fathers who deceive their wives and children by hiding meat or honey and not sharing it, and the hardships suffered by people and animals during droughts (see also Junod 1927; Earthy 1933; Stockil and Dalton n.d.).

[27] However, it is important to remember that chiefs' territories and the identities anchored to them have never been immutable, uncontested or timeless, nor necessarily are they in any way 'traditional'. Missionaries and administrators invested much effort in attempts to identify and codify, or simply invent chiefdoms in much the same way as 'tribes'.

incorporated some experience of dispossession. Soon after the Second World War Chief Tsovani's people were moved from the present day Triangle and Hippo Valley Estates area and settled in Ndanga District. Chief Chitanga was moved from the Chivumburu area to make way for ranches in 1919 and placed in Matibi I Tribal Trust Land (TTL). Mpapa was moved into Matibi II TTL from the same general area. This move separated Chitanga and Mpapa's people and caused problems of territorial control which persist to this day given that Chitanga, nominally the paramount chief, is separated from Matibi II by some 100 kilometres of commercial farms. In the 1960s Headmen Chisa and Ngwenyene were moved from near the Save and Runde rivers confluence to Sangwe and Sengwe TTLs respectively to make way for Gonarezhou National Park (Bannerman 1978).

Given the importance of the landscape as a repository of social memories and a sense of social identity, as well as to livelihood strategies, it is hardly surprising that this land alienation generated such ill-feeling, even in the lowveld where land was superficially plentiful. As we shall see in Chapter 8 the desire for restitution of these ancestral lands still runs strong and many in the lowveld vigorously push the case for the return of chief's territories and ancestral shrines in place of a nationalist attempt to reclaim land for 'the people' generally. One of the motivations for the invasion of commercial farms and Gonarezhou National Park in 2000-2001 was precisely the 'self-restitution' of ancestral land.

The post-colonial Zimbabwean state has seen the waning and waxing of chiefly authority. The ostensibly socialist government of the 1980s established Village and Ward Development Committees (VIDCOs and WADCOs) which were envisaged as replacing and modernising traditional jurisdictions (Alexander 1995). Munro (1995) describes the 'villagisation' programme of the 1980s as an attempt to reorient the political identities of rural communities away from local and traditional forms of authority that challenge the state and to ground a form of political authority that focused ultimately on the modern national state form (see also Drinkwater 1989; Robins 1994). In recent years chiefs have regained and are increasing their power (with the collapse of VIDCOs and the impoverishment of Rural District Councils). The Traditional Leaders Act of 1999 consolidated this power. But some commentators have predicted that the Act, which provides for salaried chief and village headmen posts, will serve as part of the state's attempt to extend its hegemony deeper into rural areas at a time of political discontent.[28] However, as the turbulent circumstances surrounding the land invasions of 2000-2001 (explored in Chapter 8) show, there has been a recent further twist to the complicated saga of competing political jurisdictions. The war veterans lobby – with a close

---

[28] For example, Bill Kinsey, 'Gender, traditional values and farm size': submission to a World Bank online conference on 'Land policy issues and sustainable development', 9 March 2001. Chiefs' and headmen's allowances were also substantially increased in the run-up to the 2000 election.

link to the Provincial Governor and President's Office – have to an extent usurped the role of traditional authorities in land allocation on 'fast tracked' commercial farms (Chaumba, Scoones and Wolmer 2003b).[29] These interventions have left a web of overlapping jurisdictions superimposed on the landscape. Each has been the subject of ongoing contestations as the changing nature of political authority has been mediated through constructions of landscape and territory.

Sacred landscapes

In the quote that begins this chapter, Lan (1985: 112) describes the ostensibly ahistorical landscape of the Zambezi Valley. He goes on to reveal how this 'empty' bush conceals layers of meaning. In particular:

> ... in the ritual of the bringing of the rain a powerful sense of history, of the relationship between the present and the past, suddenly appears. ... [I]t is as if the whole history of the land has come alive, linking the most recent to the most distant past and all inhabited parts of the spirit realm to each other. And there is not only one version of the past. The climax of the ritual is a battlefield on which rival historical claims fight for acceptance.

It is not only in rainmaking that a landscape's 'ritual topography' – its ensemble of meaningful features – is revealed (Schlee 1992). People tend to essentialise the sacred in terms of places occupied by it and 'to talk about the sacred is to talk and think about space' (Parkin 1991: 2). By relating such places to each other, a mapping of significant geographical space – a sacred landscape – is provided (Colson 1997). In the Shangaan-speaking lowveld this living cosmology includes the spaces occupied by ancestral spirits (*mukwembu*), territorial spirits (*masuzwa*), and disembodied spirits (*swilombo*).

As elsewhere in Zimbabwe, and much of Africa, the spirits of dead ancestors are part and parcel of land and life in the lowveld, serving ecological, social and political functions as 'guardians of the land' (Schoffeleers 1978). They take care of their descendants by guaranteeing ecological well-being through providing rain and ensuring the fertility of the soil and the health of cattle and crops. They can protect people embarking on extended labour migrations or marriage, and help to guarantee the success of hunting expeditions or the accumulation of livestock. They can also be used for more malign ends in the form of *pfuko* (what in colonial times was termed witchcraft) to make people sick (for example to force someone who has not paid *lobola* [brideprice] to pay up).

When people start cultivating their fields; when fruits or crops are ripe and ready to be eaten; or when a family is about to migrate to a new home,

---

[29] A war veterans' leader in Chiredzi went so far as to chase Chief Tsovani out of a land committee meeting because he was unhappy at his testimony in a High Court case challenging the ZANU(PF) election victory in the constituency. 'War vets besiege district administrator's office', *Daily News* 14/3/2001.

snuff is placed under a marula tree (*sclerocarya birrea*) to respect the ancestral spirits (*mukwembu*). This is known as *kuteta*. One old man described how the elders would approach the ancestral *mukwembu* before a hunting trip:

> When going on hunting parties the day before the elders should take a carved wooden container (not metal) and invite one of the ancestors to possess one of them. They spoke to him saying we have a need of relish – do you know the place where animals are grazing? The possessed man would ask what kind of animal they were in need of and tell them whether or not they are going to succeed. If they went hunting without the knowledge of *mukwembu* they would fail to kill any animals.[30]

Possession rituals involve the brewing and drinking of beer, the scattering of snuff, and dancing, singing, and clapping (see Junod 1927; Earthy 1933). The appropriate ceremonies (*kupala*) should also be performed for the *mukwembu* before collecting and eating crops, honey, fruit, nuts or certain other resources (especially marula nuts, and ilala palm). If these are not performed, ancestral spirits may come to the home in the form of lions and terrorise people and eat livestock. Portions of honey and meat (known as *kuluvela*) are kept for the chief and the *mukwembu*.

Mukwembu are associated with particular areas – marking the place at which the lineage head originally settled. These sacred places are marked by particular sounds or phenomena such as the crying of children, singing and drumming or fires burning. One such ancestral shrine is the Mapokole's at Gonakudzingwa. Gonakudzingwa is fondly remembered as being 'rich in meat, water, fields and soil'.

> [It] was a good place with plenty of fruit trees (*makanyi, tindelela, mapfilo*). [Our ancestors] built shelters in the ironwood groves. Water was close by in water holes and in the Mwenezi River. The homes were surrounded with ironwood poles and there were trapdoors attached to ropes so that when the enemy stepped on them a large log would fall down alerting them to the fact that enemies had come.[31]

The Mapokole *mukwembu* still live in these dense ironwood groves. For members of other lineages this is a fearful and dangerous place in which you would get lost if you entered without Mapokole people.[32] However, if the ancestral spirits are correctly approached it is also a place of sanctuary and safety. This was particularly true during the Liberation War of the 1960s and 1970s which was bitterly fought in the lowveld. The Rhodesian security forces herded much of the population into 'protected villages' or 'keeps' to deny the guerrillas a source of food and shelter. Many chose to take their chances and hide in the bush instead. The ironwood groves (*masimbiri*) were ideal for avoiding patrols and spotter planes.[33] They provided physical

---

[30] Interview: Chikombedzi, 22 October 1999.
[31] Interview: Chagwaliva, 31 October 1999.
[32] Sexual relations are taboo in such areas. Interview: Mrs. Ndlovu, Masukwe, 25 September 1999 (cf. Gottlieb 1992: 34-36).
[33] Although the Rhodesian Air Force made a habit of bombing these groves in the hope of hitting guerrillas – sometimes with tragic consequences. The ironwood groves of the lowveld

security and the Mapokole *mukwembu* were paid respect by the members of other lineages and by guerrillas in order to gain their protection. The *mukwembu* could ensure that when white people entered the ironwood groves they would get lost and never be able to escape.[34]

In 1964 the Rhodesian authorities built a restriction camp in a deliberately remote location near the Vila Salazar (Sango) border-post with Mozambique where many of the prominent ZAPU nationalist leaders, including Joshua Nkomo, Lazarus Nkala and Joseph Msika, were restricted without trial. Although geographically imprecise the camp was named Gonakudzingwa Restriction Camp. The restrictees, having challenged the terms of their restriction orders under the Law and Order Maintenance Act in the High Court, won the right to 'live normal lives in a tribal area' and to move around that area and receive visitors. This allowed them a relatively wide-ranging mobility and enabled them to politicise the local population and foment a near revolt against Rhodesian rule in the region, resulting in the declaration of a state of emergency in the district and the confinement of the restrictees to the camp (Wright 1972).[35] The name Gonakudzingwa is still associated, in Zimbabwe, with the nationalist cause and is a key location in the landscape of the liberation struggle. However, this landscape, newly symbolic of the nationalist political cause,[36] was layered over – and deliberately articulated with – the sacred landscape of the Mapokole *mukwembu*. Those restricted at Gonakudzingwa camp used to pay respect publicly to the Mapokole ancestors; they advocated the return of ancestral lands; they emphasised their shared 'Zulu' identity (as they were predominantly Ndebele) with Shangaan-speakers; and encouraged the expression of an openly Shangaan identity – by wearing prohibited skins and furs.[37] In the process they derived legitimacy and substantial influence locally as the authority of the *mukwembu* was conferred on them. This phenomenon is similar to that noted by Lan in the Zambezi Valley during the Liberation War where guerrillas formed strategic alliances with spirit mediums (Lan 1985; see also Bhebe and Ranger 1991). Both were able to gain political

---

[33] (ctnd) can be compared to the forests of north-west Zimbabwe where ZIPRA guerrillas made hideouts during the war and used the bushy land to their advantage, and to which many of them returned for protection as 'dissidents' post-Independence (Alexander *et al.* 2000: 11).

[34] Interview: Masukwe, by Jacob Mahenehene, 10 March 2000.

[35] Although Wright undoubtedly underestimates the development of internal nationalism in seeking to pin all the blame for 'a whole tribe subverted and on the brink of open revolt' on the insertion of 'corrupting forces into a tranquil district' (Wright 1972: 392, 358), Joshua Nkomo did assume a quasi-chiefly, almost spiritual role in the region. He was visited by thousands of people on 'mass pilgrimages' who came to see him perform 'miracles' and received homage from local chiefs and headmen. Interviews: Kraalhead, Chikombedzi, 6 July 1999; Mr. Ndlovu, Masukwe, by Jacob Mahenehene, 11 March 2000.

[36] One nationalist newspaper termed Gonakudzingwa 'the Mecca of Rhodesia' (Wright 1972: 371).

[37] NAZ ORAL/219 GC SENN – Godfrey Cassain Senn. Senn was an ICRC visitor to nationalist detainment and restriction camps.

authority at the expense of a discredited chieftaincy whose power had become inextricably connected with that of the despised colonial state.

By the time of the war the Mapokole people had already been evicted from Gonakudzingwa to make way for Gonarezhou National Park. This alienation from ancestral lands caused massive resentment which is strongly felt to this day. As one man put it:

> Long back we enjoyed drinking beer and beating drums and dancing [for the ancestors], we were happy there, our ancestral spirits were happy. Now they are not happy. They are saying that we are away from home. They are angry. Now we have difficulties respecting our ancestors. They are far away and we have to ask permission from the game wardens [to visit the shrines].

Asked if they would return to Gonakudzingwa if it were allowed, he continued: 'we would run back and celebrate for a year, but the government won't allow this'.[38] This resentment is compounded by the fact that when the elders now visit their ancestral shrines at Gonakudzingwa their numbers are strictly limited and they must be accompanied by game scouts – to check that no illicit hunting goes on. On top of this the scouts carry guns which are 'not in accord' with the ancestral spirits. This eviction from ancestral lands caused social dislocation as people no longer felt they had the full protection of their ancestors from environmental upheavals, diseases and suchlike, and the powers of community elders were undermined. It is a pattern that has been repeated across the lowveld as land was alienated to white ranchers and subsequently the national park.[39] This perception of a loss of ancestral protection feeds into narratives of declining moral values and environmental well-being symbolised by the AIDS epidemic and perceptions of deteriorating rainfall and increased drought. As Sullivan (2000) suggests, in the case of north-west Namibia, such deterioration narratives are inseparable from expressions of dissatisfaction with wider socio-political processes. They provide a powerful metaphor for portraying the impotence people feel as a legacy of colonial rule, economic decline, an extremely uncertain policy environment and – one could add in the current Zimbabwean context – political instability and violence.

> Soon after the war this area had thickets (*sihani*) of trees. This was a canopy forest. But then people came out of the keeps and immigrants moved here and cut down trees to build houses. More trees died in the [1991-92] drought. Thatching grass and building poles are now very scarce. The drought also killed our cattle, and mice and birds are attacking our crops.[40]

---

[38] Interview: Masukwe, 8 July 1999.
[39] Interestingly, it appears that in some cases people experience fewer difficulties in gaining access to ancestral shrines on commercial ranches (such as the Chumbulu Mountain on the Cold Storage Commission ranch – the Chauke sacred area) than in the national park. Interview: Chikombedzi, 28 July 1999.
[40] Interview: Mr. Chauke, Pfumari, 9 August 1997.

We have lost our culture, we are not respecting our ancestors. There is more illegitimacy and theft, sons are not obeying their fathers. Parents are not performing thanksgiving to the ancestors for looking after them when they go to South Africa.[41]

Nowadays prostitutes have abortions and throw them away, or women dispose of miscarriages without the knowledge of traditional leaders. Long back serious punishments would be given to these people to correct them and appease the ancestors. Now prostitutes just want to make money.[42]

These narratives of moral and environmental decline, and attempts to redress this deterioration, are played out metaphorically and physically in the lowveld landscape. This is well illustrated by the practise of *kuhanda kelekele* – a ritual landscape cleansing or purificatdion process. An explanation commonly advanced for drought is *mukwembu* anger at unburied human bones. Bones might be exposed during wars or other disturbances when victims of violence are left unburied or when graves are desecrated. The late arrival of the rainy season in 2001 was blamed by many on the fact that pigs and dogs had been able to dig up the shallow graves of aborted foetuses and infants near Chikombedzi hospital. Whether or not this had actually happened, it was metaphorical of a disrupted natural and political order (alongside drought, political antagonism was running high in the wake of the parliamentary election and run-up to the presidential election). In order for rain to fall, the *mukwembu* had to be appeased by cleansing this 'polluted' environment.[43] *Kuhanda kelekele* ceremonies were conducted in several villages. This is when groups of women gather up litter, in particular rags and cloth (which are associated with menstruation, miscarriages and abortions).[44] These rags are pinned to long sticks and then burnt, so that the landscape becomes ritually clean – purified of the contaminating effects of natural, moral, and political transgressions. In the process these women also deliberately transgress cultural norms – they sing explicit songs and go naked.

As well as accommodating ancestral spirits, certain features in the landscape such as caves, hills, springs, river pools and baobab trees are the abodes

---

[41] Comment made at group discussion, Pfumari, 13 August 1997.
[42] Comment made at group discussion, Chikombedzi, 10 June 1998.
[43] Similarly Alexander *et al.* (2000) describe how AIDS and drought in Matebeleland has been blamed on the pollution of war – bloodshed, gunfire and smoke; and have led to 'cleansing' initiatives.
[44] The 'taboo' nature of these items is revealed by a *n'anga* quoted by Junod: 'When a woman has had a miscarriage, when she has let her blood flow secretly and has buried the abortive child in an unknown place, it is enough to make the burning winds blow, and to dry up all the land: the rain can no longer fall, because the country is no longer right. Rain fears that spot. It can stop at that place and go no further. This woman has been very guilty. She has spoilt the country of the chief, because she has hidden blood which had not yet properly united to make a human being. That blood is taboo! What she has done is taboo. It causes starvation' (Junod 1927: 317; see Douglas 1966; Buckley and Gottlieb 1988; Parkin 1991).

of territorial spirits (*masuzwa*) who guard them, usually in the form of animals such as lions, elephants or snakes.[45] In particular, discourses on *masuzwa* reveal the symbolic importance of water in the landscape (such as *vleis*, springs and rivers) to Shangaan cognitive and symbolic geography (Bunn 1999). *Njuzi*, for example, are female water sprites (often translated as mermaids) who look after sacred pools and provide for continued availability of water.[46] They sometimes drag people into the water who then live in the pools for many years and can be seen and heard beneath the water living in a parallel world. The *njuzi* protects them from hippos and crocodiles. After some time the person's skin colour gradually changes into that of a fish. One interviewee narrated the following experience:

> Mrs Mahlekete of Malipati was possessed by *njuzi* while at home and led to Malipati pool. She stayed three months in the water. Her parents and husband were worried. They contributed money to hire a *n'anga* ['traditional' healer] to win her back from the water. The first *n'anga* they hired worked for four days and four nights while old men and women sang and beat drums, but he failed. He was paid half of the amount charged. The water started moving sideways and made waves which frightened the people. The more they sang the more waves there were. This was a sign that the possessed woman wanted to come out of the water. The second person hired was excellent and sure of what he was doing. Snuff was spread on the water and the ancestors called to take their relative from the water. The singing and dancing brought a woman out of the water. Her body was totally changed from a human being's to another skin colour which was strange and wondrous to look at. She was unable to speak for nine days and people gave her money, pins, and grass bracelets in celebration.[47]

Shangaan-speakers do not generally follow the famous Mwali cult of the Karanga and Ndebele populations of the lowveld and elsewhere, who send messengers to the oracular rainshrines of the High God cult of the Matopos in south-western Zimbabwe,[48] although some Shangaan chiefs did send emissaries to Matopos during the severe drought of 1991-92.[49] It appears that territorial cults are less of a feature amongst Shangaan populations than with many of the peoples to the north and west. This is also true of the Ndau in Zimbabwe's eastern highlands. David Hughes suggests this may be a legacy of the Gaza Nguni empire which substituted a national identity, state structure and kingdom-wide ceremonies for local territorially based symbols (cf. Liesegang 1981; Rennie 1984). This was an itinerant empire, a 'portable politics' and 'as a cause or a consequence of this mobility, the Nguni

---

[45] For a discussion of the role of territorial spirits and 'land shrines' in Central Africa see van Binsbergen (1981).
[46] In Shona these are known as *njuzu* (see Mukamuri 1995; Schmidt 1995). Many *n'anga* and prophets claim to have started their career after having lived for days or years with *njuzu* being trained - for example Mbuya Juliana (Ranger 1999).
[47] Interview: Mrs Ndiroweyi, Masukwe, by Jacob Mahenehene, 5 September 1999.
[48] See Ranger (1999) for an account of the Njelele, Dula and Dzilo shrines of the Mwali cult.
[49] Interview: Mr Masiya, Masukwe, by Jacob Mahenehene, 20 February 2000.

did not invest in landscape ... [n]or ... establish a relationship with the ancestral spirits of the land. The empire simply did not valorise land or territory' (Hughes 1999: 45). This might account for the lack of a Mwali cult equivalent amongst Shangaan-speakers although, as we have seen, they do relate closely to lineage and familial spirits that are rooted in the local landscape.

The Nguni legacy might also account, in part, for the prevalence amongst the Shangaan of spirit possession by Ndau- or Nguni-speaking disembodied spirits (*swilombo*). The twentieth century saw the increasing importance of possession cults where the invading spirits are wandering aliens who have died in battle or on journeys, were never properly buried and now roam, unattached to space. This phenomenon has caught the attention of various ethnographers studying Tsonga peoples. At the turn of the twentieth century Junod noted that:

> This disease [spirit possession] has spread enormously amongst the Thongas [sic] in the last fifty years. It is said to have been previously very rare, or even unknown; since that time it has become quite an epidemic, although it is at the present moment rather on the decrease. ... Strange to say, the gods or spirits which are credited with the power of possessing people, are not the ancestors of the Thongas themselves, the ancestor-gods, but Zulu spirits and those of the Ba-Ndjao [Ndau] tribe, who inhabit the country beyond the Sabie, and as far as the neighbourhood of Beira. It appears that the possessions which first occurred were due to the Zulu and Ngoni spirits; possibly they coincided with the invasion of the warriors of Manukosi, and with the ever-increasing exodus of young men who go to work in the diamond mines of Kimberley, or the gold mines at Johannesburg, or Natal, and travel through territory occupied by Zulus. ... We must carefully note ... these two ideas: the tormenting spirits are the *manes of strangers* and not of the people of the country, and they frequently attack Thongas who happen to be travelling in such countries, and follow them in their further migrations. (1927: 479-480) (first published in 1898)

In her study of 'Valenge Women' of Southern Mozambique, written slightly later, Earthy notes that:

> The cases of 'possession' (so-called) by Ndau or Ngoni spirits are so frequent among the natives that they may be said to be of common occurrence, and to be daily on the increase. The Ngoni spirits (of Zulu origin) are connected with the Ndau spirits, because many bands of Ndau having been taken prisoners by the Ngoni during the invasions of Gazaland and the Sabi River district, and having settled in this country, have become interpenetrated with the Zulu and Tsopi elements. There is a saying that the ghost of a Mundau never dies, meaning that if any injury has been done to a Mundau, or if he has been killed by anyone in war or otherwise, his ghost will never leave the family of the person who inflicted the injury until full redress has been obtained. (1933: 197)

More recently, Houser (1972) records that again 'Ndau spirit possession is on the increase demonstrating a new receptivity of the Hlengwe to foreign spirit possession'. *Swilombo* are not necessarily permanently rooted in the landscape but are more free floating. They do, however, tend to congregate around particular features. The spirits of dead returning labourers, for example, are said to inhabit the labour migration trails that criss-cross the lowveld. *Swilombo* reside in people of various ages, as well as trees, stones, personal articles of clothing and utensils, fish and animals. Care must be taken when touching these things. *Swilombo* can possess people at particular places and during particular activities, such as when picking up a stone or resting in the shade of a tree. For example Mrs. Chivambu is a spirit medium who, amongst others, is possessed by the Ndau-speaking spirit of a man born in Chipinge. This man (Mabunjeni) had travelled to South Africa on foot to search for work. He travelled in the summer and died of thirst on the bank of the Bubi river at Malunguje. When Mrs. Chivambu was herding her cattle she felt thirsty and she took water from a *ton'wa* plant (a vine which twists around tall trees and has a reservoir of water in its roots that is often drunk by herd-boys). The Ndau spirit had rested at this *ton'wa* and when she ate it she took the spirit from the plant and it has dwelt in her ever since.[50] Similarly she was possessed by a *madlozi* (Nguni/Zulu) spirit while fishing in Zazu pool in the Mwenzi river in Gonarezhou National Park. She caught a big cat-fish in which the *madlozi* had 'rested' and it possessed her. The game scouts found her but could not arrest her for poaching due to the spirit's influence. During possession ceremonies each spirit possesses her in sequence.

Someone possessed by a *swilombo* speaks in the spirit's language, irrespective of their own mother tongue, and should wear particular clothing (certain animal skins or cloth of a specific colour) and ornaments during the possession. Spirit mediums also acquire particular skills – those possessed by *madlozi*, for example, are renowned as skilled healers. Houser noted the increased tendency (in the 1960s and 1970s) for Hlengwe/Shangaan people to be possessed by Karanga-speaking disembodied spirits of those killed by Hlengwe warriors. He poses the intriguing question as to whether this is evidence of the Karanga peoples retaliating against the Hlengwe for dispossessing them of their land (Houser 1972). He goes on to note that:

> ... the Hlengwe are now struggling to retain their identity. In some areas the *madlozi* spirits [Zulu speaking] are replacing the Karanga *swilombo*. This may be a reaction to the incursion of Karanga speech into Hlengwe culture. I have also noted a wish to experience again the bravery of the warrior days of the Hlengwe ancestors. The conflict which began so long ago is not yet resolved between the Hlengwe and Karanga. (Houser 1972)

Indeed, possession by *madlozi* and Ndau spirits appears to be more common today than that by Karanga- and Pfumbi-speaking spirits (such as *Malembetsu* and *Valonwe*). Possession cults, in this sense, are embedded in territorial struggles, as ethnic groups seek to colonise 'spirit provinces'.[51] Possession cults are also implicated in power struggles between men and women. Lewis (1989)

---

[50] Interview: Mrs. H. Chivambu, Masukwe, 18 November 1999.
[51] Similarly Dzingirai and Bourdillon (1998) describe how the increasingly marginalised indigenous Tonga of Binga District use their religious traditions in an attempt to protect

argues that what he terms 'peripheral' possession cults[52] allow the spirit medium to behave antisocially with impunity and can be interpreted as an indirect attack on male authority and male-dominated religion (in this case *mukwembu* worship) (Maxwell 1999). There is some evidence for this thesis in the lowveld where female spirit mediums have been able to contest the patriarchal social and political order by taking on male roles to the extent of getting married to women. For example, Mrs. Phahlela Bhindzu is a married woman who is possessed by *madlozi*. When she attends beer parties her husband carries clothes for the *dlozi* which she wears when healing people. Her husband also interprets everything she says from Ndebele to Shangaan. This *dlozi* spirit decided to take a wife and got married to a young girl. *Lobola* was paid to her parents. If boys proposition the girl she can say openly that she is the wife of a *dlozi* (*nisati wasvikwembu*) and they are afraid of her. Similarly, Enia Mapimele is a *n'anga* who paid *lobola* for another woman and claimed her as her wife. The legality of this arrangement came under scrutiny when Enia was being registered as a member of the CAMPFIRE scheme (see Chapter 7). Her claim to be married to another woman and to be the head of the household was debated by the CAMPFIRE members and agreed to be true.[53]

These sacred landscapes are thus not the product of idealised, static 'traditions' but are embedded in, and shaped by, complex power struggles. It would also be a mistake to present ritual domains of the *mukwembu*, *masuzwa* and *swilombo* too tidily – as a system that fits neatly together – rather they form a varied patchwork in different people's conceptions alongside and overlapping other spiritual schema, including Christian notions of landscape to which I turn finally (cf. Wilson 1986).

Christian landscapes

Missionaries, returning labour migrants and urban evangelists have contributed to the lowveld population's long exposure to Christianity. As David Maxwell shows, Christianity in Zimbabwe has, despite global claims, been legitimated in a highly localised fashion 'pitting itself against local demons, making links with indigenous concepts of illness, and resacralising the landscape through the creation of its own holy places' (1999: 218). Churches have challenged the power of ancestral spirits but for many Christians this has resulted only in a change in the relative authority of *mukwembu* rather than a total loss of belief (cf. Fairhead and Leach 1996a: 110).

[51(ctnd)] their resources for their own use, and to maintain some political control over their country in the face of challenges from politically powerful immigrants.

[52] Peripheral possession cults are those in which the spirits are not ancestors but outside spirits where the spirits are not involved in upholding a hegemonic morality code (Lewis 1989; see Maxwell 1999).

[53] Interview: Phahlela, by Jacob Mahenehene, 15 November 1999.

As elsewhere in Zimbabwe in recent years, there has been a massive growth in membership of new Pentecostal churches such as the Apostolic Faith Mission, Zionist and Alliance Church in the lowveld.[54] In relation to landscape this trend is on the one hand encouraging a more 'mobile' spirituality that is less rooted in particular features such as sacred mountains and pools. However, certain features in the landscape are acquiring new symbolism and, in a sense, being 'converted' to Christian purposes (cf. Ranger 1997). This is particularly evident in respect of the pools in the rivers used by churches for baptisms or collecting 'holy water', and the outdoor spots used for congregations or 'revivals'.[55] Also, biblical imagery and symbolism is frequently interwoven with discourses on ancestral lands and spirits. One member of the Mapokole lineage, having been talking about the difficulties of paying respect to ancestral spirits at Gonakudzingwa, which now falls inside Gonarezhou National Park, pointed into the park saying 'our Canaan is there'. Similarly the Shangaan term *mananga* implying 'inhospitable wilderness', discussed earlier, is often elaborated in biblical terms as equivalent to the desert through which Moses led the Israelites from Egypt to Canaan.[56]

As with *swilombo* possession cults, the new churches have to some extent provided a means by which young men and women can contest the authority of patriarchal ancestor religion (Schoffeleers 1985; Maxwell 1999).[57] But the re-incorporation of traditional leaders into local administration (and ZANU(PF) party structures) appears to be countering any erosion of their claims to ritual authority. The churches (new and old) are, however, increasingly implicated in party political power struggles. In the run-up to the parliamentary election of 2000, religion and politics became highly visibly bound up in the popular imagination in and around Chikombedzi township in Matibi II communal area. Church leaders were seen by supporters of the governing ZANU(PF) as being overly supportive of the opposition Movement for Democratic Change (MDC). This had national and local causes. The established churches of mission descent had been outspoken against President Mugabe and ZANU(PF) on various occasions and were seen as very much part of the opposition coalition. Also, in the context of a financially weak and internationally unpopular state, the churches have positioned themselves as key development agents, and

---

[54] The new social groupings constituted around Pentecostal church congregations have also led to new productive arrangements on the land such as church-based agricultural work parties (*dhava*) (Wolmer, Sithole and Mukamuri 2003) (see Chapter 4).

[55] Interview: Reverend Hobani, Apostolic Faith Mission of Africa minister, Chikombedzi, 26 January 2001 (cf. Mukonyora 2000).

[56] Interviews: Mr Chauke, Ngwenyeni by Jacob Mahenehene, 24 January 2000; Mr Chauke, Chiredzi RDC, by Jacob Mahenehene 18 December 2000 (cf. Mukonyora 2000).

[57] Studies elsewhere in Zimbabwe have shown how ancestral shrines are used by local ruling lineages as a means of maintaining and re-establishing the authority of male elders and chiefs (e.g. Mukamuri 1995).

donors have increasingly chosen to channel aid through 'NGO-ised' churches. In Chikombedzi, ZANU(PF) supporters had a particular antipathy to the Free Methodist church which has strong historical links with Chikombedzi hospital (originally a Methodist mission hospital) where the MDC candidate worked as the administrator. The hospital has also had close links with a German NGO. Church leaders allege serious intimidation from ZANU(PF) supporters, 'war veterans' and the police. This intimidation extended to the new Pentecostal churches as well, and arsonists burnt an Apostolic Faith Mission church to the ground.

Conclusions

The lowveld landscape combines a multiplicity of social meanings and is riven with highly politicised territorial struggles. Contestations over territorial and political authority are simultaneously contestations over the socio-ecological control of land (cf. Fairhead and Leach 1996a), and struggles over both landscape meanings and representations, and interpretations of history, myth and tradition (cf. Moore 1993: 383; Neumann 1998; Ranger 1999).

The Zimbabwean lowveld abounds with examples of historical symbolic and political struggles over landscape. It is 'saturated with power, competing cultural meanings and historical struggles for land rights' (Moore 1998: 401-402). The history of land appropriation during the colonial period; discourses around Shangaan, Shona and Ndebele competing land uses; the establishment of Gonakudzingwa Restriction Centre and Gonarezhou National Park; the invasions of commercial farms by squatters and the accompanying rhetoric of the 2000 election and farm invasions, are all examples of moments in which the contested symbolic and political meaning of the landscape has been made manifest. These contestations are examined in detail in Parts II, III and IV.

The lowveld is constituted by an array of overlapping and sometimes competitive bounded spaces. These include ecological niches, ethnic homelands, chiefdoms, and sacred areas. To Africans in the lowveld it is a nonsense to speak in terms of a fixed 'wilderness vision'. Rather there are different landscapes to suit different contexts. In these socialised, sacred and power-ridden spaces, imagined landscapes of identity and memory are as significant as physical space and land use. However, in large part, development and conservation initiatives in the lowveld have tended to draw on the 'good and bad' wilderness dualism described in Chapter 2. As Parts II and III will show, this blindness to the multi-layered nature of landscape has had, and continues to have, implications for people's livelihoods.

Although I have presented European and African notions of landscape and nature in sequence, I do not mean to imply that they are always separate and distinct, or for that matter always competing and conflicting discourses. Rather they are often shaped by each other as 'unintentionally collaborative constructions' (White 1995). Both Europeans and Africans have frequently selectively appropriated images and techniques of representing landscape and identity from each other. These hidden dialogues have contributed to a blurring of the customary distinction between 'outside' and 'inside' perspectives. 'Both have constructed African landscapes which become part of a shared history' (Luig and von Oppen 1997: 35). Some Shangaan people have drawn on white Rhodesian mythology concerning their Phoenican or Arab origins, and their Zulu 'noble warrior' heritage in order to define an identity distinguished from the governing 'Shona'; whilst some white settlers have drawn on African notions of the sacred landscape in their representations of the lowveld as 'Nature's enchanted garden' protected by the 'Guardian Spirit of the Lowveld' (Stevenson-Hamilton 1929).

An understanding of African ways of seeing and experiencing and living in Zimbabwe's south-east lowveld is of more than simply esoteric academic concern. An awareness of this diversity of relations to, and perceptions of, landscape is vitally important to comprehending people's experiences of, and reactions to, development and conservation schemes in the lowveld, particularly given the huge political significance of land in Zimbabwe. Parts II and III investigate how particular perceptions of the lowveld landscape led to particular prescriptions for, or resistance to, land uses. Part IV examines these prescriptions in the light of the particularly charged politics of land since 2000, and points towards the policy spaces and alternative ways of framing debates on environment and development in the lowveld that are opened up by allowing the often silenced perceptions and experiences described in this chapter to be heard.

PART TWO
The Productive Landscape

4

Lowveld livelihoods
The 'suitability' of dryland cropping in the landscape

The following three chapters explore how the lowveld has been imagined and shaped by its various inhabitants, and from afar, as a 'productive landscape'. This is a zone in which dryland cropping, irrigated agriculture, and cattle ranching have historically been the main modes of production. Discourses around appropriate land use have often been in stark contrast with what actually occurs. These debates assume particular relevance in the context of the current highly charged debate – and actions – on land reform in the region, as will be discussed in Chapter 8.

The fundamentally different ways of seeing the lowveld described in Chapters 2 and 3 have had implications for the ways it has been acted upon. A legacy of colonial perceptions of landscape is the 'fixing' of landscape to a particular binary vision of wilderness. This wilderness must either be preserved in its pristine state or eradicated to serve human productive needs. But the colonial vision of the latter 'productive landscape' only allows particular land uses and activities within its framing. The space has been fixed as a particular category of land for human utilisation – in this case as 'Natural Region 5'. This designation has had, and still has, a hugely important role in Zimbabwe's land-use planning. Appropriate or suitable land-use activities were narrowly defined and deviance strongly disapproved of and legislated against. Land-use policy continues to be informed by this fixing of landscape. The lowveld is still officially designated as unsuitable for crops of economic importance, commercial agriculture has focused on extensive ranching or large-scale irrigation (Chapters 5 and 6) and dryland (or rainfed) cropping is anathema to many and is rendered as an 'inappropriate' land-use category.

Chapter 3 described very different perceptions of, and relations to, landscape. This is the space where many dynamic strategies have been played out in the pursuit of livelihoods. These activities have always been risky and subject to alteration. Changing environmental and political dynamics have led to complex accommodations and adaptations. Drought, war, land alienation, taxation and other events have shifted the significance of dryland agriculture over time, as people have moved in and out of agricultural practices with consequences for the landscape. However, despite the proscriptions attendant on Natural Region 5 status (see below) and the persistence of narratives about 'the Shangaan' being good hunters and miners but poor agriculturalists, dryland agriculture has always been a key component of people's livelihoods. Narrow definitions of appropriate land use in the lowveld have been increasingly contested by both populist political rhetoric and the actions of smallholder farmers.

This chapter describes the history of smallholder dryland agriculture and other livelihood strategies in the region and examines how land use practices have changed with population movements, colonial land alienation, agricultural extension and legislation. It traces the way in which the landscape has been represented as unsuited to dryland agriculture and its inhabitants portrayed as non-farmers. And it reveals the consistent mismatch between static, inflexible official recommendations for agricultural development and the dynamic realities of actual farming practice.

Pre-/early colonial dryland agriculture

Erratic rainfall was and is the greatest restriction on agriculture in Zimbabwe's lowveld. Frequent drought means that as many as one year in four can be a *ma lembe a ndlala* – year of hunger (Bannerman 1980).[1] The destruction of crops by locusts, quelea birds and elephants has also posed serious problems. Early colonial Native Commissioners' reports contain numerous accounts of drought and agricultural disasters as the following quotes demonstrate:

> The harvest of 1910/11 turned out to be poor all round, whilst there were practically no mealies, ground-nuts or beans. During the latter portion of the year natives are very short indeed, more especially those living in the country south of the Lundi River. These people are living mostly on roots, milk, and edible wild fruits.[2]

> The Natives are suffering from a famine, the like of which has not been experienced within human recollection. The old men say that the great famine that took place during the last years of Zonkendaba - the Swazi Chief ... is only the equal if not less than the present one. Now, as then, had there not been White people in the country to relieve their distress, the country would have been scattered with the bleached skulls of the hunger stricken people.[3]

> The natives in the south of the district ... between the Lundi and Bubi Rivers, have

---

[1] Shangaan folk stories and oral histories also frequently revolve around the experience of *ndlala* (drought/hunger). See Chapter 3; Stockil and Dalton (n.d.).
[2] NAZ N 9/1/15 NC Annual Report Chibi 1911.
[3] NAZ N 9/1/15 NC Annual Report Chibi 1912.

been, with few isolated exceptions, short of food. They live in scattered communities and are fortunately not very numerous. They are of the hunting or Bahlengwe tribe [Shangaan] and are able to obtain food from their more fortunate neighbours in the north and to live on the wild orange 'waka' and palm shoots supplemented with fish and what game they kill or take away from wild carnivores.[4]

The 1926/7 season with a total rainfall of just over 8 inches was, on the whole, a disastrous one. ...The inhabitants of Matibi No. 2 Reserve and the contiguous stretch of crown land reaping practically nothing. Shangaan natives occupying this locality subsisted throughout the year almost entirely on products of the malala palm combined with a herbaceous diet.[5]

But notwithstanding periodic drought and the scathing accounts of colonial administrators (about which more below) agricultural practices were well adapted to the environment. In the late nineteenth and early twentieth century agriculture was divided between opportunistic shifting cultivation of drylands and permanent cultivation of wetlands and riverbanks. Sorghum and millet were the staple crops, alongside green mealies, groundnuts, bambara nuts and sesame. Also pumpkins, watermelons, sweet potatoes and tobacco were grown along the riverbanks where it was possible to supplement rainfall with irrigation from the rivers. Riverine gardening offset some of the risk of dryland cropping in an uncertain climate where good crops could on average be expected only once every three or four years. But in years when there was plentiful rainfall it was possible to produce a considerable surplus of grain, which was stored in granaries to provide a crucial cushion against intervening lean years (Bannerman 1980).

At least seven different varieties of sorghum were grown.[6] This spread the risk of crop failure and each variety had favoured uses (for beer brewing and food). A large amount of labour was needed to protect these crops from monkeys, baboons and birds (particularly the clouds of tiny quelea birds) (Harries 1987: 101). A range of soil types and niches were also recognised and utilised. *Ndovolo* and *chitakataka* are black, basalt soils which are very fertile but were difficult to use before the advent of the plough, and were cultivated only on a semi-permanent basis; *thlava* are red, sandy soils on which shifting cultivation was practised and millet and sorghum grown; and *seke* are alluvial soils near rivers where vegetables (such as pumpkins, water melons and sweet potatoes) and maize (*chikafe*) for green mealies were grown (Bannerman 1980). Headman Ngwenyene, who was evicted from the Save-Runde confluence area to make way for Gonarezhou National Park extolled the virtues of the *seke* areas:

> Our country, it was marvellous country. This was because we cultivated along the small streams along the Lundi River. During the dry spells we were always assured of

---

[4] NAZ N 9/1/16 NC Annual Report Chibi 1913.
[5] NAZ S 235/505 ANC Annual Report Nuanetsi Sub-District 1927.
[6] Including *mashalani* (favoured for beer brewing, especially for ancestor propitiation), *chikombe*; *matimba, chitishi, chionda, chibedlani* and *gangala*.

having a crop. We could irrigate with water close at hand. We could grow pumpkins, maize and sweet potatoes.[7]

The annual inundations of alluvium and floodwater had such a dramatic effect on the production of maize and wild vegetables that Harries (1987) notes that several early travellers referred to the Crooks' Corner area as a 'miniature Egypt'. Similarly, travelling between the Nuanetsi and Lipalule rivers in the 1870s, Frederick Elton reported that:

> The land is highly cultivated, sesame, maize, holcus, sweet potatoes, tobacco, manioc, the castor-oil plant, the hemp plant, and ground-nuts being raised in great quantities ... The district being rich and alluvial – wild cotton grows luxuriantly, large timber borders the river, and the crops adjoining the kraals yield abundantly – it would if colonised by Europeans, rapidly become a fertile and important centre, monopolising a considerable trade with the interior. (Elton 1873: 25)

Junod also gives a positive account of agriculture among the southern Mozambican Tsonga early in the twentieth century:

> As regards Agriculture, it cannot be said that the Thonga tribe is in a very backward stage. Thongas, as well as most of the South African Natives, are essentially agriculturalists, and they succeed in obtaining their food in abundance from the soil although it is not very rich. The variety of their cereals is indeed remarkable, but they have never developed their cultivation to any great extent, because they did not wish to harvest more than was necessary for their immediate needs: there would have been no market for a surplus. (1927: 31-32)

Hoes were used for cultivation. Small hoes (*chigidani*) were smelted locally and traded for biltong (Bannerman 1980). Larger ones were obtained from Venda people in the Northern Transvaal (Stayt 1931) and sometimes used to pay *lobola*. The fertility of the basalt and alluvial soils meant they could be cultivated almost permanently without the need for crop rotations or manure applications.[8] In dry years extensive shifting cultivation was not practised as families would move entirely from extensive dryland cultivation to focus on the riverbanks – an example of opportunistic mobility across the landscape. As the Native Commissioner for Ndanga noticed in 1908: 'In the southern parts of the district, some four years ago, there were kraals scattered everywhere but now there are none away from the rivers. The whole country is dense mopani bush and quite waterless.'[9]

As we have seen, Shangaan-speakers were not the first inhabitants of the lowveld. They evicted Shona peoples from the area and instituted new agricultural regimes and livelihood strategies – and in the process remoulded the landscape. This was picked up on by the English traveller St. Vincent Erskine who passed through the area in the 1870s. His journal merits quoting

---

[7] Quoted by Bannerman (1980: 13).
[8] Hyatt (1903: 2) observed that 'so fertile does the land appear to be ... that abandoned native fields are very rarely seen, the natives raising crop after crop without impoverishing the ground'.
[9] NAZ N 9/1/11 NC Ndanga (Howman) to CNC 31 December 1908.

at some length, as he noticed:

> ... extensive patches of the dead stump of the *Umzimbiti* trees [ironwood] showing much greater extensions of those forests in times past than present. I sought by many theories to account for it, and as other bush *Umtonto* [mopane] and *Umsakari* were gradually taking up these patches I supposed that altered physical conditions were gradually eradicating this *Umzimbiti*. I suggested this theory to the Kafirs. They explained away the idea altogether that the *Umzimbiti* would ever be destroyed by natural cause but told me that at one time before the eruption of the Umhlenga tribe (mMakololo) into this country it was occupied by the 'Marongwa' [Rozvi/Pfumbi/Karanga 'Shona' peoples] and was very densely populated. They grew great quantities of sesame (inyont). As it grows best in clearances of *Umzimbiti* woods, they were accustomed to plant therein and hence these dead patches which they destroyed by fire, in clearing for their gardens.
>
> The people being driven out by the Umhlenga [Hlengwe], they preferred to plant *mapela* (sorghum) and maize and therefore selected other more suitable spots for this kind of crops. I remarked to them the great extent of these 'dead stumps patches' but they said the country was more densely populated there by Marongwas than it has ever been since and that they, the Hlengas, were not so numerous as the Marongwas. Even now since the Zulu invasions of C'Naba [Nxba] and Maunkusa [Manukosi] their own tribes had dwindled almost down to extermination from slaughter, oppression and famine caused by the Umgonis [Nguni] invaders. (Erskine 1890: 4th journey, 10)

These Nguni invaders were another risk that had to be accommodated (alongside drought, locusts and wild animals) by the survivors, and livelihood strategies were modified accordingly. It is possible that Tsonga groups resorted to hunting as a livelihood staple and adopted highly mobile lifestyles due, in part, to the insecurity of settled agriculture in the context of repeated, vicious Nguni raiding, rather than out of any 'natural' or 'traditional' predisposition to hunting. This thesis is supported by Stevenson-Hamilton (1929: 172) who describes how the violent raiding of the Nguni armies, particularly during the Mzila-Mawewe Nguni civil war:

> ... each winter so ravag[ed] the Low-Veld ... that at last it became a complete desert, inhabited only by wild animals. ... The wretched ba-Hlangane [another Tsonga group – in the Kruger National Park area of South Africa], stripped of all their possessions, were accustomed to spend the winters hiding in caves and in the thicker bush, subsisting, as best they might, on wild fruits and such animals as they could kill. In the summer, feeling comparatively safe, they would creep back to their burnt villages, and sow a little grain, with a faint hope that they might have time to reap it before the enemy's return. From bitter experience they discovered that their best chance of escape lay in abandoning all idea of village life, and in building rough grass shelters, widely separated, where single families could live together, ready to flee at the first hint of danger. This custom of dwelling in isolated huts, erected in out-of-the-way places, became so deeply rooted that the ba-Hlangane followed it from preference until the beginning of the present century. Their mode of life also turned the members of the clan into very expert hunters. ... The Ba-Hlangane were now a wild people living in the bush, and subsisting mainly by hunting. They went in fear of their neighbours.

Similarly, Erskine, travelling along the Save River in 1875, reports that:

> The right or south bank of the Sabi here is quite uninhabited, the Hlengas [Hlengwe] purposely avoiding the vicinity of water; so that the Umgonis [Nguni] may not make resting-places of their kraals. ... It is the practice of the Hlengas to desert their kraals during the dry season, and seek some spot in the bush near perennial water frequented by game. They live entirely on meat and the root of an evergreen shrub, called *umtshungutsi*, from which they also manufacture a drink, tasting like sugar and water. (Erskine 1875: 107-108)[10]

Other survival strategies included the building of stockaded villages hidden in ironwood groves or areas of denser vegetation, the concealment of food stores, minimising production, and the deliberate planting of food crops such as millet disdained by the Nguni to discourage their raiding (Rennie 1984). This was a landscape physically and symbolically moulded by fear and insecurity. Agricultural practices, and the landscape, have thus been shaped by social as well as natural history (cf. Fairhead and Leach 1996b).

Other livelihood strategies

Although it has always been of crucial importance to livelihoods, dryland agriculture has never been practised in isolation. Hunting and gathering, fishing, trading and labour migration have all been significant for different people and at different times and places, depending on drought, war, land alienation, taxes and other triggers and pressures. At one time or another state authorities have perceived many of these activities as inappropriate and they have been discouraged or actively criminalised. As Chapter 2 shows, the Shangaan population have often been caricatured as 'natural bushmen' or trackers. I would argue that their hunting reputation has been given undue priority in representations of their pre- and post-colonial economy, although it is fair to say that, given the paucity of rainfall in the lowveld, they were forced to rely on hunting and gathering to a greater extent than the Shona peoples living on the Zimbabwean plateau at this time.

Before the advent of colonial era restrictions on 'poaching', the population of the lowveld hunted widely. Most hunting was for subsistence, although ivory and cat skins were used as tributes to the Nguni and in trade to the coast.[11] A large market for furs and skins developed in the second

---

[10] Fernandes Das Neves (1879: 122-123) noted a similar scenario in Chief Chikwalakwala's area on the Limpopo in present-day Sengwe: 'These lands ... are productive to an extraordinary degree, but, notwithstanding the excellent quality of the soil, there is always more or less famine throughout the territory, owing to the continual incursions of the Zulus, who are for ever demanding tribute, which is paid for them in ivory, and demolishing the food produced by these hapless people' (see also De Laessoe 1906). The social and ecological impacts of depopulation of forested areas in times of warfare is explored by Fairhead and Leach (2001) in the West African context.

[11] One elderly informant described how ivory was taken to South Africa and traded for axes, hoes, pliers, steel wires, picks, hooks, spears which were carried back by donkey. Interview: Chikombedzi, 1 October 1999.

quarter of the nineteenth century as many adopted the dress patterns of the Nguni (Harries 1994). Biltong was also traded locally, and with plateau peoples (Duma and Ndau), and the money used to purchase grain from them in lean years (Bannerman 1980). With the development of the ivory trade came a new professionalism of elephant hunters (*amapisi*) and porters. Hunters from Ndau and other Tsonga groups migrated to Hlengwe territory and settled under Hlengwe rulers so they could carry out their chosen occupation (Bannerman 1980). Variable migrations of game encouraged mobility. As Harries (1987) shows of the Makuleke south of the Limpopo, hunting also entrenched social and political links through the distribution of meat to the various homesteads from which the hunting party was drawn, and gifts of meat and skins to the chiefs. After an elephant was killed, the local chief was supposed to receive the tusk that was on the ground when the animal died (Bannerman 1980).

A wide variety of hunting techniques were employed, including traps, snares, dogs, bows and arrows and some guns obtained from the Portuguese on the coast and later from Kimberley where many people went as migrant workers. Erskine observed in the late nineteenth century that:

> All these people are plentifully supplied with meat which they can get in the dry season, as the water is then reduced to a few pools in the river beds. They surround these pools with fences only leaving a few openings, over which they hang a heavy beam containing a poisoned spike of *Umzimbiti* wood [ironwood]. The animal passing beneath sets off a trigger which loosens the spring by which the heavy beam is hung and is transfixed by the poisoned spike. (1890: 2nd Journey, 8)

Hunting techniques reported in recent years are no less ingenious. After rain turned black soils into a sticky, muddy mass, hunters would drive game onto them with their dogs. Narrow footed antelope quickly became bogged down and could be caught by the broader footed dogs. Snares were, and are, set for everything from hares to buffalo. Ironically, snare-setting became much easier when game fencing installed by the colonial veterinary services and commercial ranchers provided a ready supply of high tensile wire. Also sharpened sticks are placed in brushwood fences around vegetable gardens to disembowel kudu or other antelope attracted by the food within. However, as Chapter 7 will show, subsistence hunting was increasingly coercively controlled in the colonial period as the authorities sought to stem this 'cruel and terrible' practice (Wright 1972). Paradoxically, sport hunting (predominantly by whites) has been advocated in recent years as the most appropriate land use in the region. Notwithstanding the punitive legislation, 'poaching' and the sale of the meat has continued to be a key livelihood strategy to some, and in the relative free-for-all since the farm invasions of 2000-2001 this increased in significance.

A large range of plants, fruits, nuts, roots and tubers were and are gathered for food, medicine, construction, firewood and beer brewing. These become particularly important during drought years. The most important include the marula, ilala palm and baobab.[12] The ilala palm, for example, is used for weaving mats, bags, baskets, and hats; as twine and thatching; and as livestock fodder; as well as being tapped for palm wine (*njemani*). Ilala palm clusters are individually owned, mainly by Shangaan men, although non-owners can often negotiate access to palms to tap sap for wine – usually paying a fee in kind, and access to palm leaves for weaving is unrestricted for locals (Mabalauta Working Group 2000).[13]

Shangaan settlement was historically focused along riverbanks and fishing, by both men and women, was another essential livelihood strategy. In pre-colonial times the two main methods of fishing were barriers and traps (Bannerman 1980). During annual fish drives (*tjeba*) barriers of reeds (*saila*) were placed across the river and fish driven against them. Smaller fish could pass between the reeds, whilst larger fish were speared or caught in floating baskets as they jumped over the barrier (Cunliffe 1993). Traps or cages (*sole*) were used, as were small bows and arrows and spears to harpoon fish. A plant known as *tsoketa* was also used to poison fish in pools. These days, where fishing is permitted at all, in pools outside the national park or commercial ranches, only fishing with hooked rods (*swinjovo*) is officially permitted by kraalheads, although nets (*masaka/mbule*), now more commonly black plastic sacks (or even donor-provided mosquito nets), are occasionally used. Fish is dried and traded locally.[14] The creation of Gonarezhou National Park put many of the favoured fishing pools off-limits but 'fish poaching' is very common, either illicitly or with the informally negotiated permission of the park wardens.

There is also a long history of local and long-distance trade in the region. As well as ivory, skins and biltong, iron, salt, gold, rubber, beeswax, copper, baskets, clay pots and cloth were traded locally and with plateau peoples and as far as the coast (Roder 1965; Pwiti 1991). In times of drought families regularly crossed borders to buy food.[15] The District Commissioner for Chipinge noted in 1931 how the population of the lowveld portion of the district had 'developed a technique of their own in the practice of *ku taunza*, a blanket-word covering barter in many forms, which enables them to get on the most advantageous terms from the Natives in the well-watered European area the grain they need but cannot grow for themselves

---

[12] See ENDA-Zimbabwe (1993); Mabalauta Working Group (2000).

[13] In Sengwe Communal Area an NGO established a women's co-operative for the production and marketing of ilala palm basketry (ENDA-Zimbabwe 1995). The project was subsequently taken over by SAFIRE.

[14] Fish caught include tilapia (*makayi*); cat-fish (*madhagweni*); eels (*tihumga*); trout (*mundungulu*); and carp (*maluhu*).

[15] For example, the Native Commissioner for Chibi wrote in his annual report for 1917: 'I consider that more natives have left the district than have come into it as, owing to the continuous drought and shortage of food, there has been a tendency of the natives who live near the Transvaal border to go with their families to the Northern Transvaal where they can buy food.' NAZ N 9/1/20 NC Annual Report Chibi 1917.

in the oft-recurring times of drought.'[16] With colonial land alienation on the plateau there was a decline in African agricultural production and barter trade with the lowveld diminished (Roder 1965). It continues to be a highly marketised rural economy with much illicit cross-border trade with Mozambique and South Africa in second-hand clothes, cooking implements, livestock, grain and vegetables. Activities such as beer brewing, brick moulding, basket weaving, pottery, and contract building are critical to the livelihoods of different people at various stages of the year. In the context of rampant inflation much trade is in the form of barter, with buckets of sorghum forming a standardised unit of currency.

Inhabitants of Zimbabwe's south-east lowveld have long had lifestyles characterised by a high degree of mobility. Whether it is an opportunistic response to famine and risk, as hunters or traders, or as refugees – moving in search of better livelihoods – geographical movement is embedded within a network of cultural strategies. Migration is thus not a recent phenomenon; it is a tradition ingrained in the pattern of everyday life. To move was 'a socially constructed reflex; a natural, accepted way of seeking to exploit the environment' (Harries 1994: 17). Liesegang (1981) estimates that in 1860 approximately 2,000 men in a population of 500,000 south of the Save in Mozambique worked part of the year as porters or elephant hunters or as self-employed traders – deriving some revenue from outside their own area. The number more than doubled after labour migration to the Natal sugar plantations started, and reached 10,000 after the Kimberley diamond fields opened. This number again multiplied several times after the opening of the Rand gold mines of the eastern Transvaal in 1886 and with the labour needs of railway construction and coal mines.[17] By 1897 the numbers of 'Shangaan' employed on the Witwatersrand totalled nearly 80,000 and by 1936 this number had almost doubled (Harries 1981). The experience in Southern Rhodesia was very similar and the movement of males onto the international labour market was encouraged – although not initiated – by land alienation and establishment of reserves (see Palmer 1977; Phimister 1986) and the imposition of hut tax.[18] Shangaan people became migrant labourers earlier, and in greater numbers, than other Zimbabwean peoples. Early on this labour migration was actively encouraged by the Rhodesian authorities. As the Native Commissioner for Ndanga put it:

> The benefits to be acquired – both to the Government and to the natives – by this exodus to the Rand are impossible to be overestimated. Firstly they are able to pay their tax without any trouble and secondly the broadening process which their minds

[16] NAZ S 235/509 NC Annual Report Melsetter/Chipinga 1931; see also Mtetwa (1976).
[17] In 1878 8000 'Shangaans' made up 30 per cent of the workforce on the Kimberley diamond diggings (Harries 1994).
[18] Notwithstanding their stereotypical reputation as good miners (Chapter 3), according to the Rev. Tillman Houser, a Methodist missionary who worked with the Hlengwe, mining was not the main form of employment of the Rhodesian Hlengwe in South Africa – they worked in the steel mills near Pretoria, as domestic servants and as farm labourers in the towns and farms of Natal and the Transvaal (Bannerman 1980).

must undergo, by intercourse with the better class natives in the South will greatly help to make them more amenable to discipline in the future.[19]

District Commissioners, however, later became perturbed that the flow of people out of the colony from the south-east would cause labour shortages on the mines and farms of Southern Rhodesia; and worried about the nefarious activities of the labour recruiters.[20] The Southern Rhodesian Government eventually prohibited the recruitment of its nationals by WNLA.[21] The Makuleke community on the South African side of the Limpopo turned this situation to their advantage by selling their identity documents (which were copies of their tax receipts) to Rhodesian workers (Harries 1987). Such dual citizenship persists to this day as many Zimbabweans use friends or illegal agents to pose as parents or family to get South African passports.

With this large-scale labour migration to the mines, repatriated wages became an important pillar of the local economy and migrant labour came to be viewed increasingly as a stage in a boy's passage to manhood (*gayisa*). Today this is still the case although there have been significant changes in the migrant labour experience. In the past, notwithstanding the activities of unscrupulous labour recruiters, there was a legitimate, licensed and organised recruitment process. Today the vast majority of labour migrants have been criminalised, as crackdowns on immigration in South Africa have forced them to become 'border jumpers', running the risk of dangerous animals and arrest as they travel at night through Kruger National Park. Most work is poorly paid and illegal, on farms or in the cities rather than in the mines. Interviews in the Chikombedzi area suggested that there have been diminishing terms of trade from the point of view of the labour migrants. While previous generations would have remitted a relatively large amount and returned with money to buy livestock and build houses, current returnees rarely bring more than a few consumer durables (such as radios and bicycles) and enough money to buy smallstock. There is also a perception, particularly among women, that many young men are just time-wasting in South Africa – spending time and money with other women and contracting HIV. However, in community meetings in Chikombedzi in 1997 women still ranked remittances as their most important source of income.[22]

Dryland cropping has thus always been one of a multiplicity of livelihood

---

[19] NAZ N 9/1/9 NC Annual Report Ndanga 1906.
[20] For example, the District Commissioner for Chipinga in 1936 complained that: 'It is estimated that for the greater part of the year at least seventy per cent of the male population is away seeking employment either at the mining centres of this colony of the Transvaal. NAZ S 235/ 514.
[21] The Witwatersrand Native Labour Association.
[22] Institute of Environmental Studies, 'PRA meeting with female youths', December 1997. Due to its illegality, exact data on income from labour migration and remittances are notoriously difficult to gather.

strategies in the lowveld. These strategies are opportunistic and changing in reaction to environmental, political and economic dynamics and emphasise mobility over the landscape as they physically shape and reshape it. I will now explore the dramatic impact of the colonial period on this landscape and people's interactions with it. The landscape, as well as being physically appropriated by the colonial settlers, was reconceptualised as suitable only for particular rigidly defined categories of land use. Hunting and fishing, and latterly cross-border labour migration, did not fit into these categories and thus were considered to be wrong and harmful and were criminalised. Dryland agriculture similarly fell outside these categories of appropriate land use and its legitimacy as a livelihood strategy in Zimbabwe's lowveld is a long contested one.

The colonial period: land alienation and its impact on African agriculture in the lowveld

The occupation of Zimbabwe by the British South African Company (BSAC) in 1890 and the delineation of the Anglo-Portuguese border with Mozambique resulted in the Shangaan-speaking people being split amongst Rhodesia, Portuguese East Africa and South Africa.[23] Within the new Rhodesian state, Shangaan-speakers comprised a small minority who were physically and linguistically isolated from the rest of the population (Cunliffe 1993). The colonial administration lost no time in imposing taxes. This caused some seasonal and permanent movement across borders to avoid it. Taxation also provided an additional stimulus for people to seek work as migrant labourers, although this practice was already widespread prior to the BSAC occupation. Shangaan-speakers were drawn into the capitalist economy at a very early stage – often paying tax and bride price with gold or money rather than cattle.

Game laws were introduced by the BSAC from 1891 onwards and in the early years of the twentieth century Africans were regularly stopped from hunting and their guns confiscated – thus criminalising one of the key components of the region's economy and reducing trade in wildlife products. This caused some migration to Mozambique where hunting was still permitted, despite the fact that taxes were higher there, causing the Native Commissioner for Ndanga to become concerned about loss of 'Shangaan labour' to the country (Bannerman 1980; Cunliffe 1993).

The greatest impact the colonial government was to have on the people of the south-east lowveld was, however, the prolonged land squeeze resulting from the system of 'land apportionment' adopted by the settler government which was to last until the late 1960s. The BSAC, on realising

---

[23] Although both Portuguese and British authorities were attempting to collect tax from the same people near the border quite some time after it was supposed to be fixed. See NAZ NVC 1/1/1 NC Forrestall to CNC, Quarterly Report, 31 January 1899.

the country was not as rich in minerals as the Witwatersrand, had decided to focus on developing the agricultural possibilities of the country (see Palmer 1977; Moyana 1984). From 1908 onwards this resulted in land alienation as Africans were denied the right to occupy areas now officially designated as 'commercial land' or 'Crown Land' and were relocated into 'Native Reserves'. Those still living on unalienated land were charged rent.[24]

Those living in the Nuanetsi sub-District of Chibi were initially relatively fortunate in their land allocation, the majority of their land being made into the enormous Matibi Reserve that stretched from the Portuguese East Africa border to the present-day Matibi I communal area in Mwenezi District. This reserve included all the land between the Runde and Mwenezi Rivers including that presently incorporated in Gonarezhou National Park and Nuanetsi Ranch. The reserve was demarcated on the recommendations of the Native Commissioner at Chibi (Peter Forrestall) who had pointed out that, although the reserve was large, it would allow room for the expansion of the population, and that much of the land between the rivers was useless from a point of view of habitation (Bannerman 1980). The lands to the north of the Runde and to the south of the Mwenezi river remained as unalienated BSAC land. The Native Commissioner for Ndanga District put forward a proposal for a second reserve in the lowveld to accommodate the Shangaan people to the east of the Runde River but this was not approved by the Native Affairs Committee.

In 1914 the Coryndon Native Reserves Commission was set up and most of its recommendations were accepted and embodied in the 1920 Native Reserves Order-in-Council. One such recommendation was for the dismemberment of the Matibi Reserve – the portion near the border with Mozambique became Gona re Zhou Forest, as the Commission thought that it was undesirable from a security point of view to have reserves along the borders of remote areas of the country. A massive chunk was also excised from the middle of Matibi Reserve and given to the BSAC Ranching Section to become Nuanetsi Ranch. The Reserve was thus reduced in extent by approximately 75 per cent, from 3,485,941 acres to 824,596 acres. Ironically, this carve-up was encouraged by the same Native Commissioner Forrestall for Chibi District who had held out the necessity of a large reserve twenty years before and who had himself since received a farm in the adjoining Ndanga District (Bannerman 1980).

Resettling Africans into reserves brought them under the umbrella of colonial authority, and the previously dispersed populations were now more easily taxed and administered. This was particularly true of the lowveld where the colonial authorities viewed the Shangaan population as very

---

[24] The Chief Native Commissioner pointed out one of the consequences of this: 'A large number of natives living on unalienated land on the borders of Portuguese territory have signified their intention to cross the border rather than pay the rent. ... The progressive policy to my mind, has always been to make every effort to get natives to live on farms.' NAZ N 9/1/11 CNC Annual Report 31 December 1908.

scattered and isolated and hence hard to control. However, as the Native Commissioner for Ndanga reveals, their resettlement into reserves threw up particular dilemmas:

> Removal into the Reserve would make for better control and efficiency and a more certain harvest, but on the other hand to leave the southern portions *unoccupied and a wilderness* until alienated has its disadvantages and will also tend to make the task of the settler more difficult when opening up.
>
> Their presence in this remote part of the district at least has the effect of preventing it from *reverting to absolute desert*, and being over-run by carnivora. Their presence also ensures an adequate supply of labour to prospective settlers.
>
> The Crown Lands cover a very large sweep of country which would be *entirely handed back to nature*, if there were no native population living there. ... [A]lthough it must be admitted that the haphazard methods of native agriculture do considerable harm to land, their cattle, at least, do good, in grazing down the veldt, and the natives themselves allow, at least, a possibility of controlling grass fires, and locust invasions. [my emphases][25]

The desire to bring this far-flung population under more rigorous control was thus tempered by the perception that a Shangaan population could provide a vanguard in the battle against wilderness,[26] holding it in abeyance until the arrival of white settlers, at which point they could be resettled or provide a supply of farm labourers as the land was progressively alienated.

The Morris Carter Commission (1925) and the Land Apportionment Act (1930) firmly entrenched the principle of racial segregation of land and defined separate areas in which Europeans and Africans could respectively and exclusively acquire land (Cunliffe 1993). The movement of Shangaan people off 'European farming areas' accelerated after the Second World War – especially with the coming of sugar estates at Triangle and Hippo Valley when taming the wilderness for productive ends became an even more lucrative endeavour for white settlers (see de Jager 1988; and Chapter 5). The resettlement of Ndebele people evicted from Filabusi in Sengwe communal area in the 1950s; the demarcation of Gonakudzingwa African Purchase Area in the 1960s (farms which went principally to Shona people) and the establishment of Gonarezhou National Park in 1975 caused further displacement and squeezing of people into a narrow band of communal land hemmed in by farms on one side and park on the other.

This prolonged land squeeze had dramatic impacts on people's interactions with the landscape. It left a curious situation of relatively very high population densities (particularly in Sangwe and Matibi II communal areas) sandwiched into arid reserves between 'empty' ranches and a national park.

---

[25] NAZ N 9/1/24 Actg NC Annual Report Ndanga 1921 (Molyneux); S 235/504 NC Annual Report Ndanga 1926; S 235/510 NC Annual Report Ndanga 1932.

[26] As Chapters 6 and 7 explore, this argument was also deployed in discourses on the control of tsetse fly infestation and foot-and-mouth disease.

As a region designated, in the argot of Rhodesian land-use planning, as Natural Region 5, it was supposed to be unable to support high population densities without the development of intensive irrigation. Traditional livelihood strategies (such as fishing and hunting) were banned in most of the landscape and constrained in the remaining niches in which they were permitted, and trade routes were disrupted. As described in Chapter 3, removal from land associated with the graves and spirits of ancestors was perceived as removal from their protective sphere – and thought to lead to the increased incidence of drought and other afflictions. Chief Gezani summed up the changes as follows:

> Our forefathers were ploughing small fields because there was plenty of meat [from hunting]. They didn't need to plant big fields. Now hunting is quite impossible, there is not enough space – it is totally occupied by people, we are in between the commercial farms and the game park. Now agriculture is more important.[27]

Land alienation, prohibitions on riverine cultivation (see below) and hunting and fishing, the increased availability of ploughs and the presence of fertile basalt soils (*ndovolo* and *chitakataka*) encouraged a spatial shift in agricultural practice with more extensive cultivation of outfields on a permanent basis. With relatively dense livestock populations, outfields (*marhimakule*) were increasingly located further away from homesteads 'to keep cattle and goats away from our crops',[28] the irony being that one of the reactions to the population being concentrated onto smaller areas was the cultivation of larger areas. This brought about a radical change in settlement patterns, from concentrations in riverine areas to being more scattered. By 1980 one senior administrator had admitted that 'development to the Hlengwe has come to mean living around a hand pump borehole in mopani scrub',[29] and as one respondent to a survey in the late 1980s put it – 'now the borehole controls our lives'.[30]

The rapid and extreme change to livelihood strategies is most clearly demonstrated by Chief Ngwenyene's people, who were forcibly evicted from the Save-Runde confluence in 1968 to make way for Gonarezhou National Park. They had been cultivating with hand hoes and sometimes donkeys (as the prevalence of tsetse fly prevented cattle ownership); fishing, hunting and fruit trees were major sources of food. They were moved further south to the tsetse-free Sengwe communal area. They had to build up cattle ownership rapidly (partly through *lobola*) in order to plough extensively. As one person put it 'the past is the past, we are now living in the modern world and not depending on fish, fruits and hunting – we are working hard in the fields'.[31] One writer is more damning of these developments:

---

[27] Interview: Chief Gezani, Gezani, 19 September 1999.
[28] Interview: Masia Makondo, Chikombedzi, 14 July 1997.
[29] T.E.F. Jordon quoted by Bannerman (1980: 30).
[30] Interview: Chirhilele Ndabani, Chipinda, by Paul de Jager, 11 February 1987 (de Jager 1988).
[31] Interview: Goliath Madoda, Chikombedzi, 6 July 1999.

[T]hey were squashed in with their sensible course of livelihood impossible. They were forced to try to turn watershed forest into fields of millet and sorghum in areas rather too dry for farming, but with astonishing rain storms and soils of low infiltration. They needed a lot of cattle in order to cope with the majority of years when they would not harvest, and to plough over the arable with the first rains to give the crops a chance. There was a lot of soil erosion. They were blamed. Now they are told they cannot be allocated more land, or be allowed to settle and use the land in the way that they want because if they do there will be environmental problems (Wilson 1988: 15).

As well as having a large portion of the landscape denied to them for settlement, Africans were faced with a raft of 'extension' advice, soil conservation initiatives and legislation prescribing and proscribing land uses in those vestiges of the landscape in which they were still entitled to live. It is to the impact of these that I now turn.

Agricultural extension in the lowveld during the colonial period

The corollary to the colonial romanticisation of the Shangaan people as skilled hunters and miners was their depiction as 'lackadaisical agriculturalists' (Wright 1972: 201). As Bannerman (1978: 493) puts it, there was a 'sort of Shangane myth' that all they ever did was fight and hunt and although they made 'good workers' they were a rather backward tribe that lived somewhere in the 'back of beyond' in the lowveld. Colonial accounts of their agricultural practice inevitably lapse into pejorative terms, as the following examples show:

> The Bahlengwe or Shangaan who live on the lower Lundi, Nuanetsi and Bubye rivers go out to work more than the Bakaranga, but are not as good agriculturalists, and let their women do most of the work in the gardens.[32]

> The district cannot be described as an agricultural one being more suitable for stock raising. The natives do not go in for extensive cultivation and with few exceptions give little thought to improving their methods. It is seldom they get a year of sufficient rain to enable them to do more than provide enough grain for their own existence and under such adversity improvements can hardly be expected.[33]

> Apart from the purchase of 63 additional ploughs, natives are, with few exceptions, apathetic when efforts are made to inculcate them with more modern methods of agriculture, appearing to consider that the extra labour involved is incommensurate with the results to be obtained.[34]

> Heedless of the exhortations of the missionaries from America to follow the example of that great country in the way of production and thrift the Natives in a large

---

[32] NAZ N 9/1/17 NC Annual Report Chibi 1914.
[33] NAZ S 235/504 NC Annual Report Gwanda 1926.
[34] NAZ S 235/505 ANC Annual Report Nuanetsi Sub-District 1927.

part of this district where the rainfall is uncertain continue their old existence of perennial underproduction.[35]

There has been no noticeable improvement in the methods of agriculture generally adopted by the natives. Stumping and manuring of land is not practised except by those natives who are working plots under the supervision of the Demonstrator and it is to be hoped that a larger number will do so as a result of the Demonstrator's presence.[36]

I feel ... more pressure should be brought to bear on the natives to adopt improved methods of agriculture. The large expanse of virgin soils in this district, plus the natives' natural inclination to a very lazy form of life and indifference to the future, make it difficult to get all the enthusiasm one might wish for improvements that require some effort. ...To illustrate this indolence I mention that some weeks after the commencement to the rains in October the larger proportion of last season's abundant crops were still lying unthreshed and unprotected. No effort had been made by a very large number of the Shangaans to build shelters, grain huts or bins. Crops were simply left to the mercy of the weather and firm action was essential to get the necessary precautions taken. ...This unconcern of the Shangaans is difficult to understand when one thinks of the terrible famine that they have just experienced.[37]

The District Commissioners continually exhorted their charges to become 'progressive' farmers and adopt 'improved methods' in the place of their 'haphazard methods which harm the land'. A great deal has been written about the 'civilising mission' of agricultural extension efforts in Zimbabwe, ranging from Emory Alvord's 'gospel of the plough' to attempts to regulate 'native land husbandry', prohibit river bank cultivation, and – most ambitiously – to designate specified cropping and grazing areas and 'centralise' dispersed African populations into 'lines'.[38] However there was disagreement about the extent to which these policies, intended principally for the densely populated reserves of the highveld, were appropriate to the lowveld context. In submissions to the Natural Resources Board Native Enquiry of 1942, Benzies asserted that it would be futile to centralise 'mopani veld' and Pole-Evans advised against 'opening up' these areas for arable and suggested that they should just be used for occasional grazing.[39] Indeed centralisation was never implemented in most of the lowveld. In most cases, attempts to introduce contour-ridging and the destumping and manuring of fields were similarly resisted, and destocking measures were avoided altogether.

---

[35] NAZ S 235/509 NC Annual Report Melsetter/Chipinga 1931.
[36] S 235/510 ANC Annual Report Nuanetsi 1932.
[37] S 235/518 ANC Annual Report Nuanetsi 1948.
[38] See, for example: Alvord (n.d.); Pendered (1955); Ranger (1985); Phimister (1986); Beinart (1989); Drinkwater (1989); Elliot (1990); McGregor (1995); Scoones (1996); Munro (1998); Moore (1999); Wolmer and Scoones (2000).
[39] Pole-Evans also argued that the country was unsuitable for permanent settlement – an issue that of course would have been strongly disputed by its inhabitants. NAZ S 988 Native Affairs: Oral Evidence – Natural Resources Board Native Enquiry, 1942, p. 44; Wilson (1988: 14).

Lower population densities, the relative abundance of arable land, inherently fertile soils and the sheer physical and conceptual marginality of the lowveld reserves conspired to blunt the missionary zeal of Alvord's agricultural 'demonstrators'. One piece of legislation to be enforced rigorously in much of the lowveld (except the Limpopo Valley) was the 1941 Stream Bank Cultivation Regulation. This banned cultivation within 100 yards of a river because of fears of soil erosion, and effectively made floodplain and riverbank gardening, so long the staples of lowveld agriculture, illegal.

However, an influential factor in encouraging the adoption of 'modern' and 'improved' methods of agriculture in the communal areas of the lowveld proved to be, not the activities of the agricultural demonstrators, but the increasing immigration of Shona and Ndebele families to the area from the 1950s. They brought maize, grew cash crops, practised 'winter ploughing' and planted in lines rather than broadcasting seeds. Initially, Shangaan-speakers rejected many of these 'modern' techniques but increasingly began to adopt some of them.[40] Ironically, given the dismissive attitudes to Shangaan agriculture and the relatively half-hearted attempts to introduce the 'gospel of the plough' to the lowveld, Shangaan-speakers were much quicker at adopting some 'modern' agricultural practices than some of their highveld neighbours (Bannerman 1980).[41] In fact the Native Commissioner for Ndanga District was to enthuse repeatedly about their 'qualities':

> The people inhabiting this southern area are the most advanced natives that I have met in Mashonaland. They are commonly called Shangaans, and, though living in the most remote corner of the district, are fast acquiring the benefits of civilisation, without its disabilities. Ploughs are being purchased readily, the ordinary native axe has ceased to exist and every kind of European tool is found in the kraals. Nearly every kraal has a sleigh, and a span of cattle broken in to pull, with which they do all the heavy carrying work. They are extremely wealthy in cattle, which are considerably finer than ordinary native cattle. These natives are physically finer than the Mashonas and are far more intelligent, particularly in their ability to follow a European's reasoning and train of thought. It is noticeable that the Mashonas living amongst them have not profited in the least from their example.[42]

In Ndanga District in 1910/11 the Shangaans owned 41 out of 51 ploughs and were even ploughing the fields of the Karanga in return for cattle or other payment; in 1916 they owned and hired out the only scotchcarts in the district and 'continued to exercise a salutary influence on the agricultural methods of the Wakaranga', 'providing a fine object lesson in the utility of the plough'.[43] Native Commissioner Forrestall in Chibi District similarly admits that the Shangaans were quicker to adopt the plough than many of the Shona to the north of them:

---

[40] Interview: Kraalhead, Chikombedzi, 6 July 1999; ENDA-Zimbabwe (1992).
[41] This issue is also examined in Wolmer, Sithole and Mukamuri (2003) and Wolmer and Scoones (2000).
[42] NAZ N 9/1/11 NC N'danga to CNC 31 December 1908.
[43] NAZ N 9/1/15 NC Annual Report Ndanga-Bikita 31 December 1911.

> In agriculture natives are commencing to use ploughs ... Hitherto ploughs have only been used by the Shangaans and natives of Matibi who have been continually in contact with the Northern Transvaal natives, but of late the Muklanga of the upper portion of the district have bought seven ploughs, and the other headmen are showing a keen interest in the matter.[44]

Bannerman (1980) ascribes this, in part, to the fact that, through migrant labour, the Shangaans came into contact with the market economy and technologies of South Africa much earlier than people to the north of them.[45] Also, in the heavy soils of the lowveld the plough had a greater comparative advantage over the hoe than on the lighter soils of the plateau, and in a dry climate the adoption of new implements was possibly far more critical than it was to people in the better-watered highlands. Ploughs were probably first bought in Messina by men working in the South African mines, but it was not until transport links improved that people were able to bring them to the area in large numbers. Mr. Macheke, a school teacher who grew up in northern Transvaal, remembers his father telling him that in the 1920s he taught his cousin, who had plenty of oxen but was still using hoes, how to team oxen to plough from his experience in South Africa.[46]

Narratives concerning the suitability of dryland agriculture in the lowveld

Alongside a discourse castigating Africans and, notwithstanding their fast uptake of certain technologies, particularly Shangaans, for their inability to farm 'progressively', was a narrative concerning the ecological inappropriateness of dryland cropping in the lowveld. This is exemplified by the national system of agro-ecological classification dating from 1960 (but picking up on earlier official discourses), when the colonial Ministry of Agriculture divided Southern Rhodesia into five agro-ecological regions (Vincent and Thomas 1960) (see Map 4.1). Classification was based primarily on rainfall and soil quality, with Natural Region 1 having the highest, most regular, rainfall (over 1000 mm a year) and Natural Region 5 the lowest and most erratic. These classifications led to prescriptions concerning the most productive and suitable land uses for the different regions, although they were never originally intended to have mandatory implications for landholders as to what land use options they might pursue on their land. The land perceived as best for arable were regions 1 and 2 (which cover less than 20 per cent of the land area of the country); region 3 was held to be suited to a mix of cattle farming and cropping, and regions 4 and

---

[44] NAZ NVC 1/1/8 NC Chibi to SON 15 December 1909.
[45] Similarly today much of the illicit employment taken up by young men in South Africa is in the agricultural sector. As a consultancy report puts it: 'This exposure to modern farming techniques in other regions has created a state of open-mindedness towards development options which are not indigenous to the area' (Salzgitter Consult GMBH and PTA Consulting Services 1993: 3).
[46] Interview: Mr Macheke, Chanyenga Primary School 5 June 1998.

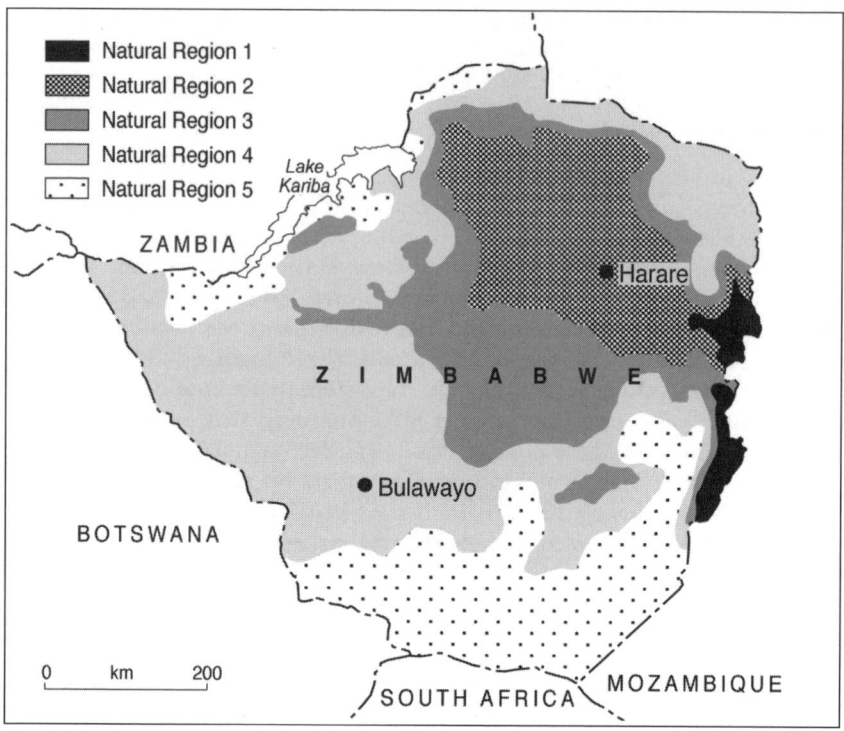

Map 4.1 Categorisation of 'Natural Regions' in Zimbabwe

5 for extensive cattle or wildlife ranching. The lowveld falls exclusively into Natural Region 5. Typically this leads to the following prescriptions:

> The only intensification in African farming possible in this Area will be where irrigation is developed, when this land should be used for the production of high-value cash crops, and protein rich feeds, silage and bean hay, for livestock. Otherwise the Area is only suitable for cultivation of extremely drought resistant varieties of sorghum and millet as subsistence crops, with legumes in limited quantities, mainly in vegetable gardens. Livestock husbandry must be extensive, except where irrigation is developed, and the indigenous breeds are most suitable in this Area for the production of meat off the rich, natural grazing.[47]

This discourse concerning appropriate land use for Natural Region 5 is alive and well today in relation to prescriptions and proscriptions for dryland agriculture in the communal areas of the lowveld. All of the recommended land uses, of course, were and are those practised by the colonial settlers rather than the African population. By extension, land uses falling outside these recommendations, those practised by the African population,

---

[47] *An Agricultural Survey of Southern Rhodesia. Part II. Agroecological Survey.* Government Printer, Salisbury (n.d) [c. 1956] - Chapter VII. African Agriculture NR V: Ranching (Section 93).

are held to be inappropriate to the fragile environment and likely to lead to environmental degradation. As early as 1906 the Native Commissioner for Ndanga was bemoaning attempts at dryland cropping in the lowveld:

> When one drops into the Sabi Valley – the eastern part of the district – the crops are very poor, *mapfundi* – Kaffir Corn – is the staple cereal in those parts and unless rain falls there I am afraid there will be the usual shortage amongst the natives. There is no reason why these natives should not leave this low-lying country and move into the mountains as there is plenty of room for them, but they prefer to risk semi-starvation every year rather than leave the country of their fore-fathers.[48]

Similar opinions were held regarding the dry south-west of the colony. Charles Murray of the Matopos Government Experimental Station, for example, insisted that families evicted from the Matopos Hills in Matebeleland should not be resettled in the lowveld which '[e]ven under good farming methods is not an area where good crops can be produced. In my opinion all that low veld country is entirely unsuitable from a land use point of view for Native occupation.'[49]

These views are still expounded by many people today and, if anything, with more vehemence. Commercial cattle and game ranchers hold particularly strong views about their neighbours in the communal areas, as the following quotes from interviews show:

> Region 5 is not a crop growing area. Growing crops [in the area] is a *political* move not an economic one. They only grow crops near the game fence so that animals come and they can get people to shoot them; or so that they can get food aid when the crops fail. You *cannot* grow crops with that type of risk factor. The average rainfall is 14 inches but most years you get very little – the norm is less. Every year they plead poverty, even in good years they get drought relief and poverty alleviation and there are always cries to have animals shot as they are devouring crops. [his emphases][50]

> There should not be any dryland agriculture practised in communal areas of the south-east lowveld. ... [The fact that the 1998/99 agricultural season was very successful] is irrelevant to the bigger picture. Unfortunately what it does is it creates in the – I won't call them farmers because I don't think you can call scrabbling a subsistence livelihood farming – it gives them unrealistic expectations, but also it creates in the minds of government planners and extension workers and whatever the suggestion that they should be growing crops down here and I think that that's absolutely wrong. ... It's their land, their livelihoods, there's actually no way that we could tell them whether they should or shouldn't be involved in dryland agriculture – whether we should be helping them do something when we have doubts about its sustainability – that's another story.[51]

> I have been here seven years and only this year has a man said he had three bags of maize. This is not a crop area it is a cattle area. But cattle were devalued by the drought

[48] NAZ N 9/1/9 NC Ndanga to CNC 31 March 1906.
[49] NAZ S 1561 46 Evidence of Charles Murray, 21/3/1949, cited by Ranger (1999: 176).
[50] Interview: Rancher, Mwenezi, 8 November 1999.
[51] Interview: Malilangwe, 13 July 1999.

and the government didn't come to help. This is cattle country – we can never be self-sufficient without cattle.[52]

The wilderness can be tamed and turned into a productive space – but only on certain terms. The legacy of the colonial gaze is that only the typically 'European' activities of ranching and large-scale irrigated agriculture are appropriate to this landscape. Dryland agriculture – even as one of many dynamic livelihood strategies – simply cannot be countenanced as a suitable land use. These oft-quoted opinions chime with the conservationist rhetoric examined in Chapter 7. The conservationist lobby would rather the wilderness was preserved than tamed, but similarly fears the landscape's 'further mutilation by unproductive cultivation' (Child 1995: 104).

These are not just the views of white commercial farmers worried by the presence of land-hungry peasants on their doorstep, and latterly inside the farm gates. It is also the officially promoted policy of the Department of Natural Resources that people should not practise dryland agriculture in Natural Region 5 – that cattle-rearing (at low stocking densities), game-ranching and irrigation should be encouraged in its place. The Director of the Department for Natural Resources for Chiredzi District told me that the 'recommended land use for the area is beef production supported by irrigation. All dry land arable should ultimately be abandoned … [it has] no future.'[53] And in the midst of land invasions in the Save Valley Conservancy in 2000 the Minister for Environment and Tourism was quoted as saying 'equitable distribution of farming land … would not work in a conservancy' as it was not suitable for cropping (see Chapter 8).[54]

Dryland agriculture in practice today

However, today as during the colonial era, many official pronouncements on appropriate farming practice in the lowveld are totally at odds with local practice. As we have seen, dryland cropping has a long, dynamic history and has always been a key element, alongside other strategies, of people's livelihoods. Agricultural practice has had to be flexible enough to accommodate major colonial interventions in the shape of massive land alienation and coercive proscriptions on and prescriptions for land use as well as repeated drought. In fact ENDA-Zimbabwe (1993), in a study of Sengwe communal area, found that there is an ongoing trend of increasing the importance of rainfed arable production, as people attempt to diversify and expand their food base. Small grains such as sorghum and millet are still the major crops grown, although maize is increasing in importance since its introduction by Shona and Ndebele settlers in the 1950s. A survey conducted in the Chikombedzi area in 1998 found that 95.5 per cent of households sampled

---

[52] Interview: Director, Mwenezi [previously Nuanetsi] Ranch, 27 July 1999.
[53] Interview: Director, Department of Natural Resources Department, Chiredzi District, 16 July 1999.
[54] *The Mirror* (Masvingo Province weekly), 3-9 November 2000.

grew sorghum and 91.5 per cent grew maize (Wolmer, Sithole and Mukamuri 2002). Average home and outfield sizes were 1.2 and 8 hectares respectively – relatively large for Zimbabwean communal areas, reflecting the extensive nature of cultivation. Not all arable land holdings are necessarily cultivated; the area actually under production depends on the availability of labour and draught power. Fertiliser and kraal manure are very rarely used. Many people maintain that they are putting more time and effort into cropping than in the past because, since the war and the major drought of the early 1990s, they lack livestock.

The increasing land and labour given over to dryland agriculture seems to belie the charge that the lowveld is unsuitable for dryland agriculture and has no future. However, the fact remains that in the pre- and post-colonial period the lowveld communal areas have been amongst the most frequent recipients of drought relief in the form of food-for-work schemes and grain 'loans'. Frost (2000) calculates that for Chiredzi district communal area populations between 1983/84 and 1992/93 the average number of people receiving food aid was 34,437 (45 per cent of the population). Over this ten-year period 37,324 tonnes of food aid was distributed in Chiredzi (and see Salzgitter Consult GMBH 1985; IFAD 1995: 2/5).

A cursory examination of farmers' own experiences also paints a bleak picture. I asked a group of farmers in Chikombedzi to rank harvest 'quality' for each year of the post-Independence period between 1980 and 1999.[55] During this 19-year period they perceived the agricultural seasons to be very 'good' only in 1998-99, 1988-89 and 1984-85; between 1989 and 1994 there were five consecutive 'bad' years, including the 1991-92 drought when practically no crops at all were harvested. This picture is a partial one, however. In the 'good' agricultural seasons massive harvests were gathered and grain stores and cash income built up (the region produced the best yields in the country in 1998-99 and grain buyers were travelling to Chikombedzi from as far as Pietersburg in South Africa). Even in 'bad' years small yields of sorghum are usually managed as farmers carefully time planting to maximise the available moisture. In 'normal' years farmers tend to get enough grain to eat, with a little to sell; and every ten years or so very severe droughts mean absolutely nothing is harvested. The situation is thus not as bad as pessimistic reports that make assertions such as 'rainfed agriculture is a non-starter – sorghum can only be harvested every 15 years'[56] make out. In this context dryland farming is not illogical or necessarily unproductive, but is a rational response to environmental dynamics.

When agricultural extension and development initiatives have conceded that dryland agriculture is not inappropriate there have been moves made to encourage the planting of 'traditional' crops – such as drought-tolerant

---

[55] Group discussion, Chikombedzi, 8 September 1999: farmers were asked to rank harvest quality between 0 (non-existent) and 10 (excellent) for maize and sorghum.
[56] Presentation to First Agenda 21 Indaba on Culture Conscious Conservation Areas, 18 May 1999.

short season varieties of sorghum – and to change farmers 'mindset' away from maize (e.g. IFAD 1995).[57] But maize is not necessarily 'inappropriate' just because the chances of a good yield are slimmer, and many farmers continually prefer to grow it. The reasons given for this are that they prefer its taste, it is less labour-intensive to grow and grind, and is more easily marketable (only a few varieties of sorghum are easy to market and maize generally receives higher prices). Again, the decision to grow maize is a rational trade-off between environmental and economic prerogatives.

Cropping patterns are highly diversified. As well as cereals, legumes (groundnuts, bambara nuts and cowpea) are grown on sandy soils, and increasingly cotton, and sunflower cash crops are planted. Often these are intercropped with cowpea, watermelons, sweet sorghum or pumpkins. Vegetable gardens are becoming increasingly popular – once the preserve of women, men are now also growing vegetables for home consumption and sale (Wolmer et al. 2002). Another increasingly common cropping scenario in the lowveld, as well as elsewhere in Zimbabwe, is for contract growing or sharecropping. Commercial seed companies or individual entrepreneurs are providing seeds or inputs to smallholders on the condition that they are sold the produce. This is most commonly organised by cotton seed companies, but Chibuku – the largest sorghum beer company in Zimbabwe – is also entering into arrangements for the growth and purchase of red sorghum, and South African entrepreneurs are providing seeds and markets for guar beans.

I have not intended to give too rosy a picture of dryland agriculture in the lowveld. Given the unpredictable nature of the environment, cropping is an inherently risky business. As one interviewee put it, pointing at his granary, 'that grain is like morning dew: it shines for a while but disappears with the rising sun.'[58] The impact of the particularly severe 1991-92 drought continues to be felt. One legacy is the ongoing shortage of draught power for cultivation which was caused by the massive-scale death of livestock. This is perceived as the main constraint to agriculture. A survey in the Chikombedzi area in 1998 found that only 26 per cent of households owned two or more draught animals. In this context a number of institutional arrangements including sharing, hiring and work parties are entered into in order to secure draught power to till the relatively large fields (Wolmer et al. 2002).[59] A further, increasingly significant, constraint to dryland agriculture is economic. Beginning with the Economic Structural Adjustment Programmes of the 1990s and continuing with the hyperinflation

---

[57] Interview: Chief Agritex Officer, Chiredzi District, 1 June 1998.
[58] Interview: Watch Mongayane, Chikombedzi, 29 July 1999.
[59] The 2000-2001 agricultural season was another potentially disastrous one. In early 2000 Cyclone Eline destroyed houses, granaries, crops and much of the maize and sorghum which survived rotted. With little maize stored for the following season an early season drought pointed towards another very poor harvest. See 'Masvingo villagers face starvation', *Daily News*, 28 March 2001.

since 2000, agricultural inputs such as seed and fertiliser have become vastly more expensive. However, in the absence of any real alternatives, other than short and long-term illicit migration to South Africa in search of work, rainfed cropping is likely to remain crucial to livelihoods in the lowveld notwithstanding its apparent 'total failure' in many years and its inherent riskiness in a drought-prone environment.

Policies in practice

Official policies concerning land use in the lowveld often contradict each other. The state has never been homogeneous, and policies emanating from the Department of Natural Resources (DNR) rooted in a way of seeing the lowveld as extensive ranchland are at odds with those of the DNPWLM and of Agritex, the agricultural extension service, which promotes standardised inputs to smallholder arable agriculture across Zimbabwe irrespective of agro-ecological zone and soil type.[60]

The official Agritex discourse differs from those of the DNR and DNPWLM, however, in that it recognises the integral importance of agriculture to livelihoods and does not write it off as simply inappropriate. Notwithstanding this, Agritex has tended to focus on either an idealised mixed farming model where large amounts of organic and inorganic fertiliser are applied to arable land (Wolmer and Scoones 2000) or capital-intensive irrigation schemes. The disjuncture between these agricultural policies and local realities is increasingly apparent to many 'street level bureaucrats' (Lipsky 1979). One Agritex official, for example, recognised that:

> The Agritex package is not at all appropriate to the lowveld. For example: more inorganic fertilisers. These are quite expensive and they don't use them because of the nature of their soils. But government packages have delivered fertiliser – which people just sell (unless they have irrigation).[61]

Amongst many extensionists there is a tacit acknowledgement that in practice people 'have their own ways of surviving' and the official recommendations have as yet had little impact outside irrigation schemes. Attempts are now being made to initiate a more flexible, client-driven agricultural extension system, focusing on encouraging needs prioritised by farmers, which recognises that 'people need food and the cheapest way of getting food [in the lowveld] is to produce it yourself.'[62]

Another discourse that has recently been brought to bear on land use in the lowveld is the ZANU(PF)/'war veteran' rhetoric on land for the people. This has seen a total inversion of the discourse on appropriate land use as dryland agriculture is being positively encouraged on existing commercial ranching land. Is this a deliberate rejection of the colonial

[60] Now AREX (Agricultural Research and Extension Services).
[61] Interview: Acting Head Agritex Provincial office Masvingo, 15 June 1999.
[62] Interview: SEDAP District Co-ordinator, Chiredzi District, 2 November 1999.

wilderness binary vision in favour of a peasant smallholder model centred on rainfed agriculture, or a strategic piece of populism intended to garner support from a disenchanted electorate? These questions will be returned to in Chapter 8.

Conclusions

There is a sharp divergence between colonially derived perceptions of the lowveld landscape as unfit for dryland agriculture, and the reality of people's livelihood strategies. The official adherence to a rigid and static 'natural region' designation is at odds with the flux and dynamism of a non-equilibrium landscape (cf. Zimmerer 2000), and many resource-users own perceptions of that landscape. Despite tentative moves into 'participatory', client-driven agricultural extension and tub-thumping populist rhetoric on land resettlement (see Chapter 8), much policy impacting on land use in the lowveld continues to draw on these 'appropriate land use' narratives. Yet rainfed cropping has always had a crucial role to play in this 'lived in' landscape, alongside labour migration and remittances and a range of other strategies; and environmental, economic and political dynamics have conspired to increase its importance. Given that recent years have seen war veterans and peasant farmers busy pegging out plots in the lowveld cattle and game ranches with the explicit support of government and a disintegrating Zimbabwean economy, it seems likely that dryland agriculture will continue to be a mainstay of livelihoods for the foreseeable future.

5

'Backwater to breadbasket'
Irrigated agriculture in the lowveld

To many in Zimbabwe the first image the lowveld conjures up is of a lush landscape characterised by the 'emerald green chequerboard of irrigated fields' (Mlambo and Pangeti 1996: 9). This is an image at odds with that of the parched landscape unsuited to agriculture explored in the previous chapter, or of the pristinely natural wilderness vision that has underpinned conservation initiatives. The lowveld has become inextricably linked, in the imaginations of many, to the massive irrigated estates of the sugar industry. This way of seeing the landscape is typified by the Masvingo Provincial Administrator's description of the lowveld as first and foremost the 'granary of the province'.[1]

The potential of the fertile soils of the lowveld to lend themselves to irrigated agriculture has long been emphasised. Together with its low altitude, frost-free conditions, and relatively low disease risk, the soils support — when irrigated — a year-round agricultural calendar 'almost perfect for the mass production of high-quality crops'.[2] As early as 1922 one Native Commissioner went as far as to assert that 'the Sabi Valley, in my opinion, carries some of the richest soil in South Africa and I quite agree with the opinion often expressed that we shall one day find this becoming a second Nile Valley'.[3] No less bullish, nearly 50 years later, was the person who wrote:

> According to legend, this was the land of King Solomon's mines, yet even King Solomon can hardly have appreciated the true wealth offered by the hills, rivers and plains of this corner of Africa... Just as Americans have always looked to their west, Australians and Canadians to their northern territories, and Brazilians to the Amazon basin as their respective lands of promise, so Rhodesians have regarded the Sabi valley (Sabi-Limpopo Authority 1970: 1).

---

[1] Interview: Provincial Administrator, Masvingo, 15 June 1999.
[2] *The Rhodesia Herald*, 5 March 1959; Williams (1981).
[3] NAZ N 9/1/25 NC Annual Report Chipinga District 1922.

This optimistic vision encapsulates one of the facets of the wilderness optic through which the lowveld has so often been viewed. This is a wild landscape that could and should be battled and tamed on a massive scale through the application of human ingenuity, hard graft and technology. Bringing water to the arid, flat landscape would transform it economically and aesthetically from a backwater to a breadbasket.

This vision has mainly been applied to the commercial agricultural sector and the large Triangle and Hippo Valley estates are the result. There have also been many plans, of varying degrees of success, to bring irrigation to the lowveld's communal areas. This chapter traces both these developments and shows how the physical and imaginative transformation of landscape has been bound up with issues of identity and with struggles for power at many levels, as various landscape representations have been appropriated and used by different actors to gain control of water or exert influence.

The lowveld sugar story

As Chapter 2 noted, popular histories of the lowveld irrigated sugar industry focus on the role of one individual – Thomas Murray MacDougall. Notwithstanding the heavily romanticised nature of these narratives, MacDougall did play a pivotal role in the introduction of large-scale irrigated agriculture to the lowveld. MacDougall arrived in Rhodesia from Scotland via South America. He became a transport rider and negotiated with the BSAC for rights to a vast 120,000 hectares of land between the Mtirikwi, Chiredzi and Runde rivers, receiving an option on the land after the First World War. He named it Triangle, after his registered cattle brand. Having had little success as a cattle rancher MacDougall, ignoring the objections of the Irrigation Department, built a weir on the Mtirikwi river and a 13-kilometre-long canal, in part tunnelled through solid granite,[4] to supply irrigation water to a small sugar plantation on his ranch during the early 1930s. In 1937 he produced the first ten tonnes of raw sugar and in 1939 completed construction of a sugar mill that had been hauled piece by piece from Natal. The hugely ambitious scheme was a financial disaster, however, and in 1944 Triangle Sugar Estates[5] had to sell out to the Rhodesian government, which formed the Sugar Industry Board to take over the concern (and its liabilities) on a caretaker basis (Saunders 1989; Mlambo and Pangeti 1996).

Under the Sugar Industry Board's administration there was a rapid expansion of the area under cane and the production of sugar. The canals were lengthened and further weirs and night storage dams built. But the

[4] Mlambo and Pangeti (1996) make the point that MacDougall is often represented in popular lore as the 'proverbial Promethean giant single-handedly hewing the tunnel' with his 'trusty claymore'. The Shona and Shangaan labourers who provided the labour, however, remain 'nameless and faceless'.

[5] MacDougall established Triangle as a company in 1938.

industry was beset with severe ecological problems (smut infestation, frost and drought) and continued to be a failure as a viable business venture. It had, however, been proved that sugar was well suited to the climate and soils of the lowveld, and was potentially profitable (Dodds 1948; Penning 1948). The government now wanted to sell Triangle back to the private sector (Mlambo and Pangeti 1996).

Interest was meanwhile being generated in the irrigable potential of the Save basin further north. After the Second World War the government was looking to the lowveld to address shortages of food. In 1947 Alexander Gibb was appointed to carry out a survey of the irrigation potential of the Save valley, particularly for the production of wheat, sugar, vegetables and fruit, and dairy produce. The Gibb Report of 1948 concluded that at least 100,000 hectares of the lowveld could be properly utilised, and recommended the building of dams, the establishment of an agricultural research station and a 10,000 hectares pilot scheme (Gibb and Partners 1948). Following the report, a small experimental area was opened at Nyanyadzi in 1949, and experimental stations were opened at 'Sabi' in 1950 and Chisumbanje in 1953 (Cunliffe 1993).

In 1954, Triangle Estates, finally profit-making, were sold to a syndicate of Natal sugar planters with the intention that a major settler-farmer scheme, involving the immigration of around 300 young, white farmers from Natal, would be responsible for growing the bulk of the cane. Three 'Pioneer Sugar Planters' were initially brought in, but before long Triangle was yet again facing severe financial difficulties. In 1957 the company was sold to the firm of a Natal sugar magnate – the Hulett Corporation. The large-scale resettlement scheme was scrapped but the three existing settler-farms were reluctantly retained. This initiated a period of major infrastructural development in the lowveld, as South African capital and technology was brought to bear in transforming the landscape (Saunders 1989; Eastwood 1996). Bulldozers, rippers and ploughs were used for large-scale bush clearances and preparation for cane planting; cement-lined canals, pumping stations and workers compounds were built; and most significantly, after negotiations between Triangle and the Irrigation Department, the government began construction of the huge Kyle Dam near Masvingo.[6]

In 1956 Ray Stockil, a local farmer and MP, established a rival concern, Hippo Valley Estates, very close to Triangle. This estate initially focused on citrus orchards but soon expanded into sugar cane with Mauritian financial backing. To accommodate the water requirements of Hippo Valley the government agreed to build the Bangala dam (completed in 1963) since the estate received only a small percentage of the Kyle Dam water. This initiated a period of bitter rivalry between Triangle and Hippo Valley, with continual fights over water allocations from the dams, which at one stage went as far as the Supreme Court (Saunders 1989; Eastwood 1996).[7] These

---

[6] This was completed in 1961.
[7] Interview: Executive Manager for Water Affairs, Triangle 8 February 2001.

conflicts were embedded in the complex and interwoven southern African regional political economy of sugar. In 1962 there was a counter take-over of the Hulett Corporation – due to machinations within the South African sugar industry – and a new consortium of Natal sugar companies owned Triangle. In the early 1960s Hippo Valley passed into the control of Anglo-American Corporation.[8]

By 1964 the recommendations of the Gibb Report of nearly 20 years earlier came to fruition with the establishment of the Sabi-Limpopo Authority (SLA). This was described as the largest and most ambitious project ever conceived in Southern Rhodesia (Sabi-Limpopo Authority 1970). Modelled on the Tennessee Valley Authority, it was a statutory body with wide powers over nearly a sixth of Zimbabwe.[9] These included: planning and co-ordinating development throughout the south-east lowveld; maintaining and operating the main water works (including investigating dam sites, basin surveys, canal alignments); controlling cropping systems; and carrying out agricultural research.[10] The SLA took over Mkwasine sugar estates[11] (the lowveld's third large-scale sugar estate) in 1965, with a view to selling it on to private plot-holders. The production of wheat was heavily subsidised at Mkwasine with the aim of establishing it as a major crop in the lowveld and producing enough for national needs (Pangeti 1986).[12] In a publication entitled 'Golden Dawn', the SLA announced its aim as being 'to develop the whole of the lowveld irrigation complex over a period of 25 years' whilst recognising that 'political difficulties' could delay progress (Sabi-Limpopo Authority 1970).

The 1960s saw further massive infrastructural development with the building of Manjirenji Dam, a new sugar mill at Triangle Mill, a tarred access road, an airport at Buffalo Range, and the entire town of Chiredzi. The construction of a new railway line to Mozambique which passed through the lowveld gave further economic impetus to the region (Fair 1964). Further dams were planned at Tokwe-Mukorsi, Tende and Manyuchi. By 1963 Rhodesia was exporting sugar, thousands of workers had been brought in from Nyasaland (Malawi) and parts of the lowveld landscape had been unrecognisably transformed. In the white Rhodesian

---

[8] Pangeti (1986) describes the maze of interlocking interests (through cross-shareholdings and intermeshing directorships) behind these two ostensibly separate interests (Triangle and Hippo Valley) and their parent companies. This, and the huge size of their multinational parent companies, has given them massive power within the Zimbabwean economy.

[9] It is also similar to the Tennessee Valley Authority in that it was set up during years of economic depression.

[10] The SLA could, in a sense, be regarded as a precursor to the Catchment Councils ushered in by the 1998 Water Act.

[11] This was originally Nandi Sugar Estates.

[12] The wheat project had proved successful by 1974 and the estate was sold to a Triangle/Hippo Valley consortium who, being more interested in profitable returns on investment than the 'national interest' in achieving self-sufficiency in food production, promptly ditched wheat and converted the Mkwasine estate to sugar cane (Pangeti 1986).

popular imagination the lowveld had become symbolic of growth, development, unlimited future potential and a badge of national pride.

Large-scale irrigation, Rhodesian identity and a new landscape aesthetic

The symbolic significance of this reshaped landscape merits closer attention. The SLA heralded a brief period of massive and optimistic ambition where the large-scale irrigated agricultural estates of the lowveld were envisaged as an economic powerhouse, not just for the region, but for the whole country and even internationally, from whence an era of productive abundance would unfold.[13] The Gibb Report of 1948 had grandiloquently laid out the challenge:

> Should the Colony make a great drive to intensify and extend production over what may be termed the present settled area, facing all the practical and administrative difficulties that this would involve, or should she take her courage in both hands and say "Here is a great unsettled area; we must bring it into production"? In biblical allegory, should she bathe in the waters of Jordan or seek to harness the more spectacular waters of Sabi? I believe the answer is both (Gibb and Partners 1948).

If the Gibb Report's projections were accurate and all the potentially irrigable area 'could be brought into full development', Southern Rhodesia, it was held, would become a food-exporting country and establish a secure foundation for industrial expansion into food processing and manufacturing using agro-industrial by-products (such as paper from cane fibre waste). This in turn would lead to the expansion of business and commerce, the establishment of new towns and villages, and the provision of more job opportunities (Fair 1964; Williams 1981). Thus, as well as transforming the lowveld, the 'agricultural revolution' would 'reorientate the Rhodesian economy'.[14] Plans were drawn up for regionally integrated economic development and attracting foreign migrant labour. The SLA predicted that the completed lowveld irrigation complex would 'support a population of 1 million people and will provide over 700,000 acres of irrigated land, growing both summer and winter crops and producing in annual value more than the present agricultural production of the whole of Rhodesia. Employment will amount to about 400,000 which is nearly half as many again as the number presently employed in the European agricultural sector' (Sabi-Limpopo Authority 1970).

One writer unwittingly captured part of the reason for the euphoria surrounding these development schemes: 'To the man in the street, the lowveld has become a symbol of good fortune, something that will avail present economic ills, and provide a golden future for Rhodesia's rapidly expanding population' (Hussey 1965: 262). 'Enterprise Valley' stood in sharp contrast to other industrial sectors 'where pessimism seems to be the

---

[13] *The Rhodesia Herald*, 5 March 1959.
[14] Quinton, Chairman of the Sabi-Limpopo Authority in Andrews (1964).

prevailing mood'.[15] The economy was in recession and the dismantling of the Federation of Rhodesia and Nyasaland in 1963 had denied Southern Rhodesia access to the substantial mining revenues generated in Northern Rhodesia. After 1965 the economy was also under siege because of the international sanctions brought about by the Rhodesian Front's Unilateral Declaration of Independence (UDI) leading to a partial closure of export markets. At the same time various commissions of inquiry had emphasised the integral present and future role of agriculture to the economy.[16] It was hardly surprising, therefore, that politicians and the media seized on the lowveld's potential to expand domestic production and bolster (white) Rhodesian pride in the face of international condemnation.[17] Politicians lined up to laud the 'biggest thing ever to happen to this country',[18] talk up the 'treasure chest' or 'showpiece' of Rhodesia[19] and usher in the future 'Birmingham of Africa'.[20] The founder of the Hippo Valley Estates, and leader of the opposition Rhodesia Party for 11 years, Ray Stockil, was interviewed on the future of the lowveld in the *Sunday Mail*. Typically, Stockil is described as picturing:

> [T]he chimneys of the vast complex of ancillary industries rising among the cane fields and citrus estates. He also sees the lowveld as a solution to African unemployment and unrest. 'So many people think of it as only an agricultural undertaking. There is enormous scope for industry. Instead of unemployment we might easily find that we no longer have enough people to develop the country'.[21]

During UDI, times were in fact very hard for the sugar industry as the British government announced a complete embargo on the export of sugar from Rhodesia and poor sugar prices compounded the difficulties. The estates were forced to diversify into wheat, cotton, bananas, maize, animal feeds, tobacco, cattle ranching and ethanol production (Saunders 1989; Mlambo and Pangeti 1996), and rescue packages had to be offered to the settler planters to keep them in business.[22]

As Chapter 2 demonstrated, representations of the lowveld's irrigated landscape were also critical to the portrayal of the white settlers as brave pioneers penetrating and taming unknown and dangerous 'empty space'. This discourse was not only applied to MacDougall and his contemporaries from 'the older pioneer days' but was also deliberately invoked in descriptions of the new round of white settlers who arrived in the emerging

---

[15] *Bulawayo Chronicle*, 28 April 1961.
[16] Such as the Phillips Commission of 1962.
[17] A decade earlier the Kariba Dam was similarly employed as a symbol of Rhodesian strength and future prosperity.
[18] H. Reedman (Minister for Roads, Tourism and Immigration) *Fort Victoria Advertiser*, 12 June 1964.
[19] *Bulawayo Chronicle*, 5 December 1961; *Bulawayo Chronicle*, 27 September 1963.
[20] *Fort Victoria News* 27 January 1950.
[21] *Sunday Mail*, 12 January 1964.
[22] *Sunday Mail*, 4 September 1966.

settlements of Triangle and Chiredzi 'in the footsteps of MacDougall' in the 1960s. As two glossy articles put it:

> These men, all sturdy individualists, carved their farms and lands from virgin bush, making do in 'pole and dagga' huts until profits allowed them to extend and improve the housing for their families. (Sabi-Limpopo Authority 1970: 41)

> [The] attitude of mind ... is so much like the way we felt years ago ... when 'time' meant that the job had to be started and finished and no-one looked at a watch or clock. (Bentley 1964: 20)

The human enterprise, endeavour and ingenuity of these white settlers were celebrated as the catalysts of progress (e.g. Fair 1964). In the face of economic difficulties and a condemning world these pioneers were pulling together to carve a new productive landscape from the wastelands. One writer went so far as to assert that:

> Civilisation had now invaded the unknown wilderness that lured MacDougall ... Here is an example of partnership in creating a microcosm of society in a formerly uninhabited wild. Empire-building as a term may have fallen into disrepute, but this is the fulfilment of all that is best in pioneer vision. The construction of something where nothing was before is the most satisfying achievement of mankind. (Lambert 1961: 12, 21)

Another theme touched on in Chapter 2 was the way in which the physical taming of the landscape was accompanied by the emergence of a new – or rather the application of an older, European – landscape aesthetic. A landscape that had seemed threatening and a site of disorder and danger was now rendered in terms of scientific and technical mastery as the hot, dry and malaria-ridden backwater was suddenly transformed into a pastoral breadbasket.

> The Lowveld ... has been a forgotten land ... There is much mopani woodland, throughout which are interspersed those strange, incredible trees, the baobabs. Big game abounds in many parts – elephant, lion, buffalo and many species of buck. Large-scale irrigation is now changing this picture dramatically. The great earth-moving machinery has rolled in and cleared and levelled large tracts of wild bush to be replaced by mile after mile of green cropland. (Andrews 1964: 19)

> Roads are being cut through the scrub. Baobabs are being yanked from the ground like giant grey molars.... A network of canals and irrigation pipes spreads wide across the land... pumping lifeblood into a once barren area.[23]

> ... the lowveld retains its character, and remains the land of the unexpected ... Most fantastic of all these contrasts is the brilliant oasis of green cane beyond the loop of the Mtilikwe, seen from the air as a miracle in the barren plain. In the dry season, the cleared earth below appears in the drab tones of cave paintings, and the rivers are disclosed as the life-lines of the country. There could be no more vivid illustration of the importance of water in this dusty waste. (Lambert 1961: 12)

[23] 'Pioneers win wealth in wastes of Hippo Valley', *Bulawayo Chronicle*, 28 April 1961.

Figure 5.1 Lake Kyle, serving the lowveld sugar estates (Source: Fair 1964)

Not only was the lush, green 'cane culture' replacing this drab and dusty waste, but order was being brought to chaos in the form of the straight edged, grid-like symmetry of the new landscape (cf. Comaroff and Comaroff 1991).[24] In books and magazine articles of the period the photographs chosen to represent this new landscape tend to dwell on aerial photographs of bulldozers dragging massive chains to rip out unruly bush, and neat grids of sugar plantations criss-crossed by endless parallel cement canals. Similarly, photographs of the brutal modernist architecture of the dams at Kyle and Bangala were popular illustrations of neo-pioneer ingenuity (see Figures 5.1-5.3). Alongside agricultural and engineering expertise, medical and veterinary science were employed to tackle the scourges of malaria, foot-and-mouth disease and trypanosomiasis in the lowveld and to domesticate the landscape previously described as 'unfit for white habitation'.

---

[24] As Sinclair (1977: 279) puts it: 'Symbolically, the war of the civilised man against the savage has always been the attack of the line against the irregular'. See Robins (1994) for another Zimbabwean example of the imposition of the 'rectangular grid of civilisation'.

Figure 5.2 Clearing bush in preparation for planting sugar cane (Source: Fair 1964)

It would be incorrect, however, to oversimplify the narratives underpinning commercial irrigated agriculture in the lowveld. There were, for example, significant differences of opinion on the relative merits of relatively small-scale white settler-based development and company estate farming backed by international capital. There were changing land allocations to these management types reflecting the contest between ideologies (although multinational capital effectively won the day) (see Williams 1981; Mlambo and Pangeti 1996).

Sanctions, a corruption scandal,[25] acrimonious in-fighting and accusations of chronic mismanagement in the SLA,[26] and the civil war of the late 1960s and 1970s took some of the shine off the lowveld agro-industrial

---

[25] There were long, drawn-out accusations of corrupt land speculation regarding the development of Nandi (Mkwasine) Estates. *Sunday Mail*, 19 September 1965, 31 November 1965.

[26] The SLA never made a profit and was increasingly accused of going beyond its original brief which was simply to co-ordinate development and provide facilities that would encourage development by private enterprise. Instead, it effectively became a farming agency in its own right. *Rhodesia Herald*, 15 August 1970; *Sunday Mail*, 1 November 1970.

Figure 5.3 Land cleared for sugar cane and uncleared bush (Source: Fair 1964)

dream. Despite rising sugar prices leading to a brief period of expansion and a return to pre-UDI profit levels in the mid-1970s, the lowveld sugar industry never regained its status as the 'showpiece of Rhodesia'. A fall in sugar prices and massively increased transport costs due to wartime closure of the Mozambican border meant the estates soon suffered a reversal of fortune. However, Zimbabwe gained independence self-sufficient in food in part due to lowveld production which by 1980 supplied 20 per cent of the country's agricultural output – 30 per cent of its wheat, 90 per cent of its sugar and 25 per cent of its cotton (Williams 1981). In 20 years the lowveld had come, for many, to stand for a totally different landscape, as a beleaguered rebel colonial state, with the financial backing of South African conglomerations, had initiated an ambitious and far-reaching economic and physical restructuring process. But this had come at a price. The vast increases in land values engendered by the sugar boom led to widespread evictions of African tenants from commercial property and a further round of land alienation. And there was the occasional prescient dissenting voice amongst the lowveld boosters. As one contributor to *The Rhodesia Herald* had the temerity to argue:

> Some of the publicity accorded to these schemes has given them misleadingly, the prestige of the discovering of a new continent. By the use of imprecise language the

---

[26] (cont.) The SLA was eventually amalgamated with the Agricultural Development Authority (ARDA) and all its remaining assets taken over and run as state farms.

general impression may have been given that everybody under the sun is going to be better off. ... It is not a couple of score European smallholdings that the country wants to see developed but thousands by all races. ... Assuming there is a future for this type of agriculture in the lowveld ... the question then turns on the accessibility of the land irrigated to large numbers of people of all races.[27]

Commercial irrigated agriculture post-Independence

Since the mid-1980s the Zimbabwean sugar industry has encountered a variety of difficulties. These have included: price control on sugar, Renamo attacks disrupting trade routes to the Mozambican ports, the increasing use of sugar substitutes in consumer countries, falling commodity prices, drought and water shortages, foreign-exchange shortages and, in recent years, tenure insecurity due to land being designated for resettlement.

The only major infrastructural development to be completed since Independence is the Manyuchi dam on the Mwenezi river. This was financed by the Mwenezi Development Corporation (see below) and completed in 1988. It was originally intended to irrigate oil palm production estates.[28] In 1995, the London-based Aberfoyle Holdings took over the entire shareholding of the Mwenezi Development Corporation in a deal billed as the biggest investment in Zimbabwe since Independence. It planned to pour £32 million into a huge irrigated palm oil project, but the project became steeped in political and financial scandal and was a failure. The water was almost totally unutilised except for an experimental palm plot and some cotton. There was a desperate series of attempts to rescue the situation including a failed government buyout and overtures from Vice-President Joshua Nkomo's Zimbabwe Development Trust (the owners of adjoining Mwenezi Ranch). After passing through various hands Triangle Estates finally bought it at a knock-down price and started growing sugar.[29]

Another ambitious scheme to get beyond the drawing board, but yet to show any likelihood of ever being completed due to severe financial difficulties, is the Tokwe-Mukorsi dam. The planned use for the water is to irrigate 22,000 hectares of the south-east lowveld in five separate schemes. The most optimistic projections are that the dam would result in a 15 per cent increase in sugar production and the creation of 10,000 new jobs, leading the Masvingo Provincial Governor to say 'this development should make us the breadbasket of Zimbabwe'[30] and one informant to talk of the region becoming a 'greenbelt'.[31] It would also free water from Lake Mutirikwe for use in Masvingo and by farmers to the north and west of the

[27] *The Rhodesia Herald*, 17 July 1961.
[28] *Commerce*, November 1987; *African Business*, December 1987.
[29] 'Happy ending for Mwenezi project', *South African Business Intelligence*, 20 October 1995.
[30] *The Herald*, 11 December 1999.
[31] Interview: Director, Mwenezi Ranch, 27 July 1999.

lake and provide flood prevention on lower reaches of the Tokwe river (Heath 1998). A consultancy report on the dam echoes the language of the 1960s in trumpeting the aesthetic improvements of irrigated land over bush:

> While the Tokwe-Mukorsi scheme will have some negative effects upon the vegetation of the area, no major damage will be caused and the establishment of selected botanical reserves or protected areas could easily offset the negative impacts. It has been pointed out by several people that the substitution of green, luscious irrigated vegetation for areas of dry and often degraded and stunted indigenous cover, can only be an improvement both visually and as a habitat for birds and other forms of life. (Heath 1998: 24)

The government rejected offers from the sugar companies to fund construction of the dam. This deal fell through for a combination of political and financial reasons. The government got cold feet because of worries that the sugar companies would then have a monopoly on the water (just as the newly implemented Water Act was intended to remove the concepts of private ownership of water and of water rights in perpetuity); and the sugar estates felt they were being asked to pay twice over for the development (with levies as well as costs).[32] The contract was instead offered to an Italian contractor. However, the contractor ceased work after completing only 40 per cent of the site in protest over the non-payment of almost Z$600 million in fees. The government was left with the task of paying this off and sourcing a further Z$1 billion to complete the project. Overtures to the Italian and Iranian governments, HSBC and the Trade Investment Bank to bail out the project were unsuccessful. The government even unsuccessfully approached Triangle and Hippo Valley estates again, a deal to resuscitate the project with a Spanish company collapsed and further construction remains indefinitely suspended.[33]

Today, visitors to the lowveld are still struck by the sheer scale of the dramatically engineered landscape. As well as the 'emerald green chequerboard' there is an impressive amount of infrastructural development. Triangle, for example, operates the only ethanol plant on the African continent, has one of the best-equipped hospitals in Zimbabwe, employs more than 8,000 people, and runs shops, eight primary schools, and three secondary schools (Mlambo and Pangeti 1996).

However, in the current political and economic climate the lowveld sugar estates are facing serious difficulties. The economic slump has resulted in erratic fuel supplies, hyperinflation, severe foreign currency shortages and industry fears that the government would reimpose price controls on sugar, and persist with a managed exchange-rate regime (Hippo Valley Estates Ltd.

---

[32] Interview: Executive Manager for Water Affairs, Triangle, 8 February 2001.
[33] 'Financiers reject government conditions on Tokwe Mukorsi dam project', *Zimbabwe Independent*, 14 June 2000; 'Construction of Tokwe Murkosi Dam suspended', *Daily News*, 12 October 2000; 'Deal to complete Tokwe-Mukorsi dam collapses', *Zimbabwe Independent*, 9 September 2001.

2000). Also, land on Triangle and Hippo Valley estates was designated for compulsory acquisition for resettlement in 1997. This was subsequently 'delisted' and the estates were initially not invaded by war veterans and other squatters to anything like the same extent as the surrounding ranches in 2000-2001, although violent labour disputes broke out on Hippo Valley. In this uncertain context Anglo-American put Hippo Valley up for sale in 2000, officially as part of a programme of disposal of 'non-core' interests to concentrate on its mining operations;[34] and Tongaat-Hulett froze their investments at Triangle.[35] In January 2004, following the passing of the Land Acquisition (Amendment) Bill, the entire Hippo Valley and Mkwasine estates were once again designated for resettlement (see Chapter 8).

The physical and imaginative transformation of the lowveld landscape from barren waste to lush land of promise was emblematic of a Rhodesian pioneering self-image. But the lone pioneer rhetoric sits awkwardly alongside the history of extensive investment by South African multinationals and a centralised, bureaucratic planning body. And there has been an ongoing tension between state attempts to promote self-sufficiency in food production and the private sector's interest in profit-maximising, export-orientated sugar production. Has this transformed landscape benefited multinational companies alone or have smallholders also been able to benefit from the development of irrigation in the lowveld? It is to plans to bring irrigation to the lowveld's communal areas that I now turn.

Irrigation in the communal areas

Irrigation is not a new technology in the lowveld and is not a European introduction. The African population had long irrigated with river water by planting crops on riverbanks and *vleis* until these practices were heavily circumscribed by colonial-era land use legislation (Bolding, Manzungu and van der Zaag 1996). Ndebele migrants from Mberengwa to Matibi II and Sengwe in the 1950s brought knowledge of vegetable gardening. They exchanged vegetables for meat or sold them at Chikombedzi hospital.[36] Today, numerous boreholes and wells are used for gardening; maize and vegetables are grown on irrigation plots and there are various small dams in communal areas to meet the needs of livestock and irrigate community gardens.

The notion that irrigated agriculture is a productive and desirable land use is one that is almost universally accepted by local communities, extension workers and politicians in the lowveld. Particularly after the severe droughts of the 1980s and 1990s the discourse on irrigation's role in transforming the landscape to productive ends is generally enthusiastically accepted. As Watch Mongayane put it to me: 'if donors brought irrigation

[34] 'Anglo-American Corp pulls out of Sugar in Zimbabwe', *Pan African News Agency*, 14 July 2000.
[35] *Financial Gazette*, 9 November 2000.
[36] Interview: Mrs Khumalo, Masukwe, by Jacob Mahenehene, 23 December 2000.

schemes we could do wonders with agriculture – [we could] feed more families – water is the best of all as far as human life is concerned. With enough water everyone could be rich – no doubt.'[37] Irrigation schemes strike a chord with people that conservation programmes do not, as they are more evidently 'useful', and irrigated agriculture has been talked up in the communal areas of the lowveld in marked contrast to the pejorative official attitudes to rainfed agriculture.

Despite the acceptance of this discourse and the presence of the large irrigated sugar industry in the lowveld and widespread irrigable soils, irrigation development in the communal areas has been fairly limited. The Agricultural Development Authority (ARDA) manages two large irrigation schemes at Tshovani in Sangwe communal area and Chisumbanje in Ndowoyo communal area. There are also a number of relatively small, government-owned irrigation schemes in the region of which six are in Beitbridge District, five in Chiredzi District and three in Chipinge District (Cunliffe 1993).[38] Many large-scale schemes that have been mooted have never materialised and many of the smaller-scale schemes have never performed as well as had been hoped.

In the dry landscape of the lowveld access to water – a scarce resource – has always been a highly contested issue. Water is obviously essential to livelihoods and control of water provides political power. In this respect the transformation of the landscape through irrigation projects is always accompanied by its layering with complex and unstable webs of power at all scales. This further complicates the messy scenario explored in Chapter 3, in which the lowveld was seen to be constituted by an array of overlapping and sometimes competitive ritual and territorial jurisdictions. From the macro-scale (e.g. water rights debates) to the micro-scale (e.g. local patronage politics in irrigation schemes) competing interests have sought to establish or shore up political power by controlling people's access to water. This section explores the rationale behind irrigation schemes in the lowveld's communal areas and examines some of these power dynamics.

Before MacDougall's much-trumpeted attempts at irrigating sugar, the first irrigation schemes in the south-east lowveld were actually in the communal areas of the Save Valley in the late 1920s and early 1930s. These schemes were initiated by Native Commissioners as social relief projects to provide work for the Africans who were being retrenched during the recession and were suffering food shortages during drought years (Roder 1965). They were soon to fall under the auspices of the recently appointed 'Agriculturalist for the Instruction of Natives' – an American missionary named Emory Alvord (Alvord n.d.). These included schemes at Nyanyadzi near the junction of the Odzi and Save rivers (in Muwushu communal area) and in

---

[37] Interview: Watch Mongayane, Chikombedzi, 8 July 1999.
[38] However, not all of these are currently operational. In January 2000 Cyclone Eline caused severe damage to some schemes, and shortages of fuel and spare parts have also hampered their smooth operation.

Mutema communal area. By the end of the Second World War there were six small irrigation schemes for Africans in the Save area (Cunliffe 1993).[39]

To Alvord, irrigation was part of a package of 'modern', 'improved' methods of agriculture that were essential for 'civilised' living and for moving from subsistence into the cash economy. Indeed he maintained that 'the difference in yield between intelligent, good farming methods and the ordinary witchcraft, spirit-worship farming methods was greatest under [the] adverse weather conditions' of the Save Valley lowveld (Alvord n.d.: 22). The adoption of mixed farming (Wolmer and Scoones 2000) and irrigation would lead to the intensification of smallholder farming on smaller areas of land. This was to be encouraged because:

> ... to give Natives now on Reserves more land at present would be most unwise. They would only ruin it and destroy its fertility in the same manner as they have already done on the land which they already have. For them the solution is not to be had in more land but in better farming the existing land. (Alvord 1948: 18-19)

In this respect intensified irrigated agriculture in the communal areas could be argued to serve several purposes for the white commercial farming sector. It was a means of staving off African land demands and freeing up more land for settler agriculture, whilst releasing labour for commercial farming, mining and industry (Palmer 1977; Drinkwater 1991). The development of irrigation projects was explicitly advocated as an effective means of confining a rapidly expanding African population into less than half the country's land area – and onto marginal land with low rainfall such as the lowveld. As the Director of Irrigation put it in 1952:

> ... to accommodate the growing Native population every available acre will have to be put to the maximum use. There are extensive dry areas particularly in the southern and south-western parts of the country where the only means to bring land into proper use will be by large-scale [irrigation] schemes.[40]

The notion that people should be confined on smaller areas of land supported by irrigation schemes is still a popular one. The Chief Agritex Officer for Chiredzi District told me that:

> The ideal situation would be one where people cultivate on smaller areas of productive irrigated land. With the dryland left as grazing land for livestock. The [planned] Tokwe dam will supply water to the District and irrigation can be encouraged in the communal areas. The only problem is that irrigation schemes attract more population.[41]

Irrigation schemes have also been justified in terms of conservation objectives. A background report prepared for the Department of National Parks and Wildlife Management Gonarezhou National Park management plan

---

[39] For details of the history of the Save Valley irrigation projects see Roder (1965), and Bolding *et al.* (1996).
[40] Report of the Director of Irrigation (1952: 11), cited by Roder (1965: 116).
[41] Interview: Chief Agritex Officer, Chiredzi District 6 July 1998.

is revealing in this regard:

> Perhaps one of the most pertinent possible benefits of irrigation development within the lowveld region is the possibilities it offers for active use as a tool to manipulate land use planning in the adjacent regions [to the national park], particularly of the communal lands. Human settlement in the communal lands of this region is often strung out along the rivers, partly because these serve as primary water supplies. This pattern of settlement is frequently detrimental to the development or maintenance of wildlife populations here, which must rely on the same water resources. Several projects are afoot ... whereby it is envisaged that pressure on riverine environments will be relieved through the willing resettlement of peoples in the vicinity of irrigation schemes, and thus freeing up the critical riverine areas for use by wildlife. (Cunliffe 1993: 51)

However, irrigation has not been advocated for the communal areas of the lowveld merely to assist the white commercial farming and conservation sectors indirectly. Even during the colonial period some described the communal areas as a land of massive promise, where black smallholder irrigated agriculture (as opposed to commercial estates) had the potential to contribute massively to national food production. Although the communal areas of the lowveld do fall into Natural Region 5 and are very arid, it would not be fair to say that they are the marginal, 'low-potential' agricultural zones that some commentators have made them out to be. As the District Commissioner for Nuanetsi (Mwenezi) District in the 1960s put it:

> There are those who maintain that Rhodesia's tribal lands are only those areas the Europeans did not want – 'baboon country' is how some describe them – all those of this opinion would be well advised to pay a visit to the vast, black, rich acres that make up most of Matibi No. 2.[42]

> The wonderful fertility of these soils ... [is] apparent – little or no fertiliser is necessary to produce really bumper crops. Only water is required but unfortunately the region has a very low and uncertain rainfall ... It is a land just made for irrigation schemes and one day many thousands of acres may well be artificially watered. (Wright 1972: 249, 20).[43]

The District Commissioner lobbied the chairman of the Sabi-Limpopo Authority requesting that the water derived from further planned dams should not be reserved solely for European land, and that 'tribal areas' should not be left out of large irrigation projects. He received an assurance that these lands would receive a fair share of the water (1972: 249). His was an ambitious vision:

> ... of a vast irrigation enterprise embracing up to twenty thousand acres of this fertile

---

[42] He describes being approached by a visiting American real estate developer keen to buy a large block of this 'Alabama cotton soil'.

[43] Wright estimated that 150,000 acres of land were available for irrigation purposes in 'tribal land'.

tribal area's plains [Matibi II communal area], using water drawn from a barrage to be flung across the Lundi river near Chipinda Pools, with a pipeline for cattle-watering snaking out to all points of that great half a million acre slab of fertile country. (1972: 248)

This high-flown concept was in keeping with the large-scale technocratic schemes being proposed at the time by the SLA. These grand modernist plans sought to replicate the aesthetically and productively transformed landscape of the sugar estates in the communal areas and were buttressed by similar top-down, managerial discourses. For example the Chisumbanje irrigation scheme was established by the SLA in 1966 with a view to catalysing 'a major break-through of Africans into irrigation farming' (Fair 1964: 200). A 1,500-acre pilot scheme was established with a view to developing 200,000 acres. But by 1967 only 7 families had taken up the offer. The SLA management did all ploughing, sowing and selling of the cotton crops – leaving tenants only to tend and harvest them. Unsurprisingly this led to a state of affairs where tenants saw themselves as little more than employees and there was a general suspicion amongst Africans that – yet again – a European company was simply alienating their land.[44]

On the whole these grand ambitions yielded few results. Other plans not to make it off the ground included schemes to dam the lower Nuanetsi (Mwenezi) River at the Samelema Gorge (now in Gonarezhou National Park), and the Chikombedzi River.[45] The former would have provided about 2,000 hectares of irrigated land for Africans on either side of the Mwenezi (Sabi-Limpopo Authority 1970: 30), but it was shelved, in part because it ran up against the counterposed pristine wilderness vision of those advocating the establishment of a national park (see Chapter 7).

The penchant for massive, engineering-driven, technocratic irrigation schemes in the lowveld communal areas endured after Independence.[46] The Zimbabwean schemes directly echoed, in their rhetoric, the Rhodesian attempts to tame and order the wilderness by 'rationalising' and 'consolidating' land use and transform the whole landscape (not just the commercial estates) into a productive region. This was exemplified by a high-profile land-use planning initiative that impinged on part of the lowveld in the early 1980s known as the Mwenezi Radical Land Reform Programme (MRLRP). This was a large-scale planned programme with funding from the EC and GTZ aimed at removing the 'impediments to development' such as scattered settlement patterns, erratic rainfall, soil erosion, and shortage of grazing land (Saunders 1986). It was a precursor to the national villagisation programme and involved the replanning of residential areas, arable lands and grazing lands, the building of dams, and the establishment of co-operatives and schools (see Cousins 1990; 1996). The

---

[44] *Financial Mail*, 21 June 1968.
[45] MRC AGR/17/4/73 DC Chiredzi (Parsons) memo - Control of Nuanetsi River 5 April 1973.
[46] Similarly Drinkwater (1991) and Robins (1994) note the ideological continuity between colonial discourses on centralisation and post-colonial discourses on villagisation.

development of irrigation schemes was a particular priority. As one District Administrator, betraying the top-down nature of the programme, put it: 'the District Planning Committee has discerned the need to revise and adjust the farming system in the area to include irrigation so as to increase the productivity of the land.'[47] The Manyuchi dam was built on the Mwenezi River and a small palm oil pilot project established. However, none of this water reached the surrounding communal areas and to this day the percentage reserved for use by Mwenezi Rural District Council is unused. The epithet 'radical' was increasingly a misnomer for the underachieving MRLRP, and by 1990 it had lost its high profile (Cousins 1996).

The MRLRP did, however, contribute to a brief explosion of interest in the communal areas of the south-east lowveld which was to fizzle out just as rapidly. Three ARDA-identified and GTZ-funded mega projects were proposed for the region: a livestock development project and massive irrigation developments at Grootvlei and along the Mwenezi River (Salzgitter Consult GMBH 1986). The latter scheme was to be based on water abstraction from an aquifer in Sengwe communal area. The aquifer was judged to have 20 million m^3 of water suitable for abstraction which could irrigate at least 1,000 hectares (Salzgitter Consult GMBH and PTA Consulting Services 1991). The feasibility study recommended the construction of infrastructure to irrigate 800 hectares and the production of a combination of food crops (maize, groundnuts and beans) and high-value cash crops (mangoes, citrus and pineapples). There would be a processing plant for agricultural and horticultural produce and export marketing by rail link to Mozambique and South Africa. The report recommended the use of stover, by-products and fodder crops grown in rotation on separate irrigation blocks for cattle fattening and the provision of reticulated water for livestock use; and the improvement of existing infrastructure, roads and water, and the provision of electric power. It described the local population as 'somewhat conservative and reluctant to change their behaviour patterns', but asserted that they would have to be resettled to 'enable them to reside closer to irrigated plots' and advocated the resettlement of further selected farmers from other parts of Chiredzi District (Salzgitter Consult GMBH and PTA Consulting Services 1993). However, like its equally ambitious colonial forerunners, the project never materialised. It is alleged that Masvingo province lacked the political clout of Mashonaland Central and that the money earmarked for the project was diverted to a dam in Guruve.[48]

In the last few years the discourse surrounding the potential impacts of the stalled Tokwe-Mukorsi dam on the communal areas of the lowveld bears a close resemblance to the policy narratives analysed above. One of the five proposed development schemes drawing on the water provided is in Matibi II communal area. According to one evaluation report this:

---

[47] MRC: L.H. Shumba. Acting DA Mwenezi (3 December 1986): Radical land reform in Mwenezi District.
[48] Interview: Director, SEDAP, Harare, 21 October 1998.

... will be the largest small scale irrigation scheme developed in Zimbabwe and its development will have to proceed in an orderly and controlled manner, with a well thought out and highly efficient management system. Families living in the area, whose main activities are currently focused around low level subsistence agriculture, will be required to undergo major changes in attitude towards intensive agriculture, managerial and technical ability, as well as social organisation. Extensive information, education and advisory campaigns will be necessary (Heath 1998: 59).

The development would also cause some families to be displaced and 'internal resettlement' is planned, leading to the establishment of six fairly large village settlements, based on the irrigation plots.

These proposals, and the colonial schemes preceding them, make many assumptions about the 'conservative' and 'cautious' farmers they set out to help. From Alvord to the consultancy reports of the last few years the characteristics of the ideal-type, modern, irrigating farmers have been fairly rigidly defined.[49] As Manzungu and van der Zaag (1996) and Rukuni (1988) describe, becoming a 'plotholder' means exactly following certain recommendations – including:
- giving up dryland farming and off-farm work to depend solely on irrigation;
- cultivating 'standard' sized plots;
- producing specified food crops for the market, and later cash crops;
- practising prescribed crop rotations, and planting on specific dates;
- applying particular quantities of particular types of fertiliser;
- paying water rates.

Irrigation schemes have thus sought to impose a planned, managerial development vision on the landscape and its inhabitants. This is a technocratic vision of bunds, check dams and boreholes with a bias towards 'high value' crops as more efficient users of irrigation investment than 'low-level' food crops (Manzungu and van der Zaag 1996). However, as was described in Chapter 4, ideal-type models of land use and farming practice rarely equate with the dynamic reality of smallholder farming livelihoods. Wetland agriculture in the south-east lowveld is an opportunistic and adaptive business, in much the same way that dryland agriculture is.

The recent history of gardening is an example of such an adaptive strategy. Given the overall shortage of formal irrigation schemes in the lowveld and the difficulties involved in getting access to plots (see below), there has been a marked trend in the last 20 years for people to make their own arrangements for micro-irrigation of garden plots. In one area near Chikombedzi township in Matibi II communal area, for example, there were five households with gardens in 1970, 15 in 1980 and 65 by 1998. Money – mainly accruing from work in South Africa – has been invested

---

[49] The creation of a yeoman class of 'Master Farmers' during the colonial period was seen to be an important way of encouraging the spread of 'civilising' ideals, but also of diffusing dissent and unrest in the African farming areas (Ranger 1985).

in personal wells and even boreholes (sunk by South African contractors) and the water used to irrigate vegetable plots. There is a large local trade in vegetables although the poor transport links and distance to major market towns militates against larger commercial enterprises. In recent years there has been a shift in the gender dynamics of vegetable gardening. It tended to be an activity dominated by women but, as draught power shortages (in the wake of the 1992 drought) have constrained extensive outfield cultivation, and vegetables have increasingly commanded premium prices in local markets, there has been more uptake of gardening by men (Wolmer, Sithole and Mukamuri 2002). There has also been a proliferation of informal sub-leasing arrangements on irrigation scheme plots. Those fortunate enough to have been allocated plots often make arrangements with others to cultivate a portion or the whole of the plot in return for payment or part of the harvest.

Numerous interviewees in Matibi II and Sengwe communal areas listed further development of irrigated agriculture as one of the main development priorities in the region and expressed strong desires for access to irrigated plots. In all cases this was thought of as an activity to complement, rather than replace, dryland agriculture or labour migration. Farmers invariably prefer to pursue a range of dynamic strategies rather than putting all their eggs in one basket. This is especially the case with irrigation plots, given the very dependent status of tenant farmers on irrigation schemes and the unreliability of water supply and tenure in the current economic and political environment (see Rukuni 1988; Manzungu and van der Zaag 1996).

The micro-politics of irrigated landscapes

A measure of the complexity of the micro-politics of irrigation schemes is given by a detailed look at Malikango and Muraba irrigation schemes near Chikombedzi township in Matibi II communal area. These have been the sites in which power struggles between 'traditional' and 'modern' authorities, between the representatives of two branches of government, and between political parties have been played out. The Malikango scheme was started in the 1950s when a small dam was built across the Mwenezi and a water extraction system set into its sandy bed (Wright 1972). During the war the scheme was put out of action and it remained unused until it was renovated in 1994 with funding from a German NGO and further irrigation plots were established nearby at Muraba. Approximately 400 plot-holders at Malikango and 70 at Muraba were soon growing maize and vegetables throughout the year.

With the departure of the German doctor at Chikombedzi mission hospital who had initiated the scheme and set up the NGO, the local councillor was able to establish *de facto* control of the projects. The schemes provided an opportunity for him to exert political patronage and for personal enrichment. Because of their 'modern' and technical nature irrigation schemes constitute a space where 'non-traditional' authorities and individuals, such as the councillor, can exert power in plot allocation at the expense of 'traditional' authorities. These are spaces that fall outside the jurisdiction of chiefs and kraalheads and, to some extent, outside the authority of ancestral spirits. In part this can be attributed to the fact that, by definition, irrigation schemes are less dependent on rainfall, and therefore rainmaking supplications to the *mukwembu* become less of a priority. But also the modern nature of irrigation schemes puts them in a physical and conceptual sphere distinct from that associated with ancestral authority. In a sense dams and boreholes 'drained meaning from the land' (Bunn 1999: 31). The physical and imaginative transformations of these niches in the landscape thus both enable and represent emergent claims to authority (cf. Vijfhuizen 1997).

The councillor was able to use his assumed patronage of the irrigation schemes to carve out a powerful fiefdom.[50] There is a commonly held perception that he has directed the allocation of plots towards his ex-ZAPU political colleagues and war veterans, as well as his friends in Chikombedzi township. Similarly, many Shona people feel that Shangaan-speakers were favoured in the plot allocations. Indeed this is hardly surprising given that the councillor has always campaigned on an explicitly tribalist pro-Shangaan ticket and states that Shangaan people should dominate Shona people in the region. In this respect he has deliberately sought to subvert the dichotomy between 'traditional' and 'modern' farming practice that continues to be layered over perceptions of ethnic identity in the lowveld (with Shona and Ndebele farmers depicted as 'progressive' and modern farmers in opposition to 'backward' Shangaans). He has represented the irrigation schemes as his personal bequest to the Shangaan people and part of a process of their empowerment *vis-à-vis* other ethnic groups and whites that will continue with the development of further schemes on their ancestral land currently inside the commercial ranches.

However the councillor's self-assumed quasi-chiefly role has been increasingly resented and questioned, particularly in the light of a litany of allegations – of mismanagement, embezzlement, stock theft, and exproprition of the schemes' tractor, solar panels and other equipment – directed at him and his family.[51] Malikango and Muraba irrigation schemes have become the spaces within which further political struggles have been played out.

The first to enter the fray was the local MP. Although they both represent the governing ZANU(PF), there is a long history of personal antipathy between the councillor and MP. They belonged to rival factions of the,

---

[50] The councillor also draws symbolic authority from the fact that he was held at Gonakudzingwa Restriction Camp in the 1960s with Joshua Nkomo and now holds a prestigious place on the ZANU(PF) Central Committee.

[51] A further cause of resentment was that Agritex extension advice and assistance came to be entirely confined to those fortunate enough to own irrigation plots.

formerly fiercely divided, Masvingo Province ZANU(PF) party. The councillor has also unsuccessfully contested the ZANU(PF) candidacy on numerous occasions. For his part the MP was keen to capitalise on the resentment surrounding his rival's appropriation of the irrigation schemes and was equally eager to secure for himself control of this conduit to donor funding and hence political patronage. Irrigation scheme meetings thereafter became bitter stand-offs between the two, with the irrigated landscape being variously invoked as emblematic of empowerment and development or of corruption and mismanagement. In the eyes of the rest of the community: 'Muraba and Malikango are just a political ground where local leaders exercise their power'[52] (cf. Moore 1998; Andersson 1999).

Many became increasingly fed up with this political football and a new committee was set up in an attempt to wrest power away from both councillor and MP. However, at this stage dramatic changes in national politics intervened. The emergence of a credible opposition to ZANU(PF) in the form of the Movement for Democratic Change (MDC) led to a rapid strategic reconciliation between the MP and councillor in the face of a common enemy. They immediately vilified the new irrigation scheme committee as an MDC front, and Malikango and Muraba became the conceptual battleground for a new round of political warfare. This was short-lived, however, as due to flood damage during Cyclone Eline and a general lack of diesel and spare parts, both schemes entirely ceased to operate in 2000 and the political struggles moved into new physical and conceptual landscapes. At the micro-level, just as in the boardrooms of the sugar industry giants, representations of the irrigated landscape are inextricably bound up with struggles for economic and political power.

Conclusions

Eradicating wilderness to make way for a carefully planned, lush irrigated landscape has been a powerful narrative in Zimbabwe's south-east lowveld in both the commercial and communal farming areas before and after Independence. The notion that irrigation is an appropriate land use in the lowveld is one that is broadly agreed upon. The irrigated estates have been lauded for their role in the Rhodesian and Zimbabwean economies alike. Local communities have not explicitly contested the establishment of irrigation schemes (except where land alienations occurred, and during the war) in the way that they have often protested against wildlife-based conservation and development schemes. As the director of an NGO working in the lowveld put it: 'irrigated farming is closer to the institutional knowledge and skills of people than tourism'.[53] Irrigation in communal areas has also been actively encouraged by the authorities in a way that rain-fed agriculture never has been.

[52] Interview: Chikombedzi, by Jacob Mahenehene, 7 September 2000.
[53] Interview: Director, SAFIRE, Harare, 5 June 1998.

However, the drive, physically and conceptually, to conquer wilderness has tended to reveal itself, in practice, in a penchant for mega-scale, hugely ambitious, technocratic developments. Some of these, with the support of large state subsidies and massive multinational investment, have been realised in the commercial sector. But various equally ambitious schemes planned for the communal areas have yet to see the light of day due to lack of finance and political will. Small-scale irrigation schemes that have been developed in the communal areas of the lowveld have tended to have overly-rigid prescriptions and often ignore the priorities of those who do not want to be full-time farmers but pursue irrigated agriculture as only one among many diverse livelihood strategies. Many of these schemes currently have operational problems due to shortages of diesel and delays in repairing pipes and pumps. This, together with local political wrangling and their relative remoteness from markets, often imposes severe constraints on their effectiveness. The appropriation and representation of these irrigated landscapes, however, is a means by which competing claims to political authority have been expressed by actors as diverse as Rhodesian sugar magnates and ex-detainee ZANU(PF) politicians.

6

Cattle country
Livestock management in the ranches and reserves

If the lush green grids of sugar cane have come to represent the vision of the lowveld as the land of irrigated agribusiness, a further signifier of the lowveld could be an Afrikander or Brahman steer. This would stand for a long-standing notion of the lowveld as 'cattle country', 'sweet veld' or 'pastoral land'. Indeed 'veld' itself literally translates from Afrikaans as pasture. The commercial farms and communal areas of the lowveld have long been described as ideal cattle ranching land. This discourse predates that on irrigation as the most suitable and productive land use in the lowveld and has been a counterpoint to the opinion that the lowveld is fundamentally unsuited to dryland agriculture.

A newspaper article in 1950 asserts, typically, that 'it is widely recognised that the lowveld is *the* cattle country of Africa'.[1] This lay 'undeveloped and unwanted' until the arrival of Europeans who carved out ranches from the bush to establish a beef industry which has historically dominated land use in the semi-arid rangelands of the south-east lowveld. Alongside this pioneer narrative is a positioning of (and by) the lowveld's African inhabitants – and Shangaan speakers in particular – as 'cattle people'. The history of cattle management on the ranches and 'reserves' of the lowveld also reveals the role played by colonial science in defining settler and African relationships to their environments and in shaping both the physical and conceptual landscape. Ecology and veterinary science have been particularly influential in parcelling veld or 'rangeland' into fenced and ordered boxes separated from disordered and disease-ridden wilderness. This science has also underpinned various policies aimed at transforming livestock management practice: defining 'off-take' rates, restricting livestock movement and 'improving' pasture. However, the history of livestock husbandry in the communal areas of the lowveld is a history of continual resistance to and contestation of these prescriptions and proscriptions for everyday prac-

[1] *Fort Victoria News*, 6 January 1950.

tice and landscape form. Livestock loaning arrangements, 'poach grazing' (where communal herds are driven through gaps cut in the ranch fences to graze on a daily basis), fence-cutting and farm invasions subvert the ranching vision of the lowveld as a patchwork of hard-edged, fenced zones, and of demarcated grazing lands and individual owner-managers of stock where livestock management is purely a technical (and never a social or political) issue.

The ranches

Before the expansion of the sugar estates and the initiation of the wildlife industry in the 1960s, cattle production was the main form of land use in the commercial farming sector in the lowveld. Soon after its arrival in Rhodesia the British South Africa Company was providing considerable assistance to aspiring cattle ranchers, primarily by making cheap and abundant land available, as well as by encouraging a plentiful supply of cattle from the peasant sector by the imposition of taxes (Cunliffe 1993). In the first decade of the twentieth century, prior to the establishment of any ranches, the BSAC was already grazing cattle in the lowveld between the Mtirikwe and Tokwe Rivers (Bannerman 1980). Elderly informants around Chikombedzi in Matibi II report that white men on horses used to employ local people to look after their cattle. Company cattle were run alongside – and interbred with – African cattle. Winter grazing was carried out in what are now Matibi II and Sengwe communal areas. District Commissioner Wright reported in the 1970s that 'the old, half-buried water troughs can be seen in these areas to this day' (Wright 1972: 231). The European and African cattle grazing areas, to begin with, were not clearly demarcated into separate, bounded zones. Instead the ranches remained unpaddocked and unfenced with African settlements and cattle populations still scattered over the ranches 'enjoy[ing] almost complete freedom from official supervision.'[2] Increasingly, however, commercial ranches came to claim exclusive grazing rights in these areas. African cattle, and whole villages, were removed, and the ranches gradually ringed by wire fences.

The first land in the south-east lowveld to be formally alienated as commercial ranching land was Chiredzi Ranch. A man called Chambers evicted eight villages and started ranching cattle just south of what is now Manjirenji dam at a time when 'lions were so plentiful he had to build 15 foot mopani kraals, surrounded by 10 foot deep thorn bush' (c. 1908).[3] Another of the first lowveld ranches was Nyazugwi Ranch which belonged to Peter Forrestall, the Chibi Native Commissioner and erstwhile defender of African lands. In 1914 the BSAC alienated a massive piece of land as Nuanetsi Ranch. This was over 3,250,000 acres, taking up a vast amount of

---

[2] NAZ S 235/517 ANC Nuanetsi Annual Report 1939.
[3] Basil Beverley in *The Hartebeast* (1998).

the south-east lowveld. Soon afterwards, in the 1920s, Devuli Ranch was established in the Save Valley by Lucas Bridges (Somerville 1976). This was soon followed by Angus Ranch (Dott), Triangle Ranch (McDougall and Spraggen), Tokwe River Ranch (Robinson), Bangala Ranch (Francis brothers) and Ruware Ranch (de la Rue).[4]

The huge Nuanetsi Ranch was bought by the Imperial Cold Storage and Supply Company (ISC) of South Africa. In 1927 the national government, after failing to interest British companies, entered into an export agreement with ISC. The company agreed to develop meat works and an export trade, in exchange for massive government concessions and subsidies. These included a ten-year monopoly on exports, favourable tax, customs duty and haulage concessions, and a guarantee that if profits fell below 10 per cent of the capital invested the government would make up the difference to a maximum of £15,000 (Phimister 1978; Child 1988).

The worldwide depression of the late 1920s caused a crash in cattle prices and hit the newly emerging lowveld ranches hard, just as they were pouring capital into purebred bulls, breeding cows, fencing, dams and other capital-intensive developments. A second set-back was the first outbreak in the country of foot and mouth disease (FMD) which broke out in the lowveld in 1931/32.[5] This caused quarantine measures to be imposed and a ban on all live exports with a consequent loss of markets (Nuanetsi Ranch used to drive cattle to Messina in South Africa for slaughter). Cattle became virtually valueless and many ranchers left the industry. To the government's concern it was particularly the large producers who were disappearing (Phimister 1978). Nuanetsi Ranch sold all but a handful of its 136,000 cattle. The government again stepped into the breach to assume ownership and management of the ISC's facilities, bringing into existence the Cold Storage Commission (CSC) in 1938 (Child 1988; Cunliffe 1993) and establishing Liebig's canning and export factory in West Nicholson by Act of Parliament (Somerville 1976).

In 1951, after much lobbying by the commercial ranchers' cattle committee, an abattoir was opened in Fort Victoria and fortunes picked up for commercial ranchers in the lowveld throughout the 1950s. This was described as a 'decade of progress and optimism, between the grey years of depression and war, and the political storms of the Sixties' (Somerville 1976: 170). However, the renewed fortunes of the beef industry in the lowveld meant further alienation of land for ranching and yet more evictions of African populations who were required to move to the reserves or become employed by ranch owners (Kelly 1973: 40). During this period there were also attempts to destock African cattle in the reserves under the coercive, ostensibly conservation-orientated, measures of the Native Land Husbandry Act (see below). Child (1988) argues that the principal logic for this policy was to extract cattle from the peasant sector and transfer them

---

[4] Basil Beverley in *The Hartebeast* (1998).
[5] NAZ S 235/509 NC Chibi Annual Report 1931.

to the commercial sector. Compulsorily purchased stock were placed on commercial farms under 'grazier agreements' to 'assist ... the under-capitalised [white/commercial] farmer to get on his feet'. The CSC marketing structure was also heavily biased towards the commercial sector (see below). These experiences engendered a long history of resentment towards the white-owned cattle ranches in the lowveld and Africans have continually contested their removal from ancestral lands and replacement by an ostensibly unproductive land use. Acts of overt resistance came to a head in the late 1970s and early 1980s. The monthly meetings of the Victoria Stockholders Association of the period report 'alarmingly high' levels of stock theft, poaching, snaring, fence-cutting and 'illegal grazing'. Between April 1979 and January 1980, for example, 3-4,000 head of cattle were abducted from two properties south of Bubi River and Mateke Hills.[6] This, of course, was at the height of the liberation war in an area where many guerrillas hid out. Stock thefts and other attacks on ranch property were a symbolic, as well as physical, contestation of the patterns of landholding and land use in the lowveld, and a deliberate strategy aimed at destabilising the white community's economic power base. Many lowveld cattle ranches were entirely abandoned by their owners during the war. Immediately after the war, stock thefts continued to be very high. Between 1981 and 1984, 547 cattle on Devuli Ranch were snared, leading one rancher to claim that 'the whole viability of the ranching area was threatened'.[7] In the run-up to, and after, the parliamentary election of June 2000 discourse and practice repeated themselves as the widespread farm invasions that spread across the lowveld were accompanied by stock thefts, snaring, poaching, firewood and thatching grass collection and deliberate starting of veld fires (see Chapter 8).

Even before the farm invasions, the lowveld's beef producers were facing a variety of difficulties. The droughts of the 1980s and early 1990s hit stocks hard and there were high interest rates for restocking finance, as CSC finance schemes had been terminated (see Jansen, Bond and Child 1992). New EU regulations such as cattle traceability schemes had increased production costs,[8] and low stocking rates had attracted political attention to the ranches as potential resettlement sites.[9] Zimbabwe's incipient economic crisis was leading to soaring costs of production without matching increases in beef prices. Many cattle ranchers had gone out of business or were shifting production into game ranching (Child 1988).

[6] Devuli Ranch (now in the Save Valley Conservancy) had 28,000 head of cattle at the start of the war and only 6,000 left in 1980. Some had been sold but the majority had been stolen. The ranch went as far as to hire mercenaries to protect its cattle (Wels 2000).
[7] Masvingo Records Centre (MRC) SBV/13/1: Hunting, poaching and snaring: Summary of proceedings of a seminar in Masvingo, organised by the Cattle Producers Association, 23 February 1984.
[8] These have been introduced in the wake of the European BSE epidemic and were widely perceived by Zimbabwean ranchers as non-tariff barriers.
[9] Interview: CFU Regional Executive, Masvingo Province, 7 August 1999.

Supporting narratives

As we have seen in Chapters 2 and 5, the ubiquitous Rhodesian 'pioneer narratives' were critical to representations of settlers' relations to the lowveld landscape. Accounts of the first white ranchers to strike off from Fort Victoria to establish ranches in the Save Valley are replete with tales of battles with lions, malaria, ticks and other evils. Typically, Somerville (1976: 153) describes how since the 1920s Devuli Ranch 'emerg[ed] from wildest bushveld into tamer pastoral county', and de la Rue reminisces that:

> Though the lion and elephant and other animals created their own hazards to ranching, nevertheless one lived in amongst them all and shared it with them. From a personal angle the lowveld acted as an enormous challenge.[10]

One elderly ex-rancher described how his grandparents were amongst the first wagon trekkers to come up from the Eastern Cape. He consciously sought to emulate their pioneering by setting out himself 'on a cattle ticket' down to the lowveld – the new frontier.[11] However, this narrative tends to play down the fact that many of these 'lone pioneers' were actually businessmen with substantial multinational investments. The Bridges at Devuli Ranch, for example, had extensive ranches in Argentina and Namibia (Somerville 1976: 153), the Whittalls at Humani Ranch had business interests in Turkey (Wels 2000), and the BSAC, and subsequently the ISC, at Nuanetsi Ranch and Liebigs in West Nicholson were obviously massive company estates, backed by international capital and generous state subsidies.[12] Most of the smaller producers were also heavily dependent on state assistance in the form of cheap land, labour and stock and guaranteed markets at fixed prices. There is thus a similar disjuncture between the rhetoric of plucky individualists and the reality of conglomerate and state interests to that found in the lowveld's irrigated agriculture sector.

The role of an emerging southern African pasture science in defining the lowveld as suitable for a particular type of livestock management is also an important one. By rendering the landscape as 'sweet veld' due to the high nutritional value of the 'natural' winter grazing, it was defined as potentially productive land for ranching provided that it was managed appropriately (see Acocks 1953; Beinart 1997). Pasture science was rooted in the notion of 'carrying capacity', and generated discourses on 'veld management' that emphasised the imminence of environmental disasters due to overgrazing (Scoones 1996).[13] Veterinary science was also employed to arrange the landscape into disease-free fenced zones buffered from the unhealthy,

---

[10] Ian de la Rue, 'Early Days – Ruware Ranch 1936', quoted by Eastwood (1996).
[11] Interview: Malilangwe 10 September 1999.
[12] See Phimister (1978) on the role of local and multinational capital and state subsidies in Southern Rhodesia's beef industry.
[13] See, for example I.B. Pole-Evans (1943) Report of the commission to enquire into the conditions prevailing, etc., in the pasturage of the colony. Southern Rhodesia. Public Records Office (PRO), DO 35/1169.

disease-ridden wilderness areas (see below and Hoppe 1995; Beinart 1997).

The 'reserves'

Before the rinderpest panzootic of 1896-97 the lowveld lay within the tsetse fly belt which prevented extensive livestock ownership. According to oral histories collected by Bannerman (1980), the Hlengwe (Shangaan) record that they entered Zimbabwe without cattle. However, John Ford (1971) notes the existence, pre-rinderpest, of a tsetse-free belt between the Save and Nuanetsi Rivers that extended into Zimbabwe along the Chefu River – and Bannerman cites archaeological evidence that people kept cattle at Malipati, on the lower Nuanetsi (Mwenezi) in the ninth century and people in North West Transvaal, just south of the Limpopo, kept cattle in the eleventh century – both areas well within the fly belt. They also record methods by which the Gaza Nguni, under Mzila and Gungunyane, coped with the tsetse fly. People and cattle were concentrated close together and game eradicated from the area; other areas were set aside for game and there were strict controls on movement of cattle and game between the areas (Swynnerton 1921; Ford 1971; Bannerman 1980). Bannerman concludes that, although the Hlengwe may not have had cattle when they entered Zimbabwe, they were familiar with them – having their own words for cattle and cattle management matters – and had kept cattle at some stage in the past. The rinderpest epidemic which swept down from East Africa wiped out much of the wildlife in the lowveld and with it most of the tsetse fly which survived only in pockets on the Mozambican coastal plain. This enabled farmers to hold stock in the region – initially acquired by raiding – and cattle became very important assets over the course of the twentieth century. The history of livestock management in the lowveld is thus a history of environmental management and its deliberate and unintended transformation. Cattle ownership was permitted by a human-induced ecosystem and the lived-in landscape kept the tsetse fly at bay. Livelihood strategies moulded and were moulded by the physical landscape (cf. Swynnerton 1921; Ford 1971; Kjekshus 1977).[14]

Herding, though, was not originally very important to pre-colonial Shangaan livelihoods, which were centred more around dryland agriculture and labour migration supplemented by hunting and gathering. In contrast with the Karanga to the north, cash earned from wage labour and trade, rather than cattle, were used for *lobola* (brideprice).[15] The emergence of an association of Shangaan identity with pastoralism and the description of them as a 'cattle people' and the lowveld as 'cattle country' is thus only a

---

[14] These studies in their different ways all embed the 'natural' history of trypanosomiasis squarely in the realm of human history (Giblin 1990).
[15] NAZ N 3/14/4 NC Chibi to Superintendent of Natives 19 October 1914. Marvin Harris (1959: 58) notes that 'even before the final pacification of the Thonga area in 1895 the English pound had already become the most prevalent form of brideprice'.

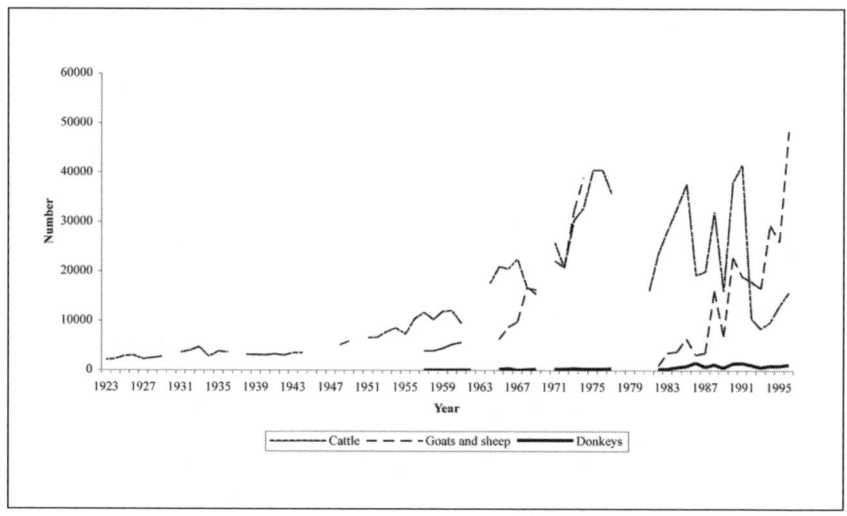

Figure 6.1 Matibi II communal area livestock populations

recent phenomenon and not one with deep historical roots in Zimbabwe.[16]

With the arrival of European settlers in the lowveld the 'communal herd' assumed a commercial importance to the formal sector that it has rarely had since. The demand for stock by Europeans contributed to a period of peasant prosperity, with the smallholder sector supplying more of the beef to the formal sector than the commercial ranchers (Child 1988). The adoption of the plough by Africans in the lowveld caused a substantial realignment in livestock management priorities. Now stock came to be primarily valued as an input to agricultural production through the provision of draught power. There was a massive increase in the communal herd and stock was brought from South Africa for breeding purposes (Bannerman 1980; Ranger 1985).

Figure 6.1 illustrates the changes in the African-owned livestock populations of the lowveld in the twentieth century by displaying the yearly livestock census data for Matibi II – one of the lowveld communal areas – from 1923 to 1997.[17]

Regular and severe droughts account for the pronounced peaks and troughs in the cattle population. For example, the Native Commissioner for Chibi noted in 1913 that: 'During the early part of the year a large number of stock was sold to buy food. I estimate that during the famine of 1912-13 the natives sold, bartered and killed 13000 head of cattle.'[18] Disease has

---

[16] In contrast with Ndebele pastoralists in south-western Zimbabwe.

[17] Detailed records of livestock numbers for communal areas have been kept since the 1920s. Some boundary changes have taken place during this period. These data were collected from the Department of Veterinary Services in the course of work conducted with Bev Sithole, Billy Mukamuri and others between 1997 and 1999 (see Wolmer, Sithole and Mukamuri 2002).

[18] NAZ N 9/1/16 NC Annual Report Chibi 1913.

also caused reductions in cattle populations, in some cases aggravated by colonial control policies. In 1934, for example, the ANC for Nuanetsi reports that FMD broke out on Nuanetsi Ranch and that 'drastic and rather severe' restrictions and quarantine methods were adopted by the Veterinary Department (especially in Matibi II):

> ... in many cases natives had to drive their cattle 100 and 200 miles to the quarantine areas where the cattle, 5000 head, were closely herded in small areas; as a result of these methods the mortality from poverty was considerably greater than in past years. ... These restrictions, combined with increased sales to dealers at the outbreak of Foot and Mouth, and the slaughter of calves during the inoculation period under Vet Dept regulations led to a reduction of cattle stock of 4161 over the previous year's total.[19]

Tsetse fly reappeared in parts of the lowveld in the 1950s (see below) and the rise in cattle populations in the late 1950s coincides with efforts by the Department of Veterinary Services to eradicate tsetse again. However, the sustained increase in cattle populations in Matibi II is more likely related to the ongoing expropriation of land by the colonial government for European commercial farms which forced people and stock into the communal area. In-migration from other parts of Zimbabwe and the establishment of Gonarezhou National Park contributed to this rise in cattle and smallstock populations between 1950 and the mid-1970s.

The massive decline in both goat and cattle populations in the mid to late 1970s was directly due to the liberation war. Notwithstanding the fact that livestock population data for this period are often not very reliable, or simply were never collected, there was clearly a marked reduction in numbers. Most of the population was forced to move into 'protected villages'. Cattle were left to wander free and many were lost. They were killed for food by families living out in the bush and by the guerrillas who also forced families to kill cattle for them. People living in the protected villages were unable to produce adequate grain for subsistence, nor could they hunt or gather, because of restrictions on their movement and strict curfews. They were therefore forced to slaughter cattle for subsistence or for sale to purchase mealie meal. The Rhodesian army also shot cattle to stop them getting to the guerrillas. Dip tanks were regularly targets for guerrilla attack[20] and livestock died from diseases due to the lack of dipping. In Sengwe communal area, for example, 80 per cent of the cattle herd was lost during the war (35,000 to 7,000) (Stubbs 1984).

[19] NAZ S 235/512 NC Annual Report Chibi 1934.
[20] The prevalence of this is shown by a letter from the Provincial Commissioner for Victoria Province to the District Commissioners dated 15 August 1979. He says: 'so far as I am concerned I will not back any request for funds to restart dipping unless you can assure me that there is no reasonable chance that the installations so repaired can be maintained in working order for a period of at least six months. We have had too many experiences of resuscitated dipping merely causing a new target resulting in the destruction of ADF [African Development Fund] fixed assets.' Mwenezi District Commissioner's files.

After the war, dipping of cattle was resumed and there was another influx of new arrivals to the region from other parts of Zimbabwe. Many of these people brought cattle with them, contributing to the recovery in cattle numbers. But drought was again to have a devastating impact on livestock populations in 1991-92. This, the most severe drought in living memory, had as massive an impact as the war over ten years earlier. As Figure 6.1 shows, the drought had a differential impact on different types of livestock, with cattle being worst hit and smallstock populations recovering more quickly. This inverted the previous pattern of most livestock consisting of cattle and resulted in an ongoing severe shortage of draught power for many farmers. It has also caused changing patterns of livestock ownership, with men now more likely to own goats than previously and investment in goats by both men and women being used as a key livelihood strategy in a context of reduced cattle holdings (Wolmer, Sithole and Mukamuri 2002).

A survey carried out in the Chikombedzi area of Matibi II in 1998 found startlingly low livestock holdings. The average number of cattle per household was only 2.1 and the majority of households sampled (74 per cent) reported owning no cattle at all (see Figure 6.2).[21] This belies any notion of the communal areas and their population currently being 'cattle country' and 'cattle people' respectively.

As Figure 6.3 shows, cattle populations have been rising again in recent years although this overall trend disguises the fact that the composition of cattle holdings is changing, with an increasingly large proportion of holdings being cows and heifers and relatively fewer oxen and steers.

Donkey populations, although remaining relatively low, have also increased over time. They were first imported from South Africa around 1905. In 1916 the Native Commissioner for Chibi was to note that: 'The natives in the southern part of the district have increased their stock of donkeys so that the number now amounts to 105. Most of these are used for pack purposes.'[22] By 1996 the livestock census recorded over 1,000 donkeys in Matibi II communal area alone. With the reduction in cattle holdings after the war and the drought of 1991-92 donkeys are increasingly used for draught power.

Livestock management in the communal areas of the lowveld has not been a static 'traditional' system, but rather has changed regularly over time in response to political, social and environmental dynamics. As Chapter 4 also described in relation to the complex accommodations and adaptations of dryland agricultural practice, drought, war, land alienation, disease and other events have shifted the significance of livestock management over time. People have moved in and out of different husbandry practices and in the process moulded and remoulded the landscape. Livestock management has

---

[21] These average numbers of cattle per household conceal a wide range – livestock ownership is markedly skewed by wealth, age and gender (see also IFAD 1995b: 4/12-15).

[22] NAZ N 9/1/16 NC Chibi Annual Report 1913.

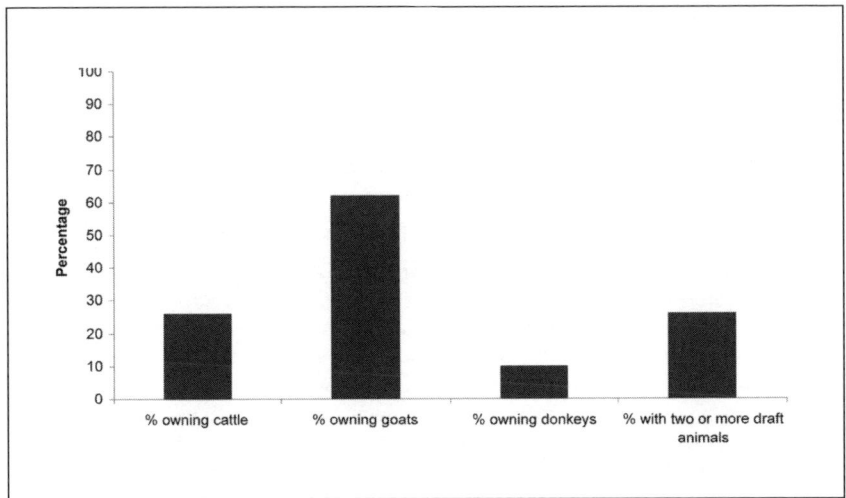

Figure 6.2 Percentage of the population near Chikombedzi owning livestock in 1998

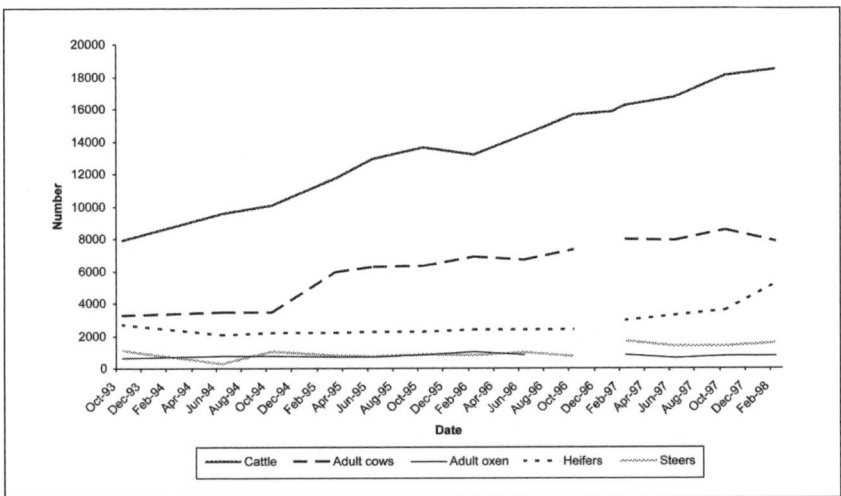

Figure 6.3 Changing composition of cattle holdings in Matibi II, 1993-1998
Source: Dip tank data

also always been a highly differentiated activity with marked changes by wealth, age and gender (Wolmer *et al.* 2002). This complexity, however, has rarely been taken on board by development initiatives that have aimed to support cattle production in the communal areas. It is to the history of these interventions, and the assumptions underpinning them, that I now turn.

Cattle country and cattle people

As European ranchers penetrated the lowveld, administrators in the reserves became increasingly appreciative of the quantity and quality of 'native cattle'. As the Native Commissioner for Ndanga put it: '[The Shangaans] are extremely wealthy in cattle, which are considerably finer than ordinary native cattle ... [and] noticeable for their size and condition in all seasons.'[23] If anything, administrators in later years were even more effusive:

> I doubt if any district in this country has better native stock than Nuanetsi. No doubt this is excellent cattle county but I am convinced that exotic blood introduced through contact with the ranch bulls over a period of years has much to do with it. The cattle are hardy, in many cases travel great distances to water, stay in good condition, and weigh more than any native stock I have seen.[24]

> Lowveld cattle are famous for their quality - the sweet grasses in this part of our land and the abundance of browse trees, put an inner lining of fat on beef animals that you just do not get in the high or middle veld. Oxen straight off the veld will produce meat of a type which only stall-feeding can ensure in other areas. (Wright 1972: 231)

Colonial definitions of the lowveld as cattle country became inseparable from representations of the Shangaans – already variously 'natural hunters' and 'good mineworkers' – as cattle people; albeit unscientific and wasteful 'traditional' cattle people. Again the imagination and transformation of the lowveld was bound up with the changing representations of its inhabitants. Interestingly there has been an appropriation of this 'cattle people' label by Shangaans themselves. As Chief Gezani put it: 'we don't want to lose our forefathers' nature of being cattle rearers'.[25] This appropriation of an essentialised identity has been used strategically to gain opportunities from colonial and post-colonial interventions – in particular to argue for restocking schemes to reinstate the 'natural' and 'culturally appropriate' stockholdings. However, in practice, many large cattle-owners in the lowveld communal areas today are ethnically Ndebele and not Shangaan.

Pasture science: veld management and destocking

Previous chapters have already alluded to the role played by colonial science in fixing particular landscapes to a prescribed usage and in defining African relationships to these landscapes. This is also evident with respect to pasture science. As in the commercial ranching sector, the concepts associated with the emerging fields of pasture science and range ecology (in particular 'carrying capacity') were to have wide-ranging effects on colonial interventions directed at the communal herd. Although the quality of native cattle in the lowveld continued to be admired, the quantity did not and nor

---

[23] NAZ N 9/1/11 NC Ndanga Annual Report 1908.
[24] NAZ S 235/518 ANC Nuanetsi Annual Report 1948.
[25] Interview: Chief Gezani, Gezani, 19 September1999.

did the 'traditional' forms of livestock keeping which were seen to be ecologically damaging and in danger of causing 'environmental collapse'. What was required was a prescribed form of planned and ordered land use (Cousins 1990; Scoones 1996). This modernising, 'improving' project had two main thrusts: destocking and veld management.[26]

Compulsory destocking was a particularly unpopular element of the Natural Resource Act and the Land Husbandry Act and was resisted across the country by the African population – becoming a cause célèbre for the emergent nationalist movement (Beinart 1984). However, many scientists and colonial administrators argued that the ecological and economic context of the lowveld was sufficiently different from the rest of the country for destocking measures to be unnecessary. Indeed, a 1943 study concluded that whilst Chibi Reserve was 49 per cent overstocked, Matibi II, Ndanga East and Sangwe communal areas of the lowveld were respectively 80, 39 and 43 per cent understocked.[27] As one Native Commissioner put it:

> Whatever view may be taken of the number of stock in relation to the limited area in which the Natives are constrained to live and have their being, it seems patent that, in relation to the needs of a people living very largely by pastoral and agricultural pursuits, the holding of cattle for each unit of population or each family cannot be held to be excessive, if there is to be any hope of a reasonable standard of living. … [N]ative cattle holdings in this part of the Colony might receive practical recognition as a potential asset capable of development in the general economic interest.[28]

To another District Commissioner, it was 'the concentration of cattle in the wrong places at the wrong times that is ruining our grazing lands, and not basic overstocking as such'. His recommended solution for winning the 'battle of the soil' was to 'remove the ever-multiplying, soil-destroying ulcers that are communal dipping tanks' (Wright 1972: 223). A more upbeat District Commissioner predicted that 'if sufficient water development could be carried out in Matibi No.2 Reserve it could carry more than treble the present number of cattle.'[29] By 1964, the administrator for Nuanetsi District was admitting that 'physical destocking is [probably] out of the question' but warning that unequal access to grazing resources was in danger of causing cattle to 'destock themselves by dying through lack of grass'. 'This "natural method" of destocking', he concluded, was 'dangerous from a political angle too. Africans whose cattle are dying through lack of food will decry the existence of grazing on adjoining European ranches and farms.'[30] A remarkably bold and prescient analysis of the stocking rates

---

[26] The 'upgrading' of 'scrub cattle' through the introduction of grade bulls was less of an issue in the lowveld than other areas due to the long history of interbreeding with the ranch bulls.
[27] NAZ S 2998/3 Destocking; 21 May 1943 – 3 July 1948.
[28] NAZ S 235/514 NC Chivi Annual Report 1938.
[29] NAZ S 235/518 ANC Nuanetsi Annual Report 1948.
[30] DC Nuanetsi Annual Report 1964, cited by Scoones (1996).

debate had been made as early as 1943 by the Bishop of Southern Rhodesia in a letter to the *Bulawayo Chronicle*:

> ... destocking is not all that is necessary, neither are the Africans the only people who are careless and inconsiderate in the matter of the use and misuses of land. But even when consideration has to be given to matters of 'restocking and destocking' equally urgent consideration should be given to what one might call 'relanding' and 'delanding' ... Overstocking in native reserves is due in some measure to the 'delanding' of the African people. There is insufficient land set aside for the African population, and ... the fact that we Europeans have crowded Africans into insufficient land makes us in no small measure responsible for the damage of these inadequate lands by overstocking. The remedy does not wholly lie in destocking but in 'delanding' the Europeans of some of their land and 'relanding' the Africans.[31]

Destocking was never implemented in the lowveld and was eventually abandoned elsewhere in the country, but the Bishop's radical call to shift the terms of debate to 'relanding' was never heeded. Instead there was a turn to the other recommendation for scientifically efficient cattle ranching – veld management. In much the same way as 'improved methods' of intensive agriculture were hoped to contain growing populations on small reserves whilst combating environmental degradation, so it was with better veld management. As one ecologist put it:

> In Matibi No. 2 Tribal Trust Land, continued intense use will lead to further deterioration of the already degraded veld. The introduction of veld management and a greater number of watering points are required to prevent continued deterioration and improve the vigour and productivity of the veld in these areas. (Kelly 1973: 203)

Veld management measures date from the Herbage Preservation Ordinance of 1913.[32] There were an increasing raft of measures for pasture improvement including paddocked grazing areas which were consolidated and divided into fenced blocks around which cattle could be rotated (Scoones 1996). These types of schemes re-emerged after Independence with the same technical rationale and donor backing. Consultancy reports in the 1980s speak, for example, of the 'maldistribution' of cattle populations with overstocking in some areas and understocking in others (Salzgitter Consult GMBH 1985: ii). The proposed solutions were couched in much the same terms as the colonial-era schemes – emphasising the need for rationalisation and order – and also included grazing schemes with short duration rotational grazing within fenced paddocks (Drinkwater 1992; Robins 1994; Scoones 1996). Many of these schemes were piloted in the lowveld as part of the Mwenezi Radical Land Reform Programme (Cousins 1990; 1996). These schemes offered the opportunity for control of the unknown (Robins 1994; Scoones 1996); coincided with political and administrative objectives (Munro 1995), and fitted with the post-colonial modernisation discourse which emphasised a planned, controlled and rationalised landscape.

[31] Bishop of Southern Rhodesia, 'A leading question', *The Bulawayo Chronicle*, 28 May 1943.
[32] NAZ N 9/1/16 NC Ndanga Annual Report 1913.

These schemes have also been buttressed by narratives about degradation and environmental collapse similar to those told since the 1930s, as a consultancy report, and many of my interviews, show:

> Signs of degradation of the vegetation due to overgrazing are several: proliferation of less desirable annual grasses at the expense of more palatable grasses, soil erosion along animal treks, and bush encroachment. The high livestock mortality during the 1991/92 drought was another indicator of overstocking. (IFAD 1995: 4/6)

> The population explosion is the problem. My father came here in the '50s. The populations were very sparse and wildlife could roam free from thunderstorm to thunderstorm. Now the perennial grasses have been devastated, the carrying capacity with annual grasses is useless as it doesn't grow - you can no longer survive drought.[33]

The ranching model

Viewing the lowveld as cattle country has had very specific connotations. This was seen as ranching land and the purpose of cattle was the production of beef. Thus notions developed for beef production in the United States and South America which were applied firstly to the commercial ranching sector in Rhodesia came to be applied to the communal sector with the aim of encouraging a process of commercialisation into the beef economy (Scoones 1996). As well as encouraging scientific veld management and optimum carrying capacities this led to an obsession with increasing 'off-take rates' – in part as a destocking mechanism, but also to turn cattle into a revenue-earning commodity. Advocates of beef production in the communal sector in the lowveld have often, in contrast to other parts of Zimbabwe, been delighted to report particularly high levels of off-take. Sengwe communal area was particularly renowned for its high level of cattle sales between the 1950s and 1970s which reached 22 per cent of total cattle holdings in some years (Wright 1972; Salzgitter Consult GMBH 1985).[34]

Much of the infrastructure developed to support and encourage African beef production was focused on the arrangement of marketing facilities such as sales pens. The first 'organised' cattle sale took place in Matibi II Reserve in 1933. Veterinary controls on the movement and sales of livestock (see below) meant these sales were disrupted for a few years, but by 1939 a licensed auctioneer was provided for public auctions with the aim of introducing a 'more equitable means of disposing of native cattle'.[35] As Munro (1998: 88) points out, 'the livestock market was a particularly

---

[33] Interview: Rancher, Mwenezi, 8 November 1999.
[34] This being about four times the national average for sales in communal areas at the time. Officials are still continually pushing for higher rates of off-take. One Veterinary Officer I spoke to even asserted that the '1992 [drought] was a good lesson for the farmer - we have seen farmers learn to sell more stock in drought years'. Interview: District Veterinary Officer, Chiredzi South, 5 June 1998.
[35] NAZ S 235/511 ANC Nuanetsi Annual Report 1933; S 235/517 ANC Nuanetsi Annual Report 1939.

conflictual arena of state-peasant relations'. To the colonial authorities cattle sales were a means or maintaining stock numbers at their 'correct' levels, while generating substantial revenue for the CSC and taxing stockholders with hefty levies. Also the cash payments were often clawed back as Africans then had to 'meet their obligations to government'.[36] As with grain marketing, the pricing and grading structures were deeply biased towards European cattle. A cattle levy of 17.5 per cent was justified as being 'absolutely necessary for, unlike the European farmer, the African puts nothing at all back into the land and spends nothing on watering points and this has to be done for him [sic]' (Wright 1972: 241). All of this caused deep resentment which was compounded by two further factors. One was the suspicion that the District Commissioner and his field staff, and the cattle graders and buyers – who would all camp together at the same rest house before cattle auctions – would conspire to ensure that African-owned cattle were sold at the lowest possible price (Wright 1972; Munro 1998). The second was the deliberate strategy of some District Administrators in the drought-prone lowveld to withhold famine-relief maize in order to force people to sell 'surplus' cattle (Wright 1972). It was, and remains, common for Africans to bring stock to sales only to spurn the offered prices and withdraw with them. However, as District Commissioner Wright admits, 'he may of course make use of the sale to ascertain the true value of his animal for some other purpose' (1972: 237). These purposes included informal deals with the cattle buyers and negotiating alternative trade or patronage arrangements with shopkeepers, butchers, and others (Munro 1998).

There are still bitter complaints at the poor terms of trade derived from the cattle auctions of Matibi II and Sengwe communal areas; suspicion at the means of estimating animals' weight; and anger at the better prices received by large-scale producers.[37] As one commercial rancher admitted, '[our] main money-spinner is buying communal area cattle, fattening on the commercial farms and selling on at the commercial farm sales for higher prices. You can more than double prices at commercial auction. With a fat steer from an African area – you wouldn't notice the difference [in quality].'[38] Indeed, as alluded to earlier, the commercial sector has long been economically reliant on the communal sector for cheap stock (as well as land and labour). The discourse on maintaining and increasing communal area off-take rates is entirely compatible with supporting the commercial ranches through the provision of cheap cattle.

Since the war and severe droughts of the 1980s and early 1990s which hammered livestock populations in the lowveld communal areas, the driving narrative behind proposed interventions in livestock management has been that this is a 'damaged' livestock area that must be rehabilitated. This

---

[36] NAZ S 235/514 ANC Nuanetsi Annual Report 1934.
[37] One reaction to these perceived poor terms of trade has been an increasing illegal transborder cattle movement to Mozambique for sale at better prices.
[38] Interview: Rancher, Mwenezi, 12 August 1999.

rehabilitation has been couched in terms of restocking – rather than destocking – the communal herd, and driving up the all-important off-take rates. The most ambitious proposal was a GTZ-funded scheme to rebuild the 'livestock economy' of Sengwe communal area. Consultancy reports envisaged that livestock numbers could be maintained at about 21400 head of cattle, and there would be a sustainable annual off-take of 20 per cent. A purely cattle-based economy with these levels of production, it was estimated, could generate sufficient income to support 60 per cent of the population of Sengwe (Stubbs 1984; Salzgitter Consult GMBH 1985). But, in common with the other potential GTZ-funded mega-projects focusing on irrigation, the restocking scheme was never implemented due to instability in the area (which was suffering from frequent raids by Renamo fighters from Mozambique); lack of finance; and poor communications between ministries (Cunliffe 1993).

However, the ranching model of commercialised beef production in the communal areas of the lowveld with high off-take rates is at odds with much local practice. Cattle have been, and continue to be, important for many reasons other than their realisable value when sold for beef. The main reason for owning cattle was and is to provide an input to arable production in the form of draught power. In a context of ongoing draught power shortage for a majority of communal area farmers, it is here that the key value of cattle (and donkeys) lies. Many households have focused on accumulating smallstock (goats and sheep) for which there is a vibrant local market (Wolmer *et al.* 2002).

Notwithstanding its flawed logic the ranching model has left a physical and conceptual imprint on the landscape. The paddocks, dams, boreholes and access roads of the grazing lands in communal areas (as well as the commercial ranches) reveal the legacy of this managerial view. One District Commissioner also explicitly reveals how ranching became a metaphor for district administration:

> I know I always looked upon the Nuanetsi district as a great 'ranch' and I took as much interest in the people, the cattle and all the other domestic animals, the crops and the land, as I would have done had I been the inheritor of some vast estate. (Wright 1972: 6)

Livestock diseases and landscape management

A further discourse that has impinged on both commercial and communal area livestock management in the lowveld is that of veterinary disease control. The cattle industry in the lowveld has historically been engaged in an ongoing battle against the twin-headed veterinary disease threats of FMD and trypanosomiasis. This battle has been physically inscribed in the landscape in the form of fences, corridors and buffer zones. It has been at the heart of ongoing ideological struggles over the meaning and purpose of the lowveld fought between the cattle and game industry lobbies and between veterinarians, ecologists and administrators rooted in different perceptions of nature and of Africans' relationships to the land. It is also illustrative of the layering and interactions between natural and political processes over time and at various geographical scales from the local to the global. Post-BSE European perceptions of food safety and risk, for example, are being played out in Zimbabwe's lowveld landscape.[39]

Veterinary science has played an important role in constructing nature and defining Africans' relationship to their environments. Hoppe (1995) describes the conjuncture between colonial biomedicine and environmental and social engineering in sleeping-sickness control policies in East Africa. Biomedicine was central to environmental colonisation by applying the value-laden contrasts of order/disorder and health/sickness to Africans' relationships and responsibilities to their environments.'[40] In colonial Rhodesia cattle health not human health was always the priority of policymakers but there are similarities in the way in which contested scientific knowledge was mapped onto the landscape. Far from being neutral or objective, scientific constructions of nature were and are highly political. For example the shift of blame for veterinary disease transmission onto African livestock 'vectors' enabled depopulation of areas and subsequent expansion of commercial ranches and protected areas.

There were 58 recorded incidents of FMD outbreak in Zimbabwe between 1931 and 1999 and nearly three-quarters of these (42) occurred in Chiredzi, Mwenezi (Nuanetsi) and Beitbridge Districts in the lowveld.[41] The first outbreak in the country was in the lowveld in 1931. This, and subsequent outbreaks, were blamed on the twin evils of 'game and uncontrolled movement of native cattle in the big Native Reserves' (Somerville 1976: 178). Chapter 7 will explore how the 'blame the game' philosophy (with respect to FMD and trypanosomiasis) fostered bitter differences of opinion in respect of land utilisation and management between veterinarians and conservationists rooted in different ways of seeing the lowveld. Here I trace the impact of FMD control measures on the latter 'evil' – cattle movement, and in particular African cattle movement.

The problem, as seen by the Veterinary Department in Ndanga Crown Lands was that:

> The native cattle in these areas cannot be kept under proper control and in outbreaks of disease, particularly FMD, they constitute a very serious menace in any measures of control that may be required. It is quite impossible to prevent illegal movement or in the event of an outbreak to check up any movements that might have taken place in these areas.[42]

The proposed solution was to 'concentrate the natives and cattle at present

---

[39] The FMD outbreak in the UK of February 2001 further exacerbated this situation.
[40] See also Lyons (1992), Beinart (1997), and Skidmore-Hess (1998).
[41] Department of Veterinary Services, Masvingo Province, manuscript, 'FMD outbreaks since 1931'.
[42] NAZ S 1542/F11/1 'FMD 1934-1939' ACVS to CNC, 7 September 1937.

scattered over a wide stretch of Crown Lands south of Ndanga into a smaller area ... with a view to obtaining more efficient supervision of cattle and breaking contact between these cattle and surrounding native and European owned herds'.[43] There were also various attempts in the lowveld at creating permanent or temporary cattle-free belts. In 1935, for example, the Chief Veterinary Surgeon insisted that cattle belonging to Chief Mahenye and his people were moved 40 miles away from their home grazing lands in order to create a cattle-free belt along the Mozambican border.[44]

However, the veterinary policy of creating cattle-free belts and concentrating livestock populations was to run up against the science of veld management and the politics of 'native affairs'. Ecologists and Native Commissioners became increasingly concerned that stringent implementation of these blanket policies – even in herds where no FMD had been reported – was leading to overstocking with the consequent dangers of veld degradation and soil erosion.[45] This was part of an increasingly bitter stand-off between the Native Affairs Department and the Veterinary Service, rooted in a fundamental difference of opinion over the place of African human and livestock populations in the lowveld landscape. To the Veterinary Service – whose principal concern was the health of cattle on the commercial ranches – these populations were essentially conceived of as vectors for FMD that could act as an infection conduit between the wild border region with Mozambique and the ranches. The Native Affairs Department, on the other hand, was broadly supportive of African settlement for a variety of administrative and political reasons.[46] However, it is interesting to note that the Native Commissioners strategically chose principally to advance 'scientific' arguments to counter the Veterinary Service. As well as deploying the countervailing science of veld management to argue that veterinary policies were causing overstocking and hence soil erosion they argued that the African population acted as a buffer (rather than a vector) between wilderness and the ranches; and that the presence of cattle was an excellent safeguard against the undetected advance of the

[43] NAZ S 1542/F11/1 'FMD 1934-1939' Minister of Agriculture and Lands to Prime Minister 13 May 1938.
[44] NAZ S 235/514 NC Melsetter Annual Report 1935.
[45] For example, NAZ S 235/514 NC Chibi Annual Report 1936.
[46] As Chapter 4 described, the African population in the lowveld was depicted by some as beneficial in that it prevented reversion to 'wilderness' or the land being 'entirely handed back to nature' (e.g. NAZ S 235/510 NC Annual Report Ndanga 1932). The NC for Zaka in 1937 was similarly against depopulation of the lowveld portion of the district: 'If that huge area of Crown Land were devoid of natives, there would be no-one handy to control grass fires or locusts and hoppers, to keep an eye on things in general, and criminals could hide away in that vast area without detection. In traversing such an area by car it is also of use at times to have someone living handy in the event of a breakdown in what otherwise would be 'no man's land''. NAZ S 1542/F11/1 FMD 1934-1939: NC Zaka to CNC 24 September 1937.

tsetse fly. Depopulation, on the other hand, brought 'wilderness conditions' and with it disease carriers such as buffalo and kudu.[47] Also, as the less than sanguine Native Commissioner for Zaka observed in relation to the scheme to depopulate Ndanga Crown Land:

> Experience has taught me that unfenced Ranch boundaries are so 'elastic' that I am not at all sure, if Native cattle are removed ... that the area that would then be cattle free would not in practice mean an extra bite for the Rancher's cattle, so there would still be 'contact' between European and Native cattle.[48]

He argued vehemently that the evacuation would cause needless hardship. However, for the Minister of Lands and Agriculture, safeguarding the health of the commercial herd was the issue of paramount importance. He decided that the 'scientific' claims of the veterinarians carried more authority than the Native Affairs Department's concerns about overstocking and land alienation through the back door, reasoning that: 'in matters of this kind I feel we must be guided by the advice of our senior Veterinary Officials, and I cannot think that the concentration will inflict any serious hardship on the natives'.[49] But the Native Commissioner's fears were realised when cattle from Angus and Devuli ranches were soon found to be occupying the areas from which African cattle had been removed to form the 'cattle-free belt'.[50]

Yet the movement of African cattle continued to be blamed for FMD outbreaks, particularly by those of a conservationist bent eager to absolve wildlife from blame. The avowedly conservationist District Commissioner for Nuanetsi in the late 1950s and 1960s, Allan Wright, for example, consistently sought to stave off the Department of Veterinary Services' game eradication measures by blaming FMD outbreaks on illegal movement of infected cattle from Mozambique to Rhodesia (where they could be sold at higher prices or were used for *lobola*). The one productive unintended consequence of a ten-strand, patrolled fence built along the Mozambican border to stop non-existent game migrations, he argued, was that it controlled these illegal movements of cattle (Wright 1972).

The FMD threat has continued to have a significant impact on the landscape and political economy of the lowveld. After the Lomé Agreement beef export deals, the livestock producing areas of Zimbabwe were divided into three zones: the vaccinated (red) zone where FMD is endemic; the buffer (green) zone where FMD outbreaks can be controlled by vaccination

---

[47] NAZ S 1542/F11/1 'FMD 1934-1939': Chief Entomologist to Secretary, Department of Agriculture and Lands, 4 March 1938; Secretary for Native Affairs to Secretary to the Prime Minister, 31 May 1938. This argument was, in fact, later to gain impeccable scientific credentials as the basis for Ford's theories about '*Grenzwildnis*' in his renowned book *The Role of the Trypanosomiases in African Ecology* (Ford 1971) (see Chapter 7).
[48] NAZ S 1542/F11/1 'FMD 1934-1939' NC Zaka to CNC, 12 April 1938.
[49] NAZ S 1542/F11/1 'FMD 1934-1939' Minister of Agriculture and Lands to Prime Minister, 13 May 1938.
[50] NAZ S 1542/F11/1 'FMD 1934-1939' CNC to Dept of Agriculture and Lands, 17 July 1938.

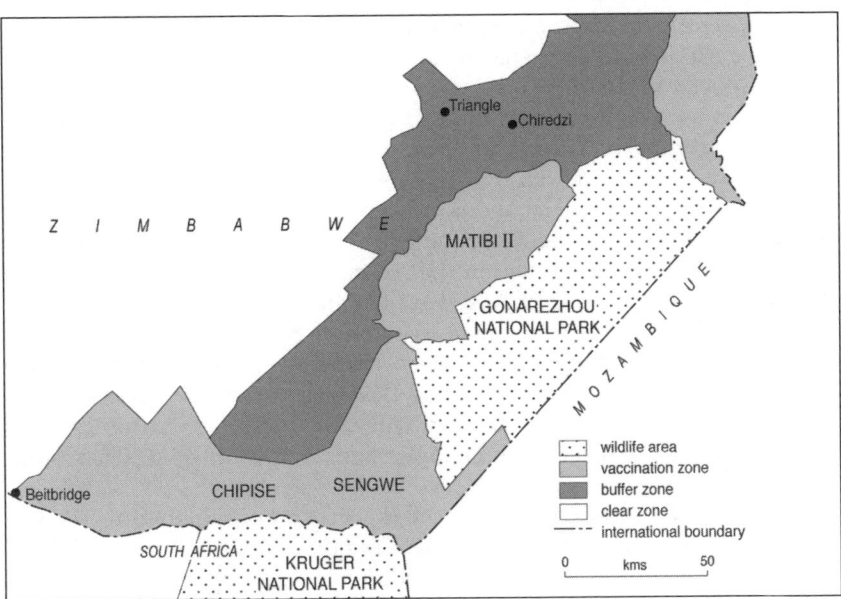

Map 6.1 Foot and mouth disease zones in the lowveld

programmes; and the clear zone from which export of animal products to the EU is permitted. Cattle within the red zone can only be moved out of it directly to an abattoir for slaughter. Cattle can move from the green to red zone, but not *vice versa* (Cunliffe 1993). The red zone is separated from the green (buffer) zone by a cattle fence that is patrolled and maintained by the Department of Veterinary Services. The bulk of the lowveld falls within the red and green zones and therefore outside of the catchment area for the EU market (see Map 6.1). The veterinary restrictions have therefore been a serious disadvantage to both commercial and communal sector cattle owners.[51] During and after FMD outbreaks strict quarantine measures are imposed. No movement of livestock is permitted, all cattle auctions are cancelled, cordons and roadblocks set up, and bans are imposed on the hunting or disturbance of game animals.

In the wake of the British BSE and FMD crises EU regulations have become increasingly strict, with the latest development being the requirement that all stock destined for export to the EU are 'traceable'. In practice this means that all stock should have officially-issued ear tags and 'animal passports' and all stock-owners should keep registers. Many in the Zimbabwean beef industry regard these regulations as non-tariff barriers[52] and they are obviously a non-starter for the communal herd.

---

[51] Although red zone cattle cannot leave the country as they may contain FMD antibodies, the export market still keeps prices higher for the domestic market. Interview: Rancher, Mwenezi, 12 August 1999.

[52] Interview: Rancher, Mwenezi, 8 November 1999.

The red zone designation theoretically has severe implications for stock-owners in the communal areas of the lowveld. It means than no live cattle can be moved into the green zone or buffer zone to the west and north and, for every five kilometres cattle are moved within the red zone, the owners are meant to get a permit. Failure to provide such a permit can lead to a fine and animals driven into the green zone are destroyed if caught.[53] Veterinary officials are strict about movements between zones but, in practice, it is impossible for them to issue permits for every movement of cattle more than five kilometres within the red zone, as this is being done every day in search of grazing land. As is described below, longer movements such as livestock loaning (*kufiyisa*) are also common. A veterinary official tacitly admitted 'there's nothing we can do - otherwise we would have to issue 1,000 permits a day'.[54] However, it is clear that veterinary restrictions on livestock movement are in conflict with the sort of opportunistic and mobile livestock management strategies and drought coping mechanisms discussed below.

Another of the stipulations for beef exports to be permitted to the EU was the erection of veterinary fencing around Gonarezhou National Park. A precedent for this was a fence around the park put up by the Tsetse and Trypanosomiasis Control Branch in the early 1980s. However, there was no consultation about the siting of this fence with local communities of Matibi II communal area or the council; it was deeply resented, and perceived as further back-door land alienation from the communal area – in this instance to the already deeply unpopular DNPWLM. This conflict was politicised and rooted in yet another difference of opinion between the Department of Veterinary Services and the District Administration and local council. To the vets:

> The expenditure of thousands of dollars to eradicate buffalo from the commercial areas appears the height of hypocrisy when over 1000 head of cattle are allowed to invade the Gonarezhou game park and mix freely with buffalo. Surely it would be simpler to have cattle removed from the park and greater surveillance of the park boundary instituted using army, police, tsetse or veterinary department personnel to patrol the boundary fence.[55]

The District Administrator's office and local councillors lobbied for gates in the fence and were angered at the frequent shooting of poachers. In the immediately post-Independence context this dispute overlaid a more deep-rooted conflict between the new black socialist administration and populist councillors, and a predominantly white veterinary service and DNPWLM seen as Rhodesian bastions. The new DA was angered by the lack of co-ordination with the local authority and consultation with people, and was at pains to point out that:

[53] Interview: District Veterinary Officer, Chiredzi South, 5 June 1998.
[54] Interview: District Veterinary Officer, Chiredzi South, 5 June 1998.
[55] MRC LAN 21/22 Letter: Government Veterinary Officer, Chiredzi to Director of Veterinary Services, 10 February 1983.

... if we are to realise our highly desired socialist goals where the masses identify with all government efforts to protect and develop their lot, the aspect of communication with the masses is crucial. It will be appreciated if the Tsetse Control Officers are made to understand this changed method of providing services to the people.[56]

The community bordering the new fence, for their part, continued to make their displeasure felt with thefts of its wire (often used for snaring) and poaching grazing cattle in the park.

Notwithstanding this controversial history of veterinary fencing in the south-east lowveld the EU had, in the late 1990s, committed €10 million for a new veterinary fence intended to streamline the landscape zoning into a wildlife zone, surveillance zone, and an uninfected zone. This would have increased the area of the lowveld from which beef exports to the EU were permitted.[57] The siting of this fence would obviously have been equally controversial. Unsurprisingly, this has been put on ice since the large-scale donor withdrawal in the wake of the farm invasions since 2000. As Chapter 8 explores, these invasions have also been accompanied by the removal of fences and their transformation into snares, and the driving of cattle into 'game' spaces. This in turn caused concern from the EU veterinarians about cattle mixing with buffalo and, indeed, with persistent and ongoing FMD outbreaks since 2001, beef exports to the EU remain indefinitely suspended.[58]

Livestock management in practice

The everyday practice of livestock husbandry by the African population of the lowveld lies for the most part outside of the ranching model, with its technical and economic rationale and spatial logic of paddocks and pens, or the veterinary vision of fences and constrained stock mobility. Livestock management is a flexible and opportunistic activity which has adapted in response to changing environmental and political dynamics. In turn it has accommodated to, and initiated changes in, the constantly remoulded lived-in landscape.

An understanding of the power-laden social dynamics of livestock management strategies in the lowveld can be gained by an exploration of the arrangement known as *kufiyisa*. This is best translated as 'livestock loaning' (Wolmer *et al.* 2002).[59] Under such arrangements a few head of cattle are lent out on a semi-permanent basis, usually to a relative. The livestock

[56] MRC DA Chiredzi to Government Veterinary Officer, Chiredzi, undated 1983.
[57] Interviews: Rancher, Mwenezi 8 November 1999; Director of Veterinary Services, Harare, 14 February 2001; Director, Wildlife Unit, Department of Veterinary Services, 14 February 2001.
[58] *Zimbabwe Independent*, 27 October 2000; 'Beef Exports to EU Unlikely to Resume Early - Vet Dept', *The Herald*, 5 February 2004. New export markets have been explored in Malaysia and Libya.
[59] The following section draws on collaborative research on crop-livestock integration in Chikombedzi. More details can be found in Wolmer, Sithole and Mukamuri (2002).

borrower gets to use the draught power and milk and in previous years, but rarely now, would receive a heifer every few years. The lender of the animals also has certain benefits: cattle in smaller groups tend to be looked after better; the reduced cost of herding and veterinary care; a decreased risk of losing the whole herd in a disease outbreak; and it avoids the necessity of building more, or larger, kraals. Before the war and recent droughts, when some farmers had extremely large herds, *kufiyisa* arrangements were particularly widespread in Matibi II and Sengwe communal areas. Makuso Siwawa, for example, moved to Chikombedzi in Matibi II from Mberengwe in 1952. He built up a herd of 800 cattle, most of which were held in *kufiyisa* arrangements by a large number of people. The general decline in livestock holdings with the war and 1991/92 drought means that today fewer animals in total are loaned or borrowed, but it appears that more people than in the past are entering into these arrangements. *Kufiyisa* is becoming smaller in scale – sometimes involving only a single beast. It is particularly common for people in Matibi II to keep part of their herds with relatives or friends in Sengwe (the adjoining communal area), where grazing land is relatively much more abundant and where many people lost all their stock in the drought and want draught animals. In some cases, though, cattle will be brought back to Matibi II for the ploughing season. The reason for the resurgence in this institution is that it is, in part, a means of spreading the risk to livestock holdings of drought – which has been perceived as more of a threat in recent years.

However, *kufiyisa* is not only interesting because it illustrates how people invest in institutional arrangements to gain access to resources and spread risk (cf. Berry 1994). It also illustrates aptly one of the means by which people have covertly resisted and undermined the ordered, boxed and bounded landscape approach to veld and stock management, and instead practised a fluid, mobile and socially-embedded livestock management system. This arrangement subverts both the ranching vision of the lowveld as a patchwork of paddocks and fences, with demarcated grazing lands and individual owner-managers of stock, and the veterinary vision of limited livestock mobility. It also implicitly contests the assumption that livestock management is purely a technical (and not a social and political) issue.

Kufiyisa has been a means by which Karanga and Ndebele stockowners from outside the lowveld have been able to run large herds in the region. It was, crucially, a means of 'hiding' livestock from official view to evade colonial era destocking and veterinary control measures. It had an international dimension, as well, as when Chauke people in Sengwe looked after cattle belonging to the Makuleke lineage in South Africa at a time when coercive FMD control measures were demanding the destruction of all Makuleke livestock (Harries 1987). It can also provide a measure of security against the rising trend of stock rustling; attempted stock thefts, particularly orchestrated from Mozambique, are a common occurrence and grazing cattle in relatively small scattered herds is one strategy used to ameliorate this.[60] *Kufiyisa* is also a means of establishing and maintaining patronage relationships whereby 'big men' – and almost always men – are able to call on people's labour, draught power and political support in a context of skewed livestock holdings (cf. Wilson 1986). This is a politicised landscape where livestock management, in practice, has been geared towards asserting and subverting power by evading and accommodating restrictions and prescriptions on livelihood strategies.

Notwithstanding the arguments of the 'new rangeland ecology',[61] or the low rates of livestock ownership and draught power shortage, there is a strongly felt perception, amongst many stockowners in the communal areas of the lowveld, that there is a shortage of grazing land.[62] This is particularly so in Matibi II communal area, which has been progressively squeezed from all sides over the years (by Land Apportionment and the establishment of the ranches, the establishment of Gonarezhou National Park, Malipati and Navasha Safari Areas, and Gonakudzingwa Small Scale Farms). The situation has been compounded by large in-migration from Chivi, Mwenezi, Zaka and as far as Mberengwa.

In interviews conducted by Paul de Jager in Matibi II in 1987 there was a litany of complaints about extensions of the boundary of Gonarezhou National Park and the consequent encroachment on grazing lands and cattle watering points, and the shooting or branding of cattle that stray into the park. Branded cattle could not be sold at formal cattle sales due to FMD restrictions and the severe reduction in grazing areas meant 'we are now witnessing a high death toll of cattle'.[63] The perceived shortage of grazing land is still strongly felt. People in the Chikombedzi area speak of feeling 'hemmed in', of being squeezed between the farms and park.[64]

The premium on grazing land necessitates all sorts of official and unofficial arrangements to negotiate access. This situation is very different from

---

[60] However, there have also been cases of litigation where loaned animals were reported stolen and the owner suspects they were secretly sold.

[61] There has been a general reassessment of many of the assumptions of range ecology and range management practice in recent years, much of which draws on research in Zimbabwe. This 'new rangeland ecology' emphasises the non-equilibrium nature of environments and questions concepts such as carrying capacity and environmental degradation. Instead it emphasises contingency, complexity and dynamism with a particular focus on mobility, opportunism and niche grazing in the landscape (Sandford 1982; Drinkwater 1992; Behnke *et al.* 1993; Scoones 1995).

[62] Indeed there is a danger, from the African point of view, that the science of the new rangeland ecology could be used to argue against land reform. Conservationists are also using this science to argue for development of conservancies (see Price Waterhouse 1994: 26; du Toit 1998: 7).

[63] Interview: Chirhilele Ndabani, Maguwa Baloyi, Chilahele Mahileke, and Timothy Sibanda, Chipinda Business Centre, by Paul de Jager, 11 February 1987 (de Jager 1988: 118-123).

[64] As far back as 1935 grazing concessions given to the ranches caused pressures on African grazing areas in the lowveld. NAZ S 235/ 514 ANC Nuanetsi Report 1935. The lack of grazing land manifests itself in repeated complaints that livestock are straying into fields and gardens and damaging crops.

the standard representation of a Natural Region 5 lowveld landscape of low population density and extensive grazing lands. In the southern portion of Matibi II the major grazing area for the dry season (even in non-drought years) for most livestock owners lies south of the Mwenezi river. This area is far less densely populated and there is, at least a perception of, plenty of available grazing land. This land, however, comes under the jurisdiction of a different chief (Chief Gezani rather than Chief Mpapa) and is in a different communal area (Sengwe rather than Matibi II), making the politics of negotiating access to it a complex, fraught and conflict-ridden affair. There are regular negotiations and disputes at the level of the chieftaincy, and interventions by the MP and locally between kraalheads on either side of the river (Batiti, Mongayani and Pfumari to the north and Masukwe and Pathela to the south) and between individual families. One result of this unofficial grazing of cattle from Batiti, Mongayani, Pfumari and further afield on the southern side of Mwenezi River is a dispute about the location of the boundary between the Matibi II kraalheads and those on the Sengwe side. The Matibi II residents maintain that the boundary should be at Gwamalala (2 kilometres south of the river) rather than the river itself (thereby extending 'their' grazing land). As kraalhead Mapfumele put it, 'the river zigzags but at Gwamalala the boundary is a straight line – so this one is official.'[65] There is a general perception north of the river that the grazing boundaries are artificial and foreign: 'long back our culture did not have boundaries on grazing – they were imposed.'[66] Yet as kraalhead Mapfumele's words reveal, people are not averse to drawing on the supposed superior authority of the straight – and therefore 'official' – line when it suits them.

Another important means of gaining access to grazing land is through negotiated access to paddocks in the commercial ranches and – in the case of Matibi II – the small-scale commercial farms at Gonakudzingwa. There is a long history of informally negotiated arrangements of this kind, particularly during drought years. During the drought of 1992, for example, Edenvale Ranch made paddocks and watering points available to the neighbouring Chompani community. This, of course, has recently happened in a far more visible – although not necessarily negotiated – way as farm invasions in the lowveld were justified in terms of grazing land shortage (see Chapter 8). Taken together with the large amount of livestock sales and exchanges between farmers in the communal areas and on the ranches this points to an interesting disjuncture between the hard-edged administrative maps of the lowveld, with their clearly demarcated land uses and the actuality of everyday practice. It appears that, in practice, there is a long history of interactions and arrangements across the boundaries between commercial farms, small-scale farms and communal areas, and that these interactions – be they illicit or semi-formalised – are increasing in frequency and scale. The sharp boundaries are actually a lot more blurred

[65] Interview: Kraalhead, Chikombedzi, 11 September 1997.
[66] Comment made at group discussion, Chikombedzi, 10 June 1998.

and fuzzy than they might at first appear. With respect to livestock grazing areas the picture that emerges is one of scattered bits and pieces of land that are officially or unofficially available to farmers, but access to them depends on such factors as their negotiating power, their location and where their relatives live.

Conclusions

As with the debates around the irrigated landscape, the notion that the lowveld is an appropriate landscape for cattle is not one simply pushed by the commercial sector and challenged by the communal sector. Differences of opinion are more likely to be over what these cattle should be for – meat, or inputs to agriculture – and the form of the rangeland landscape – fenced paddocks, cordons and buffer zones or a more open and unbounded space, maximising mobility and diversity of fodder sources. Until recently, the challenge to cattle ranching has come more from within the commercial sector itself, as a powerful lobby has increasingly pushed game rather than cattle ranching as the more economically and ecologically viable option. However, the recent farm invasions, explicitly supported by the government, are possibly evidence of a new challenge to the permanence of the ranching model's spatial logic. This is a trend symbolised by the transformation of multi-stranded steel veterinary fences into snare wire. That said, the long history of cattle loaning arrangements, livestock sales and exchanges between commercial and communal farmers, poach grazing, and cattle rustling, implies that this spatial logic has never been quite as neat or firm as is indicated by the straight lines on the map and fences in the landscape. These borders have become increasingly physically and conceptually permeable.

Development programmes need to move away from the single land use obsessions of the colonial era, deriving from prescriptions for extensive commercial ranching or irrigated agriculture estates. Reading the lowveld landscape as a multifaceted space where a variety of livelihood strategies can be, and are, played out in combination in different places leads to a reframing of the development agenda. It is not a question of promoting either commercially viable cattle ranching or large-scale irrigation schemes. Both have their role to play, but alongside a variety of other livelihood strategies. Envisaging the lowveld as a potentially productive space at least puts development (and hence livelihoods) to the forefront. However, another way the landscape has been envisaged – as a 'natural' space – has tended to emphasise conservation rather than development. It is this way of seeing, and its impact on livelihoods, that is explored in Part III.

PART THREE
The 'Natural' Landscape

7

Manufacturing wilderness
Wildlife conservation in the lowveld

A visitor to Zimbabwe's Natural History Museum in Bulawayo is encouraged to begin with its centrepiece – 'Lowveld Hall'. From the lobby you pass through a narrow cave-like entrance to emerge into a room bristling with stuffed wildlife. Under a fig tree fashioned from fibreglass is a massive elephant with drooping tusks, flanked by a stooping giraffe. On the other side of the room a pride of lions glare at you over a partially gnawed zebra with a painted backdrop of a lone baobab tree (see Figure 7.1). This impressive tableau captures perfectly the most common representation of the lowveld landscape – as a pristine wilderness emptied of humanity and prowling with game. In recent years this vision has become increasingly pervasive; elephants, lions and baobabs are today even more common signifiers in popular representations of Zimbabwe's lowveld than cane or cattle.

This way of seeing celebrates a pristine and glorious piece of national heritage that must be preserved or rehabilitated or, more often than not, manufactured. This is a different facet of the wilderness vision explored in Part II – a disease-ridden, barren and fearful landscape that must be battled and tamed to become productive. In the context of current economic imperatives, global environmental agendas and donor priorities, it is the former pristine wilderness vision or 'natural landscape' that has become increasingly hegemonic in recent years (although both continue to coexist). The pristine wilderness vision draws on many sources and is not static. With changing economic and scientific goals there has been a shift in the conservationist agenda in the lowveld from viewing protected areas as inviolate sanctuaries to looking to them as potential sources of revenue (with a consequent blurring of the boundaries between 'natural' and 'productive' spaces). This has been accompanied by a shift in emphasis from romantic narratives, to a scientific and managerial approach.

There has also been a change in emphasis from fencing protected areas into enclaves, to opening them out across administrative and national

Figure 7.1 Lowveld Hall, Zimbabwe Natural History Museum

boundaries to re-establish 'ecological integrity' in the landscape. This has involved the ongoing extension of the 'wildlife estate' beyond traditional protected areas into new spaces such as commercial farms and communal areas and the involvement of new actors such as international NGOs and businesses. This has been bound up with a seemingly oxymoronic attempt to [re]create wilderness in the region and market the lowveld as a 'wildlife landscape'. A further strand in conservationist thinking in the lowveld, as elsewhere, has been the importance attached to some form of devolution of political power and revenue to local communities. The pristine wilderness vision has encouraged and underpinned certain conservation and development initiatives in south-eastern Zimbabwe, including the 'conservancies' and a transfrontier national park. The danger is that, rather than providing a means to stimulate an economically depressed area, these initiatives will deepen antagonism over land and lead to further coercive regulations on resource use at odds with people's livelihood strategies.

This chapter asks how the 'wild' landscape of Zimbabwe's south-east lowveld has been imaginatively and physically created, battled, protected and marketed. Who has done this? Why has the 'pristine wilderness' vision come to dominate representations of this landscape? Who has contested this? What has been the impact on land use of this way of seeing? And how have representations of landscape been bound up with representations of African society? These questions are answered in relation to the debates surrounding the establishment of Gonarezhou National Park, the emergence of game ranching and wildlife conservancies, and the attempts to institute a transnational wildlife landscape and 'community-based natural resource management' initiatives.

Gonarezhou National Park

Tucked into Zimbabwe's south-east corner bordering Mozambique and South Africa, and covering 5,023 km^2, Gonarezhou National Park is the country's second biggest protected area. It is also one of the least visited. It has a reputation as a last redoubt of true pristine wilderness – remote country. However, there are several contradictions at the heart of this vision. One is that the 'vast complex' has actually been stitched together from a wide variety of land designations on the basis of *ad hoc* negotiations between various actors. It turns out to be an amalgamation of land types, including 'Forest Land', 'Controlled Hunting Areas', 'Special Native Areas', 'African Purchase Area', and tsetse control corridors. This patchwork of administrative zones has been subject to frequent boundary changes, and sections of it have been regularly proclaimed and then deproclaimed as game reserves in response to the shifting political influence of conservationists and veterinarians. A second contradiction is that large areas of this pristine wilderness have been inhabited and cultivated until quite recently, and it is still an illicit source of many natural resources. Thirdly, this 'natural' space bears the marks of large-scale human interventions in the form of tsetse control measures (such as shooting, burning, bush clearing, and insecticide spraying), and military activity (such as minefields and border fences), which have radically altered vegetation patterns and wildlife numbers and movements.

Conservationists have long been attempting to disregard these contradictions, and to rediscover — or more appropriately to create — a natural space or pristine wilderness. In his book, *Wild Places of Zimbabwe*, for example, Dick Pitman describes Gonarezhou as 'bruised and battered', a 'piecemeal hotchpotch' and a 'maze of boundaries', but reveals the power of the panoramic landscape view from the air to render it 'untouched and timeless' (1980: 18). To Pitman, 'a flight over the park reveals a wide, almost unbroken, horizon-to-horizon panorama of utterly wild, remote country about which, even today, relatively little is known' (1980: 18). Similarly, a senior park ranger, despite having detailed how the history of war, drought and poaching has affected Gonarezhou, went on to describe the park to me as 'still very intact, not yet spoiled'.[1]

The idea of an official game reserve in the south-east lowveld dates from the 1920s.[2] In 1928 the Secretary of the Wild Life Protection Society of Southern Rhodesia set out a three-point agenda for the incipient conservation lobby: to 'inculcate a sporting and humane spirit in the youth and inhabitants of this colony'; to 'ensure greater and more implicit observance of the Game Laws'; and to encourage the formation of game reserves. He went on to recommend the formation of three game reserves — in the north, west and south-east of the country. The latter would be bounded 'south-east by the Anglo-Portuguese boundary; north-east by the Lundi River, but to take in an area around the Chipinda Pools; north-west by the Native Reserve Matibi No. B [sic]; and south-east by the Nuanetsi River'.[3] In 1931 it was declared that 'portions of Gwanda and Chibi Districts lying within 25 miles from the Limpopo and those portions above 25 miles from the Limpopo, lying east of the Beitbridge — Fort Victoria [were] to be a game reserve in which it would be unlawful to hunt without the special permission of the Minister [of Agriculture and Lands]' (Masona 1987: 76). However this proclamation was nullified two years later. In 1932 the establishment of another game reserve in the Chipinda pools area was proposed (Masona 1987). These suggestions encountered resistance from some sections of the colonial administration on two grounds: the threat posed by tsetse fly encroachment to commercial ranches, and the threat to 'native interests'. The Chief Native Commissioner (CNC), for example, wrote:

... I beg to state for the information of the Honourable the Minister of Native Affairs

---

[1] Interview: Senior Ranger, Mabalauta, Gonarezhou National Park, 11 August 1999.

[2] See, for example, MacKenzie (1988), Anderson and Grove (1987), and Adams and McShane (1992) for detailed histories of the establishment of national parks in Africa; and Masona (1987) for background on colonial game policy in Zimbabwe.

[3] NAZ S 1193/P2/1 Circular letter by the Hon Secretary of the Wild Life Protection Society of Southern Rhodesia, 25 May 1928.

that, in view of the opinions expressed by the Chief Entomologist [concerning encroachment of tsetse fly], I cannot support the suggestion to proclaim a Game Reserve in the neighbourhood of Chipinda Pools. It would necessarily be adjacent to Matibi No. 2 Native Reserve, and Native interests there would be endangered in the same way as would those of neighbouring European ranchers. There are over 3000 head of cattle in Matibi No. 2 Reserve.[4]

However, the proposal to establish a game reserve in the area bounded by the southern border of Matibi II Reserve, the Lundi and Nuanetsi rivers and the border of Mozambique was renewed in 1933. The Superintendent of Natives was 'greatly in favour of the scheme', citing the tourist potential, and was not overly concerned that a total of 1,500 people would have to be evicted, as he felt they could easily be accommodated in Matibi II Reserve (Masona 1987).[5] The CNC echoed this – although he recognised that the lack of water in Matibi II restricted the population that the reserve could carry, and thought that 'those living near the border would probably move into Portuguese territory'.[6] Interestingly the CNC – the erstwhile defender of African welfare – had by this stage dropped his opposition to the game reserve on the grounds that it endangered 'native interests' but continued to oppose it because of the potential threat from 'large carnivora' to the cattle on Nuanetsi Ranch.[7]

The Minister for Commerce and Transport, R.P. Gilchrist, was very enthusiastic about the proposal on the grounds of its potential for encouraging tourism. He wrote in the *Sunday Mail* that 'the idea is that the sights of Rhodesia, which are already famed, should be approached through the greatest game sanctuary in the world' (Masona 1987). He even went as far as to anticipate contemporary attempts to establish a transboundary protected area when he wrote: 'It is possible to disclose … that the game sanctuary of Rhodesia may be a continuation of the great Union Reserve, Kruger Park, and that in addition the Portuguese will proclaim a sanctuary alongside the Rhodesian reserve' (Wolmer 2003).[8] Gilchrist had commissioned a report on the proposed game reserve from D. Townley. Despite conducting only a flying visit in which, by Townley's own admission, 'it was impossible to penetrate to the inner veld owing to lack of water and passive resistance on the part of the natives', the report took a strongly preservationist line:

> We were most impressed with the potentialities of this district as a game sanctuary. It is one of the rapidly diminishing areas in the colony within reach of the capital which

---

[4] NAZ S 138/34 1924–1934 Game: CNC to Secretary to the Premier (Native Affairs), 7 November 1932.
[5] NAZ S 1542/G1/1 Acting Superintendent of Natives to CNC 9/11/1933. The idea that game reserves could become an economic asset, by way of the tourist industry, was by 1933 beginning to gain currency (Masona 1987).
[6] NAZ S 1542/G1/1 CNC to the Minister of Commerce and Transportation, 13 November 1933.
[7] *Ibid.*
[8] *Sunday Mail*, 26 November 1933.

still contains game in quantity, and it will be a thousand pities if something is not done about it before it is too late.⁹

Townley estimated that the population of the area was 7,000, with the majority concentrated along the Chipinda-Nuanetsi road (although given the cursory nature of his examination, numbers were likely to have been much higher). But to his mind this population was 'in every way out of hand' and he took a hard line with respect to their presence in the area:

> Primarily, before even considering the possibility of making a game reserve, it will be necessary to remove the native population and transfer them elsewhere. These natives are of a most undesirable type, they do not work in Rhodesia and are not properly looked after, being apparently too far away from a Native Commissioner to be visited in person. Also they are in, or claim to be, a perpetual state of semi-starvation as the country has too little rainfall to support crops. Finally it is virtually impossible to have a game sanctuary and a native population in the same area.¹⁰

He also advanced the argument that 'moving these natives from the game reserve into the native reserve of Matibi No. 2 ... would if practicable be excellent, since it would provide an additional barrier between Nuanetsi Ranch and any possible influx of lions from the game reserve in a southerly direction'.¹¹

This report was bitterly criticised by the Assistant Native Commissioner (ANC) for Nuanetsi and the Native Commissioner for Chibi who were angered at the fact that Townley had at no point communicated with them; they felt slighted by his description of the African inhabitants as 'entirely uncontrolled', and the intimation that they never visited the area.¹² The ANC Nuanetsi responded that the water supply of Matibi No. 2 was inadequate to carry a much larger population than it already did. He agreed with Townley that 'these Natives [in the potential game reserve] are in a state of semi-starvation', but went on to argue that:

> ... unfortunately this state of affairs is not only peculiar to these Natives but also exists in No. 2 Reserve and a portion of the Nuanetsi Ranch, due mainly to low rainfall. The state of affairs will still exist if they are all moved to No. 2 Reserve, and with the possibility of relief by hunting gone on account of the establishment of the Game Reserve, they will be bound to seek relief through this office.¹³

Despite further criticism of the scheme by the Minister of Agriculture and Lands and the Chief Forest Officer (who thought it would be futile to

---

⁹ NAZ S 1532/91/2 Game 1922-1939 Vol. 2: D. Townley to Mr. Gilchrist (Minister for Commerce and Transport) 5/10/1934 – Report on proposed game reserve (Gona-re-zho). Townley was later to become the game reserve's honorary warden. Interview: Dr Colin Saunders, Malilangwe Trust 10 September 1999.
¹⁰ NAZ S 1532/91/2 Game 1922-1939 Vol. 2: D. Townley to Gilchrist.
¹¹ Ibid.
¹² NAZ S 1532/91/2 Game 1922-1939 Vol. 2: ANC Nuanetsi to NC Chibi, 21 January 1935.
¹³ NAZ S 1532/91/2 Game 1922-1939 Vol. 2: Acting ANC Nuanetsi to NC Chibi, 11 November 1934.

spend money on game protection if the area's population was as numerous as stated in Townley's report),[14] the Minister for Commerce and Transport (Gilchrist) acted on Townley's recommendation and requested that the game reserve be officially proclaimed. It was eventually formally established by Proclamation No. 3 of 20 April 1934 and was to be called the Gona-re-zhou Game Reserve (Masona 1987).[15]

Yet after the proclamation of the reserve there was no immediate eviction of its population. Echoing the ANC Nuanetsi, the CNC wrote in 1935 that:

> We have not contemplated moving the Natives who are now in the Game Reserve. Matibi No. 2 will not carry a large population. Apart from its frontages on rivers, it contains no surface water, and its soil is of poor quality. The tributaries of the Lundi and Nuanetsi, which define its boundaries, have small permanent supplies of water, only in their lower reaches: but water is an obtainable in some of them in wells at shallow depths. To develop sufficient water supplies to carry an appreciable number of Natives and their stock, would take time and the expenditure of a considerable sum of money.[16]

Before long, however, the 'administrative' advantages of having African populations concentrated in reserves, where surveillance and control was easier than when they were scattered in the bush, came to outweigh the Native Affairs Department's concerns about lack of rainfall and surface water. By 1944 the ANC Nuanetsi was to say:

> I have little sympathy with the Shangaans living in the Gona-re-zhou Game Reserve. It would be better for them, and from an administrative point of view, to move into Matibi No. 2 Reserve.[17]

In 1935 the extreme southern portion of Ndanga District, comprising the area between the Save and Runde rivers from the Chilunja hills to the Save-Runde junction, was also proclaimed as a game reserve, creating a total protected area similar to that of the present-day Gonarezhou National Park (Masona 1987; Cunliffe 1993). The reserves did not last long, however, and were deproclaimed during 1940-41 as a tsetse control hunting programme was initiated along the Save and Runde Rivers in an attempt to halt the northward and westward spread of the fly from Portuguese East Africa along the rivers into the adjacent communal and commercial farming lands (see below). A decade later, in 1950, the Save-Runde portion was again designated as a game reserve, only to be deproclaimed once more to accommodate further tsetse hunting operations (Cunliffe 1993).

---

[14] NAZ S 1532/91/2 Game 1922-1939 Vol. 2: Chief Forest Officer to Acting Secretary, Department of Agriculture and Lands, 24 November 1934.
[15] NAZ S 1532/91/2 Game 1922-1939 Vol. 2: Acting Secretary, Department of Agriculture and Lands to the Secretary to the Hon. The Prime Minister, 12 October 1934.
[16] NAZ S 1532/91/2 Game 1922-1939 Vol. 2: CNC to Acting Secretary, Department of Agriculture and Lands, 8 January 1935.
[17] NAZ S 2391/3625 Tsetse Fly, Nuanetsi. NC Nuanetsi to Provincial Native Commissioner, Fort Victoria, 25 April 1944.

District Commissioner Allan Wright

In 1953 Nuanetsi was excised from Chibi District and upgraded to full district status. In 1958 the arrival of a new District Commissioner of Nuanetsi District and self-proclaimed 'ardent conservationist', Allan Wright, marked the beginning of a concerted phase of conservationism that culminated in the proclamation of Gonarezhou National Park in 1975. At a time when the Ministry of Internal Affairs was influential and well resourced Wright managed to get them to spend large amounts on wildlife protection schemes.[18] In 1954 the bulk of the land now occupied by Gonarezhou National Park was changed in status from 'unassigned area' to become the Gonakudzingwa African Purchase Area.[19] Initially only 17 ranches of 1,700 acres each were allocated to African smallholder farmers, with a view to demarcating the remainder into 2,000-acre ranches to support more African smallholders. Wright conducted a reconnaissance survey of the area and after what he described as a 'cursory examination of topography, soils and grasses – gained from a very limited excursion', he became convinced that 'from an agricultural point of view the whole area was in the lowest category, almost wasteland' (Wright 1972: 63). Wright reveals his real reason for resisting the further development of the Gonakudzingwa African Purchase Area for the benefit of black farmers when he writes of his first panoramic view of this lowveld landscape, echoing James Stevenson-Hamilton's sentiments on first seeing the South African lowveld:

> Before me, as far as the eye could see, was the vast, empty Gonakudzingwa Purchase Area – 'empty' only in the human context for it teemed with animal life ... the great wilderness looked mysterious, haze-blue, inviting. What a heritage! What a wonderful national park this south-east corner of Rhodesia would make! (Wright 1972: 34)

Conceding that a few more farms might be fitted onto the black basalt near Chikombedzi, Wright then proceeded unilaterally to declare the whole area bounded by 'the allocated farms, the south-east railway and the Portuguese border' as a game reserve. This was to be a region where 'no shooting, hunt-

---

[18] This heralded a dramatic change in philosophy in the district. Previous Native Commissioners had been broadly 'anti-wildlife' and pro-people. In 1945, for example, the ANC for Nuanetsi wrote in desperation to the Provincial Native Commissioner in Fort Victoria: 'What is badly needed is some selected hunters to drive back the elephant which are laying waste native gardens. I am continually having visits from the Shangaans begging that something be done to check this menace, and my messenger patrols amply substantiate the great damage done. in Matibi No. 2 Reserve and on adjoining Crown Lands (Gonarezhou Forest) the Shangaans rarely have successful crops because of the low rainfall, but when the elephants flatten down the kaffir corn crops the position becomes calamitous. If natives are to progress in animal husbandry and agriculture, then this should be made possible by the elimination of all destructive wildlife from the Native Areas'. NAZ S 2391/3625 Tsetse Fly, Nuanetsi: NC Nuanetsi to Provincial Native Commissioner, Fort Victoria 25/4/1944 [9/F/44].

[19] On the history of African Purchase Areas in Zimbabwe see Cheater (1984) and Murumbedzi (1992b).

ing or camping was to take place without [Wright's] express permission' (Wright 1972: 25). By his own description he had assumed 'the mantle of unofficial game warden' and soon followed this by declaring a second and then a third *de facto* private game reserve, respectively at Manjini Pan and Malipati near the Nuanetsi River.

Far from being 'empty in the human context' there were, of course, many people living inside his new reserves and cultivating along the riverbanks. Wright assumed their continued presence could only mean that they were 'professional poachers' providing 'forward bases' for snaring parties – growing crops simply in order to attract elephants to shoot, the disadvantages of crop raiding being outweighed by the profits gained from snared meat. In his unofficial Malipati Game Reserve he banned the watering of cattle at river pools as:

> those who watered their cattle at the bridge pool did so only because they were too lazy to pump water from the boreholes in the Sengwe TTL and the driving of cattle to the river pool was a wonderful blind for snaring activities. It meant that they always had a lawful excuse for being in the big game areas ... Where there are Shangane [sic] males and wild life, there is always snaring going on *so I had to remove the Shanganes as I naturally had no desire to get rid of the wild life* [my emphasis]. (1972: 162)

This quote reveals the inherent contradiction between Wright's conservationist agenda and his role as District Commissioner. As a paternalist DC he saw his first duty as 'improving the lot of the thousands of African tribesmen who came under my care and seeing to it that no changes inimical to their long-term interests were instituted' (1972: 326). And yet in practice his way of seeing the lowveld landscape as a 'great wilderness' meant that 'naturally' wildlife had priority over people. Conservation was separate from and took priority over development.

There was one exception to this rule. When a group of people under Chief Ngwenyene were threatened with eviction during plans to expand Gonarezhou National Park, DC Wright sided with them in arguing that they should stay. His argument merits quoting at some length:

> I saw the Ngwenyene group, primitive, ultra-conservative, unspoiled Shanganes living as they had done a hundred years ago, as part and parcel of any national park scheme of the future. Tourists from overseas do not want to see dams, towns, buildings or mountains in Africa – they have a surfeit of these things at home – they do want to study wild animals and 'wild' Africans and I do not use the word 'wild' in a derogatory sense. I intend to convey a picture of all that is best in our indegenes, unspoilt by the deviousness and tarnish of so-called civilisation. Here in Gona re Zhou we had a wonderful opportunity to combine the two great attractions in a unique and beautiful setting. (1972: 329)

> ...if the presence of a group of unsophisticated Africans, who would make a wonderful tourist attraction, is considered alien to the national park concept (as distinct from a mere game reserve), then of course there can be no place for visitors themselves and their ugly rest camps, bars and restaurants. In Gona re Zhou, the object must surely

be to create a wilderness area, not as it was a thousand or even five hundred years ago but as we found it when we occupied this country nearly one hundred years ago. If there is a place for indigenous trees and plants, animals and birds, there is no reason why indigenous humans should not fit into the ecosystem, too. The presence of the Ngwenyenye people, properly controlled in the same way as all other residents of a national park must be controlled, would turn Gona re Zhou into a world-wide attraction, unique and self-contained – and a greater revenue earner. (1972: 339-340)

In order to square the presence of Africans with the vision of pristine wilderness, these Africans had to be dehumanised as another form of exotic fauna and 'managed' appropriately. This notion of suitably primitive and picturesque 'wild' Africans as potential tourist objects is echoed in contemporary 'ethnotourism' projects.[20] The quote is also interesting in that Wright reveals that there is a deliberate choice to be made about which 'wilderness' should be constructed and preserved. Wilderness, then, is not a fixed category standing 'out of time', but a political, aesthetic (and latterly economic) decision about what constitutes an appropriate landscape.

A close reading of Wright's autobiography reveals other notable tensions inherent in his way of seeing the lowveld. One such tension was between his romantic, preservationist sentiments concerning a pristine landscape with an exotic heritage of lost cities, and his more bureaucratic and technical training in land management as a District Administrator. Indeed this mirrors a more general change in emphasis in southern African conservationist thinking from romantic and paternalist notions of benevolent authority (e.g. Stevenson-Hamilton 1929) to discourses on scientifically informed management of wildlife (and later biodiversity) – implying a hard-edged, fenced landscape of artificial watering points. Wright's conservationist zeal was also blended with hard-nosed pragmatism as is evidenced by his continued 'horse-trading' over land-swap deals to add to Gonarezhou's emergent estate. His success in unilaterally establishing game reserves led to a South African company negotiating a lease with the Ministry of Internal Affairs to build a luxury lodge in Malipati game reserve. Wright's reaction to this scheme reveals a further tension between elitist and populist ways of seeing. He explains his dilemma thus:

> I certainly approved of the project but … I could not help feeling that had I still been in Nuanetsi I would have been dismayed at the thought of tourists gaping at the game animals I felt were my special charges, or a noisy hotel springing up in the deep, quiet shade of those wonderful evergreen trees which litter the Nuanetsi River's east bank at that spot. (Wright 1972: 345)

[20] See Neumann (1997) and Ranger (1999) on debates over whether Africans could be considered as part of the 'natural' environment and allowed to remain in game reserves or were alien elements to be evicted. In the 1930s, '40s and '50s the Native Reserves around-Kruger National Park in the South African lowveld were similarly advertised as a 'picturesque sort of fringe, an appropriately archaic scenic domain that formed a pleasing backdrop to a motor tour to the lowveld with the game reserve as its final destination' (Bunn 2003: 17). In this respect representations of these landscapes cannot be divorced from representations of the landscapes' inhabitants.

The populist vision won out, though, and parts of Gonarezhou came to be developed for tourists with car trails linking a network of picturesque viewing points, thatched lodges and campsites situated beside pools in the rivers or dammed water holes.[21] In 1969 the Report of the Wild Life Commission recommended that Gonarezhou should be 'elevated to the status of national park' and claimed that it 'has the undoubted potential to become one of Africa's great national parks'. In all of this, African voices were almost totally absent; they had been written out of a debate that was cast only in terms of preserving pristine wilderness or defending the productive cattle country. As Ranger puts it in the context of Matopos National Park, 'once the new Park had been created and fitted out with rest camps and picnic areas and roads the white eye triumphed over the black in "seeing" the Matopos' (Ranger 1999: 194).

African evictions

As Carruthers (1995) notes: 'In the African version of wildlife conservation history, the experience has been that game reserves are white inventions which elevate wildlife above humanity and which have served as instruments of dispossession and subjugation.' Notwithstanding Wright's early cultural tourism schemes the Ngweneyene community were soon to follow the Mapokoles, Chaukes and others and were evicted from Gonarezhou National Park. Many families forced to leave their homes were not even provided with vehicles to carry their property.[22] As well as causing the loss of riverine plots and grazing land and communities' immediate transformation into poachers, these evictions caused the separation of certain lineages from the physical basis of their identity — their ancestral land. This ancestral land, as explored in Chapter 3, was also the site for rainmaking, and the subsequent difficulties in conducting appropriate rainmaking ceremonies were blamed for ensuing droughts. The eviction of people from the Gonarezhou area into Matibi II communal area brought about an ecological and demographic inversion. Whereas previously the present Matibi II was a 'land of animals' sparsely populated by people, Gonarezhou was densely populated in part because its thicker vegetation and more varied terrain had offered better cover from Gaza raiding parties.[23] The evictions were bitterly resented, and hostility and resistance were expressed in the form of poaching, fence-cutting, snaring and so forth. African nationalists were able to exploit these grievances about land alienation and the racial

---

[21] These viewpoints were 'picturesque', in the sense described in Chapter 2, in that they met certain stylistic conventions that constituted a landscape experience (foreground and background interest, presence of water and suchlike).

[22] Interviews: Chikombedzi, 5 June 1998; W. Mavundla Chiseko by Mr Patrick Ngulube of the Department of National Archives, 5 October 1990, NAZ AOH/448.

[23] Interview: Chirhilele Ndabani, Maguwa Baloyi, Chilahlele Mahlehe, and Timothy Sambani, Chipinda Business Centre, by Paul de Jager, 11 January 1987 (de Jager 1988).

contradictions in controls on hunting, fomenting a near rebellion in the lowveld in 1965 (Wright 1972); and these covert protests fed directly into the liberation struggle of the 1970s.[24]

The tsetse challenge

Whilst the concerns of the African population remained largely ignored, the establishment of game reserves in the lowveld pitted a powerful cattle industry lobby, buttressed by veterinary science, against an increasingly internationally co-ordinated and well funded conservation lobby. The cattle lobby viewed wildlife as a threat to livestock production. Game was perceived as a reservoir for disease, a destroyer of fences, and a competitor for valuable grazing (e.g. De la Rue 1942). In particular, a 'wilderness' area was seen as a twin-headed threat to cattle in the forms of tsetse fly and foot and mouth disease (FMD). Chapter 6 has described how attempts to control FMD became (contested) attempts to control African populations and their livestock by removing whole settlements or restricting livestock movements. Similarly, contrasting visions of the lowveld landscape have been bound up with an ongoing battle with the tsetse fly and the parasite it carries. The piecemeal growth of Gonarezhou game reserve was anathema to cattle ranchers and veterinarians. It layered a perceived conflict of interest between wild animals and domestic cattle over a landscape in which European cattle and African cattle were already thought to be competing.[25] DC Wright was regularly called upon to account for his 'disease breeding ground' at ranchers' meetings (Wright 1972).

The cattle lobby was supported by those in the Ministry of Internal Affairs of a less zealously conservationist bent. Bannerman (1980: 12), following John Ford,[26] argued that 'the long-term future of the area would best be served by intensive settlement of people in certain areas ... a vast and underdeveloped game reserve can be a much poorer barrier to the spread of the fly and trypanosomiasis'. Other District Commissioners have argued for game elimination to protect African animal husbandry and agriculture.[27] The veterinary discourses and political alliances woven around tsetse control differ in certain important respects from those concerning FMD. The mainstream veterinary view of FMD was that African populations (with their attendant livestock) constituted a vector for disease spread. FMD control policies were therefore targeted at the communal areas and

---

[24] Interview: Assistant DA, Chiredzi, 15 July 1997 (cf. Ranger 1999).
[25] cf. White (1995) on sleeping sickness discourses in Northern Rhodesia.
[26] Ford (1971) argued that depopulation of areas through famine, disease or land alienation had allowed the steady spread of tsetse and wildlife reservoirs of trypanosomes into formerly cultivated areas which had been free of tsetse before the colonial period (and see MacKenzie 1988: 234; Giblin 1990).
[27] NAZ S 2391/3625 Tsetse Fly, Nuanetsi: NC Nuanetsi to Provincial Native Commissioner, Fort Victoria, 25 April 1944 [9/F/44].

were often not supported by the Native Affairs Department/Ministry of Internal Affairs who saw it as an impingement on their physical and political territory. With respect to tsetse control, however, veterinarians have tended to argue that African populations and their livestock constitute a buffer to the spread of trypanosomiasis to commercial herds and should be left alone – a position supported by the district administrators. Their interventions have instead been targeted at taming the 'wilderness' beyond – running up against the conservationists who regard this wilderness as their physical and political realm (although, as we have seen, these clear-cut differences are often blurred, in particular by the fact that one District Commissioner was an ardent conservationist).

The rinderpest epidemic of 1896-97 removed tsetse fly from the Zimbabwean lowveld for nearly 50 years. But in 1943 it was again noticed when cattle owned by the Mahenye community at the Save-Runde confluence dwindled from 650 to 150.[28] By 1953 tsetse fly had crossed the Save River and become established in the Chilunja Hills between the Save and Runde Rivers (Cunliffe 1993). The Report of the Commission of Inquiry on Human and Animal Trypanosomiasis in Southern Rhodesia of 1955 described the south-east lowveld as 'perhaps the most serious threat of all ... it is a focal point from which the fly could spread back over the whole of 20,000 or so square miles of country which it infected north of the Limpopo before the rinderpest' (Thomas 1955:15). As Allan Wright noted miserably:

> The wild animals that now roamed in ever-increasing numbers in my Valley of the Ironwoods, attracted much attention from veterinarians and from the glossinologists of our Tsetse and Trypanosomiasis Control Department. None of this attention was particularly enthusiastic and I do not think I will be contradicted if I go so far as to say that a veterinarian, or tsetse fly expert, would feel much happier if all the animals roaming in our vast Lowveld, were domesticated under his control. (1972: 250)

Wright's fears were realised with the implementation of a range of draconian measures which rapidly succeeded each other in increasingly desperate attempts to eradicate the tsetse fly from the Zimbabwean lowveld and safeguard cattle from trypanosomiasis. Initially this took the form of indiscriminate shooting of wildlife. However, in 1955 a Commission was set up as a result of public dissatisfaction with past control measures (Thomas 1955) and in 1956 John Ford was brought in from Uganda as Director of Tsetse Operations to tackle the problem without recourse to killing. As Ford himself put it, 'among a [white] community which regards hunting as a legitimate form of recreation and source of personal income, the large-scale destruction of wildlife by a government department has

---

[28] Although the ANC Nuanetsi reported in 1944 that 'Chief Ngwenyene, born in that area, assures me that to his knowledge there has never been tsetse fly, nor has he heard of their presence from the natives living on the Portuguese side of the territorial border.' NAZ S 2391/3625 Tsetse Fly, Nuanetsi. NC Nuanetsi to Provincial Native Commissioner, Fort Victoria, 25 April 1944 [9/F/44].

aroused strong feelings' (Ford 1971: 284). Despite avoiding 'game destruction policies' he was also soon unpopular with conservationists because he 'had another pet hate – trees! ... His men made an assault on every favourable forest of shady trees that they found in the main tsetse areas of Gonarezhou' (Wright 1972: 261). To conservationists such as DC Wright the bush clearance policy's 'campaign of destruction' of ironwood groves and large riverine trees caused as much upset as the earlier game slaughter: 'To [Ford], these dark groves looked ominously like ideal [tsetse fly] breeding spots. He determined to uproot these 'cancers' wherever possible and bulldozers bludgeoned hundreds of thousands of the valuable trees to the ground' (1972: 51-52). This policy, it seems, struck at the very heart of a particular way of seeing the lowveld – changing the scenery irrevocably. More recently, Pitman (1980) describes these measures as constituting a 'horrific ecological battering', and Child (1995) makes a similarly vitriolic attack on Ford.

The arrival of a new head of the Tsetse Control Branch policy (Gerald Cockbill) brought with it a new tsetse control method – that of 'controlled hunting areas' in the form of corridors or belts. These were two long strips that were totally cleared of vegetation and double fenced, then patrolled by 300 anti-tsetse staff to shoot out all the game within the corridors.[29] The Guluene-Chefu corridor ran parallel to the Rutenga-Maputo railway line, and linked up with the North-East/South-West corridor, a further fenced belt, running from the railway to the Runde river. These corridors were essentially envisaged as impermeable barriers which would halt the westward spread of the tsetse fly. They effectively cut Gonarezhou into two sections. As well as the massive corridors dividing nature and order (cf. Hoppe 1995), Gonarezhou was criss-crossed by the roads of the tsetse control teams. Thus the same strict land use boundaries that were applied outside the protected area – the complex zoned landscape of strictly delineated and subdivided boxes – had come to encroach on this supposed inviolate wilderness too.

However, as one observer wryly put it, 'naturally the fly disregards such man made rules and not reading the Government notices just treks to where blood is plentiful.'[30] By 1964 the tsetse fly was still spreading ever closer to the precious ranches and in a new attempt 'to stabilise a collapsing front and provide protection for established agriculture, particularly the rapidly developing cattle industry',[31] there was a further change of tactics in the veterinary war. In fact it was more of a reversion to the original tactic of shooting game, although with the added subtlety of focusing on eliminating six 'target species' (elephant, kudu, buffalo, bushbuck, warthog and bushpig).

---

[29] Interview: Dr Colin Saunders, Malilangwe Trust, 10 September 1999.
[30] NAZ TH 10/1/1 Blake-Thompson papers; folio 359; letter to Kenneth Radcliffe-Brown, 11 June 1958.
[31] Public Records Office (PRO) FT 3/591 Conservation problems. Southern Rhodesia: G. Cockbill to R.S.R. Fritter, Fauna Preservation Society, 22 July 1964.

Since Gonarezhou had yet to be formally gazetted as a national park the proponents of this scheme argued that this was perfectly legitimate.[32]

Ecological, as well as veterinary, science was deployed in support of this scheme. It was argued that Gonarezhou was not an 'ecological unit' and was 'used by game animals mainly as a transitory [migration] route between Mozambique and the larger rivers of the south-eastern low veldt along the Mozambique/Rhodesian border' and as such was not capable of maintaining animals 'permanently in balance with the habitat' and thus was unlikely to be successful as a nature sanctuary.[33]

The drastic culling measures posed a serious threat to the future viability of a Gonarezhou National Park and deeply scared the conservationists. The difference of opinion between conservationists and veterinarians, which had hitherto been simmering quietly, exploded into a very public row. Wright was adept at the sort of high profile campaigning and punchy, emotive lobbying that characterises the contemporary environmental movement. In a letter to Stewart Aitken-Cade (the Director of the Rhodesian Wild Life Society), he laid out his proposed tactics:

> If I could make so bold, I should like to say that I do not feel that any formal processes will make any difference to the originators of this policy. I feel that we must, by means of advertisements in the national papers such as the *Sunday Mail*, rouse the feelings and the conscience of all wild life lovers throughout the country and we must encourage each and every one of them to register a protest. ... I realise that a full-scale appeal to emotionalism, to all those in this country on our side, will be the only way to stop the slaughter. ... I am absolutely convinced that we must stir up a hornet's nest throughout the country. (Wright 1972: 314-315)

Wright put this into practice when, writing under a pseudonym in the *Sunday Mail*, he consciously echoed Grzimek's (1965) emotive call to action in East Africa: 'like the Serengeti of Tanganyika, Gona re Zhou, the place of the elephant, must not die'.[34] This was followed by an article in the *New York Times* which briefly drew the world's attention to Gonarezhou's plight and international conservation organisations such as IUCN, WWF, US National Parks Association, the Fauna Preservation Society, and the Rhinoceros Group joined the fray in campaigning to 'save' Gonarezhou.[35] Their lobbying campaign became increasingly shrill as the game cull exercise was portrayed as the 'thin end of the wedge aimed eventually at all game reserves and national parks thus establishing control of all game by the

---

[32] PRO FT 3/591 Conservation problems. Southern Rhodesia: P. Gordon Deedes (Chairman NRB) to Anthony Wayne Smith, President, National Parks Association, USA, 21 July 1967.
[33] PRO FT 3/591 Conservation problems. Southern Rhodesia: P.E. Glover to Dr M. Newman, IUCN, 22 February 1965. Interestingly, similar 'ecological unit' arguments are today being used to justify the incorporation of Gonarezhou into a transboundary protected area also encompassing contiguous parts of Mozambique and South Africa (see below).
[34] *Sunday Mail*, 22 March 1964.
[35] *IUCN Bulletin*, Oct/Dec 1964, p. 2.

agricultural interests',[36] and there were further accusations that the policy stemmed from fears within the cattle industry of an economic challenge from the emerging game ranching industry. Warming to the theme, the *Sunday Mail* pronounced that 'any government which can tolerate the implementation of a barbaric campaign like this is neither civilised nor responsible.'[37]

Eventually, insecticide spraying drove 'the fly' back into Mozambique. Hunting was halted in December 1970. Estimates of the number of animals killed during the whole tsetse-fly control hunting period range from 12,738 (Cunliffe 1993) to 55,015 (Pitman 1980). The intensive lobbying by the conservationists did, however, have a lasting effect. Gonarezhou was proclaimed a fully-fledged National Park in 1975.

Gonarezhou National Park after Independence: Wars, drought and political intrigue

During the liberation war of the 1970s the newly established national park became a militarised space over which regular skirmishes were fought. By 1976 the lowveld had become 'the new and bitterly-contested 'sharp-end' of the war' (Godwin and Hancock 1997: 156). Tourists were barred from the park and a permanent encampment of Rhodesian soldiers attempted to patrol guerrilla 'infiltration routes' from Mozambique, and scattered landmines along the border. Guerrillas and those avoiding coerced resettlement in the 'protected villages' hid from patrol planes in Gonarezhou's ironwood thickets. The Rhodesian soldiers burnt out large areas of bush to remove cover and closed down artificial watering points; cattle were left to wander freely inside and outside the park and suffered predation from wildlife, guerrillas and Rhodesian soldiers. This period saw the return of a discourse on the lowveld landscape that had not been heard since the era of the blackbirders of Crooks' Corner nearly 50 years earlier. Again the lowveld – and Gonarezhou National Park in particular – came to be described as a savage land of desperados and dissidents: a wild place with similarly wild and ungoverned inhabitants, hiding on the margins from the state's authority and making occasional incursions from their remote lair (Ford 1971; Ellis 1994).

With Independence came a government formed of former guerrillas who had been opposed to colonial notions of conservation and had used the grievances of land alienation for parks and racist 'poaching' legislation to recruit people to the nationalist cause. But much to the surprise and chagrin of communities bordering Gonarezhou, who had hoped for the return of ancestral lands, the pristine wilderness vision survived undimmed.

---

[36] PRO FT 3/591 Conservation problems. Southern Rhodesia: A. Mossman, Secretary, Game Ranchers Association, to Sec Gen, IUCN, 1 March 1964.

[37] *Sunday Mail*, 1 March 1964. This sentiment was, of course, the subtext of much reporting in the independent and international press of the poaching accompanying the farm invasions in the conservancies and ranches of the lowveld in 2000 (see Chapter 8).

The colonial commitment to maintaining national parks in their 'untouched' state endured, and in some cases former Rhodesian soldiers became Parks Department staff. The result of all this was that the National Parks authorities were bitterly resented by local communities in the lowveld. When, for example, the DNPWLM proposed a land transfer in 1983 – to incorporate the Chipinda Pools area of Matibi II into the park in return for excising an area from the park along the Mazvikote River – there was deep-rooted hostility and resistance. The Gonarezhou National Park resident ecologist commented that:

> The tribespeople concerned stated that, if National Parks were not involved in this exchange, then they would have no hesitation in leaving the Chipinda Pools area at the request of the DA. They went so far as to indicate their willingness to move, provided the Chipinda Pools area would be taken over by the District Council and not by National Parks. ... The DA used every possible means in an effort to persuade the people to move but it was clear that the underlying feeling was 'If it's National Parks, then we are not interested'. This hostility is probably understandable when one considers the persistent problems of poaching, cattle encroachment and destruction of the crops by hippo and elephant. I doubt that there is a single family in the Chipinda Pools area that has not had, at one time or another, a member apprehended for contravention of the Parks and Wildlife Act. Furthermore the forced eviction of people from the Lower Lundi when the Park was gazetted is still a very sore point.[38]

Hostility was magnified by the apparently wasteful culling of over 2,000 elephants by DNPLWM at the same time as coercive controls on poaching were being enforced. This hostility manifested itself in a big increase in poaching (aided by the relative availability, post-war, of guns), fishing, deliberate veld burning, poach grazing, wire-cutting, and wood and thatching-grass gathering in the national park (as was happening on the ranches bordering the communal areas to the west at the same time). Local narratives celebrated the notorious activities of Shadrack the poacher – a folk hero who is estimated to have killed 20-30 large elephant bulls each year for 15 years. The DNPWLM, in turn, stepped up raids and arrests of poachers. In one raid in Mahenye in 1982, 81 arrests were made and ivory, skins, and traps recovered from many houses (Zimbabwe Trust 1990).

Not long after Independence, Gonarezhou was again heavily militarised as the stage for intense army and guerrilla activity. This time the rebels were the MNR/Renamo from Mozambique. As was the case during the liberation war, Gonarezhou came to be perceived as a mysterious and forbidden place – it was once more a land of desperados and dissidents.[39] Between 1987 and 1990 the park was again closed to Zimbabwean visitors (and until 1994 to foreign tourists), and became a 'frozen zone' under the command

---

[38] MRC LAN 1/16 Letter: G.J. Sharp (ecologist) to The Director of National Parks and Wild Life Management, re: Boundary dispute – Matibi II Communal Land, 28 March 1983.

[39] Gonarezhou's reputation as a fearsome lair for dissidents bizarrely came to the fore again in early 2001 when the government security services allegedly rounded up opposition MDC supporters and dumped them inside the national park. *Daily News*, 10 January 2001.

of the Zimbabwean army (ZNA). This was a particularly murky and contentious period in Gonarezhou's history. The park became a haven for large-scale commercial poaching of elephant and rhinoceros as well as smuggling. The 'elephant killing field' was principally attributed to the actions of the 'bands of Renamo guerrillas [who] roamed the park with AK47 and G-3 automatic rifles'[40] although there were also allegations and rumours surrounding South African army and ZNA involvement (with the complicity of wildlife officials) in large-scale ivory poaching (Environmental Investigation Agency 1992; Ellis 1994; Duffy 1999).[41]

There was to be an even more dramatic impact on the fortunes of Gonarezhou National Park in the shape of the 1991-92 drought, which caused the death of much wildlife and made headlines around the world.[42] This ecological crisis was to have political reverberations when the plight of the park's drought-stricken fauna – and in particular the emotive and highly visible elephant – caught the attention of local and international conservationists. The resulting 'Save Our Wildlife Heritage Campaign', supported by GTZ, the US Department of Fisheries and Wildlife and various NGOs, included a dramatic elephant rescue campaign involving the capture and translocation of complete breeding herds to private game ranches and conservancies in the lowveld and further afield, including South Africa. This was to become highly controversial and expose the racialised politics of wildlife management, as nationalist elements within ZANU(PF) perceived the white warden of the park to be transferring state assets into the hands of white farmers. An enquiry was launched to establish whether elephants had been illegally exported and funds expropriated (Duffy 2000). The controversy exposed the existence of bitterly opposed factions within the DNPWLM and, as it played out, the Director and two senior officials of the department were sacked.

Wars, mines, drought, poaching, politics, and remoteness conspired to keep tourists away from Gonarezhou National Park and fostered a generally negative image of the park. An article in *The Herald* entitled 'Wildlife falls into oblivion' pointed out that 'for years, the country's second largest wildlife sanctuary has been nothing more than a demarcation on the map'.[43] Gonarezhou has not made a significant impression on Zimbabwe's tourism sector and by the 1990s the DNPWLM generally was facing financial collapse, low morale and allegations of corruption, patronage and in-fighting.[44]

[40] 'Wilderness of Myth: Gonarezhou National Park', in *Impressions of Africa* 4 (4). In 1984, for example, the Warden at Mabalauta reported 25 elephants lost to ivory poaching with automatic weapons (Phil Palmer, in *The Hartebeest* 1984, no. 16); and the DNPWLM record the illegal hunting of 896 elephant between 1969 and 1993.

[41] A Grenada Television documentary, *A Place of Skulls*, exposed the clandestine ivory poaching activities of a number of high-ranking South African army officers.

[42] For example: Richard Boston, 'A country dying of thirst', *The Guardian*, 2 September 1992.

[43] Nelson Chenga 'Gonarezhou National Park fails to attract tourists' *The Herald*, 30 December 1998.

[44] Interviews: Senior Ranger and Warden, Mabalauta, Gonarezhou National Park, 11 August 1999.

In the face of this seemingly terminal decline, there were occasional arguments for radical reform such as 'the re-classification of the park into a multi-use game management area on a parastatal or profit motivated basis with more direct benefits to the neighbouring communal lands'.[45] Whilst any attempts at reclassifying Gonarezhou have been stridently resisted, the profit-driven ethos is one that has been increasingly embraced. More broadly, the national park has come to be envisaged as having an important role as 'a catalyst for socioeconomic development in the lowveld, thereby improving livelihoods of people in an impoverished area' (DNPWLM 1998: 46). This reflects a new philosophy – conservation as development. It is markedly different from DC Wright's elitist concerns with preserving game for his own aesthetic pleasure and his distrust of 'progress'. Conservation now encompassed economic concerns – and protected areas such as Gonarezhou should be seen to be making money. It was now potentially economically, as well as ecologically, an integral part of the region.

Yet the DNPWLM in general, and Gonarezhou National Park in particular, was still perceived as underfunded, mismanaged, and deteriorating.[46] In 1998 Gonarezhou was to receive a windfall in the form of the World Bank Global Environmental Facility (GEF).[47] Funding of US$67.5 million was approved for the 'Zimbabwe Park Rehabilitation and Conservation Project'. This money was targeted particularly at 'strengthening the institutional and organisational capacity' of the DNPWLM. The GEF component also committed US$5 million specifically to improve biodiversity conservation and management in Gonarezhou National Park and the surrounding area. Key features of this project are described as: 'protection of adequate range for mobile wildlife; protection of vegetation from destruction by fire and other impacts created by humans; protection of water resources; re-establishment of migration corridors; protection of wildlife from illegal killing; and minimisation of conflict between wildlife and agriculture or other land uses outside the park.'[48] What this meant in practice was the provision of vehicles and computers, plans (as yet unfulfilled) for electrification, and rehabilitation of the road network, water supplies and staff accommodation (Wolmer 2003).[49]

---

[45] Phil Palmer, *The Hartebeest* 1984, no. 16. As one particularly radical commentator put it to me 'parks can only survive by being privatised ... [you should] leave security in the hands of parks and privatise everything else'. Interview: Director, Wildlife Management Services, Triangle, 3 November 1999.
[46] See, for example, Gonarezhou National Park Management Plan (DNPWLM 1998).
[47] This fund was established after the 1992 Rio Summit to provide finance for environmental projects. It was the subject of much debate. Broadly speaking, as Duffy points out, 'developing states wanted GEF to be controlled by United Nations Environment Programme (UNEP), while the Western states were keen to see it in World Bank hands. After much wrangling GEF was placed under the auspices of the World Bank' (Duffy 2000: 136).
[48] The World Bank Group Press Release, 2 June 1998, No. 98/1791/AFR.
[49] An EU funded de-mining project was also initiated along the Mozambican border but all donor-funded projects were put on hold in the post-2000 Zimbabwean government-

Attempts to rehabilitate Gonarezhou National Park typify the seemingly contradictory attempt to manufacture wilderness in order to market the lowveld as a tourist destination. This has been particularly concerned with two aims: selling 'wilderness quality' and establishing a regional 'wildlife landscape'. The notion of a wildlife landscape is one I will examine in more detail below. Given Gonarezhou's turbulent history (of anti-tsetse operations, wars and drought) there are relatively few animals in the park and its promoters have therefore had to look elsewhere for its 'comparative advantage'. A read through the guest books at Swimiwuni Rest Camp in the park reveals that time and again it is its 'wilderness quality' that guests (for the most part white South Africans and Zimbabweans) are impressed by: 'it is so wild and remote', 'it felt as if we had a whole section of the country to ourselves', 'keep your wilderness and remoteness'. This is also a wilderness that visitors feel must be protected from 'unnecessary development' and commercialism and remain 'unspoilt'. This has been recognised by consultants such as Schuerholz and Moore (1993), who define the 'product' which Gonarezhou and its 'support zone' have to offer as a 'wilderness experience' (see also Robford Tourism 1999). As a result, the park's management plan states that 'the park's remoteness and rugged, harsh environment are special qualities that will be sustained for park visitor experiences' (DNPWLM 1998: v). This is supported by a survey conducted for the UK Department for International Development which concluded that: 'being in a wild landscape' ranked as more important than seeing wildlife by visitors to Gonarezhou surveyed and as the most important activity (Goodwin et al. 1997). There are various interpretations of what precisely this wilderness experience or wilderness quality should consist of. A selection from my interviews includes the following:

> Tourists are not into 'faux-ethnic' cultural tourism. They are not in the lowveld because of the Shangaans. They are there because it is a wild, remote area [they are] in search of a wilderness experience. The real primary attraction is wilderness not wildlife – the area is unable to attract people on the basis of wildlife as it has much less than the nearby Kruger National Park. But it can create the illusion of emptiness – a Wild Africa feeling.[50]

> Land has got to have wilderness quality – a feeling of space, that you are away from technology – the Garden of Eden feeling. You can create that with aesthetically pleasing roads, hidden phone lines and so on.[51]

Where this experience does involve people 'the product the tourists would like to see is the past, rather than new shiny houses'.[52] But in essence as one interviewee astutely put it, 'wilderness quality is what the market believes it is'.[53] This quest for wilderness quality is particularly ironic as Gonarezhou

---

[49 (cont.)] donor political impasse.
[50] Interview: Director, SAFIRE, Harare, 25 June 1999.
[51] Interview: Rancher, Chiredzi, 15 August 1999. [52] Interview: Malilangwe Trust, 13 August 1999.
[53] Interview: Dr Colin Saunders, Malilangwe Trust, 10 September 1999. This interviewee also

National Park was, as I have described, until the late 1960s, inhabited and farmed, and is still visibly 'scarred' by the fading impression of homesteads and fields as well as the corridors and tracks of tsetse fly control teams. However, as all the quotes above reveal, there is a recognition by those promoting tourism in the lowveld that this wilderness is as much artifice as 'natural' and has to be actively and self-consciously created in its own image, and then managed, in order to attract tourists. 'Nature' has been progressively commodified.[54]

Commercial wildlife management in the lowveld

This manufacturing and marketing of wilderness is particularly evident on private game ranches and in the so-called conservancies of the lowveld, where former cattle ranchers have gone to new lengths in the creation of a wilderness spectacle. A relatively new – and inherently political – dimension to the long-running 'cattle versus wildlife' dispute over appropriate land use (and ways of seeing landscape) is the large-scale move by former cattle ranchers in the lowveld into game ranching, either exclusively or alongside cattle. Before 1960 the presence of wildlife was generally considered detrimental to cattle ranching. The Department of Veterinary Services, the Department for Conservation and Extension and the National Farmers Union were universally advocating the elimination or considerable reduction of game as 'one cannot ranch in a zoo' (Child 1988).[55] As I have described, game was perceived as a reservoir for disease, and a competitor for scarce grazing. Also the danger of predation necessitated the kraaling of stock at night, leading to loss of animal condition and vegetation damage at certain concentration points. Wildlife was hunted or indirectly destroyed through reduced availability of grazing land and access to waterholes due to fencing (Child 1988). However, in the 1960s some influential studies by Fulbright scholars[56] on game meat production, and a change in legislation encouraging landowners to use their wildlife for profit, encouraged a steady growth in game meat and hide production, pioneered in the lowveld on Buffalo Range and Lone Star ranches. By 1964 there were more than 1.5 million acres registered for commercial wildlife production in the south and south-east lowveld (Gwanda, Beitbridge, Nuanetsi, Chibi, Victoria, Ndanga and Bikita districts) (Roth 1964). The industry began to stagnate because of difficulty in marketing game meat due to stringent veterinary

---

[53] (cont.) observed that a wilderness landscape is not always more aesthetically pleasing: 'If you do not manage big game areas carefully you will end up with three things: elephant, impala and gulleys.'

[54] This equates with the UK experience of the 'heritage industry' and the deliberate manufacture of appropriately historical landscapes (Hewison 1987).

[55] See for example De la Rue (1942); 'Zebras threaten cattle lands', *Bulawayo Chronicle* 13 October 1966.

[56] Such as Dasmann (1961).

and food-hygiene controls, and pressure from the powerful and partially subsidised beef industry. But the fortunes of the emergent industry rose in the 1970s with the lucrative development of safari hunting (Child 1988), and in 1975 the Parks and Wildlife Act, which decentralised 'appropriate authority' over wildlife to the landowner, was another major catalyst for private sector wildlife conservation – fundamentally changing the attitudes of many ranchers who now perceived wildlife as an economic asset.

The last twenty-five years have seen the accelerated development of the wildlife industry in the lowveld. This was underpinned by two further game products: live game sales (which after 1995 were severely restricted) and 'non-consumptive utilisation' (i.e. tourism).[57] Other contributory factors behind the increasing popularity of game ranching include: the relative decline in beef prices; the difficulties faced in restocking cattle after the devastating 1991-92 drought; and the collapse of the Zimbabwe dollar (as 'like roses or tobacco, game sticks to the US dollar').[58] The fortunes of the wildlife industry have also been reflected and encouraged by various upbeat and highly favourable comparisons of the industry's prospects with those of beef production (e.g. Child 1988; Jansen et al. 1992; Bond 1993; Price Waterhouse 1994). By 1994 wildlife ranching was one of the fastest growing new uses of commercial farming land in Zimbabwe, with 20.7 per cent of white commercial farms under some sort of wildlife utilisation (Hill 1994). Cattle ranching – which had previously been the officially recommended land use in 'Natural Region 5', including the lowveld – was now being cast as ecologically destructive in this 'fragile' environment. Over-grazing of cattle was held to be leading to soil erosion and loss of perennial grasses – mixed game would be far more ecologically appropriate. The pristine wilderness vision was gaining ground at the expense of cattle country.

The game ranching trend reached its apogee with the development of conservancies in the late 1980s and early 1990s. These are amalgamations of privately owned ranches devoted to wildlife production (both consumptive – game cropping and safari hunting, and non-consumptive – photographic tourism) with internal fences removed. They emerged as a result of negotiations between neighbouring ranchers without the formal involvement or approval of government authorities and have no statutory definition. The south-east lowveld came to be particularly associated with the conservancy concept because of the existence of Zimbabwe's first three conservancies in the region. In the early 1990s a donor-funded and DNPWLM-supported black rhino conservation scheme provided the catalyst for this new trend for large-scale natural resource management on commercial property. Rhinos at threat from poaching in the Zambezi valley were translocated to the relative safety of private land in the Save Valley, Chiredzi River and Bubiana 'rhino conservancies' in order to establish 'secure nuclei' as an

---

[57] Tourism was encouraged by the regional stability emanating from post-apartheid South Africa and post-conflict Mozambique.
[58] Interview: Rancher, Chiredzi, 15 July 1999.

Map 7.1 The Save Valley Conservancy and surrounding districts

'insurance policy' against their being poached out on the DNPWLM's estate (du Toit 1998).[59] Save Valley Conservancy subsequently made a complete land use transition from cattle ranching to wildlife operations. Comprising 24 properties and with a total area of 3,387 km^2 it has become the largest private wildlife reserve in Africa (du Toit 1998) (see Map 7.1). The consolidation of the conservancies was encouraged by the very severe drought of 1991-92, and their relative irreversibility (it became difficult to revert to cattle once FMD-carrying buffalo, fence-destroying elephant and wilderness-seeking hunters and tourists had been introduced). The new arrangements had various attractions for the commercial farmers: wildlife was less labour-intensive; it was supported by donor funding;[60] it allowed

---

[59] Conservancies had first been developed in apartheid-era South Africa in the 1970s (Wels 2000: 151).
[60] The Beit Trust provided a considerable grant for electrified game fencing around Save Valley and Bubiana Conservancies, an anti-poaching unit and a 'Community Liaison Officer'. This grant was conditional on the conservancy matching it with expenditure on

hunting and tourism operations on a larger scale than on individual ranches without having to negotiate with Rural District Councils or the DNPWLM for hunting concessions and access fees; and it allowed pooling of anti-poaching operations with shared game guards. Since the establishment of the conservancy, new land owners buying into the scheme have been specifically interested in hunting or tourism and not cattle.

Attempts to manufacture 'wilderness quality' are particularly evident in conservancies and game ranches where – as on former (and sometimes current) cattle ranches – cattle troughs, dip tanks, water pipelines, fence lines, paddocks and other legacies of the industry are sometimes all too obviously visible to tourists and trophy hunters. One dilemma is that artificial water supplies are necessary if ranches want to stock large numbers of game all the year round, leading one game ranch to invest much time and effort in transforming artificial water supplies from dams and boreholes 'to more aesthetically pleasing, more 'natural' looking pans'.[61] As Ranger describes in the case of tourist lodges on ranches adjoining Matopos National Park, 'now that scenery is for sale … even though all these farms were originally intended for the exploitation rather than the preservation of the environment, these safari camps enthusiastically represent the Matopos [landscape] as "nature"' (1999: 271). Alongside their newly pristine wild landscapes the conservancy ranchers and other operators need to stock up on the appropriate fauna and reintroduce previously hunted-out species. As one advisor to the SVC put it, '… we need to buy in wildlife *to create the spectacle that tourists want to see*' [my emphasis].[62] And 'to return to a natural system requires capital investment' (Goodwin *et al.* 1997: 245). This is most spectacularly illustrated by the spending spree of the Malilangwe Trust, a former lowveld cattle ranch turned exclusive ecotourism and 'low-key and high quality' bow hunting development bankrolled by an American billionaire. The estate is, relative to other tourism concerns in the lowveld, hugely well-endowed.[63] It incorporates a new US$5.5 million 'flagship' luxury safari lodge, an older refurbished lodge, an 'artists' village', an environmental education facility and a helicopter landing pad. It describes its vision as one where habitats and wildlife populations are restored and maintained in their 'former pristine state' and provides a spectacle that supports top-quality tourism. To this end 1998 saw the import and stocking on the ranch of

---

[60 (cont.)] restocking (du Toit 1998). The conservancies have also received powerful ideological and financial backing from influential international conservation organisations such as WWF and IUCN (Wels 2000).

[61] Malilangwe Trust, Annual Report (1999: 2).   [62] Interview: Harare, 14 June 1999.

[63] Malilangwe Trust is a game ranch rather than a conservancy as it consists of only one former cattle ranch and not an amalgamation of ranches. As of March 2000 the Trust had received US$21.2 million in donor funding (Annual Report 1999). Malilangwe Trust management are keen to stress that it is not owned by an American – merely funded by private American money. There are similar examples of northern millionaires buying up and manufacturing wilderness playgrounds in Mozambique and South Africa (such as Richard Branson's Ulusaba Game Reserve bordering Kruger National Park).

28 black rhinoceros from Kwazulu-Natal, for US$1 million, in 'what is believed to be the biggest ever single private transaction involving wildlife'; 33 roan antelope from Malawi; and 20 Lichenstein's hartebeest.[64]

The SVC has also received a US$1 million loan from the International Finance Corporation (IFC) for 'restocking' purposes. This was underwritten by the Delta Corporation[65] which had significant investments in the SVC in the shape of its subsidiary Zimbabwe Sun, which operates two tourist lodges in the conservancy. Large amounts of money and significant multinational investments have thus been marshalled to the cause of manufacturing a wilderness landscape in the lowveld.

Despite their success in the lowveld in terms of land coverage game ranching and the conservancies have always been highly controversial. One of the first ventures into a form of game ranching in the lowveld occurred in the 1950s when the ailing Nuanetsi Ranch sold off much of its land to South African real estate companies who carved it into dozens of smaller plots which were advertised in the South African press as 'shooting boxes'. This was at the time of the copper belt boom and many South Africans bought them sight unseen as private hunting grounds. This was vehemently disapproved of by Allan Wright and other conservationists. Wright (1972) also notes how in the 1950s some cattle ranchers strategically marshalled themselves under the 'soiled banner of game ranching' in order to get permits from the Department of Wild Life to destroy game.

Game ranching came under even more bitter and sustained conflict from many in the cattle ranching lobby. The risk of veterinary disease was, as we have seen, a very powerful narrative. Particularly contentious was the presence of 'dirty buffalo' (thought to be FMD carriers) on ranches. Although there were, and still are, major disagreements over the precise science of FMD contamination, the cattle lobby and veterinarians have always squarely blamed the buffalo (alongside African cattle – see Chapter 6) with the resulting policy of separating all buffalo from cattle.[66] This meant fencing off the Gonarezhou and Limpopo area and eliminating all buffalo on commercial ranches. One game rancher claims to have 'saved buffalo for the lowveld' by taking the Ministers of Land and Internal Affairs to court to

---

[64] Malilangwe Trust Annual Report 1998. By 1999 Malilangwe Trust had spent US$2.4 million on introductions ranging from 233 buffalo to 15 white rhinoceros. This is particularly ironic when the former owner of the ranch admits to shooting over 200 lion and leopard in his first decade on the ranch. Interview: Retired rancher, Malilangwe, 10 September 1999. In the SVC there have frequently been disputes among ranchers about which animals should be introduced and in what numbers (particularly regarding large predators).

[65] Zimbabwe's third largest company with interests in drinks, retailing and tourism (Wels 2000).

[66] As also became clear in the FMD outbreak in the UK in 2001, the science of FMD transmission is deeply disputed and politicised. In Zimbabwe the 'wildlife lobby' argue that DNA fingerprinting techniques prove that some outbreaks in Zimbabwe originated from carrier cattle rather than game (Griffen 1999).

protect the buffalo on his land. He negotiated a deal whereby he was fenced into the dirty buffalo area and abandoned cattle entirely, although by his own admission he 'became a pariah among fellow cattle ranchers' in the process.[67] The eradication of buffalo outside the fence has had severe implications for the profitability of game ranching. Buffalo, alongside elephant, lion and leopard, as a dangerous and prestigious trophy, commands much larger fees from hunters than plains game but, after their eradication, they were denied to game ranchers. 'Clean buffalo' (FMD-free) are now available but prohibitively expensive to most game ranchers. After drawn-out negotiations the Department of Veterinary Services (DVS) was persuaded to relax FMD control restrictions in the Save Valley Conservancy and allow the reintroduction of buffalo on condition that ranchers disposed of any cattle they still owned and that stringent requirements for electrified perimeter double fencing were enforced (a decision which has caused conflicts on various fronts – see below) (Anderson and Foggin 1994). However, the DVS still views the conservancies with suspicion and many vets are angered that 'now we have dirty buffalo right in the middle of the country'.[68] There is a long history of rows between the conservancy, the Cattle Producer Associations, vets, and surrounding communal area farmers,[69] and even between ranch owners, and these are inevitably politicised. A rancher in Mwenezi admitted that 'game causes big bust ups at farmers meetings'.[70] There have been bitter disputes between game and cattle people and between those who are not utilising game and those who are perceived to be overutilising it – leading to the frantic erection of fences between properties to prevent game moving off people's land (an interesting reversal of the conservancy concept).[71] After the farm invasions in 2000 – with sensitivities raised by the UK FMD outbreak – there was heightened concern that the breaching of the veterinary fence and the driving of communal area cattle into the SVC would lead to a disease outbreak.[72]

[67] Interview: Retired rancher, Malilangwe, 10 September 1999.
[68] Interview: Provincial Veterinary Officer, Masvingo, 15 November 1999. Save Valley Conservancy was blamed for FMD outbreaks in 1997 and 1999. Interview: Regional Chairman CFU, Masvingo Province, 8 September 1999.
[69] Farmers in Matsai communal area in Bikita District, bordering the conservancy, were perplexed and angered that their cattle – rather than conservancy buffalo – were slaughtered during a FMD outbreak in 1997. The slaughter of cattle trained as draught animals was particularly resisted (Wels 2000).
[70] Interview: Rancher, Mwenezi, 12 August 1999.
[71] Interview: CFU Regional Executive, Masvingo Province, 7 August 1999. This is overlaid over a certain amount of tension between English- and Afrikaans-speaking ranchers (the Masvingo Province CFU executives have been mainly English although in Mwenezi District they constitute a minority). Afrikaners are perceived by some English-speaking ranchers as 'racialistic' and backward, a closed community who 'culturally like to hunt' – this contributes to the storminess of farmers meetings. Afrikaners also tend to be perceived by the government as foreigners with closer allegiances to South Africa than Zimbabwe.
[72] See *Daily News*, 11 August 2000 'Farm invasions to cut country's beef exports'; *Zimbabwe Standard*, 22 October, 2000 'Imminent outbreak of foot and mouth disease'; *Zimbabwe*

The presence of buffalo is thus symbolic of the deeply political and contested process of manufacturing wilderness in the lowveld.

Although initially supported by the DNPWLM the conservancies have since also been contested and hindered by factions within the department. This is due to a complex interplay of economic and political factors. After World Bank-driven reforms of the DNPWLM in the 1990s gave the department a newly commercial focus, the conservancies came to be viewed by some as direct competitors and as being counterproductive to the department's own commercial interests.[73] Faction fighting within the department – set in the context of Zimbabwe's fraught racial politics – and the controversy surrounding the denunciation of the translocation of elephants from Gonarezhou to Save Valley Conservancy during the 1991-92 drought as economic sabotage and the squandering of 'state assets' (du Toit 1998), were other reasons for this antipathy (see above). The DNPWLM has done much to frustrate game ranching enterprises by increasing regulations and bureaucracy surrounding the capture and sale of live game. Live game exports were banned entirely in 1995 and very little domestic capture and sale is permitted.[74] The only available buffalo to stock the conservancies are found on the DNPWLM estate and no sales of buffalo have been permitted. As one person involved in game translocation sees it, 'National Parks would rather let game starve than go into a conservancy'.[75] The inability of the conservancies to purchase buffalo from the DNPWLM has been a major setback for hunting revenues – and has put them in a double bind as they are unable to run cattle alongside their few re-introduced buffalo but must provide expensive veterinary cordons.[76] On the other hand, Duffy (2000) sees the conservationist wing of the Parks Department as tacitly supporting privatised conservation in an attempt to wrest control over wildlife from corrupt government officials. Some commercial farmers describe the conservancies as inevitably replacing the role that national parks are currently playing – leading a *de facto* privatisation of much of the region's wildlife estate – although still drawing on Gonarezhou National Park as part of the 'lowveld package'.[77] In this case it is not the pristine wilderness vision itself that is contested, but state and private sector actors are fighting over who gets to represent the landscape in this way and garner the potential proceeds.

The pristine wilderness vision has, however, run up against an alternative

---

[72] (cont.) *Independent*, 27 October 2000, 'Zim faces removal from EU beef protocol'.
[73] *The Herald*, 7 July 1996; Wels (2000).
[74] DNPWLM's strict controls on the movement and sales of game echo the Department of Veterinary Service's control of cattle movement and sales.
[75] Interview: Director, Wildlife Management Services, Triangle, 3 November 1999. On the plus side for Save Valley Conservancy the relative lack of predators has allowed rare wild dog packs to establish themselves unassisted and these have proved to be a major tourist pull.
[76] Some of the lowveld-based safari companies circumvent the lack of dangerous large game for hunting by also operating hunting concessions in the Zambezi Valley.
[77] Interview: CFU Regional Executive, Masvingo Province, 7 August 1999.

way of seeing the lowveld landscape, one rooted in contrasting political priorities. The conservancies have been politically controversial because they encapsulate the volatile Zimbabwean land issue in microcosm. Groups of white commercial farmers are building a continuous fence between themselves and the communal area farmers, creating an island with low population densities and a rich habitat surrounded by densely populated areas (Goodwin *et al.* 1997). In this light, rather than being portrayed as the most economically lucrative and environmentally sustainable form of land use in the lowveld (Price Waterhouse 1994), they have been seen by some as 'de-development, economic sabotage, a demonstration of white luxury – indulging their whims by turning land into large game parks'.[78] In this reading, wildlife conservation in conservancies is more self-indulgence by white farmers than a properly productive land use; they represent and reinforce Zimbabwe's existing racially unequal distribution of land and money. The stark visibility in the landscape of electrified veterinary fencing compounds the controversy – symbolically dividing nature and culture and 'writing whites' power in lines' on the landscape (Metcalfe 1996; Wels 2000: 258). There is a key difference between the nature of the boundaries between conservancies and communal areas and national parks and communal areas in this regard. The conservancies (in particular the SVC) – notwithstanding their proposed revenue-sharing projects (below) – are strictly hard-edged, with electrified double fences patrolled by well-organised and armed game guards (until the farm invasions of 2000 dramatically changed the scenario). Gonarezhou National Park's boundary has, on the other hand, *de jure* and *de facto* become softer as communities are legitimately able to benefit from animals that stray outside (via CAMPFIRE – see below). Also, since the fence is non-electrified, poorly maintained and in some places simply non-existent, and the park rangers thin on the ground, crossing the fence to poach, or collect thatching grass, firewood or building poles has tended to be relatively easier than in the conservancies.

The conservancies are also are perceived as attempts by large-scale farmers to 'hide and privatise wildlife',[79] thereby challenging the state's control over wildlife and exploiting a 'national heritage'. In the mid-1990s the Minister of Environment and Tourism pledged to curb the 'unplanned and uncontrolled mushrooming' of private conservancies in areas suited to subsistence farming and commercial agriculture in order to prevent them 'threatening food security',[80] and was at pains to emphasise that:

> Government will not allow the privatisation of wildlife resources through the back door, that is, through unplanned and uncontrolled private conservancies. We are fully aware of such Machiavellian plots to privatise wildlife resources from Kenya to South Africa.[81]

---

[78] Interview: International conservation organisation member of staff, Harare, 14 June 1999.
[79] Chiredzi Rural District Council – Master Plan 1997.
[80] Minister for Environment and Tourism (Chen Chimutengwende) in *Hansard*, 14 February 1996, 3967-3971.
[81] Address to staff seminar on private conservancies and game ranches and the conditions for

This relates to a broader suspicion of the highly visible white-controlled safari hunting and tourism industries which are accused of channelling profits into the pockets of very few, or out of the country, with little or no benefit going to Zimbabwe or local communities.[82] This has been reflected in attempts to levy, tax and control the industry (such as the closure of foreign-exchange accounts).[83] There has long been talk of 'indigenising' the wildlife industry[84] which has often been perceived – particularly by whites and the international community – as potential cronyism and lacking transparency (and as conflicting with resettlement aims). It is with respect to resettlement that the government has had the greatest current and potential impact on the lowveld conservancies and game ranches. Under the terms of the 1992 Land Acquisition Act the government can compulsorily purchase land that it defines as derelict or under-utilised. This cuts to the core of whether wildlife production is considered by the government as a politically or economically legitimate form of land use on the lowveld ranches, a question that will be returned to in Chapter 8. Many white game ranchers perceived their properties as particularly vulnerable to designation for resettlement on this score: 'with game it looks like you are doing nothing, [that] it is not profitable farming, so they are going to take the land'.[85] This logic encouraged one Mwenezi bow-hunting game ranch owner to grow a plot of oranges under irrigation as a 'productive' front.[86] The logic was borne out by the land designation exercises and farm invasions of 1997 and 2000 which targeted a great many Mwenezi and Chiredzi game ranches, including some within the conservancies, for resettlement – official or otherwise. The 'game as more economically productive and ecologically appropriate' narrative that underpins the pristine wilderness way of seeing was being challenged by an understanding of the landscape that ostensibly emphasises equity and food security.

Even before the farm invasions there was a certain amount of disquiet amongst conservancy ranchers at the lack of revenue coming in, particularly given the low levels of tourism.[87] At the same time the economics of cattle ranching was changing, with the value of stock massively increasing.

---

[81] (cont.) their establishment and growth, Mushandike Training Centre, Masvingo, 3-6 October 1995.
[82] Interview: Head of Water and Sanitation, Masvingo Province, 15 November 1999. And see Ranger (1985) on guerrilla opposition to the wildlife industry during the war.
[83] See, for example, *The Herald*, 14 March 1997, 'Charge private wildlife farmers'.
[84] In the SVC, for example, apart from an ARDA-managed property, there were no black owned ranches in 2000.
[85] Interview: Commercial farmer, Mwenezi, 12 August 1999. Jansen *et al.* (1992), alongside their advocacy of game ranching as more economically productive, reveal that game ranchers employ approximately half the staff of cattle ranchers. As Hill (1994) notes, in a recession-strapped economy this has obvious political ramifications.
[86] Interview: Commercial farmer, Mwenezi, 12 August 1999.
[87] Zimbabwe Sun's operations at Save Valley were making massive losses even before the national collapse (Chapter 8).

This was making beef tempting again for some, and with the increased value of calves farmers could not afford to write as many off to wildlife (such as when leopards eat them).[88] Cattle ranching, particularly in the context of the ongoing insecurities, was perceived by some as more secure than a game industry dependent on fickle foreign visitors.[89] It is also interesting to note that, by 1998, four properties within the SVC had started growing plots of cash crops (particularly citrus and paprika) and one property had brought back cattle for fattening because the conservancy was not making the kind of money hoped for and projected. It remains to be seen whether there will be further movement by remaining ranchers towards agriculture or back to beef – although the substantial amount invested in conversion to wildlife will probably militate against this. Yet ranchers are not, in essence, loyal to the cause of conservation – only to the most lucrative land use. As one cattle and game rancher put it, 'the fuel is the US dollar – there is no ethos about greenness, [or] the good of the world, [it's] pure economics'.[90] Future land uses on all the lowveld commercial property are, however, contingent on the working through of the politics of, and policies on, land – as I shall explore in the next chapter.

The wildlife landscape

As well as attempts to manufacture wilderness in particular enclaves of the lowveld (the national park, game ranches and conservancies), the entire region has increasingly been represented and marketed as a 'wildlife landscape'. When in 1933 the Minister of Commerce and Transport (Gilchrist) envisaged a proposed game reserve in Rhodesia's south-east as a continuation of the South African Kruger Park, and a further contiguous 'sanctuary' on the Mozambican side of the border he was drawing on General Smuts' typically grandiose notion of a 'a great fauna and tourist road through Africa'.[91] In recent years the idea of a regional 'wildlife landscape' has re-emerged in the form of what has been termed a 'Peace Park' or Transboundary Protected Area (TBPA).[92] Although there has been conceptual continuity since the colonial period there has also been an escalation (in terms of scale and the number of actors involved) of the political and economic dynamics. Transfrontier conservation is a particularly apt development with respect to my theoretical approach in this book because 'landscape' has explicitly become a key conceptual category with potentially wide-ranging impacts.

[88] Interview: Regional Executive, CFU, Masvingo, 7 August 1999.
[89] Interview: Rancher, Mwenezi, 12 August 1999.
[90] Interview: Rancher, Chiredzi, 15 July 1999.
[91] NAZ S 1194/1608/1/1 Minutes of meeting of National Public Relations Advisory Board, Salisbury, 14 January 1947 – A.W. Redfern: memorandum on 'National Parks and Places of Scenic or Other Attractions'
[92] The following section draws on Wolmer (2003), where I examine the politics of the Great Limpopo Transfrontier Park in greater detail.

In October 1999 the Zimbabwe, Mozambique and South African governments signed a memorandum of understanding noting that 'ecosystems transcend national boundaries' and recognising 'the need for transborder cooperation in the conservation and management of shared natural resources'. The agreement aimed to 'promote biodiversity and socio-economic development in the area ...The Banhine-Zinave [or Gaza]/Kruger/Gonarezhou Peace Park will create one of the most impressive conservation regions in the world, with an area totalling a massive 95,700km^2.'[93] This encompasses a substantial amount of the lowveld regions of all three countries, although only 7 per cent of the total protected area falls inside Zimbabwe.[94] In December 2002 the three heads of state signed a treaty to establish the less cumbersome and more marketably named Great Limpopo Transfrontier Park.

This wildlife landscape concept is informed by both traditional preservationist notions of wildlife management, and ecocentric environmental philosophies with an emphasis on biodiversity and 'bioregionalism' (Duffy 1997; Wolmer 2003). This leads to a discourse on preserving the ecological 'integrity' or 'robustness' of 'eco-zones', '-regions' or '-spaces', 'heartlands' or, indeed, landscapes, by opening 'biological corridors for megafauna'.[95] The lowveld is one such ecological entity. However, this ecospace is perceived as at threat from, or already damaged by, habitat fragmentation, as:

> Environmentally arbitrary barriers to the fluxes of biotic and economic resources act in the region in the form of administrative boundaries such as those dividing protected areas from commercial farms and communal lands as well as those separating various districts and other local and regional administrative units.[96]

This threat to biodiversity, it is held, can only be reversed by the creation of large 'wildlife complexes' (Price Waterhouse 1994) and a regional approach to ecological management; the wilderness of old has become 'technified' as pristineness is replaced by ecological integrity as the natural and desired attributes of landscape.[97] This bioregionalist logic has also been used to justify the development of the conservancies:

> The restoration of some cattle ranching areas to full-scale multi-use wildlife operations potentially *enhances connectivity* between private wildlife areas and state wildlife areas and enhances the conservation of biodiversity. ... The present pattern of land-use in the Lowveld does offer opportunities for an enlightened *ecologically appropriate*

---

[93] *The Herald*, 25 October 1999. The proposed protected area was larger than Portugal.
[94] 21 per cent is in South Africa and 72 per cent in Mozambique, *BBC News Online*, 10 November 2000.
[95] 'Ecospaces' were the theme of the IUCN's Second World Conservation Congress in Amman, October 2000. See, for example, Pirot *et al.* (2000)
[96] CESVI (Draft Nov. 1997), unpublished Project Concept Paper.
[97] Although transboundary protected area advocates are not averse to deploying the odd bit of romantic rhetoric alongside all this science. The Peace Parks Foundation, for example, describes its 'dream of ancient migration trails trodden deep by an instinct that time has never contained' and the African Wildlife Foundation talks in terms of 'heartlands'.

zonation of activities ... In particular, there is the possibility of joining the Save Valley and Chiredzi River conservancies onto a corridor of commercial wildlife ranches extending to Gonarezhou National Park [and beyond that the Transfrontier Conservation Area]. [my emphases] (Price Waterhouse 1994: 22-23)

Again, a way of seeing and representing the lowveld leads logically towards a particular way of acting: a portioned ecospace must be allowed to regain its integrity through the opening up of 'artificial' boundaries. But this technical conservation biology discourse occludes politics and economics. The Great Limpopo Transfrontier Park represents a constellation of overlapping interests knitted together into strategic coalitions. This scheme is more than simply a bioregionalist agenda – it is rooted in economic and political imperatives (see also Simon 2003; Wolmer 2003).

One of the major driving forces behind the TBPA is its potential for private sector opportunities– and in particular increased tourism revenues. Alongside the drive to market 'wilderness quality' examined above there has been much talk of promoting the entire lowveld as a new regional tourist landscape or 'Wildlife Empire' – which feeds directly into the TBPA concept. In the late 1990s attempts were begun to market it as a destination on an alternative tourist route around Zimbabwe, particularly in the light of the GEF rehabilitation programme for Gonarezhou National Park. This 'southern circuit', with wildlife and wilderness as the main attractions, was intended to mop up the overspill of the rapidly overcrowding Victoria Falls vicinity in western Zimbabwe (Goodwin et al. 1997; Willis and Pangeti 1998).[98] At its most ambitious this logic envisages 'a major wildlife zone, including commercial, communal and state land [which] will stretch 300 km along the Limpopo and then 300 km northwards.'[99] This vision was being pushed by a grouping of private tourist operators (including the Save Valley Conservancy and Malilangwe Trust) under the banner of the Gazaland Tourist Initiative (GTI), which had the objective of promoting tourism in the Zimbabwean lowveld and the coastal resorts of southern Mozambique in a 'surf and turf' package, 'offering quality wildlife and pristine marine wilderness'. Potential attractions would be easy access for South African self-drive tourists to Zimbabwe's lowveld via a border crossing at Crooks Corner and a network of four-wheel-drive trails and campsites; and the option of being whisked away to the sandy beaches of the Mozambican coast.[100] Heavy promotion of the Great Limpopo National Park as a wildlife and wilderness landscape would be a huge boon to these forays into ecotourism. An advisor to Save Valley Conservancy also made the argument that – provided it had been fully stocked with wildlife – the

---

[98] See Safari Lodges of Africa News Flash, May 1999: New regional safari circuit unveiled.
[99] B.A. Child (1993) Proposal: Beitbridge, Chipinge, Chiredzi and Gonarezhou Joint Committee. DNPWLM, Harare.
[100] One consultancy report even suggests developing the liberation war battle sites of the lowveld into places of interest for tourists – particularly curious ex-combatants – to visit (Robford Tourism 1999).

conservancy could act as a wildlife reservoir. It would then be able to sell progeny to restock the transfrontier park.[101]

Private sector interest in the Great Limpopo Transfrontier Park is epitomised by the role of the Peace Parks Foundation. This ostensibly conservation-orientated institution was launched by Anton Rupert with his own money in 1997 with a mandate 'to facilitate establishment of Transfrontier Conservation Areas'. Rupert is a very wealthy South African businessman (head of Rothmans International tobacco company) with interests in tourism ventures, and is a former chief executive of WWF-South Africa (Ellis 1994; Duffy 2000). Rupert has been a major player in the development of the TBPA; it was he who initiated talks with President Chissano of Mozambique in 1990 concerning the transborder conservation initiative. He was also instrumental in interesting the World Bank in the project and securing financing (Hanks 1997). One of the main stated aims of the Peace Parks Foundation is to promote the commercial development of peace parks. The Peace Parks Foundation has secured funding from the private sector and the German Development Bank and has the personal endorsement of Nelson Mandela – it has also garnered a great deal of publicity for the scheme.[102] But as a member of an international conservation NGO put it to me, the widely held perception – given its provenance – is that it is 'in the pocket of big business' – specifically Rupert's pocket (see Bonner 1993; Ellis 1994; Duffy 2000).[103] Other players in South Africa's tourism and safari industries saw the economic potential of marketing a 'Kruger-plus' concept. Kruger National Park was rapidly approaching saturation and the industry was looking for new markets and a label with which to continue increasing Kruger's pulling power – being part of the largest protected area in Africa would be just such a marketing opportunity. A massive new park would also accommodate many more tourists, provide economies of scale and make for lucrative safari concessions within it and on its fringes. In the optimism surrounding the prospects for tourism in the region with the end of apartheid and the Mozambican civil war, Kruger was envisaged as a springboard for increased tourism in the region.[104]

Behind the bioregionalist conservation discourse there are thus major economic interests lurking. Private capital is being channelled into the domain of nature through a range of new commercialised ventures (Broch-Due 2000). This may also account for the massive financial backing to the TBPA and associated developments from donors, usually more concerned with economic development than biodiversity protection. The way in which romantic and ecocentric discourses somewhat surprisingly articulate with an explicitly neoliberal free trade agenda is revealed by the United

---

[101] Interviews: Director, Malilangwe Trust, 13 July 1999; Staff member, WWF, Harare, 14 June 1999.
[102] Such as: 'Elephants parking space', *Financial Times*, 9 April 1988; 'Game without Frontiers', *Time*, 14 May 2001; 'Without Borders', *National Geographic Magazine*, September 2001.
[103] Interview: Conservation NGO staff member, Harare, 10 June 2000.
[104] South African Ministry of Environmental Affairs and Tourism (www.environment.gov.za).

States Agency for International Development's (USAID) ambitious and well-funded Initiative for Southern Africa, which has a dual commitment to establishing regional economic integration and promoting ecological integrity. This programme explicitly aims to drive through 'market-orientated' reforms to the policy and regulatory environment in the region (such as privatisation and macroeconomic liberalisation), and 'reduce barriers to broader participation in the regional market', promoting the free flow of goods, services, capital and labour across borders and opening up US export and investment opportunities. TBPAs sit comfortably with this integrationist agenda for cross-border collaboration, and its potential for providing widespread tourism investment opportunities enables it to be portrayed as an 'engine to propel economic development'.[105]

TBPAs are also conceptually compatible with another high profile neoliberal initiative in the region: the Spatial Development Initiative (SDI) and development corridor programme launched by the South African government in 1997. Government funds are being used to leverage private sector involvement in the development of certain contiguous areas and to stimulate cross-border trade. There is a particular emphasis on investments in tourism, and public–private and private–community partnerships are encouraged. These are envisaged as potential major employment generators.

A range of political agendas are explicitly or implicitly bound up with the lowveld transfrontier park. Officially, one of the main goals has been described as ameliorating political tensions related to disputed borderlands and strengthening or re-establishing good political relations between neighbouring states, thereby warding off the threat of violent conflict 'by giving governments an agenda for mutual action on issues of common concern'[106] – hence the term 'peace parks'. This conventional wisdom has it that TBPAs will establish transboundary co-operation. However, as Rosaleen Duffy has documented in the case of the Great Limpopo Transfrontier Park, political realities tend to be more complex and less harmonious. The Zimbabwean government was long opposed to the scheme because of worries about the erosion of its sovereignty. There have been fears about losing sovereignty to South Africa (fed by the fact that the tranfrontier is commonly talked of in terms of creating a 'bigger Kruger Park') and to suprastate donors (conceived of as potentially a form of ecological imperialism) (Magome and Murombedzi 2003). Within government, the parks department has viewed the transfrontier park as a threat to its control of lucrative wildlife resources (legitimate and illicit) in the region (Duffy 1997; 2000; see also Ellis 1994). Some analysts have cast TBPAs as a mechanism for the extension of state power into marginal regions (Duffy 1997; Singh 2000; cf. Murombedzi 1992a; Hill 1996) (and see below).

[105]Deputy Minister of Environment and Tourism, Zimbabwe, Dialogue on Transboundary Natural Resource Management, Holiday Inn, Harare, 20-21 February 2001.
[106]Melanie Gosling 'Peace Parks urged for conserving ecosystems', *Cape Times*, 22 September 1997.

However, given the current economic context, and donor and private sector power relative to the state in southern Africa, TBPAs might be better envisaged as mechanisms for the extension of private sector interests into state land (cf. Moyo 2000b). The wildlife landscape concept deriving from the wilderness vision provides justification for their territorial claims across national and administrative boundaries.

A further, oft-stated, logic for the creation of TBPAs is an apparently ethnographic one. They are described as a means of re-establishing the 'cultural integrity', or achieving the 'cultural harmonisation', of divided ethnic groups. Removing the artificial national boundaries dividing ethnic groups, it is hoped, would 're-establish historical links' and 'foster a cultural renaissance' (Griffen 1999). In the Great Limpopo case this would, presumably, mean the 're-unification' in some shape or form of the Shangaan people of Zimbabwe, South Africa and Mozambique. However, as we shall see below, such representations of Shangaan identity have tended to focus only on a marketable 'exotic, traditional and primitive' version rather than emphasising the Shangaan people's history as dynamic players in an international economy. As one study admits, for local communities transfrontier natural resource management is 'not a new fad but a daily reality' (Griffen 1999: 32). Between Zimbabwe, Mozambique and South Africa there is a massive amount of informal trading and labour migration (both legal and illegal) by the Shangaan people and others. But, despite nebulous talk about re-establishing cultural identity, there has been little practical discussion of opening up human (as opposed to elephant) migration corridors to free movement.[107] Indeed, human migration is very often characterised as a problem, alongside 'squatting', which 'effective and efficient' transborder natural resource management will somehow solve (Mbizvo and Guveya 1999: 7). As the Great Limpopo Transfrontier Park plans stand, there is a danger that it might do more to threaten than encourage these mobile livelihood strategies.

Community-Based Natural Resource Management

Lying awkwardly alongside the technical bio-regionalist discourse about 're-establishing key ecological functions' in the form of a lowveld wildlife landscape (and its attendant multiple political and economic agendas) is a decentralisation discourse.[108] As well as safeguarding biodiversity and bringing socio-economic development, creating a regional wildlife landscape

---

[107] Although the Southern African Development Community treaty theoretically promotes liberalised border policies that eliminate obstacles to free movement among member states of capital and labour, goods and services, *and of the region's peoples* (SADC 1992: Article 5, para 2b).

[108] This is one of various strange juxtapositions of discourse including 'deep-green' ecocentrism alongside sustainable utilisation of wildlife; and free-market-driven commercial development alongside 'bottom-up' rural development.

in the lowveld, it is held, will incorporate the devolution of authority to 'communities'.

Zimbabwe has been at the forefront of attempts to promote decentralised or 'community-based' natural resource management (CBNRM) through the CAMPFIRE scheme (Communal Area Management Programme for Indigenous Resources). CAMPFIRE has been represented as an antidote to the colonial 'fortress conservation' discourse which undermined people's control over their environment and criminalised their use of game (Alexander and McGregor 2000). Instead, communities are cast as 'partners in conservation'. The central tenets of this scheme, which has become something of an icon among conservation agencies and international NGOs, are that neighbouring communities must receive direct benefits from protected areas and have some say in wildlife management and use if conservation policies are to be effective (Zimbabwe Trust 1990; Peterson 1991; Child 1995). This implies the 'sustainable utilisation', rather than preservation, of wildlife with a portion of hunting or tourism revenues disbursed to local authorities. The CAMPFIRE model has achieved the status of conventional wisdom in the southern African region and internationally, endorsed by a range of generous donors. It has spawned a research industry and has been the subject of countless workshops, conferences and glossy publications.[109]

CAMPFIRE projects in Zimbabwe have been mainly associated with the Zambezi Valley area. However, in the south-east lowveld, Chiredzi, Chipinge and Beitbridge Rural District Councils have the 'appropriate authority' to utilise wildlife and other natural resources within their jurisdiction. In practice this principally means leasing hunting rights to certain areas (either in designated 'safari areas' or in parts of the communal areas along the Limpopo river and bordering Gonarezhou National Park). Thus, in parallel to developments on commercial land, there has been a shift in certain actors' logic of what constitutes an appropriate land use in the lowveld communal areas incorporating wildlife management.

An early proto-CAMPFIRE initiative involved the Mahenye community at the confluence of the Save and Runde rivers. What started off as a hunting-revenue-based scheme has since 1994 incorporated a joint ecotourism venture with the private sector.[110] The Mahenye community initiative is now regarded as a model site and has been the location of numerous donor-funded SADC exchange visits of regional parliamentarians, permanent secretaries and 'CBNRM practitioners'. Zimbabwe Sun Limited lease land from the Mahenye community for two safari lodges on the fringe of Gonarezhou National Park and give a percentage of the annual turnover to

[109] The community conservation discourse entered the mainstream after the 1992 World Congress on National Parks and Protected areas.
[110] See Peterson (1991), Dalton (1992), Goodwin (1997) and Murphree (2000) for detailed descriptions of the Mahenye experience. These writers devote much space to romantic accounts of the integral role of a local Shangaan-speaking white rancher – Clive Stockil (also a key figure in representations of the Save Valley Conservancy's history).

Chipinge Rural District Council who in turn remit a percentage to the Mahenye community.[111] The project aptly illustrates the centrality of the wilderness vision to conservation and development initiatives in the lowveld. Included in the lease agreement is a clause prohibiting the watering of cattle in front of the lodges – 'destroying the ambience of the wild' for international tourists (Goodwin *et al.* 1997: 184). Also, according to the manager of Chilo Lodge, 'when our guests see cultivation on the riverbanks next to the national park, they get upset. ... [C]ommunity members must be prepared for an element of change'.[112] As in the conservancies, the appropriate degree of wilderness quality must be consciously manufactured.

As well as taking tourists into the national park, the safari vehicles make 'cultural tours' through Mahenye village. As the publicity brochure puts it, 'the Shangaan community are an integral part of the safari product at Chilo and Mahenye', alongside game drives, bird watching and thatched, open-fronted bedrooms.[113] Similarly, an NGO working in the lowveld claims that 'the way of life of the Sengwe and Sangwe [communal area] communities, i.e. the tradition, the cultural beliefs, the way the homesteads are constructed, the language etc. are a resource which can be closely linked to the potential for ecotourism in the area'.[114] These sentiments echo DC Wright's scheme for the viewing of 'wild animals and wild Africans' of 40 years earlier. Shangaan identity is packaged, commodified and marketed as an add-on attraction. A particularly common representation, as Chapter 2 shows, is of Shangaan people as natural hunters and 'trackers' with an almost primaeval instinctive connection to the land and wildlife.[115] Unsurprisingly, suitably 'traditional' and historic Shangaan villages are hard to find these days and the logical outcome – in parallel to the creation of suitably wild scenic views – has been to build 'traditional villages' that look '100 per cent the way a Shangaan village should'.[116] This has been attempted at Mahenye, and in a communal area bordering the Save Valley Conservancy and is planned by the Malilangwe Trust. As the manager of tourist operations at Malilangwe explained, having built a traditional thatched, 'pole and dagga' style village you can:

> ...staff it with families which are out of work, bring a few chickens and goats and every damn thing along. Bring a few craftspeople – they can sit there and make stuff.

---

[111] One might cynically conclude that the presence of the two luxury lodges goes a long way towards explaining the popularity of Mahenye as a 'model site' for VIP exchange visits.
[112] Simon Rawson, Chilo Lodge, General Manager, 'Implications of the private sector involvement in Mahenye and CBNRM generally'. Presentation in the SADC Natural Resources Management Programme, *Report of the 7th Exchange Visit Seminar for Parliamentarians from Mozambique*, Chilo Lodge, Mahenye, 7-10 July 1998.
[113] River Lodges of Africa brochure: Mahenye Safari Lodge.
[114] *SAFIRE News* No. 2, December 1998.
[115] In Kruger National Park African park rangers also tended to be referred to generically as dutiful 'Shangaans' (Bunn 1999).
[116] Interview: Manager, Tourism Operations, Malilangwe Trust, 13 July 1999.

Our guests can come and barter – they love that – they'll buy it!¹¹⁷
Malilangwe Trust's dilemma is that they have two sets of neighbours – Sangwe communal area and Chizvirizvi Resettlement Area. They do not want to be seen to be favouring one of them for the location of this traditional village, but reason that 'the TTL would be more traditional'.¹¹⁸ However, a similar attempt to build a 'traditional village' with the Gudo community outside the SVC ran into serious difficulties. The development was perceived as a land-grab, with white ranchers extending their commercial operations further onto Gudo territory. The development met with ongoing resistance, and ultimately was burnt down before its completion (Wels 2000). These projects also reflect changing discourses surrounding Africans and protected areas. Indigenous populations were initially equated with wildlife and allowed to remain (as envisaged by DC Wright – above); then they were held to be anathema to the wilderness experience expected by safari hunters and tourists, and were removed; and now they are seen as a useful adjunct to wildlife for 'ethnotourism' on the fringes of protected areas as long as they are visually pleasing. Community-based tourism has meant the community becoming the objects of tourism. Landscape and its inhabitants have been imaginatively transformed together (Neumann 1999; see Gordon 1992; Neumann 1997; Ranger 1999).

I do not want my account of these cultural tourism initiatives to give the impression that all Shangaan people are necessarily dismissive of, or offended by, this kind of caricatured identity. Indeed, as Chapter 3 shows, many people have not been averse to taking on the 'traditional hunter' Shangaan identity deliberately to suit certain ends. And others see traditional villages as a potentially very important income-earner. Yet many people at Mahenye and elsewhere in the lowveld are deeply disillusioned with the CAMPFIRE project on other grounds – in particular a feeling that it has not delivered on its promises to transfer either money or political authority to the local level.¹¹⁹ In Mahenye there have been ongoing complaints about money being tied by Chipinge RDC bureaucracy (or worse) and only released for particular 'projects' over which they have little control.¹²⁰ Dissatisfaction is even more marked in Chiredzi District, which lacks a prestigious ecotourism development and where substantially less wildlife-related revenue is being generated. Interviewees in Matibi II and

---

[117] Interview: Manager, Tourism Operations, Malilangwe Trust, 13 July 1999. Similarly the Governor of Masvingo Province told me that Shangaan people 'are part of the attraction [of the lowveld] – with bare bodies wrapped in wrappers, small huts, pole and dagga. [It] all adds to what tourists would like to see. The tourist must be able to go to a typical Shangani village.' Interview: Provincial Governor, Masvingo, 9 September 1999.
[118] Interview: Manager, Tourism Operations, Malilangwe Trust, 13 July 1999.
[119] Interview: Chief Gezani, Gezani, 19 September 1999.
[120] In the context of declining central government funding CAMPFIRE has become a vitally important source of revenue for Rural District Councils – and they are keen to hang on to as much of it as possible.

Sengwe communal areas repeatedly alleged that the small revenues accruing to members of CAMPFIRE committees did little to offset the damage caused by marauding elephants or carnivores; the removal of hunting as a source of protein; the loss of grazing lands; or restrictions on cutting poles and reeds, collecting firewood and fishing. It remains more lucrative to poach an animal than to wait for the CAMPFIRE dividends. As one disillusioned informant from Sengwe put it:

> CAMPFIRE promised us school buildings, clinics, elephant and buffalo meat, grinding mills, job creation, grazing areas, and to kill elephants that destroy our crops. But to our surprise they target only the elephants coming to our fields which they say are of trophy quality – meaning having big ivory which they can sell for more. The elephants which destroy our crops are not of trophy quality. The people are bored with the political approach to us [derogatory use of 'political']. The CAMPFIRE programme has taken our grazing areas and we no longer have as much grazing land. As time goes on they [CAMPFIRE officials] go against their promises. They have only employed three people (a resource monitor, a grinding mill operator and a ticket writer). They are giving money to individuals – Z$350 per year – which is not enough to allow a home to survive hunger for a whole year. Elephants can destroy tonnes and tonnes of our crops in one night. The money given to individuals can be used by that person in a day drinking local beer! The money should be channelled to people on a monthly basis not annually. The yearly payments are used by the family elders who are buying *porosi* [beer] and the children are not getting any benefit from the CAMPFIRE money.[121]

Particularly galling was the debacle in 1999 when the CEO of a bankrupt Chiredzi Rural District Council (RDC) plundered the banked CAMPFIRE receipts to pay the salaries of angry striking council workers. At the village level membership of CAMPFIRE committees is often regarded as something of a poisoned chalice because of the degree of local political infighting, corruption and jealousies it can bring. CAMPFIRE was regularly described to me as a 'political issue' which tends to carry scathingly pejorative connotations in Zimbabwe.

The CAMPFIRE programme in the communal land surrounding state-owned protected areas is mirrored by attempts by the private sector operatives of the SVC and Malilangwe Trust to establish community trusts and 'neighbour outreach' programmes. This is in recognition of the fact that, particularly in the current political context, 'the negative political image of the electrified fencing and upmarket ecotourism adjacent to over-populated communal lands must somehow be converted into a positive context for local communities' (du Toit 1998: 10). Indeed in 1996 the Minister for Environment and Tourism stated in a written answer to parliamentary questions that conservancies should only be allowed if they were able to generate a 'formal and meaningful relationship' with neighbouring communities.[122] To this end there have been bold attempts by advocates for

---

[121] Interview: Masukwe, 1 October 1999. For an even more vitriolic response to a CAMPFIRE project see Alexander and McGregor (2000).

[122] Minister for Environment and Tourism (Chen Chimutengewende) in *Hansard*, 14 February 1996, 3967-3971.

the conservancies to assert that the wildlife industry has greater potential to diminish the poverty of the people in the neighbouring communal lands than any alternative land use.

There have been various attempts in the SVC to establish trusts through which the neighbouring communities could be somehow seen to benefit from the conservancy. The first involved trustees chosen by the SVC and a Joint Committee of representatives from the five surrounding RDCs who would 'represent beneficiary interests'. This was criticised for delivering a 'take-it-or-leave-it' blueprint with no prior consultation. The second attempt was a so-called 'community wildlife endowment' scheme whereby the trust (with trustees now nominated by the RDCs) would use donor funding to purchase wildlife which would be released within the conservancy. The conservancy would then be obliged to buy their progeny each year at the prevailing market rate. This money could then be used to finance community projects (Metcalfe 1996; du Toit 1998; Wels 2000). Wels (2000) argues that these schemes are no more than strategic tokenism and would, in practice, be far more beneficial to the few ranchers than the thousands in the neighbouring communities. He intimates that the schemes were actually exercises in 'spin', intended to secure political and social legitimacy for the conservancy from the government and put pressure on a reluctant DNPWLM to supply buffalo for a 'good cause'. In applications for donor funding the trust was pushed to the foreground. A 'formal and meaningful' relationship with neighbouring communities, ranchers thought, would help stave off the threat of land designation (and subsequent redistribution). Yet for many in the surrounding RDCs this was missing the point. Land redistribution and the return of inalienable ancestral lands inside the fence was precisely what they wanted – not some form of co-operation on the conservancy's terms, and ownership of 'free' wildlife (Wels 2000). This difference of opinion came to a head in 2000, as we will see in Chapter 8.

The well-endowed Malilangwe Trust also operates a neighbour outreach programme. This is principally envisaged as an interim development scheme – a means or maintaining harmonious relationships with neighbouring communities before the envisaged knock-on benefits of ecotourism development come on stream.[123] Its aims include: supporting social welfare; stimulating the development of rural enterprises; 'capacity building'; fostering sustainable use of land and other sustainable resources; recognising and developing 'cultural soul';[124] and co-ordinating and planning activities within the context of wider district-level initiatives by the government and other development agencies.[125] As such it makes no claims to be either community-based or participatory. In practice this has meant

---

[123] Interview: Director, Malilangwe Trust, 13 July 1999.
[124] Malilangwe Trust has a 'Shangaan cultural promotion' programme 'aimed at making sure that the Shangaan culture down here isn't swamped and assimilated into the broader Shona culture that surrounds it'. Interview: Director, Malilangwe Trust, 13 July 1999.
[125] Malilangwe Trust Annual Report 1998.

handouts of school fees and uniforms; a subsidised tillage programme; sponsoring a 'Shangaan dancing' competition for local primary schools; the development of a theatre group for disseminating conservation messages; and a 'traditional ceremony' involving Chief Tsovani and tribal elders to bless the new luxury lodge.

It is also important to note that the GEF-funded Gonarezhou National Park rehabilitation plans and the Great Limpopo Tranfrontier Park plans incorporate much talk of communities being not only beneficiaries but also partners in conservation. As an early proposal for developing the lowveld as a wildlife landscape explains:

> ... local involvement and smaller-scale local initiatives are critical, with local people running less capital intensive ventures such as campsites, walking trails, bird-watching and cultural tourism. This will develop a strong proprietary interest and pride in their wildlife. Voluntary consolidation of settlement is expected around such centres at community-managed irrigation schemes which provide both employment and food security. These *consolidated settlements* make available land for tourism and also provide ideal sites for the development of business adding more wealth and employment [my emphasis] (Child 1993).

The GEF project laid aside US$2 million for 'out-of-park' projects to 'support community and development activities that promote conservation and sustainable use of habitat and wildlife' such as the 'development of innovative and participatory wildlife utilisation on Communal Lands and on small-scale commercial farms adjacent to the Gonarezhou National Park'. These schemes would '*thus effectively extend the wildlife conservation estate over a broad area*' [my emphasis].[126] These quotes, notwithstanding their talk of involvement and participation, make critical assumptions: that the extension of the wildlife estate is a desirable state of affairs, with communal areas and game ranches constituting some sort of infill or cement between 'traditional' protected areas; and that even displacement in the form of 'consolidated settlements' would be a desirable means of achieving this. This has associations, in Zimbabwe, with coercive colonial and postcolonial attempts at centralisation and villagisation respectively and would be likely to awake painful memories of eviction (cf. Moore 1998). This scenario lends weight to David Hughes' controversial contention that the 'logic of CAMPFIRE culminates in eviction' and that CAMPFIRE 'has come to denote an expensive public-private partnership for latter-day colonisation' (2001: 18, 27).

Ostensibly, CBNRM programmes are allowing multiple resource use in the communal areas (wildlife, livestock and crops) and yet their driving philosophy tends to be a conservation one not a development one (a means of decreasing poaching). CAMPFIRE started life as a DNPWLM initiative – and Neighbour Outreach programmes were initiated by the SVC and

---

[126] Global Environmental Facility, South-east Lowveld Co-ordinating Committee Project (GEF-SELCC) Project Operational manual – First Draft, Dec. 1998.

Malilangwe Trust – and as such they are arguably not equipped to deliver substantial development results. Development remains a subservient goal to conservation. The lowveld – at root, according to the all-pervasive pristine wilderness vision that informs these initiatives – is a wildlife/wilderness landscape and should be maintained, or rehabilitated, as such. As a 'community-based' initiative, CAMPFIRE might be supposed to have grown instead out of more locally-grounded notions of landscape like those explored in Chapter 3. To date, however, CAMPFIRE and ecotourism initiatives have constituted a new rhetorical scaffold supporting and reproducing (and attempting to enlist communities to) the wilderness vision rather than an alternative way of seeing the lowveld landscape.

Conclusions

To set out, deliberately, to manufacture a wilderness area in the image of a romanticised imagined landscape is, on the face of it, a strange thing to do – if not a fundamental contradiction in terms. This chapter has investigated why this has been attempted, by whom, how, and with what impact. This is an inherently political debate and, as discussed at the beginning of this book, like so many political debates in Zimbabwe it ends up being about land – power over land and the power to define what constitutes an appropriate land use.

Early attempts at conservation in Zimbabwe's south-eastern lowveld were rooted in a romantic notion of the lowveld as the abode of wild Africa and proving ground of settler masculinity and pioneering spirit. The 'lure of the lowveld' encouraged a paternalistic view of benevolent authority over the most seemingly pristine areas and their animal and human inhabitants. This was a natural space that was defined in opposition to the productive spaces of the cattle ranches and sugar estates. The inhabitants of these game reserves were evicted and the enclaves were fenced off and policed to protect a heritage perceived as threatened for future generations. But from the time a protected area was first proposed for the south-east of the country there was also an eye for the future tourism development and hence revenue-generating potential of such a scheme, which ran up against the elitist instincts of many conservationists. The incremental alienation of land into the conservation estate also upset the cattle lobby who traded veterinary and ecological science discourses with the conservationists in a drawn-out battle to define appropriate land uses.

In recent years there have been a number of significant developments. One has been the ongoing commoditisation of nature in Zimbabwe. Starting with the emergence of game ranching on commercial ranches in the 1950s and '60s and gathering momentum with the ascendancy of CBNRM since the late 1980s and early 1990s, a wide variety of actors has come together in a 'discourse coalition' around the sustainable utilisation of wildlife as new ways of appropriating value from the landscape have been explored (Hajer 1995). These actors included local, global and regional conservationists, private entrepreneurs, donors and the state. This has conspired to encourage a shift in the conservationist agenda from viewing protected areas as inviolate sanctuaries to looking to them increasingly as potential sources of revenue. In this respect any division between 'natural' and 'productive' spaces is an increasingly artificial one as the boundaries have blurred. In order to attract trophy hunters and tourists, a great deal of effort has been invested in manufacturing landscapes with the appropriately 'wild' flora and fauna, rustic architecture and 'primitive and traditional' African neighbours. This wilderness experience has been marketed through the deployment of the old narratives on the romance and 'lure' of the lowveld of the colonial imagination.

Alongside this, developments in conservation biology have encouraged a bioregional approach to biodiversity management. This advocates the removal of arbitrary barriers to the movement of biotic resources in order to re-establish the ecological integrity of ecospaces across administrative and national boundaries. Ecocentric philosophies and neoliberal economic agendas have found common cause in the promotion of a wildlife landscape which is spreading from 'traditional' protected areas (in this case Gonarezhou National Park) to impinge on previously separate constituencies – commercial farms and communal areas. Whereas in the past the communal areas of the lowveld have often been represented as a buffer separating commercial ranches from the veterinary disease threat of the wilderness areas, now they are coming to be conceptualised more in terms of interstitial connective zones, cement, or corridors between wildlife areas (e.g. DNPWLM 1998: 42). CAMPFIRE has also contributed to a blurring of previously hard-edged racial boundaries between land use zones in Zimbabwe, as white entrepreneurs have been able to penetrate black spaces with safari operations (Hughes 2001).

It has become a conventional wisdom that a new lowveld wildlife landscape will be a much needed means to stimulate an economically depressed area with few industries and little potential for anything else but wildlife development (Duffy 1997). However, the money so far generated by wildlife enterprises has not been enough to establish viable commercial concerns on private farms and in the national park, let alone to pass substantial knock-on benefits to communities. Even before the collapse of the Zimbabwean tourist industry in 2000 the only economically viable wildlife zones were those like Malilangwe Trust, which is the playground of a single foreign donor with deep pockets and a yearning for a chunk of pristine Africa – but is this politically viable? For the black population of the lowveld, wildlife enterprises deliver the occasional small bonus to some but this is very far from constituting an alternative livelihood. It remains more lucrative to work in South Africa (and hope for a similarly radical attitude to human migration to that now suggested for elephants), and take one's chances with dryland cropping and livestock. The danger is that, at best, the drive towards CBNRM or 'neighbour outreach' means a few jobs in safari lodges and 'Shangaan' dance troupes and, at worst, will impose more coercive regulations on resource use, stretching livelihood systems yet further in the opaque interests of bioregionalism and 'ecological integrity'.

These developments raise serious questions about power. On whose terms is this wildlife landscape being developed? Various writers have argued that the extension of the conservation estate in this manner represents the covert penetration of coercive state power into remote and marginal areas (cf. Ferguson 1990).[127] But the Zimbabwean state is far from monolithic; central and local government and different departments, and civil servants, have very different agendas, and the economic crisis is fast eroding the state's capacity for large-scale interventions. The lowveld wildlife landscape could alternatively be read as an expansion of the realm of the private sector – which is penetrating previously 'communal' spaces with arrangements such as private-public joint ventures. In practice, the complex coalition of interests that constitutes the private sector includes 'state' actors such as MPs, Councillors, and civil servants, acting in an individual capacity as entrepreneurs. The expansion of the realm of the private sector into this lowveld wildlife landscape is ostensibly at odds with the ZANU(PF) government's noisy post-1995 (and particularly post-2000) attempts to address the highly unequal racial pattern of land ownership and economic power. The wildlife industry in particular has acted as a crucible for racial politics. Power, as ever in Zimbabwe, is related to power over the representation and meanings of land, meanings that are encouraged and underpinned by particular ways of seeing the landscape, as we shall see in the following concluding chapter.

[127]Examples include: Murombedzi (1992a); Peluso (1993); Neumann (1997); Hitchcock (1995); Hill (1996); Schroeder (1999); and Gibson (1999).

PART FOUR
The Politics of Land(scape)

8

Reclaiming the wilderness?
Farm invasions in the lowveld

Events in 2000 catapulted Zimbabwe into the headlines and brought the volatile 'land question' to the world's attention. The sudden emergence of a radicalised land reform programme, involving the seizure of largely white-owned commercial farmland, dramatically altered the physical landscape. In the conservancies and game ranches of the lowveld, where so much effort had been put into manufacturing a wilderness landscape, these were particularly dramatic. Some of these newly pristine spaces are now criss-crossed by footpaths and cart tracks, trees had been felled, huts built, fences pulled down, fires started, fields cleared and ploughed, and wildlife hunted. It is particularly the latter manifestation of this seemingly direct attack on the wilderness vision that generated international outrage and many an apocalyptic headline as we saw at the beginning of this book.

This concluding chapter examines these radical developments in the light of the history of the conflicting perceptions of the lowveld landscape that I have explored. To recap briefly on my central thesis: one legacy of the colonial period in Zimbabwe's lowveld is what I have described as a particular 'way of seeing' the landscape – the wilderness vision. This has had particular consequences for the ways in which this landscape has been defined, represented and acted upon, including the design and implementation of development and conservation schemes. Initially the wilderness vision had a binary logic – it was either a wilderness to be tamed and made productive, or a pristine space to be preserved in its natural glory. In both manifestations of this wilderness vision African people were written out of the landscape. The wilderness vision continues to be extremely influential in informing projects and plans for the lowveld. However, there has been one important change. The binary wilderness vision of separate productive and natural spaces has to some extent been elided by the emergence of a game ranching industry and a discourse on sustainable utilisation of wildlife that holds that the lowveld landscape can be simultaneously natural and productive. Over time the wilderness vision has been buttressed by a range of narratives, including the pioneer experience, modernisation, efficient ecological utilisation and, most recently, bioregional ecological integrity. This way of seeing has played out in the form of the lowveld landscape – a landscape ostensibly boxed into hard-edged, single-use zones.

Despite its all-pervasive influence, this understanding does not always fit with local perceptions and experiences, as the preceding chapters have shown. Dryland agriculture in the lowveld has been regularly dismissed as a waste of time, rather than one of many crucial elements of livelihoods systems. Plans for irrigation schemes have been biased towards mega-scale developments which have yet to see the light of day outside of the commercial sector. Livestock management strategies that fall outside the large-scale commercial ranching model have not been supported – and have often been actively discouraged by constraints on livestock mobility. Wildlife utilisation schemes have delivered minimal returns to communities and have imposed further coercive restrictions on other livelihood activities. Multiple livelihood strategies that encompass a variety of activities in a range of spaces do not fit into such an understanding of boxed and bounded single-use areas. The wilderness vision excludes other African understandings of landscape too. There is no room in it for transcending the division between nature and culture – recognising a landscape which is inextricably bound up with identity through its embodiment of ancestral spirits and its role as a repository of social memories.

Since June 2000, however, there has seemingly been a dramatic and highly visible physical and conceptual challenge to the logic of the wilderness vision in the lowveld. Widespread farm invasions, underpinned by revolutionary rhetoric and the initiation of a 'fast-track' resettlement process, have radically altered the previously strictly demarcated landscape. These developments raise important questions. Do the current developments on the 'land question' in Zimbabwe generally, and the lowveld specifically, have the potential to replace the wilderness vision with a new paradigm to underpin development and conservation initiatives? Can they avoid the problems referred to above and write people back into the landscape? Will local visions be included and the diversity of perceptions of landscape reflected?

An overview of 'the land question' post-Independence

The turbulent politics of land in Zimbabwe is a subject that has received much academic attention (e.g. Palmer 1977; Moyana 1984; Palmer 1990; Moyo 1995). The 'land question' has constantly simmered and has periodically approached boiling point. With Independence in 1980 decolonisation was not accompanied, as one might have expected, by radical land reform incorporating large-scale redistribution, restitution or reparations. Rather, the colonial status quo was legalised in the Lancaster House Constitution: land transfer would have to be on the basis of full compensation in foreign exchange according to the notorious 'willing seller, willing buyer' formula, and National Parks were safe-guarded, which effectively ruled out significant land redistribution (Palmer 2000).

During the 1980s there was a general lack of commitment on the part of the major players to move forward on the land question. Donors – particularly the British government – downplayed assurances of financial assistance for resettlement; the powerful CFU stalled land reform at every stage; and the ZANU(PF) government cynically alternately downplayed and legitimised land claims in response to electoral imperatives. Notwithstanding this, and largely unfavourable academic and media accounts of the resettlement process (including accusations of cronyism as members of the ruling elite acquired land), 71,000 families had been resettled by 1996, and a further 20,000 given access to additional grazing lands (Kinsey 1999). Throughout the 1980s there were also sporadic and low profile farm invasions by the land hungry.

In the early 1990s Zimbabwe entered the neoliberal era of 'ESAP'[1] which had important implications for the land reform programme. The free-market ideology held that land transfers should be based on acquisition through market mechanisms (rather than compulsory land acquisition by the state). ESAP also brought export-orientated sectoral policies (for agriculture and tourism for example); and macroeconomic policies geared towards trade liberalisation, domestic market deregulation, exchange-rate devaluation and privatisation. Together these had the effect of further entrenching the inequitable land ownership structure, restraining the land redistribution agenda and encouraging land use conversions towards wildlife management, horticulture and livestock exports (Moyo 2000c). ESAP exacerbated inequality, unemployment and poverty (Scoones et al. 1996; Alwang et al. 2001; Jenkins and Knight 2002). The increasing lack of alternatives to land and natural resource-based livelihood strategies exacerbated land hunger and contributed to mounting frustration at the slow pace of land reform – keeping the land question high on the political agenda (Moyo 2000c).

The controversial 1992 Land Acquisition Act theoretically enabled compulsory land acquisition at controlled prices and abandonment of the willing seller/willing buyer principle. But these powers were not used until 'Mugabe's land grab' (Palmer 1998) of 1997 when a swathe of 1,471 farms were designated for compulsory acquisition in an attempt to answer the clamour for land reform once and for all and shore up the waning popularity of the former liberation movement party, ZANU(PF). This rapidly became a complex, bureaucratic and expensive process. By 1998, 510 farms (42 per cent of the designated properties) had been degazetted after appeal

---

[1] The Economic Structural Adjustment Programme implemented by the International Monetary Fund (IMF).

or court challenges, and 500 of the 847 farms remaining on the list were struck off by the Administrative Court in 1999 (Moyo 2000b). But these designations had provided a strategic political opening for claims to land – triggering some farm invasions by 'squatters' and war veterans. They also forced donors into a more engaged approach and in September 1998 there was a well-attended conference on Land Reform and Resettlement. The government presented its 'Phase II' plan – aiming to acquire five million hectares from the commercial farming sector for redistribution to 91,000 families. Agreement was reached amongst all stakeholders on the intrinsic need for land reform, and 118 farms were offered up voluntarily as part of an 'inception phase'. However, soon afterwards the technical, donor-approved Phase II process unravelled. It was derailed by a combination of domestic political imperatives, donor anxiety at some government actions and pronouncements, and a series of diplomatic rows between Zimbabwe and Britain (potentially the main donor).

ZANU(PF) suffered an unexpected political rebuff in 2000 when its proposed new constitution (incorporating a clause obliging the former colonial government rather than the Zimbabwean government to pay compensation for compulsory land acquisition) was rejected in a referendum. Taken together with the rapid emergence of a strong opposition (the Movement for Democratic Change) in advance of the parliamentary election, and popular dissatisfaction at the desperate state of the economy and Zimbabwe's involvement in the war in the Democratic Republic of Congo, this forced ZANU(PF)'s hand on the land issue. Falling into typical electioneering mode, it sought to capitalise on deep-seated grievances on the emotive land issue (and particularly demands for action from the war veterans' lobby) and fought the election under the slogan 'land is the economy and the economy is land'. After the referendum and during and after the election there were large-scale spontaneous and orchestrated farm invasions as various coalitions of actors, gathered under the banner of 'war veterans', stepped up a previously low-level campaign of occupying commercial farms and some state-owned land. This was paralleled by the announcement of the government's official 'fast-track' resettlement process. Upping the stakes from 1997, 2,159 farms were now gazetted for compulsory acquisition.[2] The implementation of this fast-track resettlement process was hampered by bureaucratic confusion, lack of technical capacity and shortages of staff, transport and fuel. There were also increasing donor concerns over lack of transparency, cronyism, and the general collapse of the rule of law in Zimbabwe, leading to the freezing of bilateral and multilateral aid programmes. ZANU(PF) had become increasingly politically and economically isolated and belligerent – doing battle with 'imperialist' interference in national sovereignty, the judiciary and the independent press.

---

[2] After a new constitutional amendment the government was only obliged to compensate for improvements to land (as had been put forward in the rejected constitution).

Competing discourses concerning land

Relationships between black and white in Zimbabwe are often characterised as being dominated by struggles over the possession and use of land and defined by competing claims of 'belonging'. Land is often portrayed by writers and politicians as *the* defining theme of black/white relations (e.g. Moyo 1995). This is the favoured discourse of the ZANU(PF) government. The fast-track resettlement exercise was underpinned by a revolutionary discourse of picking up where the liberation struggle left off, with a 'Third Chimurenga'. Appeals were made to nationalism, indigeneity and patriotism. Land is a signifier of nationhood and is explicitly racialised – the war was fought against the whites for land, and there is an ongoing need to address colonial imbalances and put right an historical injustice. White concessions to that point were seen as inadequate compensation for the historical crime of land alienation. The British government, as the former imperial power was, and is, singled out for particular opprobrium. Interestingly, what is lacking is an argument for land restitution in the South African sense, whereby land is returned specifically to the communities alienated from it, rather than to citizens generally.

Countering the government's populist and moral discourse on land rights is a technical, scientific and legal discourse used by the commercial farming lobby and most donors. This emphasises title deeds and market-based acquisition. It favours a gradual land reform process that does not hinder productivity and, in particular, foreign-exchange earning. Land reform is cast as a technical, rather than a political, issue. Conversely, commercial farmers perceive ZANU(PF)'s agenda as an explicitly political one rather than being about land reform *per se*. An extreme reading is that it is a 'Maoist tactic to break up land for peasant agriculture ... destroying all forms of wealth and establishing a peasant society forever dependent on the government.'[3]

As well as a divergence between the visions of donors and the government for the appropriate means of land reform, there has been tension within government – between politicians and technocrats. Should resettlement be implemented immediately with a minimum of unwieldy bureaucracy and technical planning or should it be a measured, orderly, efficient and rational process? In 2000, political and economic imperatives appeared to have shifted the balance of power to the former argument, and the technical arm of government, so central to the resettlement models of the 1980s and early 1990s, appeared largely sidelined.[4]

---

[3] Interview: Masvingo Province CFU member, 22 January 2001.
[4] Although as Chaumba, Scoones and Wolmer (2003a) show, the formal and technical tools and discourses of land-use planning were deployed to a remarkable extent even in the midst of violent ostensible disorder and chaos.

The land question in the lowveld

As Parts I and II described, the process of land alienation in the lowveld was triggered by the movement of 'pioneer' white farmers off the highveld to carve out cattle ranches. This constituted a second, relatively more recent phase of land alienation as the prime agricultural land in the highveld had already been taken by the colonialists. The movement of Africans off the 'European farming area' in the lowveld accelerated after the Second World War – especially with the coming of the sugar estates at Triangle and Hippo Valley. Evictions continued in the lowveld until the late 1960s with the establishment of Gonarezhou National Park.

It is worth stressing that, compared to other parts of Zimbabwe, land has always been relatively available, and population densities relatively low, in the south-east. Particularly in the south of Matibi II and in Sengwe communal areas there is not a massive pressure on arable land (although there is pressure on grazing land in some years and seasons). Grievances around colonial interventions tended to focus more on the alienation from ancestral lands, destruction of traditional livelihood strategies (such as fishing and hunting) and the disruption of trade routes. In common with elsewhere in Rhodesia land was a major rallying point for the nationalist movement in the lowveld. As former District Commissioner Allan Wright notes in his memoirs, Joshua Nkomo, who was interned at Gonakudzingwa Restriction Camp, 'made very intelligent and effective use of [the] attitude of the tribesmen to old [alienated] hunting lands' in the process garnering widespread support from the local population (Wright 1972: 143). The removal of people from the former protective sphere of their ancestors was also, and continues to be, a particularly contentious issue.

Having said that shortage of arable land is not a major issue in the communal areas of the lowveld it is important to add the proviso that, in certain areas where population is concentrated, there are strongly felt perceptions of land shortage. This is particularly true of the area around Chikombedzi township in the south of Matibi II communal area. The township is located in a bottleneck between the commercial ranches to the west and the Gonakudzingwa small scale farms and Gonarezhou National Park to the east. People feel literally squeezed in. Typical was Mr Makondo:

> If I had power I would say people should make the commercial farms smaller and give up a portion of Gonarezhou National Park to use so our houses can be 1 km apart. This overcrowding is encouraging disease, we need space.[5]

Post-Independence land reform initiatives in the lowveld have been quite limited despite the fact that in the early 1980s the radical Mwenezi land reform exercise was a precursor to the countrywide 'villagisation programme'. The only two resettlement schemes to have been imple-

---

[5] Interview: Mr Makondo, Chikombedzi, 8 June 1998.

mented in the lowveld were in Chiredzi district at Chizvirizvi, bordering Sangwe communal area, Gonarezhou National Park and Malilangwe Trust, and Nyagambe bordering the current Save Valley Conservancy and Mkwasine Estate.[6]

However, in the last several years there has been a flurry of formal and informal activity concerning land reform and resettlement in the lowveld. In the 1997 land designation exercise more than 15 per cent of all land identified for resettlement was in Mwenezi District, mainly on the grounds that these farms were 'under-utilised' (Moyo 1998).[7] Other categories prioritised for designation were derelict land, multiply owned land, foreign owned land and land contiguous to communal areas (Moyo 1998).[8] Much of this land was subsequently delisted.[9]

Before considering the turbulent developments since 2000 it is important to stress that the boundaries separating white commercial and black communal land in the lowveld are not always as hard-edged as they appear on the map or, for that matter, in the landscape. Some writers have laid great emphasis on the symbolic nature of the fences in the lowveld landscape which bound the landscape into delineated, straight and visibly exact zones, separating single function land uses (e.g. Wels 2000). This is read as symbolic of the division between white and black spaces, productive and natural spaces, order and disorder, healthy and diseased spaces, culture and nature. But this strict binary division of white and black spaces should not be overplayed. Even before, and alongside, the highly visible farm invasions, a variety of less high-profile activities have often blurred these boundaries making them more permeable than they appear. Farmers in the communal areas of Matibi II and Sengwe, for example, regularly negotiated agreements with neighbouring white commercial farmers about access to certain natural resources on their properties. Informal agreements were reached about collection of mopane worms, firewood, thatching grass, poles, quelea birds, and ilala palm. The degree of latitude within these agreements depends on the relationship between the communities and the individual commercial farmers, with some having a reputation for generosity and others harshness. One rancher, for example, made some of his paddocks available for communal cattle grazing during the severe drought of 1991-92; whilst his neighbour threatened to shoot any cattle – or people – wandering onto his land. The landscape's spatial logic has thus never been quite as neat or firm as the impression given by the straight lines on the map or the fences divid-

---

[6] Devure Resettlement Scheme also borders the Save Valley Conservancy but falls outside the lowveld in Bikita District.
[7] But only 3.3 per cent of the designated farms were in Mwenezi district (indicating the extensive nature of the holdings).
[8] The now legislated 'farm size ceiling' in Natural Region 5 (into which the lowveld ranches fall – see Chapter 4) is 3,000 hectares (Moyo 2000b).
[9] 23 per cent of the land subsequently delisted was in Mwenezi District – including the massive Nuanetsi Ranch (owned by the Development Trust of Zimbabwe led, at the time, by Vice President Joshua Nkomo) – at 319,711 hectares this is Zimbabwe's largest landholding.

ing it. These 'cross-fence' resource flows are dynamic and constantly changing, depending on season and on the personal dynamics of particular communities and farmers, and can range from formally negotiated arrangements to illicit 'poaching'.

Similarly, as Hughes (2001: 5) has demonstrated elsewhere in Zimbabwe, 'white' activities are increasingly no longer confined to white spaces – commercial farms – but are encroaching onto 'black' land – communal areas – in a potential 'territorial scramble similar to but more inventive than that of the 1890s'. As Chapter 6 described, commercial ranchers in the lowveld have long operated in the communal areas: sourcing stock from auctions for fattening and resale. In recent years some ranchers have diversified into buying goats (many destined for export to Mauritius) – spending days travelling around and camping in Matibi II, Sengwe, Chipise and Diti communal areas.[10] Another means by which white entrepreneurs have 'penetrated' communal lands is through the contract growing of cash crops – particularly guar beans, but also red sorghum and tomatoes. However, white commercial activity in the communal areas is most strikingly apparent in the wildlife industry. The CAMPFIRE programme is premised on the activity of mainly white-run safari operations in communal areas, in the process redefining black entitlement to land in communal areas as merely a claim competing with those of other stakeholders (Hughes 2001). The quasi-CAMPFIRE activities of the Save Valley Conservancy and Malilangwe Trust have also focused on the expansion of tourism and hunting operations into communal areas. These activities have contributed to a blurring of the ostensibly hard edges dividing commercial and communal land in the lowveld.

Further theoretically hard but practically porous boundaries in the landscape are the international borders separating Zimbabwe, Mozambique and South Africa. As Chapter 4 examined, illicit cross-border movements of people and goods are absolutely crucial to livelihoods in the region. The Zimbabwe-South Africa border is regularly crossed by 'border jumpers' who must negotiate the electric fence, crocodiles in the Limpopo and lions in Kruger National Park in their night-time attempts to avoid border guards. There is also extensive trade in goods with Mozambique and an increasing amount of illegal movement of livestock to Mozambique for sale – either stolen or smuggled by their owners.

Farm invasions in the lowveld

Squatting, poaching and arson on commercial property are not new phenomena in the lowveld. The latter two were tactics deployed by the guerrillas during the liberation war to target the isolated white ranchers. Post-Independence these tactics have also been used at various times as

---
[10] Interview: Commercial farmer, Mwenezi, 17 August 1999.

political messages – signifying resistance or punishment (deliberately started veld fires are also used as a poaching strategy – driving animals towards poachers and distracting game guards). Between 1997 and 1999 there was a noticeable escalation of farm invasion incidents. Squatters moved onto Levanga and Angus ranches in the Save Valley Conservancy, as well as Faversham and Ngwane Extension ranches near Chiredzi, and 120,000 acres were burnt out in Chiredzi Conservancy.[11]

However, as described above, it was in the run-up to the 2000 election that farm invasions started happening in large numbers across Zimbabwe. In the lowveld these invasions started later than elsewhere (April), but they rapidly picked up momentum after the election in June. By July they were on a massive scale; and by September/October the lowveld ranches of Masvingo Province, particularly around Chiredzi,[12] were probably the most seriously affected farms in the country – huge areas had been burnt out, cleared, and poached of game and by November the occupied farms were being ploughed and planting with maize.[13]

Who were the invaders?

The catch-all description of 'farm invasions' masks a great range of different dynamics, as different combinations of actors have occupied different properties for different reasons in different ways. Although much of the international media have unfairly caricatured the farm invasions as an exclusively politically-driven process, political orchestration has undoubtedly played an important part in the farm invasions in the lowveld. That ZANU(PF) should fight the election under the slogan 'the economy is land' and crank up the rhetoric on resettlement is no surprise given the history of election campaigning in Zimbabwe, and particularly given the existence of serious opposition for the first time. What is more surprising is that the electioneering rhetoric persisted and segued into a drawn-out presidential election campaign. This was accompanied by active political support and encouragement for the farm invasions from the government. In the lowveld the principal actors were the Provincial Governor and the ZANU(PF) MPs for Chiredzi North and South. They all had something to prove. The Governor had long been bound up in a bitter ZANU(PF) faction fight for control of Masvingo, and both MPs had very closely fought election campaigns in which they made extensive promises for land delivery. The Governor and Chiredzi South MP, in particular, have on numerous occasions addressed rallies exhorting people to invade farms – on occasion going as far as to arrange transport. The Governor and MPs gained crucial

---

[11] Interview: Director, Wildlife Management Services, Triangle, 3 November 1999.
[12] Particular hotspots were: Angus/Mukwazi/Mukazi ranches in the SVC; Buffalo Range, Fair Range, Chipimbi and Bangala in Chiredzi District.
[13] *Zimbabwe Standard*, 8 October 2000.

support from a relatively new, and very powerful, political grouping – the war veterans. These war veterans were loose groupings of genuine ex-combatants, ZANU(PF) apparatchiks, and unemployed youths led by charismatic 'big-men' (in Masvingo Province these have included Boniface Mutemachani, Kid Muzenda, Captain Zimuto, Makaye, and 'Black Jesus'). Interestingly, as appears to be the case elsewhere in Zimbabwe, a new loop of governance came to the fore – incorporating the Governors, MPs and war veterans, but by-passing other institutions (such as the Councillors, chiefs and District Administrators), and apparently beyond the reach of the law.[14] The war veterans acted as ZANU(PF) enforcers. Not only have they been crucial in mobilising the farm invasions and allocating plots (becoming *de facto* land patrons),[15] but they have played a key role in 'campaigning' for the elections, most notably in the Bikita West by-election of January 2001. The war veterans are symbolically useful to ZANU(PF) too, as they emphasise the links between the land invasions and the 'unfinished business' of the liberation war. There was a deliberate use of wartime rhetoric and terminology: for example, alongside the war vets were *chimbwido* (women who cook for guerrillas) and *mujiba* (frontier youth or guerrilla auxiliaries), political opponents were labelled 'sell-outs', and war songs were frequently sung. Roadblocks and bush camps also evoked recent memories of landscapes of war. Similarly, the white farmers fell back into wartime language and practice: establishing 'Agric-alert' radio networks, travelling in convoys, and producing regular 'sitreps' (Situation Reports) – these days posted on the internet (see Chaumba, Scoones and Wolmer 2003a and 2003b for more detail on these dynamics).

However, as in the liberation war, the degree of political unanimity should not be exaggerated (cf. Kriger 1992). There were many, sometimes competing, constituencies. This was true within government also – as we shall see below, the Ministry of Environment and Tourism and the DNPWLM were often speaking to different agendas from the President's Office, Governor and MPs. From this dynamic and confused situation various political opportunists – such as the Provincial Governor and the 'big-men' – were able to carve out powerful positions.[16] Lines of political

---

[14] The police were wary of involvement in 'political crimes' like farm invasions.

[15] Farm invaders were not supposed to go independently onto the farms but were supposed to register formally to become a group member. The official procedure was that a list of potential settlers should be compiled by district committees comprising traditional leaders, councillors and war veterans and submitted to a provincial land allocation committee. In practice land allocation was often administered exclusively by the war veterans (providing them with possibilities for patronage and leading to allegations of profiteering by selling plots). Disputes between war veterans and district land committees over land allocation intensified. *Daily News*, 14 February 2001; *Sunday Mail*, 22 April 2001. The emergent lines of political authority during this period in the Sangwe communal area of the lowveld are explored in detail in Chaumba, Scoones and Wolmer (2003b).

[16] This is admitted by the government's own Report of the Presidential Land Review Committee which concedes that certain 'war veterans and politicians' were able to exert

authority became even more overlapping, complex and contested than usual as war veterans usurped some of the powers of traditional leaders (such as land allocation) (Chaumba, Scoones and Wolmer 2003b).

The micro-politics of the farm invasions revealed contrasting local dynamics. Certain commercial farmers had their properties specifically targeted — either as a punishment by the war veterans/ZANU(PF) for openly supporting the opposition MDC; or as a means of retaliation by community members for past actions and perceived injustices. One game ranch owner near Chikombedzi was particularly unpopular with both the government and his communal area neighbours. He was reputed to have a brutal war record and was locally rumoured to have poisoned an eland found in a snare on his property which was subsequently eaten at a wedding party, killing several and severely poisoning others. He had always had a very intolerant attitude to requests for firewood and pole collection on his land; and when the farm invasions started in 2000 he openly threatened to shoot any person he found on his farm and throw their body down an ant bear's hole.[17] None of this endeared him to the local community and he also made enemies in government by working actively as an MDC fund-raiser and campaigner (at one stage scattering MDC leaflets and money from his plane as he flew over Chikombedzi). It was an open secret that his farm was due to be targeted by the local and non-local war veterans but his fearsome reputation was enough to deter large-scale invasions of his property until mid-2001. Another rancher, in Mwenezi, played up his liberation war credentials (he had actively supported guerrillas with food) and took the MP to court arguing that the farm occupiers on his property should be removed because he too was a war veteran.[18]

However, this discussion of politically motivated and targeted land invasions should not obscure the movement of genuinely land-hungry people from outside the lowveld onto the ranches of the lowveld. This was most evident on Chiredzi ranches such as Bangala, Buffalo Range, Nuanetsi, Fair Range, and Chipimbi where landless settlers from the overcrowded communal areas of Bikita, Zaka, and Chivi settled in large numbers. Similarly there were movements from Maranda and Matibi I communal areas onto the neighbouring ranches in Mwenezi. There was also a massive movement of poor urban, unemployed people from Chiredzi township onto nearby ranches (particularly Buffalo Range which by August 2000 had thousands of settlers and was soon visibly partitioned into small stands). In a desperate economic environment the urban poor are particularly vulnerable, so many of them jumped at the opportunity of acquiring land.

There were also movements onto neighbouring farms from the communal areas within the lowveld. This is particularly the case in the relatively

---

[16] (cont.) considerable 'unprocedural' influence in Masvingo Province and particularly Chiredzi and Mwenezi districts during the land reform process (Utete 2003).
[17] Interview: Farm worker, Mwenezi, by Jacob Mahenehene, 25 July 2000.
[18] Interview: Muraba, by Jacob Mahenehene, 29 November 2000.

densely populated (by lowveld standards) Sangwe and Matibi II communal areas. In Chompani (in Matibi II), for example, there was a lot of movement onto the immediately neighbouring commercial farms (Edenvale and Jaula). Given the close proximity it was possible for people to plough and graze their animals on the ranches without leaving their communal area homestead – allowing a daily migration onto the ranches. On the ranch discussed above, where the owner was particularly feared, there were initially weekly invaders who would leave the property when they heard the owner's aeroplane at weekends.

Another feature of the farm invasions that received much media attention was the opportunist asset stripping from commercial ranches. Local and non-local entrepreneurs took advantage of the police's *laissez-faire* attitude and the ability to move over commercial property relatively unhindered. The resulting asset stripping included: large-scale poaching (with snares, dogs and bows and arrows); cattle rustling; fish poaching; the collection of poles, firewood, thatching grass, ilala palm, fencing wire and posts, sand and even sugar cane,[19] for re-sale. One ranch in Mwenezi, for example, lost 700 cattle between July and December 2000.[20] Piles of wood and thatching grass were sold along the Ngundu-Chiredzi road; firewood carted to Tsovani township in Chiredzi; meat sold house to house in the communal areas; and there were reports of new butcheries opening near Save Valley Conservancy to process the poached meat.[21]

The people who were best able to benefit from this situation were those most well-endowed with capital (financial and social): relatively wealthy individuals who are politically well-connected to the local ZANU(PF) hierarchy. They included many war veterans, who received cash disbursements and regular pensions from the government in 1997,[22] local businessmen and salaried black middle-classes (such as Triangle and Hippo Valley Estates managers, and urban-dwellers from further afield – Masvingo and even Harare). Political connections ensured the allocation of plots by the war veterans, and financial capital enabled the hire of labourers to clear fields and the provision of transport. Those in a position to take advantage of new land needed to have sufficient draught power, ploughs, scotchcarts and other equipment to spare (as well as access to labour) – since the government was not yet providing infrastructure, credit or any other assistance to settlers, only the asset rich were able to take full advantage.

A further rationale for land occupiers, one that has received less attention, is the desire to return to one's ancestral lands and to re-establish ties with lineage history and culture. This desire for land restitution is particularly

[19] 125 tonnes of sugar cane was reported stolen from Levanga ranch by people from the Gudo area of Sangwe communal area. *Daily News*, 15 August 2000.
[20] Interview: Rancher, Mwenezi, 27 January 2001.
[21] 'Wildlife becomes victim of Zimbabweans' grab for land'. *Financial Times*, 16 August 2000.
[22] After violent demonstrations in 1997 a newly powerful war veterans lobby secured Z$50,000 each in gratuities and Z$2000 a month pensions as well as a guarantee of land in the resettlement process.

powerful amongst the Shangaan population of the lowveld and especially those old enough to have memories of eviction.[23] The removal from the protective sphere of the *mukwembu* (ancestral spirits) is bitterly resented and often blamed for leading to a perceived increased incidence of drought and other misfortunes. The return of ancestral lands would allow rainmaking and other ceremonies to be carried out unhindered. The Mateke Hills and Chiumbulu Mountain in the Mwenezi commercial ranches; the pools on Levanga ranch in the Save Valley Conservancy; and the Chilunja and Gonakudzingwa hills in Gonarezhou National park are all examples of sacred sites and lineage 'homelands' that are coveted by former inhabitants. The desire for restitution of ancestral land goes beyond the desire to re-establish spatial and spiritual connections with *mukwembu*. There is also a powerful notion of wanting to be back in one's own place and therefore no longer 'foreign' (*valuveli*) or tribute (*kukondza*) to another chief or headman. Narratives of land restitution are associated with nostalgic notions of a golden past – a landscape where hunting and rain were plentiful – but also express a practical desire to return to particular key resources such as river banks, and grazing lands, that are well known and missed. This desire for restitution of particular pieces of land is distinct from wanting resettlement to anywhere; and it is not solely targeted at land that is currently commercial property, but also includes 'state land' in National Parks. The sentiments have been particularly strongly felt in recent years because people closely followed the experiences of the Makuleke community in South Africa.[24] This is another lowveld Shangaan community immediately bordering Zimbabwe who, in a well-publicised case, won back the land they were evicted from in the 1960s with the establishment of Kruger National Park (see Harries 1987; Steenkamp 1999; Reid 2001).

The dynamics of the farm invasions

Farm invasions in Mwenezi and Chiredzi Districts were thus a product of both political orchestration and spontaneous opportunism. Although much of the media coverage portrayed the farm invasions as uniformly violent, many were peaceful. Where there was violence this was directed at a variety of groups, including farmers, farm workers, 'unofficial' poachers and most commonly game scouts. The invasions were fluid, dynamic affairs, with numbers of occupiers fluctuating as different groups arrived and departed. Some farms were occupied, abandoned and reoccupied on several occasions.

Some farm invasions were of a purely symbolic nature. There was minimal interference with the landscape other than the leaving of symbolic markers (such as pegging field boundaries, ring-barking trees and building

---

[23] Interviews in Chikombedzi and Masukwe.
[24] For example: Interview: Councillor, Chikombedzi, by Jacob Mahenehene, 21 December 2000.

shelters) with no attempt made at cultivating the land. Other invasions caused more aggressive damage (such as fence-cutting, clearing fields, maiming cattle, fire-setting, poaching, and occupying safari camps), and the landscape was physically transformed from mopane 'bush' into ploughed fields.[25] The literal appropriation of boundary fences and their remoulding as snares can also be read as a symbolic attempt to erase the white signature in the landscape (Wels 2000).

Another interesting dimension is the ethnic dynamics of the farm invasions in the lowveld. There was a marked perception that Shona people are more actively engaged in the farm invasions than Shangaan people. This is borne out when one compares the Karanga-dominated Chompani/Chanyenga area in Matibi II with the nearby Shangaan-dominated Chikombedzi area; or similarly the Ndau Gudo area with the Shangaan Chitsa area in Sangwe communal area. In both cases the Shona-dominated areas were much more actively engaged in movements onto the commercial farms. This could be explained by the relatively higher population densities in those areas. However, both Shona and Shangaan people I asked about this trend tended to explain it in terms of ethnic stereotypes: 'Shona people grew up in an agricultural set-up; they are good farmers and hungry for land ... Shangaan people are not real agriculturalists... they have small fields and big herds'; 'Shangaan people have no need of land – they are hunters and gatherers'. A further ethnic stereotype invoked was that 'Shona people are more political – farm invasions are for them; Shangaan people are not interested in politics'.[26] The Chompani/ Chanyenga area is certainly a strong ZANU(PF) area (compared to the MDC-dominated Chikombedzi) and more openly politicised.[27] This notion is also interesting in that it reveals that originally many people perceived the farm invasions as primarily an exercise in political symbolism and were wary of getting dragged into 'politics'.

Another broad ethnic generalisation that appears to be borne out in practice is that Shona and Ndebele 'immigrants' to the lowveld tended to be interested in receiving any land – preferably nearby to their existing homesteads – but not necessarily 'their land', except in the broad nationalist sense. Yet many Shangaan people explicitly demanded restitution of 'their' ancestral land from which they or their forefathers were alienated (see above). These ethnic dimensions to the land invasions were picked up on and exploited by local politicians. The MP for Chiredzi South, for example, regularly admonished Shangaan people for being 'lethargic' in the farm occupations. Addressing a post-election rally he reportedly said: 'Please, people of my race [i.e. Shangaan], let's make sure that we go and occupy

---

[25] At one stage it was reported that invaders would be issued with red flags to mark them out as 'peggers not poachers'. *CFU Situation Report*, 30 July 2000.

[26] Interviews: Chikombedzi, January-February 2001.

[27] Driving through relatively well-watered fields in Chanyenga one informant from the more drought-ridden Chikombedzi said to me 'now even the rain is political!'

the farms which are nearer to us. If we delay, people from faraway places will come and occupy the farms and we will fail to get them.'[28]

Competing groups of invaders were not just divided along ethnic lines. There were conflicts between invaders from different administrative areas. For example Jabula Ranch, despite bordering Matibi II communal area, falls into Mwenezi District, and was invaded by people from the relatively distant Shindi, Dare, Ngundu, and Maranda, as well as by people from the adjoining Matibi II (in Chiredzi District). This triggered quarrels between the invaders themselves, and between the MPs and District Administrators from Chiredzi and Mwenezi – and it was eventually decided that the ranch should be reserved for Chiredzi people.[29] The ranches of Triangle/Chiredzi were similarly balkanised with invaders from the Zaka/Bikita communal areas claiming one half, and those from the Chiredzi communal areas the other. There were reports of competing factions of war veterans led by different 'big-men' driving each other off farms.[30]

There were also post-invasion conflicts between invaders and farm owners over various issues. These included water access for the invaders' cattle; access to grazing land (particularly where many cattle have been driven in and veld fires have been started, putting grass in short supply); damage to invaders fields by ranchers' cattle; the spreading of tick-borne diseases between invaders' and ranchers' cattle; and particularly poaching (see below).

In Matibi II and Sengwe many people did not participate in the farm invasions. The reasons given for this revealed a high level of political awareness and cynicism. The most common reason put to me was fears over the permanency of tenure on squatted plots. Will they keep them when formal allocation of land occurs? Or will the land go only to war veterans, those with political connections or holders of 'Master Farmer' certificates? As one person put it, 'land hungry people are all swimming in the pool of doubts'.[31] People were wary of being used as political pawns, many were disillusioned at having campaigned for land for so long without the government fulfilling its promises – and distrusted the MP who was perceived to be opportunistically using land as a campaigning issue. An analogy commonly made is with the antbear – which digs many holes that other animals (such as porcupines, jackals, bush pigs and wild dogs) take advantage of (*sasela vanungu*).[32] Others admitted to being scared off the farms by the perceived 'disorderly' and sometimes violent occupation process or by potential intimidation from farmers and their game guards.[33]

---

[28] Interview: Mutende, by Jacob Mahenehene, 9 August 2000.
[29] Interview: Muraba, by Jacob Mahenehene, 29 November 2000.
[30] CFU situation report, Merrievale, 10 July 2000; 'Chivi, Mwenezi villagers clash over land', *Daily News*, 30 October 2000.
[31] Interview: Chikombedzi by Jacob Mahenehene, 19 December 2000.
[32] Interview: Masukwe by Jacob Mahenehene, 7 March 2001.
[33] In August 2000 many farm occupiers on Edenvale Ranch from Chompani and Chanyenga fled when they heard radio reports that occupiers had been forcefully evicted from farms

Farm occupiers were also being told not to hunt, cut trees and grass, or mould bricks (although this was rarely being enforced). But people asked why they are being given land with strings attached – 'when a person who has given me something turns to give me instructions on how to use it – has that thing really been given to me, or is it a fake kind of giving? That is just the same as [the way] the government has given farms to the people.'[34]

Notwithstanding the different motivations for farm invasions, their contested nature, and the fact that not everyone participated in them, they dramatically revealed fundamentally different ways of seeing the landscape. The crucial question remains whether the current land reform programme will improve the livelihoods of people in the lowveld communal areas and incorporate their alternative perceptions of landscape. Does it have the potential to replace the wilderness vision with a new paradigm? The remainder of this chapter attempts to answer these questions in relation to the land-use themes explored in Chapters 4-7: dryland agriculture, water, cattle, and wildlife.

Dryland agriculture and land

As Chapter 4 examined, discourses on the 'productivity' of land in the lowveld have been essential props to land-use planning. The landscape has been zoned in such a way as to define dryland or rainfed agriculture as simply ecologically inappropriate. This discourse continues to hold sway despite the importance of this type of agriculture – as one strand amongst many strategies – to rural livelihoods. Defining 'appropriate land uses' is an inherently political exercise and no more so than when used as the rationale for the suitability or unsuitability of land reform and resettlement programmes. Indeed precisely this argument has been advanced by many in the commercial farming sector and wildlife lobby to promote the case that large-scale resettlement is inappropriate due to the 'limited agricultural potential' of the lowveld – it will exacerbate, not alleviate, poverty and environmental degradation. However, this way of seeing is being directly challenged by both ZANU(PF)'s populist political rhetoric and the actions of farm invaders.

Commercial farmers typically used arguments about efficient 'economic scale', food security concerns, undermining export markets, the dangers of environmental degradation, and the existence of hidden political agendas to make the case against resettlement in the lowveld, as the following quotes show:

> When you talk to sensitive people like the DA they say the region is not suitable for

[33] (cont.) near Harare and their belongings burnt. Interview: Chanyenga, by Jacob Mahenehene, 26 August 2000.
[34] Interview: Chikombedzi, by Jacob Mahenehene, 30 July 2000.

land resettlement because of drought. Moving people into the region means feeding more people. For every 10 tonnes of grain moved out of the area 90 tonnes is brought in. It consumes more grain in the long-run than it grows.... Why go against the natural system? Nature is forcing people out. There will be problems if you resettle people here — it's just politics. Better to resettle people on land suitable for cultivation north of the Lundi River.[35]

It's all very well taking a ranch and subdividing it into resettlement plots. Once the trees have been chopped down and people start agriculture the government will be subsidising people because it isn't sustainable unless they get at least 10 acres of irrigated land.[36]

I don't believe in dishing out land willy-nilly because one ethnic group has more land than the other when you consider that land down here can't be utilised without irrigation and the interest to do something. If guys are given 0.2 ha they can't do anything but grow vegetables for their family. With the cost of inputs commercial production is unsustainable. This is 'political' — to get more people on a smaller area. ... Down in this part of the world we've got huge areas of land. We're very prone to drought. The only way people can make it is livestock or wildlife. You need roughly 1 beast per 30 hectares. If it's overpopulated you have a problem.[37]

Of course it is no less 'political' to have fewer people on a larger area — just different politics. There is also anger at the way in which farm invasions disrupt the aesthetics of landscape — in effect the disorder of communal areas is intruding on previously rationally ordered commercial property or wilderness. As one journalist commented on viewing the Chiredzi farm invasions: 'Everywhere squalid daub-and-wattle hovels and sparse crops of under-nourished mealies; often tasselling less than knee high, spoiled what were highly productive farms'.[38] Another inverviewee was even more explicit: 'Huts are popping up like fever blisters as pristine areas are invaded'.[39]

As Potts (2000: 50) notes, the knee-jerk labelling of such dramatic environmental changes as 'degradation' suggests either ignorance of previous land uses or an underlying agenda to denigrate resettlement.[40] The fact that in the 2000-2001 season the rains came very late, leading to large-scale crop failures in the communal areas and the farm occupiers' new plots on the ranches, provided further ammunition to the anti-resettlement lobby.

Challenges to the unsuitability of dryland agriculture argument have

---

[35] Interview: Commercial farmer, Mwenezi, 12 August 1999.
[36] Interview: Commercial farmer and councillor, Chiredzi, 2 November 1999.
[37] Interview: CFU Chairman, Masvingo Province, 22 January 2001.
[38] Dusty Miller, *Zimbabwe Standard*, 11-17 February 2001.
[39] Interview: Environmental consultant, Harare, 15 November 2001.
[40] These statements can be located in a broader narrative — particularly influential in the 1980s — which assumed that the conversion of commercial farms to smallholdings was to cease significant commercial production in favour of subsistence production. This is belied by the rapid post-Independence expansion in smallholders' marketed output in Zimbabwe (Eicher and Rukuni 1994) and Kinsey's (1999) evidence of substantial productivity gains in resettlement areas compared to communal areas (Potts 2000).

come from two areas. One, to which I will return, was the government's newly rediscovered enthusiasm for peasant agriculture. The other concerned the shift to participatory, client-driven approaches in agricultural extension. Donor priorities and funding constraints have pushed Zimbabwean agricultural extension towards a more 'bottom-up' rhetoric. In the south-east lowveld this is exemplified by the activities of the South-Eastern Dry Areas Project (SEDAP) funded by the International Fund for Agricultural Development (IFAD). Rather than dismissing dryland agriculture as ecologically inappropriate or economically inefficient, its importance is actively recognised and attempts made to support it – by 'enhancing drought-coping strategies', enabling restocking of draught power animals, and providing micro-finance (IFAD 1996). There has also been a great deal of community consultation. However, in common with almost all donor-supported programmes in Zimbabwe, it is currently stalled, and further funding is threatened before it has delivered very much on the ground. But SEDAP's activities have contributed to and reflected a changed mood in policy circles in Zimbabwe towards supporting existing agricultural livelihood strategies in the lowveld – and away from irrelevant blanket recommendations geared more towards the commercial than the communal sector.

The statements given by ZANU(PF) politicians since 2000 appear directly to counter the CFU arguments about the inappropriateness of dryland agriculture in the lowveld. The Masvingo Provincial Governor and MPs have been actively encouraging people to plough up commercial cattle and game ranches. The MP for Chiredzi South made much of the good soil fertility on the ranches in the region and persistently tried to persuade people to get onto the ranches and exploit it – even donating seeds. However, as we have seen, the question asked by a cynical electorate is whether this enthusiasm for smallholder dryland agriculture is symbolic or permanent. Is it a deliberate rejection of the colonial wilderness binary vision in favour of a peasant smallholder model centred on rainfed agriculture or a strategic piece of populism intended to garner support in the face of an invigorated political opposition?

Given the problems experienced with overly technical and bureaucratic resettlement schemes in the past in Zimbabwe (Drinkwater 1989; Robins 1994), the ostensibly chaotic and slightly anarchic nature of the fast-track resettlement process worked to many people's advantage. The relative lack of enforcement of formal rules or technocratic plans allowed for a large measure of flexibility and opportunism by the land 'self-provisioners'. A rigorously planned and managed process would undoubtedly have hindered these opportunistic strategies by enforcing bans on riverbank and wetland cultivation, for example. However this *laissez-faire* approach stemmed from political and economic imperatives rather than a radical change of philosophy from a government with an instinctively technocratic and managerial bias towards land-use planning (Drinkwater 1989; Alexander 1994;

Chaumba *et al.* 2003a). The government had insufficient time and money to implement a more rigourous and formally planned process, given that it was keen to show results in advance of a presidential election, and lacked donor support. Notwithstanding this, by early 2001 the government was keen to draw a line under the time of '*jambanja*'[41] and land invasions, and the agricultural extension department was frantically drawing up maps for parcelling out ranches to smallholders and surveying and pegging plots in an attempt to impose a patina of order on a land allocation process that had, in some cases, already been conducted by the farm invaders themselves. In the process they were recasting invasions as resettlement, legitimising settlers' presence with long-familiar codes of land-use planning. The danger for the new settlers is that this reassertion of technocracy will mean the reimposition of coercive land use regulations, rigid categorisations and static recommendations that are at odds with their dynamic livelihood strategies (Chaumba *et al.* 2003a).

A further way in which government priorities on land diverge from those of many in the lowveld communal areas is on the actual need for further arable land. As mentioned above, these areas are crucially different from the communal areas further north – arable land shortage is a progressively less severe issue as you move south (with some important exceptions). Water is hard to find away from rivers and boreholes on many of the lowveld ranches; and the lack of rain early in the 2000-2001 season provided even less incentive for people to move onto the farms. This is compounded by the draught power shortage which makes ploughing even existing arable land difficult for many. Resource-poor people wanted to concentrate their farming efforts on the safe bet – the land they farm in the communal areas with relatively secure tenure. That said, they may be keen to exploit certain key areas for agriculture such as particular *vleis*, patches of fertile soil, and to utilise the newly available natural resources and grazing lands on the farms (as well as desiring the restitution of ancestral lands). In Matibi II and Sengwe communal areas, the farm invasions provided more of an opportunity for further extensification of dryland fields by the asset-rich and politically well connected than a means of relieving the poverty of the very poor (this can be contrasted with the more densely populated Sangwe communal area, to the north, where many poor and landless people did indeed gain land (Chaumba *et al.* 2003b)).

Water and land

During the recent round of land 'self-provisioning' and designations of lowveld game and cattle ranches for resettlement, small-scale irrigated agri-

---

[41] This literally means violence or angry argument and has been popularly used to describe the time and space of confusion, disorder and chaos surrounding the farm invasions or politically instigated violence (Chaumba *et al.* 2003a).

culture was surprisingly rarely mentioned as a potential resettlement model. The lush, green and productive lowveld has not been portrayed as a panacea to the land issue in the way that it was held up as Rhodesia's economic saviour and a promised land for (white) settlers in the 1960s. Interestingly, however, the arguments put forward by young white agricultural students at that time to justify their allocation of plots in the Hippo Valley, Triangle and Mkwasine settler agriculture schemes sound not dissimilar to the ZANU(PF) rhetoric of today. A newspaper headline in 1970, for example, quotes agricultural students referring to the lowveld: 'This land is our land, say Gwebi [Agricultural College] young farmers.'[42]

Before his death, Joshua Nkomo's vision for Nuanetsi/Mwenezi ranch (owned by the Development Trust of Zimbabwe which he chaired) was for it to become 'the hub of a new settlement scheme drawing agro-minded technocrats such as water engineers, agronomists, trainee farmers and economic planners — among others — to create a new crop of black commercial farmers.' His plan, finalised in 1996, in association with the neighbouring commercial sugar estates, envisaged the systematic resettlement of thousands of new farmers on 100 hectares each to produce sugar and cotton.[43]

Others within government have also argued forcefully for an irrigation-based resettlement model in the lowveld. The ZANU(PF) MP for Mwenezi, for example, writing to the Minister of Lands and Agriculture in early 1999 about any future resettlement on commercial farms in Mwenezi stresses that 'it is imperative that water for irrigation, even domestic use, be provided before settlers are moved in', and:

> Unless the proposed Manyuchi Irrigation Project is established, settling of people on farms acquired by government in Mwenezi will not, unfortunately, resolve our current problems, in fact it will turn out to be a very costly exercise as government again will end up feeding those families resettled on these farms.[44]

However, expensive capital-intensive irrigation schemes were at odds with the minimal infrastructure fast-track resettlement scheme. Again this stems from political and economic imperatives. Long-term investment in infrastructure was not a priority, given the short-term political desire to maintain symbolic occupations of commercial properties in the run-up to presidential elections and the subsequent desire to roll out the resettlement programme as fast as possible. The government was, and remains, simply unable to fund large-scale irrigation schemes (the Tokwe-Mukorsi dam remains stalled because of lack of funds) or attract donor support in the current political climate and, until legislative change in early 2004 (see below), appeared unwilling to jeopardise foreign investment any further by wholesale appropriation of land from the large-scale sugar estates.

[42] *Financial Gazette*, 22 May 1970.
[43] 'Nkomo's allies fight for Nuanetsi' *Financial Gazette*, 4 July 2002.
[44] MP for Mwenezi to the Minister of Lands and Agriculture, 16 February 1999.

Where irrigation-based resettlement schemes have been considered there have been disagreements over the appropriate size of individual plots. These disputes reflect, in microcosm, the conflicting logic of different ways of seeing the lowveld. The government wants the maximum number of people to be resettled and therefore argues for small plot sizes; whereas the members of the commercial farming lobby argue for larger plot sizes using a discourse on 'economic' and 'uneconomic' units for commercial agriculture reminiscent of debates around the implementation of the Native Land Husbandry Act.[45] As the Regional Executive of the Masvingo Province Commercial Farmers Union put it: 'Resettlement programmes don't give them enough resources to [farm] commercially ... A two hectares irrigation plot provides food but not enough to put you on your feet. It's not enough to generate enough money to pay for inputs. You would need at least 10 hectares.'[46] The CFU were lobbying for a commercial resettlement programme based on 100-hectare irrigated sugar and cotton smallholdings on Nuanetsi Ranch with a view to further out-grower schemes in neighbouring communal areas (the same scheme that Joshua Nkomo had long championed). Resettlement in this manner fits with the CFU's productive economic holdings model and their wish to avoid 'upsetting the delicate economic base of commercial farming' by giving up productive ranching land.[47]

Another potential model for irrigation-scheme-based resettlement would be for smallholder out-grower schemes on the large sugar estates. There is a precedent for this at Mkwasine estate (owned by a consortium of Triangle and Hippo Valley Estates) where 'small-scale' African farmers were settled on ten-hectare plots on condition that they delivered all their cane to the company mills, the companies retaining 35 per cent of the value of the sugar cane milled (Pangeti 1986). The UK Department for International Development (DFID) had been in discussion with Triangle Estates about the possibilities for this kind of arrangement. But in the current political climate Triangle has been very worried about offering any land up for resettlement, fearing that it will open the floodgates to further claims.[48]

Although some government supporters were directing anti-imperialist rhetoric towards the sugar estates,[49] farm invasions on these properties were relatively limited during 2000-2001. However, disgruntled cane cutters at Hippo Valley did take advantage of the turbulent context in May 2000 to demonstrate against poor wages. Two foremen were killed and over 1,000 hectares of sugar cane burnt in violent protests (Hippo Valley Estates Ltd.

---

[45] See, for example, Phillips *et al.* (1962).
[46] Interview: CFU Regional Executive, Masvingo Province, 7 August 1999.
[47] Interview: CFU Regional Chairman, Masvingo Province, 8 September 1999.
[48] Interview: DFID, Harare, 15 February 2001.
[49] For example: 'If the Anglo-Americans pack and go to their motherlands Britain and America and leave Hippo Valley and Triangle Mills, China is willing to come and take over running those mills without any problems'. Interview: Ponyoka, by Jacob Mahenehene, 2 August 2000.

2000). Large parts of Triangle and Hippo Valley were initially gazetted for resettlement, but the Minister for Lands, Agriculture and Resettlement later said this had been an error.[50] The government appeared unwilling to sanction resettlement on land owned by companies that have Zimbabwe Investment Centre certificates.[51] Notwithstanding this, by late 2001 cane farms within Triangle, Hippo Valley and Mkwasine estates were pegged and settled under the Model A2 resettlement scheme, leading to legal disputes over the ownership of standing sugar cane.[52] In 2002, the government used land on the sugar estates for the high-profile and controversial winter cropping of maize in an attempt to stave off drought-induced food shortages – a scheme which was subsequently abandoned.[53] And in January 2004, following the passing of the Land Acquisition (Amendment) Bill which empowered the government to acquire agro-businesses with Zimbabwe Investment Centre certificates and repealed the 1964 Hippo Valley Agreement Act ceding land and water rights to the estate, the entire Hippo Valley and Mkwasine estates were once again designated for resettlement – although the government's intentions for this land remain unclear.[54]

A further proposed development for the lowveld – ominously echoing the grandiloquent and ill-fated schemes for large-scale communal area irrigation from the 1960s to the 1990s and the 'greenbelt' and 'breadbasket' rhetoric described in Chapter 5 – is the hugely ambitious proposal to grow 150,000 hectares of winter maize on the land on Nuanetsi Ranch that Joshua Nkomo had earmarked for his sugar and cotton scheme. Like many previous *Grands Projets* in the region, this scheme, the brainchild of the Provincial Governor, has been mired in ZANU(PF) faction-fighting and has had difficulty keeping its Chinese contractors, given fuel shortages and payment difficulties.[55]

Despite this scheme, and the transfer of some irrigated sugar estate land to relatively affluent and politically well-connected 'Model A2' farmers – for the relatively asset poor, improving access to existing smallholder irrigation schemes through existing informal sub-leasing arrangements may be of greater help to livelihoods than large-scale irrigation-based resettlement which, in practice, appears unlikely to materialise in the short to medium term.

---

[50] *Daily News*, 22 September 2000.
[51] Interview: Acting DA, Acting CEO, Chiredzi, 29 January 2001.
[52] The Model A2 resettlement schemes are envisaged as a means of 'deracialising' agriculture by providing small-scale, self-contained commercial production units for black entrepreneurs. These A2 settlers are relatively affluent and politically well-connected. According to the Presidential Land Review Committee (2003) there were 401 A2 settlers on irrigated plots on former sugar estate land by the end of 2003.
[53] 'Experts predict winter maize project will fail', *Daily News*, 19 April 2002.
[54] 'Anglo's bid to save plantations fails', *Zimbabwe Independent*, 13 February 2004.
[55] 'Nkomo's allies fight for Nuanetsi', *Financial Gazette*, 4 July 2002; 'Chinese firm abandons Nuanetsi project', *Zimbabwe Independent*, 1 August 2003.

Cattle and land

As with debates about the productivity of dryland agriculture, ecological arguments about appropriate stocking rates of livestock on rangeland are inherently political. Perceptions of the 'correct' management of livestock – particularly cattle – diverge markedly and, as with arguments about the suitability of dryland agriculture, they are deployed to argue for and against resettlement in the lowveld. Many advocates of large-scale resettlement in government have long pointed to 'under-utilised' ranches with low stocking rates,[56] whilst commercial farmers have argued that the lower, uncertain, and variable rainfall of 'Natural Region 5' necessitates extensive ranches with low stocking rates (1:20 hectares). They contrast this with the 'environmental destruction', and low productivity on 'overstocked' communal areas.

As Chapter 6 described, the fact that livestock management provides a potentially important land use in both the commercial and communal areas of the lowveld is not in doubt. What is in question is what these livestock should principally be for – meat, inputs to agriculture, or both? And what form should the rangeland landscape take: fenced paddocks, cordons and buffer zones or a more open and unbounded space maximising livestock mobility and the diversity of fodder sources?

The farm invasions of 2000-2001 brought these questions to the fore. The most common, and most popular, form of land invasion in the lowveld was poach grazing. Grazing land, as opposed to arable land, is in short supply in many areas of the lowveld, particularly during dry years, and this illicit access enabled much more wide-ranging opportunistic grazing of cattle and goat herds and was welcomed by livestock owners. Also the collapse in enforcement of veterinary controls on livestock movement permitted livestock mobility over wider areas, allowing improved 'tracking' of key resources (cf. Scoones 1995).

These developments particularly benefited relatively wealthy owners of large numbers of livestock, and those living close to the commercial farms. But they are the main way – other than the short-term provision of cheap meat – that the farm invasions and their aftermath have improved livelihoods in the lowveld's communal areas. However, this is probably only a narrow window of opportunity before the government reimposes strict enforcement of livestock movement controls and official stocking rates. The fast-track resettlement scheme technically has formal plans for the organisation of livestock-based resettlement areas. In Natural Region 5, a 10-15 unit beef herd on 180 hectares is officially recommended.[57] Whether this will ever be implemented – or whether calls to halt illegal movements of

---

[56] Such as during the 1997 land designation exercise when a large number of Mwenezi ranches were listed.

[57] This is the 'three tier model': 'designed for drier areas where livestock ranching is the suitable form of land use [in the absence of developed irrigation facilities]. Under this model,

cattle will be heeded because of the veterinary concerns of the cattle industry – remains to be seen. It seems unlikely that the current situation, which is so advantageous to many livestock owners in the communal areas, will be allowed to carry on much longer. Indeed the Report of the Presidential Land Review Committee in 2003 called for the replanning and reorganisation of some resettlement areas of the Masvingo Province lowveld 'such that they would revert to the original [i.e. ranching-based] land use patterns' and for the reintroduction of 'punitive measures against unauthorised livestock movement' (Utete 2003: 60, 91).

Wildlife and land

It is with regard to the 'wildlife landscape' of the lowveld that the turbulent events of recent years have revealed the most starkly contrasting ways of seeing the landscape. The wilderness vision has been brought into sharp contradistinction with other conceptualisations of landscape. The legitimacy of the white-dominated private wildlife industry in the game ranches and conservancies has come under sustained political, moral and physical attack from politicians, war veterans and some communities. The validity of the drive to manufacture wilderness on private land, and to some extent on state land, has been called into question.

As Chapter 7 described, the conservancies, in particular, have always been hugely controversial and highly politicised. It is hardly surprising then, that the Save Valley Conservancy became a well-publicised flashpoint for farm invasions in 2000. In 1997 the depth of political feeling surrounding the conservancies is revealed by a typical article in the state-controlled newspaper which urged the government 'never-ever to spare the so-called conservancies in this [land designation and acquisition] exercise which must be ongoing'.[58] Between 1997 and 2000 government attitudes towards the game ranches and conservancies appeared to be softening. In 1999 the Governor of Masvingo Province, whilst maintaining that indigenisation of the wildlife industry was a priority, told me that:

> Drought paved the way for tourism. We shall not have a lot of cattle in the south-east. There isn't much left. It has moved away from ranching into conservancies. I see in the future cattle giving way to game.[59]

The MP for Chiredzi South argued, similarly, that: 'this area is not good for resettlement ... Most farms [in the lowveld] are properly utilised. Wildlife counts as proper utilisation. Government has promoted tourism so farmers

---

[57] (cont.) settlers are granted commercial grazing rights and the scheme is designed for incremental livestock stocking.' Some schemes will have communally managed grazing, other units will be self-contained and individually managed (Government of Zimbabwe 1998: vi; 2001).
[58] *The Herald*, 22 November 1997; cited by Wels (2000: 201).
[59] Interview: Provincial Governor, Masvingo, 9 September 1999.

are preparing for it. So government can't say it's not viable.'[60] However, this was to change in the run-up to, and aftermath of, the general elections of 2000. With the support and encouragement of the Governor and MPs for Chiredzi North and South there was a wholesale invasion of the SVC, and other conservancies and game ranches. Game scouts were attacked, fields were pegged, fences removed, cattle driven in, and poaching, burning, removals of firewood and thatching grass intensively carried out by local communities and opportunist entrepreneurs. There were increasingly violent stand-offs between game guards and war veterans[61] and escalating poaching and, by mid-June 2000, 'no-go' areas had been established by the veterans.

The precise dynamics of these invasions of the SVC properties merit closer attention. Most of the activity has been focused on a relatively small number of 'hotspots'. Levanga Ranch, adjacent to Gudo in Sangwe communal area, was the first property to be invaded (April 2000). This was followed in May by invasions of Sango Ranch (adjacent to Devure Resettlement Area); Msapas Ranch (also near Sangwe communal area); and the adjoining Angus, Mukwasi and Mkwasi ranches (bordering Matsai communal area). By late June there were 1,000 settlers on Mukwasi and by late August 5,000 settlers from Gudo on Levanga.[62] In October, Mukwasi was completely burnt out and an inspection by the Department of Veterinary Services found the perimeter fence breached in 50 places and substantial numbers of cattle inside the conservancy.[63]

Levanga and Humani ranches (in the south-east of the conservancy) and Angus, Mukwasi and Mkwasi ranches (in the south-west) have consistently been the key hotspots, where most of the reported invasions, poaching, wire-cutting and harassment have taken place. Research into the history of the relations between these farms and their neighbouring communities conducted by Harry Wels in 1997-98 reveals that the current invasions are rooted in long-term contests over the landscape. The ethnically Ndau Gudo people in Sangwe communal area have ancestral burial sites and ritual pools, and have conducted an annual fishing festival, on what is currently Levanga Ranch. Before 1986 the Levanga area was classified as State Land to which the Gudo people had relatively free access in order to visit their ancestral shrines, hunt, fish or graze their cattle. Since the ranch was bought in 1986 there have been conflicts over access to ritual sites and natural resources and the Gudo people's position hardened from a desire to negotiate access to certain pieces of land to an outright land claim. This antagonism has been made manifest in acts of resistance such as the starting of veld fires, fence-cutting, thefts of sugar cane, the burning of a 'traditional village' (see Chapter 7) and then the farm invasions (Wels 2000;

[60] Interview: Chiredzi South MP, Chikombedzi, 13 August 1999.
[61] 'Farm guards shoot group of occupiers', *The Herald*, 15 February 2001.
[62] *Daily News*, 21 August 2000; CFU situation reports (URL: www.samara.co.zw/cfu/farmininbul.htm).
[63] CFU situation reports April – October 2000.

Wolmer, Chaumba and Scoones 2004).[64] On Angus, Mukwasi and Mkwasi ranches the roots of the farm invasions are somewhat different. These were formerly a single property known as Angus Ranch and most of the farm workers were drawn from the neighbouring Matsai communal area. These farm workers were given a small plot of land to plant their own food crops. During the war the ranch was abandoned and the former workers took the opportunity to settle on the property and remained there after Independence, claiming it was their right as retired workers. However in 1983, 33 families were evicted and their houses burnt by the Bikita District Administrator on the grounds that they never 'officially worked for Angus'. Soon after that the District Administrator was transferred and families came back onto the property and in 1993 72 squatting families were granted rights to land (Hill 1994; Wels 2000). The land claims in Angus were not rooted in a narrative about access to ancestral land – the Matsai community's claims to the land span only a generation and there are no ritual sites on the property; rather, land claims are represented as the rightful entitlement of former ranch employees – or families of employees. When Angus became part of the SVC the controversy was reawakened and the siting of the veterinary fence was a particular point of conflict. This soon became highly politicised as, during 1998 (long before the recent invasions), the Matsai people started to invade Angus (now Angus, Mukwazi and Mkwazi) repeatedly and the issue was picked up as a cause-célèbre by the Provincial Governor. The invaders were eventually evicted by the police who used tear-gas, tore down shelters and arrested people.

A closer look at the recent invasions of the SVC reveals, then, that the conservancy was not uniformly targeted. There were flashpoints where there are histories of antagonism between particular ranches and their neighbouring communities, as well as a certain amount of politically motivated 'symbolic' occupation and intimidation of farmers and game scouts. Large sections of the conservancy have never been occupied. One possible reading of poaching in this context is that it is a deliberate political strategy or 'weapon of the weak' by which peasants display resistance (Scott 1985; cf. Bonner 1993; Peluso 1993).[65] This may be partially the case here – although in some cases poaching could also be interpreted as a political strategy by agents of the state intent on running down white businesses. However, in most cases, poaching has been simple opportunism as people take advantage of the lack of enforcement.

The high-profile media coverage of the SVC invasions tended to give a less nuanced picture. As we saw at the beginning of this book, many news-

---

[64] The SVC annual report for 1997-98 reported that the 'Gudo area has ... been identified as an area posing the biggest threat to the SVC in terms of illegal hunting, veld fires, thefts etc.' (Wels 2000: 294).

[65] Bonner (1993) interprets the deliberate and systematic attacking of elephants and rhinos by Maasai residents as a tactic used in order to pressure conservation groups to take Maasai claims seriously and expose the coercive conservation policies of the Kenyan state.

paper articles focus on an emotive narrative in which Eden becomes wasteland as 'poachers feed on Zimbabwe's land crisis'[66] and there has been a 'systematic annihilation of every game species' in 'one of Africa's most important conservation zones'.[67] Particular outrage is reserved for the use of snares and there are fears for the safety of the iconic rhino and endangered wild dogs. As well as threatening biodiversity the farm invasions are held responsible for other environmental ills such as soil erosion due to 'slash and burn' agriculture. As one conservancy member sees it, 'a whole ecosystem is being destroyed'.[68] This is particularly ironic when, by the conservancy ranchers' own admission, few of the wild animals existed on the 'degraded' cattle ranches until very recently. But the pristine wilderness vision is a powerful and persuasive one – the self-consciously manufactured wilderness landscape has, in a matter of years, assumed the status of an inviolate sanctuary of original and irreplaceable nature under threat of extinction from poaching and burning.

The SVC invasions have also been depicted as causing a massive financial loss and as posing a threat to 'a post-Independence success story and ecotourism money spinner'.[69] One newspaper estimated that 'the fast track resettlement programme will cost the country in excess of [Z]$1 billion through the resettlement of people in the Save Conservancy area'.[70] Undoubtedly there has been a total collapse in tourism and hunting revenues nationally,[71] but is it the case that the SVC was a 'success story' or a 'money spinner' before the invasions? In fact Zimbabwe Sun's operations in the SVC were already making massive losses which, according to their auditors, 'cast significant doubt on the company's ability to continue as a going concern'.[72] The lowveld was not yet on the tourist map and certainly now, given international media exposure, the SVC, and the lowveld generally, has a particularly severe negative perception to overcome which poses a serious threat to its potential for achieving a critical mass of tourism development.[73]

The extensive media coverage of the invasions perhaps gave the impression that the SVC has been targeted more than properties elsewhere. This is not the case. However, as Chapter 7 discussed, there has long been a great deal of political antipathy towards it, and towards the wildlife industry in general (Hill 1994). The attempts by the SVC to set up a trust in order to develop a 'meaningful relationship' and share benefits with neighbouring

[66] *BBC News Online*, 7 September 2000.
[67] 'Wildlife becomes victim of Zimbabweans' grab for land', *Financial Times*, 16 August 2000.
[68] Rob Style, Vice Chair, Save Valley Conservancy, quoted in *Mail and Guardian*, 7 November 2000; and see *Zimbabwe Independent*, 25 August 2000.
[69] *Mail and Guardian*, 25 August 2000.
[70] *Zimbabwe Standard*, 22 October 2000.
[71] Interview: Director, Malilangwe Trust, 2 February 2001.
[72] River Lodges of Africa's net loss for 1999-2000 was Z$13,833,663; Price Waterhouse Coopers Ltd. River Lodges of Africa (Private Ltd) 31 March 2000, Financial Statements.
[73] Interview: Director, Malilangwe Trust, 2 February 2001.

communities had, it seems, been a spectacular failure. The scheme was 'shallow and mistrusted', 'more promise than progress' and the invaders had no idea that such a plan even existed.[74] Only after the invasions was the obvious alternative – formally giving communities shares in the land inside the fence – being discussed.[75] After some complex horse-trading, four properties in Bikita (outside the SVC) and the long contested Angus, Mukwasi and Mukazi River ranches in the south-west of the conservancy were offered up for resettlement. This was on the condition that these properties were divided north-south along the line of an old fence boundary – with the west used as a resettlement zone on the standard agriculture-based model and the area to the east (about three-quarters of the land) as a wildlife concession area for the community. The SVC perimeter fence would thus be realigned through this area between the separate land uses.[76] As the Wildlife and Tourism Advisory Council put it: 'The CAMPFIRE-type deal helps dilute the whites-only image of the conservancy. We also want properties to be bought by black indigenous businessmen.'[77] Initially the government accepted the offer of the ranches but was unwilling to negotiate on land uses, although there appeared subsequently to be moves to accept a variation on this scheme as part of an emergent policy on 'wildlife-based land reform' for indigenising the conservancies (Wolmer et al. 2004).[78]

The political dynamics around the farm invasions in the SVC revealed that 'government' is highly heterogeneous and fissured. The President's Office, the Minister of Land and Agriculture, the Minister and Deputy Minister of Environment and Tourism, two Ministers for Home Affairs, the Masvingo Provincial Governor, and local District Administrators, MPs, and Councillors made often contradictory pronouncements on the situation. The conservancy had official visits from such dignitaries as Vice Presidents Msika and Muzenda, the Minister of Environment and Tourism, the Minister of Youth Development, Gender and Employment Creation, and the Masvingo Provincial Governor. The confusion stemmed in part from the wide range of actors seeking to make political – and in some cases financial – capital from the situation. In particular, the politicians and technocrats appeared to be working to different agendas rooted in different ways of seeing the landscape. The Minister of Environment and Tourism publicly announced that the conservancies were not suitable for resettlement and that the army would have to be called in to clear squatters; DNPWLM rangers were sent in to protect wildlife.[79] Yet the minister and the

[74] Interviews: Zimbabwe Wildlife and Tourism Advisory Council (ZWTAC), Harare, 14 February 2001; Malilangwe Trust, 5 February 2001; *Daily News,* 11 September 2000.
[75] This is explored in more detail in Wolmer et al. (2004).
[76] Interviews: ZWTAC, 14 February 2001; WWF, Harare, 19 January 2001.
[77] Interview: ZWTAC, 14 February 2001.
[78] See 'State putting final touches on conservancies policy', *The Herald,* 12 February 2004; 'Govt moves to acquire private conservancies', *The Independent,* 19 March 2004.
[79] *Daily News,* 21 May 2001. The Deputy Director (Research) DNPWLM came out strongly

DNPWLM had been sidelined by the newly powerful loop of governance running directly from the President's Office to the Governor and war veterans (Chaumba et al. 2003b). This grouping was pushing for resettlement of the conservancy for smallholder agriculture or, at the very least, indigenisation of the businesses (to become black-owned cattle or game ranches). After being assaulted and disarmed by war veterans and denied police support, the DNPWLM rangers were withdrawn.[80] Similarly, the Governor pulled rank on veterinarians, dismissing EU veterinary regulations as irrelevant.[81]

The desire expressed by commercial farmers and the wildlife lobby was to get out of this politicised arena and return to dealing with the technocrats: 'We need to get back to the technical people in government rather than starting with the politicos.'[82] One risky tactic used by the wildlife lobby to shift the debate onto 'technical' grounds was to talk up the danger of an FMD outbreak to encourage the government to prevent cattle and people moving onto the conservancy in order to safeguard lucrative beef exports to the EU,[83] the risk being that the government would instead advocate the complete removal of game – particularly buffalo.

Alongside the high-profile invasions of game ranches and conservancies there has been a quieter land occupation in the lowveld, one that has not been trumpeted to the same extent by international environmentalists, commercial farmers or the government. This was an invasion by the Chitsa people of Sangwe communal area of a northern portion of Gonarezhou National Park. The Chitsa people were evicted from this land in the 1960s during the establishment of the park and have been 'invading' the land since Independence – mainly by driving their cattle into the park as a poach grazing strategy. Some of the Chitsa community took advantage of the febrile atmosphere surrounding the ongoing farm invasions to step up the amount of poach grazing and to establish plots and huts inside the park. This remained relatively low-profile compared to the conservancy invasions, initially attracting no support from the war veterans or politicians.

---

[79] (cont.) in support of this view: 'Save Conservancy is a well managed enterprise fulfilling the twin objectives of creating employment and sustainable utilisation of wildlife resources. To reduce such an area to subsistence agriculture is a development motivated more by political exigency than economics or conservation', *The Mirror* (Masvingo Province weekly), 3-9 November 2000.

[80] Interview: Provincial Warden, DNPWLM, Masvingo, 9 February 2001; *Daily News*, 25 October 2000.

[81] Into these shifting political sands new actors were able to insert themselves as important players. The newly formed Zimbabwe Wildlife and Tourism Advisory Council, for example, stepped into the vacuum left by a politically marginalised Commercial Farmers Union to act as a conduit between the ranchers and government.

[82] Interview: Conservation NGO staff member, Harare, 19 January 2001.

[83] *Daily News*, 11 August 2000, 'Farm invasions to cut country's beef exports'; *Zimbabwe Standard*, 22 October 2000, 'Imminent outbreak of foot and mouth disease'; *Zimbabwe Independent*, 27 October 2000, 'Zim faces removal from EU beef protocol'. Foot and mouth disease did indeed break out in 2001.

The situation was finally noticed by the ever-zealous Provincial Governor and Chiredzi MPs who immediately moved to get the contested portion of the park officially demarcated for resettlement.[84] This development was severely censured by the Ministry of Environment and Tourism and the DNPWLM, who saw it as 'undermining the integrity of parks' estates' and potentially jeopardising the Great Limpopo Transfrontier Park plans (see Wolmer et al. 2004).[85]

This is not the only contested portion of Gonarezhou National Park. Further south, in Sengwe communal area, the Mapokole community are keen for restitution of their land now inside the park. As Yingwani Madyahasi complained to me:

> We were not given the go-ahead by government to go and occupy the game park [unlike the commercial farms] – we are hungry for that. We do not want the farms but our ancestors' place. We need to stick to our side. If given the go-ahead we would occupy our original place. Plenty of people are longing for that.[86]

Many in government – and not only the Ministry of Environment and Tourism – appeared distinctly uncomfortable with the developments in Gonarezhou National Park because ZANU(PF) has been keen to portray the battle for land as one of re-nationalising white-held commercial land. The national parks had been ignored – there is less political capital to be made in arguing for land reform there. In 2003 the Presidential Land Review Committee argued that 'all self-settled land occupiers in any part of the National Parks Estate should be removed and the protective game fences restored without further delay' (Utete et al. 2003: 7), and indeed attempts were made to evict the Chitsa from the park in early 2004.[87] However, grudges over land in the lowveld are not with commercial farms per se, but with the process of alienation from ancestral lands and the accompanying disruption of livelihood strategies.

Conclusions

This book has explored contrasting perceptions of the lowveld landscape – some of which are mainstream and some of which tend to remain hidden. One of the key questions posed at the beginning of the book was: what policy spaces and alternative ways of framing debates on land reform in the lowveld are opened up by allowing silenced perceptions and experiences of landscape to be heard? There are two key answers to this question; they point in different directions, but are not necessarily contradictory. The first is the need for land reform to support flexible and mobile livelihood strategies that cut across single land-use zones and hard boundaries; the second

---

[84] *Zimbabwe Independent*, 11 May 2001.
[85] *The Herald*, 1 June 2001.
[86] Interview: Masukwe, 24 January 2001.
[87] 'Govt relocating illegal Gonarezhou settlers', *Financial Gazette*, 22 January 2004.

is the need for a debate on the restitution of ancestral land in Zimbabwe's lowveld. With the ongoing dramatic developments surrounding land in the lowveld, is there the potential to replace the development and conservation initiatives underpinned by the wilderness vision with new initiatives that write people back into the landscape and address these issues? With respect to the first issue – supporting flexible and mobile livelihood strategies – the answer is yes, but probably only in the short term, and this is likely to benefit some more than others. Attempts to deliver the restitution of ancestral land, on the other hand, although possible, are most unlikely.

The lowveld landscape cannot be characterised as rainfed agricultural land, sugar country, cattle country or pristine wilderness alone. Rather it constitutes a mosaic of contested spaces with multiple land-use options. Reading the lowveld landscape as such a multifaceted space where a variety of livelihood strategies can be, and are, played out in combination in different places by different people leads to a reframing of the land agenda. Land reform rooted in such an understanding would seek to support existing livelihoods and coping strategies. This might involve resettling those who want to move; making grazing land available; and removing constraints on the mobility of livestock and utilisation of certain natural resources.

Despite the subsequent emergence of an official fast-track resettlement policy, Zimbabwe's land reform process since 2000 has been a seemingly chaotic and unplanned affair (although see Chaumba *et al.* 2003a). There was political control of some of the farm occupations via the war veterans and encouragement of MPs, but much of the activity was opportunist.

The lack of planning, the unwillingness (on the part of game guards, national parks staff and the police) to enforce legislation, and the rapid escalation of momentum provided opportunities for many. The *de facto* situation was one where many were still able to pursue flexible, mobile and opportunistic livelihood strategies without fear of punishment. Access to meat, fish, and grazing land opened up in the short term. Access to grazing land was particularly welcome. However, it tended to be the relatively wealthy, politically well-connected and least scrupulous who benefited most from this situation. Others feared that sooner or later the government would revert to technocratic type and exclude all but the politically connected and 'expert' farmers, as the symbolic occupations give way to a formal land allocation process.

ZANU(PF)'s rejection of the developmental agenda of the 1980s and '90s in favour of liberation-era rhetoric means they are making a generic appeal for land for 'the people'. This is a nationalist agenda which makes appeals to patriotism and 'Zimbabwean-ness', or even Pan-Africanism, rather than addressing the desire for restitution of specific ancestral lands. Gonarezhou National Park, for example, according to this rationale, had already been returned to the people with majority rule (cf. Ranger 1999). There is no political will to implement a slow, costly and potentially bureaucratically cumbersome land restitution programme and it is very unlikely to happen

(Moyo 2000a). There is also the potential danger that a restitution debate will exacerbate ethnicised politics and provide a rationale for the eviction of 'outsiders' alongside the return of ancestral land.[88]

But restitution of ancestral land need not necessarily imply resettlement – it also provides opportunities for recasting the wildlife utilisation debate. It could involve joint wildlife management arrangements between communities and the private sector (in the SVC for example) or between communities and the DNPWLM (as has happened with the Makuleke community and South African National Parks). The South African experience has set a regional precedent for the expansion of 'tribal land' onto the wildlife estate (both state and privately owned), rather than *vice versa*. Land claims against national parks have been particularly successful, as state land is easier to return to the dispossessed than private land, and has usually not threatened the conservation status or economic utilisation of the land because it is often leased back to the state (Carruthers 1999). This type of land reform could go beyond the emerging South African model for 'contractual national parks' (Reid 2001) where communities have gained title to land, but with highly restricted use rights that ensure that they are still kept separate from 'their' newly restituted land and natural resources (despite notionally controlling them). Instead it might embrace the notion of multiple land uses in the former 'parks estate' – and allow alternative land uses to tourism such as commercial hunting and the collection of natural resources (ilala palm, mopane worms, quelea birds, thatching grass and suchlike), or, for that matter, some agriculture and livestock-based livelihood strategies (Wolmer 2003).

It is important to remember that no land reform programme can provide a panacea to the problems faced by people in the communal areas of the lowveld. Land and natural resources are not the only factors important to livelihoods, nor are they always the most important ones. Particularly in the context of Zimbabwe's current economic collapse, labour migration, remittances and transborder trade are mainstays of livelihood systems for many in the lowveld and are often more important than the natural resources (from wildlife to ilala palm) so beloved of donor and NGO programmes. Policies to support cross-border movements of goods and people would have the potential to improve livelihoods dramatically. The irony is that one contemporary initiative with the potential to open up the 'boxed' landscape, permit multiple land uses and transborder movements may in fact have the opposite effect because it derives its logic from the wilderness vision. This is the Great Limpopo Transfrontier Park, discussed in Chapter 7, which is attracting significant donor interest and financial support. To date its advocates have been more interested in facilitating animal than

---

[88] The 2000 resettlement programme led Chief Gezani in Sengwe to argue for the eviction of people 'who were not born here' and resettlement in 'their own lands' now that the government is making land available. Interview: Masukwe, by Jacob Mahenehene, 3 August 2000.

human transborder migration; and encouraging multiple land uses translates in practice as attempting to expand the wildlife landscape further into the communal areas through joint-venture ecotourism arrangements.

Using a nuanced understanding of landscape as the analytical lens through which to view the lowveld has revealed multiple layers of meaning. This is much more than a physical space, or an environment devoid of culture, history and politics. As landscape it falls firmly into the human realms of agency, imagination and power. It has been appropriated and represented by different actors who have made claims to control the land and define appropriate land uses. These claims have been continually contested as different ways of representing the landscape have gained the ascendancy – and hence the ability to influence policy – at particular moments in time. Historically, the hegemonic way of representing the lowveld landscape has been as wilderness – a vision that derives from white settlers' experiences and priorities. But this vision has recently come under its most severe attack as the privately owned game ranches and conservancies of the lowveld have been invaded, and the politics of land and the needs of black smallholders pushed to the top of the political agenda. And yet the wilderness vision is simultaneously being promoted with more enthusiasm than ever by donors and the government in the national park and communal areas of the lowveld, threatening to obscure once more the history and politics of land and landscape.

Bibliography

Abramson, A. (2000). 'Mythical land, legal boundaries: wondering about landscape and other tracts'. In A. Abramson and D. Theodossopoulos (eds). *Land, Law and Environment: Mythical Land, Legal Boundaries*. London, Pluto Press.
Acocks, J. P. H. (1953). *Veld Types of South Africa*. Pretoria, Botanical Research Institute.
Adams, B. and Hulme, D. (1998). 'Conservation and communities: Changing narratives, policies and practices in African Conservation'. *Community Conservation in Africa: Principles and Comparative Practice*. Working Paper No. 4. University of Manchester, Institute for Development Policy and Management.
Adams, J. S. and McShane, T. O. (1992). *The Myth of Wild Africa. Conservation without Illusion*. New York and London, W.W. Norton.
Alexander, J. (1994). 'State, peasantry and resettlement in Zimbabwe'. *Review of African Political Economy* 61: 325-45.
Alexander, J. (1995). 'Things fall apart, the centre can hold: Processes of postwar political change in Zimbabwe's rural areas'. In N. Bhebe and T. Ranger (eds). *Society in Zimbabwe's Liberation War*. Harare, University of Zimbabwe Publications and Oxford, James Currey.
Alexander, J. and McGregor, J. (2000). 'Wildlife and Politics: CAMPFIRE in Zimbabwe'. *Development and Change* 31 (3): 605-627.
Alexander, J., McGregor, J. and Ranger, T. (2000). *Violence and Memory: One Hundred Years in the 'Dark Forests' of Matebeleland*. Oxford, James Currey.
Alvord, E. D. (1948). 'The progress of Native Agriculture in Southern Rhodesia'. *The New Rhodesia* 15: 18-19.
Alvord, E. D. (n.d.). 'Development of Native Agriculture and Land Tenure in Southern Rhodesia'. Unpublished manuscript.
Alwang, J., Ersado, L. and Taruvinga, N. (2001). 'Changes in poverty in Zimbabwe between 1990 and 1996: worsening conditions under adverse conditions'. Development Bank of Southern Africa 15 (5).
Anderson, D. and Grove, R. (1987). 'The scramble for Eden: past, present and

future in African conservation'. In D. Anderson and R. Grove, (eds). *Conservation in Africa; People, Policies and Practice*. Cambridge, Cambridge University Press.

Anderson, E. and Foggin, C. (1994). 'Animal disease control factors arising from the change from cattle ranching to wildlife conservancy'. In Price Waterhouse, (ed.). *The Lowveld Conservancies: New Opportunities for Productive and Sustainable Landuse*. Save Valley, Bubiana and Chiredzi River Conservancies.

Anderson, P. R. (1993). 'The human clay: an essay in the spatial history of the Cape Eastern frontier'. M. Litt. thesis, Oxford University.

Andersson, J. A. (1999). 'The politics of land scarcity: Land disputes in Save Communal Area, Zimbabwe'. *Journal of Southern African Studies* 25 (4): 553-578.

Andrews, B. (1964). *The Lowveld: an Economic Survey*. Salisbury, Ramsay, Parker Publications.

Andrews, M. (1999). *Landscape and Western Art*. Oxford, Oxford University Press.

Badenhorst, C. and Mather, C. (1997). 'Tribal recreation and recreating tribalism: Culture, leisure and social control on South Africa's gold mines, 1940-1950'. *Journal of Southern African Studies* 23 (3): 473-489.

Bannerman, J. H. (1978). 'Towards a history of the Hlengwe people of the south of Rhodesia'. *NADA* 11 (5): 483-496.

Bannerman, J. H. (1980). 'A short political and economic history of the Tsovani, Chisa and Mahenye: dynasties of the Ndanga, Chiredzi and Chipinga Districts to ca. 1950'. Unpublished manuscript.

Barnes, T. J. and Duncan, J. S. (1992). *Writing Worlds : Discourse, Text and Metaphor in the Representation of Landscape*. London, Routledge.

Beach, D. (1994). *The Shona and their Neighbours*. Oxford, Blackwell.

Behnke, R. H., Scoones, I. and Kerven, C. (1993). *Range Ecology at Disequilibrium: New Models of Natural Variability and Pastoral Adaption in African Savannas*. London, Overseas Development Institute.

Beinart, W. (1984). 'Soil Erosion, Conservation and Ideas about Development: a Southern African Exploration, 1900-60'. *Journal of Southern African Studies* 11 (1): 52-83.

Beinart, W. (1989). 'The politics of conservation in Southern Africa'. *Journal of Southern African Studies* 15 (2): 143-162.

Beinart, W. (1997). 'Vets, viruses and environmentalism: the Cape in the 1870s and 1880s (South Africa)'. *Paideuma* 43: 227-254.

Beinart, W. (2000). 'African history and environmental history'. *African Affairs* 99: 269-302.

Beinart, W. and Coates, P. A. (1995). *Environment and History: the Taming of the USA and South Africa*. London, Routledge.

Bender, B. (1998). *Stonehenge: Making Space*. Oxford, Berg Publishers.

Bender, B. (1999). 'Subverting the Western Gaze: mapping alternative worlds'. In P. J. Ucko and R. Layton (eds). *The Archaeology and Anthropology of Landscape*. London and New York, Routledge.

Bentley, B. (1964). 'Our 1964 pioneers'. *You* July Issue: 20-21.

Berger, J. (1972). *Ways of Seeing*. Harmondsworth, Penguin.

Berry, S. (1993). *No Condition is Permanent: The Social Dynamics of Agrarian Change in Sub-Saharan Africa*. Madison, WI, University of Wisconsin Press.

Berry, S. (1994). 'Resource access and management as historical processes –

conceptual and methodological issues'. In C. Lund and H. Secher Marcussen (eds). *Access, Control and Management of Natural Resources in Sub-Saharan Africa – Methodological Considerations*. Occasional Paper No. 13. International Development Studies, Roskilde University.

Bhebe, N. and Ranger, T. (eds). (1991). *Society in Zimbabwe's Liberation War*. University of Zimbabwe, International Conference on Zimbabwe. London, James Currey.

Blaikie, P. (1995). 'Changing environments or changing views? A political ecology for developing countries'. *Geography* 80 (348 Pt3): 203-214.

Bolding, A., Manzungu, E. and van der Zaag, P. (1996). 'Farmer-initiated irrigation furrows: observations from the Eastern Highlands'. In E. Manzungu and P. van der Zaag (eds). *The Practice of Smallholder Irrigation: Case Studies from Zimbabwe*. Harare, University of Zimbabwe Publications.

Bond, I. (1993). *The economics of wildlife and land-use in Zimbabwe: An examination of current knowledge and issues*. WWF Multispecies Production Systems Project Paper No. 35. Harare, WWF.

Bonner, R. (1993). *At the Hand of Man: Perils and Hope for Africa's Wildlife*. New York, Vintage.

Brandon, P. (1998). *The South Downs*. Chichester, Phillimore.

Braun, B. and Castree, N. (eds). (1998). *Remaking Reality: Nature at the Millennium*. London, Routledge.

Bridges, E. L. (1948). *Uttermost Part of the Earth*. London, Hodder and Stoughton.

Broch-Due, V. (2000). 'Producing nature and poverty in Africa: an introduction'. In V. Broche-Due and R. A. Schroeder (eds). *Producing Nature and Poverty in Africa*. Uppsala, Nordiska Afrikainstitutet.

Bryant, R. (1992). 'Political ecology: an emerging research agenda in Third World Studies'. *Political Geography Quarterly* 11 (1): 12-36.

Bryant, R. (1997). 'Beyond the impasse: the power of political ecology in Third World environmental research'. *Area* 29 (1): 5-19.

Buckley, T. and Gottlieb, A. (eds). (1988). *Blood Magic: The Anthropology of Menstruation*. Berkeley, University of California Press.

Bulpin, T. V. (1954). *The Ivory Trail*. Cape Town, Howard B. Timmins.

Bunn, D. (1994). '"Our wattled cot". Mercantile and domestic space in Thomas Pringle's African landscapes'. In W. T. R. Mitchell (ed.). *Landscape and Power*. Chicago, Chicago University Press.

Bunn, D. (2003). 'An unnatural state: tourism, water and wildlife photography in the early Kruger National Park'. In W. Beinart and J. McGregor (eds). *Social History and African Environments*. Oxford, James Currey.

Carlaw, C. A. (1962). 'Ethnology'. In *Gona re Zhou Expedition*. Salisbury, Rhodesian Schools Exploration Society.

Carruthers, J. (1989). 'Creating a National Park, 1910-1923'. *Journal of Southern African Studies* 15 (2): 188-216.

Carruthers, J. (1995). *The Kruger National Park. A Social and Political history*. Pietermaritzburg, University of Natal Press.

Carruthers, J. (1999). 'Past and future landscape ideology. The Kalahari Gemsbock National Park and Uluru - Kata Tjuta National Park compared'. Paper presented at the conference African Environments: Past and Present, 5-8 July, St. Antony's College, Oxford.

Chamberlain, G. A. (1923). *African Hunting Among the Thongas*. New York and

London, Harper and Brothers.
Chaumba, J., Scoones, I. and Wolmer, W. (2003a). 'From jambanja to planning: the reassertion of technocracy in land reform in south-eastern Zimbabwe'. *Journal of Modern African Studies* 41 (4): 533-554.
Chaumba, J., Scoones, I. and Wolmer, W. (2003b). 'New politics, new livelihoods: agrarian change in Zimbabwe'. *Review of African Political Economy* 98: 585-608.
Cheater, A. P. (1984). *Idioms of Accumulation: Rural Development and Class Formation among Freeholders in Zimbabwe*. Gweru, Mambo Press.
Child, B. (1988) 'The role of wildlife utilisation in sustainable economic development'. D.Phil. thesis, Oxford University.
Child, B. (1993) Proposal: Beitbridge, Chipinge, Chiredzi and Gonarezhou Joint Committee. Unpublished report for DNPWLM, Harare.
Child, G. (1995). *Wildlife and People: the Zimbabwe Success. How the conflict between animals and people became progress for both*. Harare, Wisdom Foundation.
Coetzee, J. M. (1988). *White Writing: On the Culture of Letters in South Africa*. New Haven, CT, Yale University Press.
Cohen, D. W. and Atieno Odhiambo, E. S. (1989). *Siaya. The Historical Anthropology of an African Landscape*. London, James Currey.
Collingwood, R. G. (1945). *The Idea of Nature*. Oxford, Clarendon Press.
Colson, E. (1997). 'Places of power and shrines of the land'. *Paideuma* 43: 47-58.
Comaroff, J. V. and Comaroff, J. L. (1991). *Of Revelation and Revolution: Christianity, Colonialism and Consciousness in South Africa*. Chicago, University of Chicago Press.
Comaroff, J. L. and Comaroff, J. V. (1997). *Of Revelation and Revolution: The Dialectics of Modernity on a South African Frontier*. Chicago, University of Chicago Press.
Conrad, J. (1925). 'Heart of Darkness'. In *Youth and Two Other Stories*. Garden City, NY, Doubleday.
Cosgrove, D. (1984). *Social Formation and Symbolic Landscape*. London, Croom Helm.
Cousins, B. (1990). 'Livestock production and grazing rights in Communal Lands and settlement schemes in Zimbabwe', Paper submitted to the World Bank Agricultural Sector Mission.
Cousins, B. (1996). 'Collective decision-making in the Communal Area grazing schemes'. Ph.D. thesis, Centre for Applied Social Sciences, University of Zimbabwe.
Croll, E. and Parkin, D. (1992). 'Anthropology, the environment and development'. In E. Croll and D. Parkin (eds). *Bush Base: Forest Farm. Culture, Environment and Development*. London, Routledge.
Cronon, W. (1991). *Nature's Metropolis: Chicago and the Great West*. New York, W.W. Norton.
Cronon, W. (1996). 'The trouble with wilderness; or getting back to the wrong nature'. In W. Cronon (ed.). *Uncommon Ground: Rethinking the Human Place in Nature*. New York, W.W. Norton.
Cunliffe, R. N. (1993). 'Land use in the southeast lowveld'. In B. Downie (ed.). *Gonarezhou National Park Management Planning Programme. Background Data Reports*. Harare, Department of National Parks and Wildlife Management.
Curtin, P. D. (1964). *The Image of Africa: British Ideas and Action, 1780-1850*. Madison, WI, University of Wisconsin Press.

Dalton, J. (1992). 'The Mahenya CAMPFIRE Project. Environmental Reality. The Mahenya Project in Zimbabwe: Its History, Establishment, Enigma and Future'. Unpublished monograph.
Daniels, S. (1989). 'Marxism, culture and the duplicity of landscape'. In R. Peet and N. Thrift (eds). *New Models in Geography. Volume II.* London, Unwin Hyman.
Daniels, S. (1993). *Fields of Vision: Landscape Imagery and National Identity in England and the United States.* Cambridge, Polity.
Dasmann, R. F. and Mossman, A. S. (1961). 'Commercial utilization of game on a Rhodesian ranch'. *Wild Life* 3: 7-17.
de Jager, P. (1988). 'Environmental degradation in communal land'. M.Sc. thesis, Department of Biological Sciences, University of Zimbabwe.
De la Rue, I. H. (1942). 'Can game and ranching run together?'. *Vuka* 2 (11): 34-35.
De Laessoe (1906). 'Journey down the Lundi and Sabi Rivers'. Unpublished monograph in the National Archives of Zimbabwe (BE 8/11/2).
Demeritt, D. (1994a). 'The nature of metaphors in cultural geography and environmental history'. *Progress in Human Geography* 18 (2): 163-185.
Demeritt, D. (1994b). 'Ecology, objectivity and critique in writings on nature and human societies'. *Journal of Historical Geography* 20 (1): 22-37.
Descola, P. (1996). 'Constructing natures: Symbolic ecology and social practice'. In P. Descola and G. Palsson (eds). *Nature and Society: Anthropological Perspectives.* London, Routledge.
Descola, P. and Palsson, G. (1996a). 'Introduction'. In P. Descola and G. Palsson (eds). *Nature and Society: Anthropological Perspectives.* London, Routledge.
Descola, P. and Palsson, G. (eds). (1996b). *Nature and Society: Anthropological Perspectives.* London, Routledge.
Dickens, V. (1907). 'Journeys in South-Eastern Mashonaland'. *Geographical Journal* 29 (1): 15-23.
DNPWLM (1998). *Gonarezhou National Park: Management Plan.* Harare, Department of National Parks and Wildlife Management.
Dodds, H. (1948). 'Memorandum on the Triangle Sugar Estate'. Salisbury, Department of Agriculture.
Douglas, M. (1966). *Purity and Danger: an Analysis of the Concepts of Pollution and Taboo.* London, Routledge.
Doyle, D. (1891). 'With King Gungunhana in Gazaland'. *Fortnightly Review* 50: 112-117.
Drinkwater, M. (1989). 'Technical development and peasant impoverishment: Land use policy in Zimbabwe's Midlands Province'. *Journal of Southern African Studies* 15 (2): 287-305.
Drinkwater, M. (1991). *The State and Agrarian Change in Zimbabwe's Communal Areas.* London, Macmillan.
Drinkwater, M. (1992). 'Cows eat grass don't they? Evaluating conflict over pastoral management in Zimbabwe'. In E. Croll and D. Parkin (eds). *Bush Base: Forest Farm. Culture, Environment and Development.* London, Routledge.
du Toit, R. (1998). 'Case study of the policies that support sustainable development in Africa: The Save Valley Conservancy, Zimbabwe'. Paper presented at the workshop on African perspectives of policies which support sustainable development, Scandinavian Seminar College, Harare 28-30 September.

Duffy, R. (1997). 'The environmental challenge to the nation-state: superparks and national parks policy in Zimbabwe'. *Journal of Southern African Studies* 23 (3): 441-451.

Duffy, R. (1999). 'The role and limitations of state coercion: Anti-poaching policies in Zimbabwe'. *Journal of Contemporary African Studies* 17 (1): 97-121.

Duffy, R. (2000). *Killing for Conservation: Wildlife Policy in Zimbabwe*. Oxford, James Currey.

Duncan, J. S. (1990). *The City as Text: The Politics of Landscape Interpretation in the Kandyan Kingdom*. Cambridge, Cambridge University Press.

Duncan, J. S. (1995). 'Landscape geography, 1993-94'. *Progress in Human Geography* 19 (3): 414-422.

Duncan, J. S. and Ley, D. (1993). *Place/Culture/Representation*. London, Routledge.

Dzingirai, V. and Bourdillon, M. F. C. (1998). *Religious ritual and environmental control in the Zambezi Valley: The Case of Binga*. CASS Working Paper – NRM Series; CPN 98/98. Centre for Applied Social Sciences, University of Zimbabwe.

Earthy, E. D. (1933). *Valenge Women: The Social and Economic Life of the Valenge Women of Portuguese East Africa*. Oxford, Oxford University Press.

Eastwood, J. H. R. (1996). *After MacDougall: From Tick Bird to Guinea Fowl. The recollections of a 'Pioneer Sugar Planter' (1954-1964) of the beginnings of the Rhodesian lowveld sugar industry*. Triangle, Zimbabwe, Triangle Limited.

Eicher, C. and Rukuni, M. (eds). (1994). *Zimbabwe's Agricultural Revolution*. Harare, University of Zimbabwe.

Elliot, J. (1990). 'The mechanical conservation of soil in Rhodesia/Zimbabwe'. In D. Cosgrove and G. Petts (eds). *Water, Engineering and Landscape*. London, Belhaven.

Ellis, S. (1994). 'Of elephants and men: politics and nature conservation in South Africa'. *Journal of Southern African Studies* 20: 53-69.

Elton, F. (1873). 'Journal of an Exploration of the Limpopo River'. Paper read before the Royal Geographical Society during the session 1871-72. London, Royal Geographical Society.

ENDA-Zimbabwe (1992). 'An indicative report of the socio-economic and natural resource survey of Sengwe Communal Lands, Zimbabwe'. Harare, ENDA-Zimbabwe.

ENDA-Zimbabwe (1993). 'Report of the socioeconomic and natural resource survey of Sengwe Communal Lands, Zimbabwe. Facilitated by the World Bank'. Harare, ENDA-Zimbabwe.

ENDA-Zimbabwe (1995). 'Women and Crafts Project in the Sengwe Communal Lands'. Harare, ENDA-Zimbabwe.

Environmental Investigation Agency (1992). *Under Fire: Elephants in the Front Line*. London, EIA.

Erskine, St. V. (1875). 'Journal of a Voyage to Umzila; King of Gaza, 1871-72'. *Journal of the Royal Geographical Society* 45: 35-45.

Erskine, St. V. (1890). 'Five Journeys of Exploration in South-Eastern Africa'. Manuscript, Royal Geographical Society archives.

Escobar, A. (1996). 'Construction nature – elements for a poststructuralist political ecology'. In R. Peet and M. Watts (eds). *Liberation Ecologies: Environment, Development, Social Movements*. London, Routledge.

Escobar, A. (1999). 'After nature: steps to an antiessentialist political ecology'.

Current Anthropology 40 (1): 1-16.
Fair, T. J. D. (1964). 'Rhodesian lowveld: source of new economic strength'. Optima 14 (4): 191-201.
Fairhead, J. and Leach, M. (1995). 'False forest history, complicit social analysis: rethinking some West African environmental narratives'. World Development 23 (6): 1023-1035.
Fairhead, J. and Leach, M. (1996a). Misreading the African Landscape. Society and Ecology in a Forest-Savanna Mosaic. Cambridge, Cambridge University Press.
Fairhead, J. and Leach, M. (1996b). 'Enriching the landscape: Social history and the management of transition ecology in the forest-savannah mosaic of the Republic of Guinea'. Africa 66 (1): 14-36.
Fairhead, J. and Leach, M. (2001). 'History, memory and the social shaping of forests in West Africa and Trinidad'. Paper for the Workshop 'Changing perspectives on forests: ecology, people and science/policy processes in West Africa and the Caribbean', 26-27 March at the Institute of Development Studies, University of Sussex.
Ferguson, J. (1990). The Anti-Politics Machine: 'Development', Depoliticization and Bureaucratic State Power in Lesotho. Cambridge, Cambridge University Press.
Fernandes Das Neves, D. (1879). A Hunting Expedition to the Transvaal. London, George Bell and Sons.
Fitzpatrick, P. (1907). Jock of the Bushveld. London, Longmans, Green and Co.
Ford, J. (1971). The Role of the Trypanosomiases in African Ecology: A Study of the Tsetse Fly Problem. Oxford, Clarendon Press.
Foster, J. (1998). 'The poetics of liminal spaces: Landscape and the construction of white identity in early 20th century South Africa'. Ph.D. thesis, London University.
Foucault, M. (1972) The Archaeology of Knowledge. London, Sheridan Smith.
Foucault, M. (1977). Discipline and Punish: The Birth of the Prison. Harmondsworth, Penguin.
Frost, P. G. H. (2000). 'Environmental and socio-economic overview of the Communal Areas of Beitbridge and Chiredzi Districts'. In Institute of Environmental Studies (ed.). Summary Report. Prepared for the CESVI Sustainable Development and Natural Resources Management in Southern Zimbabwe Project. Harare, Institute of Environmental Studies, University of Zimbabwe.
Gandy, M. (1996). 'Crumbling land: the postmodernity debate and the analysis of environmental problems'. Progress in Human Geography 20 (1): 23-40.
Garlake, P. S. (1983). 'Prehistory and ideology in Zimbabwe'. In J. D.Y. Peel and T. O. Ranger (eds). Past and Present in Zimbabwe. Manchester, Manchester University Press.
Gibb, A. and Partners (1948). 'Sabi-Lundi Development'. Salisbury, Government of Rhodesia.
Giblin, J. (1990). 'Trypanosomiasis control in African history – an evaded issue?' Journal of African History 31 (1): 59-80.
Gibson, C. C. (1999). Politicians and Poachers: The Political Economy of Wildlife Policy in Africa. Cambridge, Cambridge University Press.
Gillmore, P. (1890). Through Gazaland and the Scene of the Portuguese Aggression. Journey of a Hunter in Search of Gold and Ivory. London, Harrison and Sons.
Glacken, C. (1967). Traces on the Rhodian Shore: Nature and Culture in Western Thought from Ancient Times to the End of the Eighteenth Century. Berkeley, University of California Press.

Godwin, P. and Hancock, I. (1997). *'Rhodesians Never Die': The impact of war and political change on white Rhodesia, c. 1970-1980.* Harare, Baobab Books.

Goodwin, H. J., Kent, I. J., Parker, K. T. and Walpole, M. J. (1997). 'Tourism, conservation and sustainable development, Volume IV, the south-east lowveld, Zimbabwe. Final report to the Department for International Development', Durrell Institute of Conservation and Ecology, Institute of Mathematics and Statistics, University of Kent.

Gooneratne, W. and Mosselman, E. E. (1996). 'Planning across the borders: border regions in Eastern and Southern Africa'. *Regional Development Dialogue* 17 (2): 136-151.

Gordon, R. (1992). *The Bushman Myth: the Making of a Namibian Underclass.* Boulder, CO, Westview Press.

Gottlieb, A. (1992). *Under the Kapok Tree: Identity and Difference in Beng Thought.* Bloomington and Indianapolis, Indiana University Press.

Government of Zimbabwe (1998). 'Land Reform and Resettlement Programme Phase II: A Policy Framework and Project Document'. Harare, Government of Zimbabwe.

Government of Zimbabwe (2001). 'Accelerated Land Reform and Resettlement Implementation Plan - 'Fast Track''. Harare, Government of Zimbabwe.

Greider, T. and Garkovich, L. (1994). 'Landscapes - the social construction of nature and the environment'. *Rural Sociology* 59 (1): 1-24.

Griffen, J. (1999). *Study on the Development and Management of Transboundary Conservation Areas in Southern Africa.* Lilongwe, Malawi, USAID Regional Centre for Southern Africa.

Grillo, R. D. (1997). 'Discourses of development: the view from anthropology'. In R. D. Grillo and J. Stirrat (eds). *Discourses of development: Anthropological Perspectives.* Oxford, Berg.

Grzimek, B. and Grzimek, M. (1965). *Serengeti Shall not Die.* London, Hamish Hamilton.

Guha, R. and Spivak, G. (eds). (1988). *Selected Subaltern Studies.* Delhi, Oxford University Press.

Haarhoff, D. (1991). *The Wild South-West: Frontier Myths and Metaphors in Literature Set in Namibia, 1760-1988.* Johannesburg, Witwatersrand University Press.

Haila, Y. (1997). 'Wilderness and the multiple layers of environmental thought'. *Environment and History* 3: 127-147.

Hajer, M. A. (1995). *The Politics of Environmental Discourse: Ecological Modernization and the Policy Process.* Oxford, Oxford University Press.

Hamilton, C. (1998). *Terrific Majesty: The Powers of Shaka Zulu and the Limits of Historical Invention.* Cambridge, MA, Harvard University Press.

Hanks, J. (1997). 'Protected areas during and after conflict: the objectives and activities of the Peace Park Foundation'. Paper presented to the Parks for Peace: International Conference on Transboundary Protected Areas as a Vehicle for International Co-operation, 16-18 September, Somerset West, South Africa.

Harries, P. (1981). 'The anthropologist as historian and liberal: H-A. Junod and the Thonga'. *Journal of Southern African Studies* 8 (1): 37-50.

Harries, P. (1987). 'A forgotten corner of the Transvaal: reconstructing the history of a relocated community through oral testimony and song'. In B. Bozzoli (ed.). *Class, Community and Conflict.* Johannesburg, Ravan Press.

Harries, P. (1988). 'The roots of ethnicity: Discourse and the politics of language construction in south-east Africa'. *African Affairs* 87 (346): 25-52.
Harries, P. (1989). 'Exclusion, classification and internal colonialism: the emergence of ethnicity among of the Tsonga-speakers of South Africa'. In L. Vail (ed.). *The Creation of Tribalism in Southern Africa*. London, James Currey.
Harries, P. (1993). 'Through the eyes of the beholder: H. A. Junod and the notion of the primitive'. *Social Dynamics* 19 (1): 1-10.
Harries, P. (1994). *Work, Culture, and Identity: Migrant Labourers in Mozambique and South Africa c. 1890-1910*. Johannesburg, Witwatersrand University Press.
Harries, P. (1997). 'Under alpine eyes: constructing landscape and society in late pre-colonial south-east Africa'. *Paideuma* 43: 171-192.
Harris, M. (1959). 'Labour emigration among the Mocambique Thonga: Cultural and political factors'. *Africa* 29 (1): 50-65.
Harvey, D. (1993). 'The nature of the environment: the dialectics of social and environmental change'. *The Socialist Register* 1: 1-51.
Heath, R. (1998). 'The Tokwe-Mukorsi Project: A Summary of its Environmental Impacts', unpublished report.
Hewison, R. (1987). *The Heritage Industry: Britain in a Climate of Decline*. London, Methuen.
Hill, K. (1994). 'Politicians, Farmers and Ecologists: Commercial Wildlife Ranching and the Politics of Land in Zimbabwe'. *Journal of African and Asian Studies* 29: 226-247.
Hill, K. (1996). 'Zimbabwe's wildlife utilisation programmes: grassroots democracy or an extension of state power?' *African Studies Review* 39 (1): 103-122.
Hippo Valley Estates Ltd. (2000). *Annual Report 2000*. Chiredzi, Hippo Valley Estates Limited.
Hirsch, E. and Michael, O. H. (eds) (1995). *The Anthropology of Landscape: Perspectives on Place and Space*. Oxford, Clarendon Press.
Hitchcock, R. K. (1995). 'Centralisation, resource depletion and coercive conservation among the Tyua of the Northwestern Kalahari'. *Human Ecology* 23 (2): 169-98.
Hoppe, K. A. (1995). *Lords of the flies: British sleeping sickness policies as environmental engineering in the Lake Victoria region 1900-1950*. Working Paper No. 203. African Studies Centre, Boston University.
Hoskins, W. G. (1955). *The Making of the English Landscape*. London, Penguin.
Houser, T. (1972). 'The extent of Karanga speaking spirit possession among the Hlengwe in Rhodesia'. Paper presented at the History of Central African Religious Systems Conference, Lusaka, August 30-September 8.
Hughes, D. M. (1999). 'Frontier dynamics: struggles for land and clients on the Zimbabwe-Mozambique border'. Ph.D. thesis, Department of Anthropology, University of California, Berkeley.
Hughes, D. M. (2001). 'Rezoned for business: How eco-tourism unlocked black farmland in Eastern Zimbabwe'. *Journal of Agrarian Change* 1 (4), 575-599.
Hussey, D. E. (1965). 'The Rhodesian lowveld'. *The Geographical Magazine* 38 (4): 249-262.
Hyatt, S. P. (1903). 'The Lower Sabi Valley'. Unpublished manuscript, Royal Geographical Society.
Hyatt, S. P. (1917). *The Old Transport Road*. London, Andrew Melrose.
Hyatt, S. P. (n.d.). *Off the Main Track*. London, Werner Laurie.
IFAD (1995). *Republic of Zimbabwe, South-Eastern Dry Areas Project Appraisal*

Report. Volume 2: Working Papers, Rome, International Fund for Agricultural Development.
IFAD (1996). *Republic of Zimbabwe, South-Eastern Dry Areas Project Appraisal Report. Volume 1: Main Report and Annexes*, Rome, International Fund for Agricultural Development.
Institute of Environmental Studies (1999). 'Summary Report. Prepared for the CESVI Sustainable Development and Natural Resources Management in Southern Zimbabwe Project', Institute of Environmental Studies, University of Zimbabwe.
Jansen, D., Bond, I. and Child, B. (1992). *Cattle, wildlife, both or neither: results of a financial and economic survey of commercial ranches in southern Zimbabwe*. Multi-species Animal Production Systems Project, Project Paper No. 27. Harare, Worldwide Fund for Nature.
Jenkins, C. and Knight, J. (2002). *The Economic Decline of Zimbabwe: Neither Growth nor Equity*. Basingstoke, Palgrave.
Jenkins, G. and Palmer, E. (1978). *The Companion Guide to South Africa*. London, Collins.
Junod, H. A. (1927). *The Life of a South African Tribe*. London, Macmillan.
Kelly, R. (1973). 'A comparative study of primary productivity under different kinds of land use in southeastern Rhodesia'. Ph.D. thesis, Department of Botany. Salisbury, University of Rhodesia.
Kinsey, B. H. (1999). 'Land reform, growth and equity: emerging evidence from Zimbabwe's resettlement programme'. *Journal of Southern African Studies* 25 (2): 169-92.
Kjekshus, H. (1977). *Ecology, Control and Economic Development in East African History: The Case of Tanganyika, 1850-1950*. Berkeley, University of California Press.
Kriger, N. (1992). *Zimbabwe's Guerrilla War. Peasant Voices*. Cambridge, Cambridge University Press.
Lambert, Y. (1961). *The Story of Triangle*. Durban, Hammett and Hodge.
Lammas, R. C. (1996). 'Portraits of placelessness: British nineteenth-century images of the African landscape'. *Singapore Journal of Tropical Geography* 17 (1): 40-51.
Lan, D. (1985). *Guns and Rain: Guerrillas and Spirit Mediums in Zimbabwe*. London, James Currey.
Layton, R. and Ucko, P. J. (1999). 'Introduction: gazing on the landscape and encountering the environment'. In P. J. Ucko and R. Layton (eds). *The Archaeology and Anthropology of Landscape*. London and New York, Routledge.
Leach, M. and Mearns, R. (eds). (1996). *The Lie of the Land: Challenging Received Wisdom on the African Environment*. London, James Currey.
Lewis, I. (1989). *Ecstatic Religion. A Study of Shamanism and Spirit Possession*. London, Routledge.
Liesegang, G. (1981). 'Notes on the internal structure of the Gaza kingdom of southern Mozambique, 1840-1895'. In J. B. Peires (ed.). *Before and after Shaka: Papers in Nguni History*. Grahamstown, Institute for Social and Economic Research, Rhodes University.
Lipsky, M. (1979). *Street Level Bureaucracy*. New York, Russell Sage Foundation.
Longden, H. W. D. (1950). *Red Buffalo: The Story of Will Longden, Pioneer, Friend and Emissary of Rhodes*. Cape Town, Juta.
Lovell, N. (ed.). (1996). *Locality and Belonging*. London, Routledge.

Luig, U. and von Oppen, A. (1997). 'Landscape in Africa: process and vision. An introductory essay'. *Paideuma* 43: 7-46.

Lyons, M. (1992). *The Colonial Disease: a Social History of Sleeping Sickness in Northern Zaire, 1900-1940.* Cambridge, Cambridge University Press.

Mabalauta Working Group (2000). *The Ecology, Control and Economics of Ilala Palm in Sengwe Communal Area, Zimbabwe.* Harare, Institute of Environmental Studies, University of Zimbabwe.

MacKenzie, J. M. (1988). *The Empire of Nature. Hunting, Conservation and British Imperialism.* Manchester, Manchester University Press.

Magome, H. and Murombedzi, J. (2003). 'Sharing South African National Parks: Community land and conservation in a democratic South Africa'. In W. Adams and M. Mulligan (eds). *Decolonizing Nature: Strategies for Conservation in a Post-Colonial Era.* London, Earthscan.

Manzungu, E. and van der Zaag, P. (1996). 'Continuity and controversy in smallholder irrigation'. In E. Manzungu and P. van der Zaag (eds). *The Practice of Smallholder Irrigation: Case Studies from Zimbabwe.* Harare, University of Zimbabwe Publications.

Marcus, G. E. (1995). 'Ethnography in/of the world system: the emergence of multi-sited ethnography'. *Annual Review of Anthroplogy* 24: 95-117.

Masona, T. (1987). 'Colonial game policy: A study of the origin and administration of game policy in Southern Rhodesia - 1890-1945'. M.Sc. thesis, University of Zimbabwe.

Matless, D. (1998). *Landscape and Englishness.* London, Reaktion Books.

Maxwell, D. (1999). *Christians and Chiefs in Zimbabwe: A Social History of the Hwesa People.* Edinburgh, Edinburgh University Press.

Mbizvo, C. and Guveya, E. (eds). (1999). *Proceedings of the Transborder Natural Resources Management Workshop Held at the Bronte Hotel, Harare (18-19 August 1999),* IUCN Regional Office for Southern Africa.

McDowell, L. (1994). 'The transformation of cultural geography'. In D. Gregory, R. Martin and G. Smith (eds). *Human Geography: Society, Space and Social Science.* Basingstoke and London, Macmillan.

McIvor, D. (1906). 'The Rhodesian ruins'. *Geographical Journal* 27.

McGregor, J. (1995). 'Conservation, control and ecological change: the politics and ecology of colonial conservation in Shurugwi, Zimbabwe'. *Environment and History* 1 (3): 257-279.

Metcalfe, S. (1996). 'Enhancing capacity for neighbouring communities to benefit from the proposed Save Valley Conservancy Trust'. First Draft Project Identification Plan prepared for RDCs surrounding the Conservancy: Chiredzi, Chipinge, Bikita, Zaka, Buhera. Chiredzi, SVC Trust/Zimbabwe Trust.

Mitchell, W. J. T. (1994). 'Introduction'. In W. J. T. Mitchell (ed.). *Landscape and Power.* Chicago, University of Chicago Press.

Mlambo, A. S. and Pangeti, E. S. (1996). *The Political Economy of the Sugar Industry in Zimbabwe 1920-1990.* Harare, University of Zimbabwe Publications.

Moodie, J. (1999). 'Preparing the waste places for future prosperity? The New Zealand pioneering myth and adaptation to recent change'. Paper presented at Landscapes of Memory: Oral History and the Environment Conference, 15-16 May 1999, University of Sussex.

Moore, D. S. (1993). 'Contesting terrain in Zimbabwe's Eastern Highlands: political ecology, ethnography, and peasant resource struggles'. *Economic Geography* 69 (4): 380-401.

Moore, D. S. (1998). 'Clear waters and muddied histories: environmental history and the politics of community in Zimbabwe's Eastern Highlands'. *Journal of Southern African Studies* 24 (2): 377-403.

Moore, D. S. (1999). 'The crucible of cultural politics: reworking 'development' in Zimbabwe's eastern highlands'. *American Ethnologist* 26 (3): 654-689.

Moore, H. L. (1986). *Space, Text and Gender: An Anthropological Study of the Marakwet of Kenya*. Cambridge, Cambridge University Press.

Moore, H. L. and Vaughan, M. (1994). *Cutting Down Trees. Gender, Nutrition, and Agricultural Change in the Northern Province of Zambia, 1890-1990*. Portsmouth, NH, Heinemann.

Mosse, D. (1997). 'The ideology and politics of community participation: tank irrigation in colonial and contemporary Tamil Nadu'. In R. D. Grillo and R. L. Stirrat (eds). *Discourses of Development*. Oxford, Berg.

Moyana, H. V. (1984). *The Political Economy of Land in Zimbabwe*. Gweru, Mambo Press.

Moyo, S. (1995). *The Land Question in Zimbabwe*. Harare, Sapes Books.

Moyo, S. (1998). *The Land Acquisition Process in Zimbabwe (1997/8)*. Harare, UNDP.

Moyo, S. (1998). 'The political economy of land redistribution in the 1990s'. Paper presented to the Centre of African Studies, University of London, SOAS and Britain Zimbabwe Society seminar on Land Reform in Zimbabwe: The Way Forward, 11 March, School of Oriental and African Studies, University of London.

Moyo, S. (2000a). 'The Interaction of Market and Compulsory Land Acquisition Processes with Social Action in Zimbabwe's Land Reform'. Paper presented at the SARIPS of the Sapes Trust Annual colloquium on Regional Integration: Past, Present and Future, Harare Sheraton Hotel and Towers, 24-27 September.

Moyo, S. (2000b). 'The political economy of land acquisition and redistribution in Zimbabwe, 1990-1999'. *Journal of Southern African Studies* 26 (1): 5-28.

Moyo, S. (2000c). *Land Reform Under Structural Adjustment in Zimbabwe: Land Use Change in the Mashonaland Provinces*. Uppsala, Nordiska Afrikainsitutet.

Mtetwa, R. M. G. (1976). 'The political and economic history of the Duma people of south-eastern Rhodesia from the early eighteenth century to 1945'. Ph.D. thesis, Department of History, University of Rhodesia.

Mukamuri, B. (1995). 'Local environmental conservation strategies: Karanga religion, politics and environmental control'. *Environment and History* 1 (3): 297-311.

Mukonyora, I. (2000). 'The sacred wilderness: a study of the role of women in shaping the Masowe thought pattern'. Paper presented at 'A View of the Land' international conference, Bulawayo, 3-6 July.

Munro, W. (1995). 'Building the post-colonial state: villagization and resource management in Zimbabwe'. *Politics and Society* 23 (1): 107-140.

Munro, W. (1998). *The Moral Economy of the Sate: Conservation, Community Development and State Making in Zimbabwe*. Athens, OH, Ohio University Center for International Studies.

Murombedzi, J. (1992a). *Decentralisation or Recentralisation? Implementing CAMPFIRE in the Omay Communal Lands of Nyaminyami District*. CASS Natural Resource Management Working Paper No. 2. Harare, CASS, University of Zimbabwe.

Murombedzi, J. (1992b). 'Socio-economic background study of the Gonakudzingwa small scale commercial farming area'. Report prepared for the World Bank and The Department of National Parks and Wildlife Management. Harare.

Murphree, M. W. (2000). 'The Lesson from Mahenye'. In J. Hutton and B. Dickson (eds). *Endangered Species, Threatened Convention: The Past, Present and Future of CITES*. London, Earthscan.

Murray, M. J. (1995). "'Blackbirding' at 'Crooks' Corner": illicit labour recruiting in the Northeastern Transvaal, 1910-1940'. *Journal of Southern African Studies* 21 (3): 373-397.

Nash, R. (1982). *Wilderness and the American Mind*. New Haven, CT, Yale University Press.

Neumann, R. P. (1995). 'Ways of seeing Africa: colonial recasting of African society and landscape in Serengeti National Park'. *Ecumene* 2 (2): 149-169.

Neumann, R. P. (1996). 'Dukes, earls, and ersatz Edens: aristocratic nature preservationists in colonial Africa'. *Environment and Planning D: Society and Space* 14: 79-98.

Neumann, R. P. (1997). 'Primitive ideas: protected area buffer zones and the politics of land in Africa'. *Development and Change* 28: 559-582.

Neumann, R. P. (1998). *Imposing Wilderness: Struggles over Livelihood and Nature Preservation in Africa*. Berkeley, University of California Press.

Neumann, R. P. (1999). 'Disease, development, and conservation: changing images of people and place in colonial Tanganyika'. Paper presented at the conference African Environments: Past and Present, 5-8 July, St. Antony's College, Oxford.

Noyes, J. K. (1991). *Colonial Space: Spatiality in the Discourse of German South West Africa 1884-1915*. Reading, Harwood Press.

Noyes, J. K. (2000). 'Nomadic fantasies: producing landscapes of mobility in German Southwest Africa'. *Ecumene* 7 (1): 47-66.

Oeschlaeger, M. (1991). *The Idea of Wilderness. From Prehistory to the Age of Ecology*. New Haven, CT, Yale University Press.

Okoye, I. S. (1997). 'History, aesthetics and the political in Igbo spatial heterotopias'. *Paideuma* 43: 75-92.

Oliver, C. P. (1957). *Many Treks Made Rhodesia*. Cape Town, Howard B. Timmins.

Olwig, K. (1984). *Nature's Ideological Landscape*. London, George Allen and Unwin.

Palmer, R. (1977). *Land and Racial Domination in Rhodesia*. London, Heinemann.

Palmer, R. (1990). 'Land reform in Zimbabwe, 1980-1990'. *African Affairs* 89 (335): 163-181.

Palmer, R. (1998). 'Mugabe's "land grab" in regional perspective'. Paper presented to the Centre of African Studies, University of London, SOAS and Britain Zimbabwe Society seminar on Land Reform in Zimbabwe: The Way Forward, 11 March, School of Oriental and African Studies, University of London.

Palmer, R. (2000). 'Robert Mugabe and the rules of the game'. URL: http://www.oxfam.org.uk/landrights/resource.htm/Southern Africa.

Pangeti, E. S. (1986). 'Agribusiness in colonial Zimbabwe: The case of the lowveld'. In A. Teichova (ed.). *Multinational Enterprise in Historical Perspective*.

Cambridge, Cambridge University Press.

Parkin, D. (1991). *Sacred Void: Spatial Images of Work and Ritual among the Giriama of Kenya*. Cambridge, Cambridge University Press.

Peet, R. and Watts, M. (1996). 'Liberation ecology: development, sustainability and environment in an age of market triumphalism'. In R. Peet and M. Watts (eds). *Liberation Ecologies: Environment, Development, Social Movements*. London, Routledge.

Peluso, N. L. (1992). *Rich Forests, Poor People. Resource Control and Resistance in Java*. Berkeley, University of California Press.

Peluso, N. L. (1993). 'Coercing conservation? The politics of state resource control'. *Global Environmental Change* June Issue: 199-217.

Pendered, A. and von Memerty, W. (1955). 'Native Land Husbandry Act of Rhodesia'. *Journal of African Administration* 7 (3): 99-109.

Penning, C. J. (1948). 'Report on the Triangle Sugar Estates and Factory'. Salisbury, Department of Agriculture.

Peterson, J. H. (1991). *CAMPFIRE: A Zimbabwean Approach to Sustainable Development through Wildlife Utilisation*. Harare, University of Zimbabwe.

Phillips, J., Hammond, J., Samuels, L. H. and Swynnerton, R. J. M. (1962). *The Development of the Economic Resources of Southern Rhodesia with Particular Reference to the Role of African Agriculture. Report of the Advisory Committee*. Salisbury, Mardon.

Phimister, I. R. (1986). 'Discourse and the discipline of historical context: conservationism and ideas about development in Southern Rhodesia 1930-1950'. *Journal of Southern African Studies* 12 (2): 263-275.

Phimister, I. R. (1978). 'Meat and monopolies: beef cattle in Southern Rhodesia, 1980-1938'. *Journal of African History* 19 (3): 391-414.

Pirot, J.-Y., Meynell, P.-J. and Elder, D. (2000). *Ecosystem Management: Lessons from around the World. A Guide to Development and Conservation Practioners*. Gland and Cambridge, IUCN.

Pirow, O. (n.d.). *Shangani*. Johannesburg, Dagbreek Book Store.

Pitman, D. (1980). *Wild Places of Zimbabwe*. Bulawayo, Books of Zimbabwe.

Pollock, N. C. (1968). 'Irrigation in the Rhodesian lowveld'. *Geographical Journal* 134 (1): 70-77.

Posey, D. A. (1985). 'Indigenous management of tropical forest ecosystems: the case of the Kyapo Indians of the Brazilian Amazon'. *Agroforestry Systems* 3: 139-158.

Potts, D. (2000). 'Environmental myths and narratives: case studies from Zimbabwe'. In P. Stott and S. Sullivan (eds). *Political Ecology: Science, Myth and Power*. London, Arnold.

Pratt, M. L. (1992). *Imperial Eyes. Travel Writing and Transculturation*. London, Routledge.

Price Waterhouse (1994). *The Lowveld Conservancies: New Opportunities for Productive and Sustainable Landuse*, Save Valley, Bubiana and Chiredzi River Conservancies.

Proctor, J. D. (1998). 'The social construction of nature: relativist accusations, pragmatist and critical realist responses'. *Annals of the Association of American Geographers* 88 (3): 352-376.

Pwiti, G. (1991). 'Trade and economics in Southern Africa: the archaeological evidence'. *Zambezi* 18 (2): 119-129.

Ranger, T. (1985). *The Invention of Tribalism in Zimbabwe*. Gweru, Mambo.

Ranger, T. (1985). *Peasant Consciousness and Guerrilla War in Zimbabwe*. Harare, Zimbabwe Publishing House.
Ranger, T. (1987). 'Taking hold of the land: Holy places and pilgrimages in twentieth-century Zimbabwe'. *Past and Present* 117: 158-194.
Ranger, T. (1989). 'Missionaries, migrants and the Manyika: The invention of ethnicity in Zimbabwe'. In L. Vail (ed.). *The Creation of Tribalism in Southern Africa*. London, James Currey.
Ranger, T. (1997). 'Making Zimbabwean landscapes: painters, projectors and priests'. *Paideuma* 43: 59-74.
Ranger, T. (1999). *Voices from the Rocks: Nature, Culture and History in the Matopos Hills of Zimbabwe*. Oxford, James Currey.
Ravi Rajan, S. (1997). 'The ends of environmental history: some questions'. *Environment and History* 3: 245-52.
Reid Daly, R. (1982). *Selous Scouts: Top Secret War. As Told to Peter Stiff*. Alberton, South Africa, Galago Publishing.
Reid, H. (2001). 'Contractual National Parks and the Makuleke Community'. *Human Ecology* 29 (2): 135-155.
Rennie, J. K. (1984). 'Ideology and state formation: political and communal ideologies amongst the south-eastern Shona, 1500-1890'. In I. Salim (ed.). *State Formation in East Africa*. Nairobi, Heinemann.
Roberson, G. M. M., Tickner, L., Bird, J., Curtis, B. and Putnam, T. (eds). (1996). *Future Natural: Science/Nature/Culture*. London, Routledge.
Robford Tourism (1999). *Development Plan for Sustainable CBT for Gaza Tourism Sub-region*. Cape Town, Robford Tourism.
Robins, S. (1994). 'Contesting the geometry of state power: a case study of land-use planning in Matebeleland, Zimbabwe'. *Social Dynamics* 20 (2): 91-118.
Rocheleau, D. (1999). 'Commentary on After Nature by Arturo Escobar'. *Current Anthropology* 40 (1): 22-23.
Roder, W. (1965). *The Sabi Valley Irrigation Projects*. Department of Geography Research Paper No. 99. Chicago, University of Chicago Press.
Roe, E. (1991). 'Development narratives, or making the best of blueprint development'. *World Development* 19 (4): 1065-1069.
Rose, G. (1992). 'Geography as a science of observation: the landscape, the gaze and masculinity'. In F. Driver and G. Rose, (eds). *Nature and Science: Essays in the History of Geographical Knowledge*. Cheltenham, Historical Geography Research Group.
Roth, H. H. (1964). 'Game utilisation in Rhodesia'. *Mammalia* 30: 397-427.
Rukuni, M. (1988). 'The evolution of smallholder irrigation policy in Zimbabwe: 1928-1986'. *Irrigation and Drainage Systems* 2: 199-210.
Sabi-Limpopo Authority (1970). *Golden Dawn*. Harare, SLA.
SADC (1992). *Declaration Treaty and Protocol of the Southern African Development Community*. Gaborone, Botswana, Southern African Development Community.
Said, E. W. (1978). *Orientalism. Western Conceptions of the Orient*. London, Penguin Books.
Said, E. W. (1993). *Culture and Imperialism*. London, Chatto and Windus.
Salzgitter Consult GMBH (1985). 'Sengwe Cattle Development Project, Chiredzi District, Masvingo Province. Report prepared for GTZ', Republic of Zimbabwe, Federal Republic of Germany.

Salzgitter Consult GMBH (1986). 'Grootvlei (Gwatobi) Irrigation Scheme Feasibility Study: Phase 1, Final Report'. Government of Zimbabwe, Ministry of Lands, Agriculture and Water Development, Agriculture and Rural Development Authority.

Salzgitter Consult GMBH and PTA Consulting Services (1991). 'Study of the Irrigation Potential Along the Mwenezi River, Sengwe Communal Land, Masvingo Province. Interim Report'. Government of Zimbabwe, Ministry of Lands, Agriculture and Water Development, Agriculture and Rural Development Authority.

Salzgitter Consult GMBH and PTA Consulting Services (1993). 'Study of the Irrigation Potential Along the Mwenezi River, Sengwe Communal Land, Masvingo Province. Feasibility Report'. Government of Zimbabwe, Ministry of Lands, Agriculture and Water Development, Agriculture and Rural Development Authority.

Sandford, S. (1982). 'Livestock in the communal areas of Zimbabwe'. Report prepared for the Ministry of Lands, Resettlement and Rural Development, Harare.

Sauer, C. O. (1925). 'The morphology of landscape'. *University of California Publications in Geography* 2: 19–54.

Sauer, C. O. (1969). 'The morphology of landscape'. In J. Leighley (ed.). *Land and Life. A Selection from the Writings of Carl Otwin Sauer*. Berkeley, University of California Press.

Saunders, C. (1989). *Murray MacDougall and the Story of Triangle*, Triangle, Triangle Limited.

Saunders, D. A. (1986). 'Project proposal: an analysis of development strategy in Zimbabwe. A case study of the Mwenezi Development Plan (1982-1986)'. Unpublished report.

Schama, S. (1995). *Landscape and Memory*. London, Harper Collins.

Schlee, G. (1992). 'Ritual topography and ecological use: The Gabbra of the Kenyan / Ethiopian borderlands'. In E. Croll and D. Parkin (eds). *Bush Base: Forest Farm. Culture, Environment and Development*. London, Routledge.

Schmidt, H. (1995). '"Penetrating" foreign lands; contestations over African landscapes. A case study from Eastern Zimbabwe'. *Environment and History* 1 (3): 351-376.

Schoffeleers, J. M. (ed.) (1978). *Guardians of the Land: Essays on Central African Territorial Cults*. Gwelo, Mambo Press.

Schoffeleers, M. (1985). *Pentecostalism and Neo-Traditionalism: the Religious Polarisation of a Rural District in Southern Malawi*. Amsterdam, Free University Press.

Schroeder, R. A. (1999). 'Geographies of environmental intervention in Africa'. *Progress in Human Geography* 23 (3): 359-378.

Schuerholz, G. and Moore, A. (1993). 'Tourism Sector'. In B. Downie, (ed.). *Gonarezhou National Park Management Planning Programme. Background Data Reports*. Harare, Department of National Parks and Wildlife Management.

Scoones, I. (1995). 'New Directions in Pastoral Development in Africa'. In I. Scoones (ed.). *Living with Uncertainty: New Directions in Pastoral Development in Africa*. London, Intermediate Technology Publications.

Scoones, I. (1996). 'Range management science and policy: Politics, polemics and pasture in Southern Africa'. In M. Leach and R. Mearns (eds). *The Lie of the Land: Challenging Received Wisdom on the African Environment*. London, James Currey.

Scoones, I. (1997).'Landscapes, fields and soils: understanding the history of soil fertility management in Southern Zimbabwe'. *Journal of Southern African Studies* 23 (4): 617-636.

Scoones, I., Chibudu, C., Chikura, S., Jeranyama, P., Machaka, D., Machanja, W., Mavedzenge, B., Mombeshora, B., Mudhara, M., Mudziwo, C., Murimbarimba, F. and Zirereza, B. (1996). *Hazards and Opportunities. Farming Livelihoods in Dryland Africa: Lessons from Zimbabwe.* London, Zed Books.

Scott, J. C. (1985). *Weapons of the Weak. Everyday Forms of Peasant Resistance.* New Haven, CT, Yale University Press.

Scott, J. C. (1998). *Seeing Like a State. How Certain Schemes to Improve the Human Condition have Failed.* New Haven, CT, and London, Yale University Press.

Seidal, G. (1985).'Political discourse analysis'. In T. van Dijk, (ed.). *Handbook of Discourse Analysis*, 4. London, Academic Press.

Short, J. R. (1991). *Imagined Country: Society, Culture and Environment.* London, Routledge.

Simon, D. (2003). 'Regional development-environment discourses, policies and practices in post-apartheid southern Africa'. In J. A. Grant and F. Soderbaum (eds). *New Regionalisms in Africa*, Aldershot, Ashgate.

Sinclair, A. (1977). *The Savage: A History of Misunderstanding.* London, Weidenfeld and Nicholson.

Singh, J. (2000). 'Transboundary conservation in the African context: A threat to sovereignty?' Paper presented at the Border Regions in Transition - IV conference: Rethinking Boundaries, Geopolitics, Identities and Sustainability, 20-24 February, Chandigarh, India.

Sithole, B., Hwenha, S., Kozanayi, W., Manyeu, M. and Munyaradzi, W. (1999). 'People, livelihoods and options for development. A socio-economic analysis based on PRAs conducted in Sengwe Ward and Chikwarakwara village. Report prepared for CESVI'. Institute of Environmental Studies, University of Zimbabwe.

Skidmore-Hess, C. (1998). 'Wilderness and witchcraft: perceptions of health, land and development in Northern Botswana (1900-1950)'. Paper presented at a conference on Science and Society in Southern Africa, 10-11 September, at the Centre for Southern African Studies, University of Sussex.

Somerville, D. (1976). *My Life was a Ranch.* Salisbury, Kailani Books.

Soper, K. (1996). 'Nature/'nature''. In G. M. M. Roberson et al. (eds). *Future Natural: Science/Nature/Culture.* London, Routledge.

Soule, M. E. and Lease, G. (1995). *Reinventing Nature? Responses to Postmodern Deconstruction.* Washington, DC, Island Press.

Sparrow, A. L. (1977).'A lowveld rite: a Shangaan circumcision lodge'. *NADA*, 394-396.

Stanley, H. M. (1890). *Through the Dark Continent.* London, Sampson, Low, Marston, Seale and Rimington.

Stayt, H. A. (1931). *The BaVenda.* London, International African Institute.

Steenkamp, C. (1999). 'The Makuleke land claim: Power relations and CBNRM'. Unpublished manuscript.

Steibel, L. (2000). 'Creating a landscape of Africa: Baines, Haggard and Great Zimbabwe'. Paper prepared for a conference on 'Views of the Land', Bulawayo, 3-7 July.

Stevenson-Hamilton, J. (1929). *The Lowveld: Its Wildlife and its People.* London, Cassell and Company.

Stevenson-Hamilton, J. (1937). *South African Eden: From Sabi Game Reserve to Kruger National Park.* London, Cassell and Company.

Stockil, C. and Dalton, M. (n.d.). *Shangani Folk Tales: a collection of Shangani folk stories.* Harare, Jongwe Printing and Publishing.

Stott, P. and Sullivan, S. (2000). 'Introduction'. In P. Stott and S. Sullivan, (eds). *Political Ecology: Science, Myth and Power.* London, Arnold.

Strang, V. (1999). 'Competing perceptions of landscape in Kowanyama, North Queensland'. In P. J. Ucko and R. Layton (eds). *The Archaeology and Anthropology of Landscape.* London and New York, Routledge.

Struthers, R. B. (1991). *Hunting Journal 1852-1856 in the Zulu Kingdom and the Tsonga Regions.* Pietermaritzburg, University of Natal Press.

Stubbs, A. T. (1984). 'Feasibility study to rehabilitate the livestock economy in Sengwe Communal Land (Chiredzi District)'. Masvingo, Agricultural and Rural Development Authority.

Sullivan, S. (2000). 'Getting the facts right, or introducing science in the first place? Local 'facts', global discourse - 'desertification' in north-west Namibia'. In P. Stott and S. Sullivan (eds). *Political Ecology: Science, Myth and Power.* London, Arnold.

Sullivan, S. (2001a). 'The "wild" and the known: implications of identity and memory for "Community-Based Natural Resource Management" in a Namibian landscape'. Paper presented at Landscapes and Politics – a cross-disciplinary conference, Edinburgh, 23-25 March.

Sullivan, S. (2001b). 'Anthropology of landscapes and land rights: social constructions of environment'. Reading list for Masters course, Department of Anthropology and Sociology, School of Oriental and African Studies, University of London.

Swynnerton, C. F. M. (1921). 'An examination of the tsetse problem in North Mossurise, Portuguese East Africa'. *Bulletin of Entomological Research* 11: 323-5.

Thomas, E. (1955). *Report of the Commission of Inquiry on Human and Animal Trypanosomiasis in Southern Rhodesia.* Salisbury, Government Printer.

Thompson, M., Warburton, M. and Hatley, T. (1986). *Uncertainty on a Himalayan Scale.* London, Ethnographica.

Tiffen, M., Mortimore, M. and Gichuki, F. (1994). *More People, Less Erosion: Environmental Recovery in Kenya.* Chichester, John Wiley and Sons.

Turner, F. J. (1920). *The Frontier in American History.* New York, Henry Holt.

Tyler, R. (1983). *Visions of America: Pioneer Artists in a New Land.* London, Thames and Hudson.

USAID-RCSA (1998). *RCSA Strategic Plan 1991-2003: Regional Integration through Regional Partnership and Participation.* Gaborone, Botswana, USAID-RCSA.

Utete, C. et al. (2003). *Report of the Presidential Land Review Committee on the Implementation of the Fast Track Land Reform Programme, 2000-2002.* Harare, Government of Zimbabwe.

Vail, L. (1989). 'Introduction: ethnicity in Southern African history'. In L. Vail (ed.). *The Creation of Tribalism in Southern Africa.* London, James Currey.

van Binsbergen, W. J. M. (1981). 'Explorations in the history and sociology of territorial cults in Zambia'. In W. J. M. van Binsbergen (ed.). *Religious Change in Zambia: Exploratory Studies.* London, Kegan Paul International.

Van der Post, L. (1984). 'Wilderness: a Way of Truth'. In V. Martin and M. Inglis (eds). *Wilderness: the Way Ahead.* Forres, The Findhorn Press.

Vijfhuizen, C. (1997). 'Rain-making, political conflicts and gender images: a case study from Mutema chieftaincy in Zimbabwe'. *Zambezia* 24 (1): 31-49.
Vincent, V. and Thomas, R. G. (1960). *An Agricultural Survey of Southern Rhodesia. Part 1: Agro-Ecological Survey*. Salisbury, Government Printer.
Vitebski, P. (1993). *Dialogues with the Dead: the Discussion of Mortality, Loss and Continuity among the Sora of Central India*. Cambridge, Cambridge University Press.
Warnke, M. (1994). *Political Landscape: the Art History of Nature*. London, Reaktion Books.
Webb, H. S. (1954). 'Preface'. In Lowveld Regional Development Association, *A Survey of the Resources and Development of the Southern Region of the Eastern Transvaal*. Lowveld Regional Development Association.
Wels, H. (2000). 'Fighting over fences: Organisational co-operation and reciprocal exchange between the Save Valley Conservancy and its neighbouring communities'. Ph.D. thesis, Free University, Amsterdam.
Whiston Spirn, A. (1996). 'Constructing nature: The legacy of Frederick Law Olmstead'. In W. Cronon (ed.). *Uncommon Ground: Rethinking the Human Place in Nature*. New York, W.W. Norton.
White, L. (1995). 'Tsetse visions: narratives of blood and bugs in colonial Northern Rhodesia, 1931-9'. *Journal of African History* 36: 219-245.
Williams, O. (1981). 'Irrigation farming in the southeast lowveld of Zimbabwe: retrospect and prospect'. *Geography* 66 (3): 228-231.
Williams, R. (1973). *The Country and the City*. London, The Hogarth Press.
Williams, R. (1980). 'Ideas of nature'. In R. Williams, (ed.). *Problems in Materialism and Culture*. London, Verso.
Williams, R. (1988). *Keywords*. London, Fontana Press.
Willis, J. D. and Pangeti, G. N. (1998). *The Limpopo Riverine Tourist Project: Feasibility Study Prepared for WWF Harare*. Harare, Geckoconsult – WWF.
Wilson, K. B. (1986). 'History, ecology and conservation in southern Zimbabwe'. Paper delivered at a seminar, Department of Sociology, University of Manchester, 12 February.
Wilson, K. B. (1988). 'Indigenous conservation in Zimbabwe: soil erosion, land-use planning and rural life'. Paper submitted to the panel session 'Conservation and Rural People', African Studies Association of UK Conference, Cambridge, 14 September.
Wolmer, W. (2003). 'Transboundary conservation: the politics of ecological integrity in the Great Limpopo Transfrontier Park'. *Journal of Southern African Studies* 29 (1): 261-278.
Wolmer, W., Chaumba, J. and Scoones, I. (2004). 'Wildlife management and land reform in southeastern Zimbabwe: a compatible pairing or a contradiction in terms?'. *Geoforum* 35: 87-98.
Wolmer, W. and Scoones, I. (2000). 'The science of "civilised" agriculture: The mixed farming discourse in Zimbabwe'. *African Affairs* 99: 575-600.
Wolmer, W., Sithole, B. and Mukamuri, B. (2002). 'Crops, livestock and livelihoods in Zimbabwe'. In I. Scoones and W. Wolmer (eds). *Pathways of Change: Crops, Livestock and Livelihoods in Africa. Lessons from Ethiopia, Mali and Zimbabwe*. Oxford, James Currey.
Worby, E. (1994). 'Maps, names, and ethnic games: The epistemology and iconography of colonial power in northwestern Zimbabwe'. *Journal of Southern African Studies* 20 (3): 371-392.

World Bank Preparation Mission (1992). 'Zimbabwe: proposed wildlife management and environmental conservation project'. Washington, DC, World Bank.

Wright, A. (1972). *Valley of the Ironwoods: a Personal Record of Ten Years Served as District Commissioner in Rhodesia's Largest Administrative Area, Nuanetsi, in the South-Eastern Lowveld*. Cape Town, T.V. Bulpin.

Zimbabwe Trust (1990). *People, Wildlife and Natural Resources: The CAMPFIRE Approach to Rural Development in Zimbabwe*. Harare, Zimbabwe Trust.

Zimmerer, K. S. (2000). 'The reworking of conservation geographies: nonequilibrium landscapes and nature-society hybrids'. *Annals of the Association of American Geographers* 90 (2): 356–369.

Index

Aberfoyle Holdings, 103
Abramson, A., 11
Acocks, J.P.H., 120
Adams, B., 31, 40, 38
Adams, J.S., 31
Agricultural Development Agency, 106
agriculture, 2, 7, 16, 20, 36-7, 44, 68-115, 188; commercial, 2-4 *passim*, 6, 15, 21, 68, 94, 103-5, 115, 117, 190, 201; communal, 2-4 *passim*, 6, 17, 105-12, 115; contract, 193; dryland, 16, 17, 68-73, 78-92 *passim*, 121, 187, 201-4; shifting/slash and burn, 44, 70, 71, 212
Agricultural Development Authority 106, 110
Agritex, 15, 91, 107
aid, 189
AIDS, 59
Aitken-Cade, Stewart, 156
Alexander, J., 37, 47, 53, 55, 177, 203
Alvord, Emory, 83-4, 106-7
Alwang, J., 188
Amazon, 8
America, North, 24, 34, 38
ancestral spirits, 2, 54, 56-60, 64, 81, 113, 187, 1911, 198, 215
Anderson, D., 11, 13, 22, 38, 40
Anderson, E., 167
Anderson, P.R., 23, 34
Andersson, J.A., 114
Andrews, B., 99
Andrews, M., 9
Anglo-American corporation, 96, 105

Angus Ranch, 118, 134, 194, 210, 211, 213
Arabs, 29, 42, 67
arson, 193
Atieno Odhiambo, E.S., 43, 48-9
Australia, 24, 34

Badenhorst, C., 51
Baines, Thomas, 23
Bangala Dam/Ranch, 95, 100, 118
Bannerman, J.H., 5, 6, 50, 53, 55, 69-71 *passim*, 74, 75, 78, 79, 82, 84, 85, 117, 121, 122, 153
Barnard, Cecil, 24-5
Barnes, T.J., 10
Beach, D., 50
beef industry, 116, 118, 129-31, 163, 171, 214
Behnke, R., 11
Beinart, W,. 11-13 *passim*, 31, 47, 120, 121, 127
Bemba, 51
Bender, B., 15, 49
Bentley, B., 99
Benzies, 83
Berger, John, 9
Berkeley school, 7, 8
Berry, S., 10, 138
Bhebe, N., 58
biomedicine, 132
'blackbirding', 25, 157
Blaikie, P., 8, 10
Blake-Thompson, 'Tommy', 27
Bolding, A. 105

Bond, I., 119, 163
Bonner, R., 174, 211
Brandon, P., 8
Braun, B., 7, 11
Bridges family, 120
Bridges, Lucas, 33n22, 118
Britain, 188-90 *passim*; *see also* colonial era
British South Africa Co., 20, 36, 78, 94, 117, 120
Broch-Due, V., 13, 14, 41, 174
Brown, Capability, 8
Bryant, R., 10
buffalo, 134, 136, 137, 155, 164, 166-8 *passim*, 181, 214
Bulpin, T.V., 24-6 *passim*, 31
Bunn, D., 12, 33, 42, 61, 113
Burchell, William, 23
bushbuck, 155
bushpig, 155

Caldwell, Edward, 30
CAMPFIRE, 17, 53, 64, 169, 177, 179-80, 182-4, *passim*, 193, 213
Carlaw, C.A., 29
Carruthers, J., 12, 31, 152, 217
carrying capacity, 126, 129
Castree, N., 7, 11
cattle, 17, 21, 116-41, 153, 157, 208-9; movement 132-7, *passim*, 208-9, 214
CFU, 188, 203, 206
Chaumba, J., 56, 195, 196, 204, 211, 214, 216
chiefdoms, 53-6
Chikombedzi, 18, 53, 88, 90, 117, 124, 138, 139, 191, 199
Child, B., 88, 118-19, 122, 155, 162, 163, 177, 182
Chipinda Pools, 145-6, 158
Chiredzi, 106, 179, 194, 196, 198, 200; Ranch, 117
Chissano, President, 174
Chitanga, Chief, 55
Chitsa, 214, 215
Christianity, 64-6
churches, 65-6
circumcision, 48
citrus, 21
clans/lineages, 53-4
Coates, P.A., 13, 31
Cockbill, Gerald, 155
Coetzee, J.M., 9, 13, 23, 24, 34
Cohen, D.W., 43, 48-9
Cold Storage Commission, 118-19, 130
colonial era, 2, 5, 20-41, 69-73, 78-88; post-, 12, 22, 55; pre-, 69-73
Colson, E., 56
Comaroff, J. and J., 12, 22, 36, 100
communal areas, 3-4, 17, 37, 41, 105-12, 121-41, 169, 193, 204, 217
compensation, 189
conservancies, 144, 162-9, 172, 180-1, 186, 209-10, 213, 214, 218
conservation, 2, 17, 31, 40, 82, 93, 107-8, 114, 141-83; Department for - and Extension, 162
corruption, 101
Cosgrove, Dennis, 9
cotton, 90, 109, 205, 206
Cousins, B., 109, 110, 127, 128
Croll, E., 43, 45, 46
Cronon, W,. 8, 12, 15, 34
cronyism, 189
'Crooks Corner', 25, 157, 173
culture, 6-9 *passim*
Cunliffe, R.N., 4, 5, 50, 75, 78, 80, 95, 106-8 *passim*, 117, 118, 131, 135, 148, 154, 157
Curtin, P.D., 13, 38
Cyclone Eline, 114

Daniels, S., 7, 9, 12
de Jager, P., 80, 139
de la Rue, Ian, 120, 153
decentralisation, 176-83
degradation, environmental, 36, 40-1, 128-9, 133, 201, 202
Delta Corporation, 166
Demeritt, D., 8, 11
Democratic Republic of Congo, 189
Descola, P., 7, 43, 46
destocking, 118, 127-9 *passim*, 138
devaluation, 188
Devuli Ranch, 118-20 *passim*, 134
DFID, 206
Dickens, V., 32
dipping, 124, 127
disease, cattle, 121-3 *passim*, 131-8 *passim*, 153-7, 200
Dodds, H., 95
donkeys, 124, 131-7
donors, 2, 137, 164, 174, 181, 188-91 *passim*, 203, 217
draught power, 122, 124, 131, 139, 204
Drinkwater, M., 37, 55, 107, 128, 203
drought, 4, 40, 41, 59, 60, 69, 70, 89, 90, 103, 119, 124, 129, 130, 138, 140, 152, 159, 164, 168, 192
du Toit, R., 164, 168, 180, 181
Duffy, R., 159, 168, 172, 174, 175, 184

Dunbar, 20
Duncan, J.S., 6, 7, 9, 10

Earthy, E.D., 57, 62
Eastwood, J.H.R., 33, 95
economy, 94-8, 102
elections, 194, 210
elephants, 21, 155, 158, 159, 164, 168, 180, 183
Ellis, S., 157, 159, 174, 175
Elton, F., 22, 71
ENDA-Zimbabwe, 88
Environmental Investigation Agency, 159
Erskine, St V,. 23, 26, 30, 31, 44, 71-3
ESAP, 188
Escobar, A., 9, 11
European Commission/Union, 109, 119, 134-7 *passim*, 214
evictions, 81-2, 102, 117, 118, 148, 152-3, 182, 191, 215, 217
exports, 118, 134-7 *passim*, 168, 188, 214
extension, 82-5, 91, 203-4

Fair, T.J.D., 96, 97, 99, 109
Fairhead, J., 8, 11, 15, 19, 43, 46, 64, 66, 73
fences, 117, 131, 134-7 *passim*, 141, 166, 167, 169, 192, 211; cutting, 117, 119, 152, 199, 210
Ferguson, J., 10, 185
fishing, 44, 73, 75, 81, 158, 191, 210
Fitzpatrick, Sir Percy, 29-30
Foggin, C., 167
food aid, 89
food for work, 89
food security, 201
foot and mouth disease (FMD), 118, 123, 131-8 *passim*, 153-4, 166, 167, 214
Ford, John, 37, 121, 153-5 *passim*, 157
foreign exchange, 103, 190
Forrestall, Peter, 79, 84-5, 117
Fort Victoria, 118, 120
Foster, J., 12
Foucault, Michel, 9, 36
Frost, P.G.H., 89
furs/skins, 73-4, 162

game, 21, 73, 74, 119, 121, 131, 132, 141, 153, 155-7, 162, 168, 209, 214; laws, 78, 145; ranches, 2, 162-71, 186, 209-10, 214, 218; reserves, 144-53 *passim*, 183
Gandy, M., 11
gardening, 105, 111-12
Garkovich, L., 8

Garlake, P.S., 28
gathering, 44, 73-5 *passim*, 121
Gaza Nguni, 26, 27, 50, 52, 61-2, 121, 152
Gazaland, 26-8; Tourist Initiative, 173
GEF, 15, 160, 182
Gezani, Chief, 81, 126, 140, 217n88
Gibb, Alexander, 95; Report, 95-7 *passim*
Gichuki, F., 11
Gilchrist, R.P., 146, 148, 171
Gillmore, P., 23
goats, 123, 124, 131, 193, 208
Godwin, P., 37, 157
Gohlawayo Purchase Area, 6
Gona re Zhou Forest, 79
Gonakudzingwa, 4, 18, 50, 57, 59, 65, 140; African Purchase Area, 80, 139, 149; Restriction Camp, 37, 58, 66, 191
Gonarezhou National Park, 3, 17, 18, 23, 38, 40, 55, 59, 66, 75, 79-81 *passim*, 107-8, 123, 136, 139, 144-9, 153-62 *passim*, 168, 169, 173, 182, 191, 214-16 *passim*
Goodwin, H.J., 161, 165, 169, 173, 178
Gordon, R., 179
Gottlieb, A., 47
grazing, 17, 117, 128, 139-41, 153, 188, 191, 192, 200, 208, 216; 'poach' 117, 140, 141, 158, 208, 214
Great Limpopo Transfrontier Park, 172-6 *passim*, 182, 205, 217-18
Great Zimbabwe, 27-8, 51
Greider, T., 8
Griffen, J., 176
Grove, R., 11, 13, 22, 38, 40
Grzimek, B. and M., 40, 156
GTZ, 109, 110, 131, 159
Gudo, 210
Guha, R., 12
Guluane-Chefu corridor 155
Gungunyane 32, 50, 121
Guveya, E. 176

Haarhoff, D., 12, 34
Haggard, Rider, 27
Haila, Y., 14
Hajer, M. C., 184
Hamilton, C., 27
Hancock, I., 37. 157
Hanks, J., 174
Harley, T., 11
Harries, P., 5, 12, 23, 24, 36, 51, 53, 54, 70, 71, 74, 76, 77, 138, 198
Harvey, D., 11

Heath, R., 104, 111
Herald, The, 159
Herbage Preservation Ordinance, 128
hides, 162
Hill, K., 163, 175, 211, 212
Hippo Valley, 80, 94-6 passim, 104, 105, 191, 205-7 passim
Hirsch, E., 7
Hlengwe, 4, 27, 44, 50, 62, 63, 72-4 passim, 81, 121
Hoppe, K.A., 121, 132, 155
Hoskins, W.G., 7
Houser, T., 62, 63
Hughes, D.M., 20, 61, 62, 182, 184, 193
Hulett Corporation, 95, 96
Hulme, D., 31
Humani Ranch, 210
hunting, 30-2, 44, 72-4 passim, 78, 81, 121, 154, 157, 165, 168, 177, 191, 193, 212, 217; safari, 163, 170
Hussey, D.E., 97
Hyatt, S.P,. 23, 27, 29, 33

IFAD, 89, 90, 129, 203
Imperial Cold Storage and Supply Co., 118, 120
infrastructure, 4, 95-7, 103-4, 129, 205
Institute of Environmental Studies, 32
International Finance Corporation, 166
invasions, land 2, 17, 53, 55-6, 66, 88, 105, 117, 119, 137, 140, 141, 167, 169, 170, 187-9, 193-214 passim, 218
investment, foreign ,103, 105, 205
irrigation, 6, 16-17, 21, 35, 68, 70, 81, 86, 91, 93-165 passim, 187, 204-7
ivory 73, 74, 159

Jansen, D., 119, 163
Jenkins, C., 188
Jenkins, G., 33
'jumpers', border, 193
Junod, H.A., 46, 49, 57, 62, 71

Karanga, 6, 61, 63, 84, 121, 138
Kelly, R., 41, 118, 128
Kenya, 48-9
Kerven, C., 11
Kinsey, B.H., 188
kinship links, 49
Kjekshus, H., 121
Knight, J., 188
Kriger, N., 195
Kruger National Park, 39, 77, 146, 171, 174, 175, 198
Kudu, 134, 155

kufiyisa, 117, 136-41 passim
Kyle Dam, 95, 100

labour, 20-1, 25, 51-2, 70, 76-7, 121, 217; WNLA, 77
Lambert, Y., 35, 99
Lammas, R.C., 13, 24
Lan, David, 42, 56, 58
Lancaster House Constitution, 188
land, 1, 3, 17, 80, 186-218; acquisition, 188-9; Acquisition Act, 170, 188; Acquisition (Amendment) Bill, 105, 207; alienation, 6, 16, 20, 21, 36, 49, 54-5, 59, 66, 76, 79-82, 102, 114, 117, 118, 123, 128, 134, 136, 152, 157, 183, 190, 191, 215; ancestral, 18, 197-9, 216-17; Apportionment Act, 80; designation, 170, 181, 189, 192, 204; Husbandry Act, 36-7, 118, 127, 206; Presidential - Review Committee, 209, 215; reform, 2, 4, 17, 109, 186-92 passim, 201, 215-17; Mwenezi Radical - Programme, 109-10, 128, 191; restitution, 198, 216-17; tenure, 103; use, 1, 2, 5, 16, 44, 66, 68, 85-92 passim, 110-11, 127, 183, 201, 204, 215-18 passim
landscape, aesthetic, 22-4, 99-100; cultural, 6-8; definition of, 6-7; imagined, 8-12; lowveld, 1-67; politics of, 186-218; productive, 68-141; types, 45; wildlife, 161, 171-6, 183-5, 209
Layton, R., 7
Leach, M., 8, 11, 15, 19, 40, 43, 46, 64, 66, 73
Levanga Ranch, 210
levy, cattle, 130
Lewis, I., 63-4
Ley, D., 10
Liebig, 118, 120
Liesegang, G., 61, 76
lions, 147
Lipsky, M., 91
livelihood strategies, 2, 17, 43-4, 68-92, 187, 188, 191, 203, 204, 215, 216
livestock, 2, 17, 116-42, 153, 193, 208-9; loans, 117, 136; movement of, 132-7 passim, 153, 187, 208-9, 214, 216
lobola, 121
Lomé Agreement, 134
Lovell, N., 7. 43
Luig, U.12, 21-2, 34, 43, 47, 67
Luo 48-9

Maasai, 39

Mabalauta Working Group, 75
MacDougall, Thomas Murray, 34, 94, 98, 99
MacKenzie, J.M., 31
Madyahasi, Yingwani, 215
Magome, H., 175
Mahenehene, Jacob, 18-19
Mahenye, 133, 177-9 *passim*
maize, 88-90 *passim*, 105, 130
Makulele, 138, 198, 217
Malkango irrigation scheme, 112-14
Malilangwe Trust, 165-6, 173, 178-81 *passim*, 184, 193
Malipati Game Reserve, 150, 151; Safari Area, 3, 6, 139
mananga, 47-8, 65
Mandela, Nelson, 174
Manyuchi dam project, 103, 110, 205
Manzungu, E., 105, 111, 112
Mapfumele, kraalhead, 140
Mapokole, 57-9 *passim*, 65, 215
Marcus, G.E., 18
marketing, 119, 129-31
Masona, T., 145, 146, 148
'master farmers', 111n49, 200
Mather, C., 51
Matibi II communal area, 3, 6, 18, 53, 80, 105, 108, 111-14, 117, 122-4, 127, 130, 136, 138-40, 146-8 *passim*, 152, 179, 191-3 *passim*, 197, 199, 200, 204; Reserve, 79
Matless, David, 7, 12
Matopos National Park, 152, 165
Maxwell, D., 64, 65
Mbizvo, C., 175
McDowell, L., 12
McGregor, J., 47, 177
McShane, T.O., 31, 38, 40
Mearns, R., 11, 40
meat, 162, 208
Metcalfe, S., 181
Michael, O.E., 7
migration, 15, 21, 25, 49-52, 73-8 *passim*, 92, 105, 121, 123, 139, 176, 184, 217-18
millet, 70, 73, 88
mining, 20, 21, 51-2, 76-7
missionaries, 36, 52, 74-6
Mitchell, W.J.T., 7, 12
Mkwasi Ranch, 210, 211
Mkwasine Estate, 205-7 *passim*
Mlambo, A.S., 93-5 *passim*, 98, 101, 104
Mongayane, Watch, 105-6
Moodie, J., 34, 35
Moore, A., 161

Moore, D.S., 10, 11, 20, 37, 46, 49, 66, 114, 182
Moore, H. L., 19, 51
Morris Carter Commission, 80
Mortimore, M., 11
Mosse, D., 10
Movement for Democratic Change, 65-6, 114, 189, 196
Moyana, H.V., 20, 79, 187
Moyo, S., 20, 175, 187-90 *passim*, 192, 217
Mozambique, 38, 62, 76, 78, 121, 131, 134, 138, 157, 172, 173, 176, 193; civil war, 54; MNR/Renamo, 38, 103, 131, 158-9
Mpapa, Chief, 55, 140
Msika, Joseph, 58
Mtetwa, R.M.G., 5, 51-2
Mugabe, Robert, 65, 188
Mukamuri, B., 89, 112, 124
Mukonyora, I., 13
Mukwasi Ranch, 210, 211, 213
Munro, W., 36, 55, 128, 129
Muraba irrigation scheme, 112-14
Murombedzi, J., 175
Murray, Charles, 87
Murray, M.J., 25
Mwenezi, 192, 196, 198, 200, 205; Development Corporation, 103; Radical Land Reform Programme, 109-10, 128, 191
Mzila, 50, 121

Namibia, 59
Nash, R., 13, 14, 34
National Farmers Union, 162
National Parks, 2, 3, 17, 36, 39, 109, 143, 157-8, 168, 188, 215, 217, 218; Department of 3, 136, 158-61 *passim*, 165, 168, 181, 182, 184, 213, 215, 217
nationalism, 127, 152, 159, 190, 191
'Natural Region 5', 68-92 *passim*, 108, 140, 163, 208
Natural Resources Act, 127; Board, Native Enquiry, 83;
natural resources management, community-based 176-83, 185
Ndanga, 148
Ndau, 5, 50, 61-3 *passim*, 74, 210
Ndebele, 6, 15, 16, 27, 43, 47, 61, 66, 80, 84, 88, 105, 113, 126, 138, 199
Neighbour Outreach programmes, 182, 184
Neumann, R.P., 9, 12, 14, 24, 31, 39, 53, 66, 179

NGOs, 143, 159
Nguni, 26, 27, 32, 44, 49, 50, 61-2, 72-4 *passim*
Ngwenyene, Chief, 81, 150
Nkala, Lazarus, 58
Nkomo, Joshua, 37, 58, 191, 205-7 *passim*
Noyes, J.K., 12, 36, 42
Nuanetsi, 53, 79, 108, 126, 127, 131, 149; Ranch, 21, 79, 117-18, 120, 123, 146, 147, 166, 205-7 *passim*
Nyazugwi Ranch, 117

off-take rates, 116, 129
Okoye, I.S., 12, 22, 42
Oliver, C.P., 20
Olmstead, Frederick Law, 8
out-grower schemes, 206
overgrazing, 120, 128-9, 163
overstocking, 128, 133, 134, 208

palm oil, 103, 110
Palmer, E., 30, 76, 79, 107, 187, 188
Palmer, R., 20
Palsson, G., 7, 46
pan-Africanism, 216
Pangeti, E.S., 93-6 *passim*, 98, 101, 104, 206
Pangeti, J.N., 173
Parkin, D., 43, 45, 46, 48, 56
Parks and Wildlife Act, 163
pasture science, 116, 120, 126-9
patronage, 113-14, 139
Peace Parks Foundation, 174
Peet, R., 11
Peluso, N.L., 10, 211
Penning, C.J., 95
Peterson, J.H., 177
Phimister, I.R., 76, 118
Pirow, J.-Y,. 26
Pitman, Dick, 145, 155, 157
poaching, 21, 41, 73-5 *passim*, 119, 137, 152, 158, 159, 193, 194, 197, 199, 200, 210, 211; anti-, 165
Pole-Evans, I.B., 83
politics, 52-6, 65, 112-14, 133, 186-218
Pollock, N.C., 35, 38
Posey, D.A., 8
Potts, D., 202
Pratt, M.L., 42
Price Waterhouse, 163, 169, 172-3
prices, 102-4 *passim*; cattle/beef, 118, 119, 130, 163; control, 103, 104
privatisation, 188
private-public joint ventures, 185; *see also* Malilangwe Trust
Proctor, J.D,. 8, 11
protected areas, 2, 17, 39, 41, 42, 142-9, 177, 179, 182, 184; *see also* individual parks; Transboundary PA, 171-6
PTA Consulting Services, 110
Pwiti, G., 75

quarantine, 123

rainfall, 4, 44, 69, 70
rainmaking, 152, 198
ranching/ranches, cattle, 2, 4, 17, 21, 33-4, 68, 88, 117-21, 129-31, 141, 157, 163, 166, 170-2 *passim*, 191, 193; game, 2, 162-71, 183, 186, 209
Ranger, T., 5, 12, 14, 23, 37, 43, 47, 54, 58, 65, 66, 122, 152, 165, 179, 216
Reid, H., 198, 217
Reid Daly, R., 37
religion, 56-66
remittances, 15, 77, 92, 217
Rennie, J.K,. 61, 73
Reserves, Native, 36, 76, 79-82, 121-6, 148; Coryndon Commission, 79
resettlement, 92, 95, 103, 105, 110, 170, 187-92, 201-9, 212-17 *passim*; Model A2, 207
restocking, 131, 163, 166, 203
rhinoceros, 157, 163, 166, 212
Rhodes, Cecil, 32
Rhodesia, 20-41
Rhodesian Herald, 102-3
rinderpest, 121, 154
rituals, 48, 56-60 *passim*
Roberson, G.M.M., 11
Robford Tourism, 161
Robins, S., 34, 36, 55, 128, 203
Rocheleau, D., 10
Roder, W,. 75, 76, 106
Rose, G.G., 10
Roth, H.H., 162
Rukuni, M., 111, 112
Rupert, Anton, 174

Sabi-Limpopo Authority, 93, 96, 97, 99, 101, 108-9
Said, E.W., 5, 12
sales, cattle, 129-31 *passim*
Salzgitter Consult, 89, 110, 128, 129, 131
Sango Ranch, 210
Sangwe, 3, 55, 80, 106, 179, 197, 199, 204, 210, 214
Sauer, Carl, 7, 8

Saunders, C., 27, 34, 94, 95, 98
Saunders, D.A., 109
Save Valley, 3, 95, 106-7, 118, 120, 163; Conservancy, 164-8 *passim*, 171, 173, 178, 180-1, 193, 194, 197, 209-13, 217
Schama, S., 13
Schlee, G., 56
Schmidt, H., 34
Schoffeleers, M., 56, 65
Schuerholz, G., 161
Scoones, I., 11, 37, 44, 56, 91, 107, 120, 127-9 *passim*, 188, 195, 196, 208, 211
Scott, J.C., 36, 211
SEDAP, 203
Selous Scouts, 37
Sengwe, 3, 6, 18, 53, 55, 80, 81, 88, 105, 110, 112, 117, 123-4, 129-31 *passim*, 138, 140, 180, 191-3 *passim*, 200, 204, 215
Serengeti National Park, 39
settlers, 20-41 *passim*, 94, 98-9, 120, 122; pioneers, 22-35 *passim*, 98-9, 105, 120, 191
Shaka, 27
Shangaan, 2, 4-6, 15, 16, 26, 27, 29, 31-2, 43, 45-53 *passim*, 61-2, 66, 67, 73, 75, 78, 79, 82-5 *passim*, 113, 121, 126, 150, 176, 178, 179, 198, 199
sharecropping, 90
Shona, 15, 16, 27, 28, 43, 46, 47, 50, 52, 66, 71, 73, 84, 88, 113, 199
Short, J.R., 13, 14
Shoshangane, 50
Simon, D., 173
Singh, J., 175
Sithole, B., 32, 89, 112, 124
Siwawa, Makuso, 138
sleeping sickness, 132
smuggling, 159, 193
snaring, 119, 150, 152, 212
soil erosion, 129, 133, 163, 212
Smuts, Gen. Jan, 39, 40, 171
Somerville, D.M., 33, 118, 120, 132
Soper, K., 7
sorghum, 70, 88-90 *passim*
South Africa, 4, 35, 39, 51, 76-7, 85, 166, 172, 174-6 *passim*, 184, 190, 193, 198, 217
Sparrow, A.L., 48
Spatial Development Initiative, 175
spirit possession, 62-4
Spivak, G., 12
squatters, 189, 193, 194, 211
Stayt, H.A., 71

Steencamp, C., 198
Steibel, L., 28
Stevenson-Hamilton, J., 23, 39-40, 48, 67, 72, 149, 151
Stockil, Ray, 95, 98
Stott, P., 11
Strang, V., 34
Stubbs, A.T., 123, 131
sugar, 2, 21, 34, 76, 93-8 *passim*, 102, 103, 117, 191, 205-7 *passim*
Sullivan, S., 10, 11, 15, 52, 59
Summers, Roger, 27
Sunday Mail, 156, 157
sviumbiwa, 46
Swynnerton, C.F.M., 121

taxation, 76, 78, 117, 130
territorial spirits, 60-1
theft, stock, 119, 138, 141, 197
Thomas, R.G., 85, 154
Thompson, M., 11
Tiffen, M., 11
Tokwe-Mukorsi dam, 103-4, 107, 110-11, 205
Tongaat-Hulett, 105
tourism, 146, 150-2 *passim*, 159, 161, 163, 165, 170, 173-5 *passim*, 179, 183, 188, 193, 212
Townley, D., 146-8 *passim*
trade, 73-6, 121, 175, 188, 217; routes, 103, 130-1, 191
Traditional Leaders Act, 55
Triangle Estates, 80, 94, 95, 103-5 *passim*, 191, 205-7 *passim*
tribute, 54
trypanosomiasis, 121n14, 131, 136, 153, 154
tsetse fly, 121, 123, 134, 145, 148, 153-7; control, 136, 145, 148, 153-7
Tsonga, 4, 53-4, 62, 71-2, 74
Tsovani, Chief, 55
tumbuluko, 46
Turner, F.J., 34

Ucko, P.J., 7
UDI, 93
unemployment, 98
United States, 14, 175
Utete, C., 209, 215

vaccination, 134-5
VaDuma, 6
Vail, L., 5
van der Post, L., 14
van der Zaag, P., 105, 111, 112

Vaughan, M., 19, 51
vegetables, 105, 112
veld burning, 119, 158, 194, 200, 210
veld management, 128-9, 133
Venda, 6, 71
veterinary science/veterinarians, 116, 120-1, 132-7, 153-6, 166, 183, 214; Department of Veterinary Services, 162
Victoria Reserve, 6
VIDCOs, 55
Vijfhuizen, C., 113
villagisation, 36-8 *passim*, 55, 109, 123, 182, 191
Vincent, V., 85
Vitebski, P., 46
von Oppen, A., 12, 21-2, 34, 43, 47, 67

WADCOs, 55
war, liberation, 37, 48, 50, 53, 57, 58, 101-2, 114, 119, 123, 153, 157, 193, 195
war veteran,s 56, 91, 92, 189, 195-7 *passim*, 200, 210, 214, 216
Warburton, M., 11
Warnke, M., 7
warthog, 155
water supply, 104, 106, 147, 148, 165, 200, 204-7; Act, 104
Watts, M., 11
Webb, H.S., 35
Wels, H., 120, 179, 181, 192, 199, 210, 211
Whiston Spirn, A., 8
Whittaalls, 120
White, L., 67
wilderness, 2, 8, 12-16, 68, 142-83 *passim*, 218; vision, 12-13, 20-42, 68, 109, 142-4, 157, 163, 168-9, 183, 186-7, 201, 209, 212, 216-18
wildlife 1, 17, 117, 142-83 *passim*, 186-7, 193, 209-15, 217; commercial management of, 162-7
Wildlife and Tourism Advisory Council, 213
Williams, O., 97, 101, 102
Williams, Raymond, 6n4, 8, 9
Willis, J.D., 173
Wilson, K.B., 64, 82, 139
wire cutting, 158, 210
witchcraft, 56
Wolmer, W., 37, 56, 89-91 *passim*, 107, 112, 124, 125, 131, 137, 146, 160, 172, 173, 195, 196, 211, 213, 215, 217
women, 60, 64, 77, 112

Worby, E., 5
World Bank, 168, 174
Wright, Allan, 29, 31, 32, 40, 58, 74, 82, 108-9, 112, 117, 126, 127, 129-31 *passim*, 134, 149-54, 156, 160, 166, 178, 179, 191

Zambezi Valley, 3, 18, 42, 58, 163, 177
Zambia, 51
ZANU(PF), 65-6, 91, 113, 114, 159, 188-90, 194-6 *passim*, 203, 215, 216
ZANLA, 37
Zimbabwe Development Trust, 103, 205
Zimbabwe Sun Ltd, 177, 212
Zimbabwe Trust, 158, 177
Zimmerer, K.S., 92
ZIPRA, 37
ZNA, 159
zvisikwa, 46